Social Work with Groups

A Process Model

Joseph Anderson
Norfolk State University

 LONGMAN

An imprint of Addison Wesley Longman, Inc.

New York • Reading, Massachusetts • Menlo Park, California • Harlow, England
Don Mills, Ontario • Sydney • Mexico City • Madrid • Amsterdam

Social Work with Groups: A Process Model

Longman, 10 Bank Street, White Plains, N.Y. 10606

Executive editor: Pamela A. Gordon
Associate editor: Hillary B. Henderson
Editorial assistant: Jennifer A. McCaffery
Production editor: Linda Moser
Academic consulting editor: Howard J. Karger
Production supervisor: Edith Pullman
Cover design: Joseph DiPinho
Compositor: Digitype

Library of Congress Cataloging-in-Publication Data

Anderson, Joseph
    Social work with groups : a process model / Joseph Anderson.
        p.   cm.
    Includes bibliographical references and index.
    ISBN 0-8013-1837-8
    1. Social group work.   I. Title.
    HV45.A727   1997
    361.4 — dc20   96-15770
                                                                          CIP

1 2 3 4 5 6 7 8 9 10-MA-0099989796

To the group that supports and challenges me to love more fully each and every day:
Wanda, Bailey, Sean, and Caitlin

Contents

CHAPTER 3   GENERALIST PERSPECTIVE AND PRACTICE   **33**

CHAPTER 4   MULTICULTURAL PERSPECTIVE   **49**

CHAPTER 5   SMALL GROUP DYNAMICS PERSPECTIVE   **77**

PART II   THE PROCESS MODEL   **107**

CHAPTER 6   OVERVIEW OF SOCIAL WORK PRACTICE THROUGH GROUP PROCESS   109

CHAPTER 7   PREAFFILIATION STAGE: TRUST THEMES   123

PART III IMPLICATIONS   241

CHAPTER 12 **DIRECT PRACTICE GROUPS**   243

CHAPTER 13 **TASK GROUPS**   255

CHAPTER 14 **PRACTICE EVALUATION**   263

Preface

This book is about theory and skills for social work practice through group process. It presents a model of group process and of generic skills for this practice. The approach promotes the enabling of stages of group development. The group's growth toward mutual aid, facilitated by the developmentally appropriate functions and skills of the practitioner, is the medium through which members are empowered to meet their individual needs. The model is compatible with historical, generalist, and multicultural perspectives. Research on group process and outcome variables, leader variables, and the stages of group development ground this approach.

The model centers around the sequential stages (and themes) of group process: Preaffiliation (Trust), Power and Control (Autonomy), Intimacy (Closeness), Differentiation (Interdependence), and Separation (Termination) (J. Anderson, 1984; Garland, Jones, and Kolodny, 1973). Each stage informs particular practice functions and skills. Social workers facilitate the group process through the disciplined and creative use of these skills. The methodology addresses all major elements of group process—the members ("I's"), the group ("We"), and the purpose and content ("It")—and presents practice skills in operational terms. As in all effective professional practice, readers can find direction in these principles, concepts, and skills; but each reader must find his or her own unique way of using this approach.

I wrote the book especially for classroom and practicum learning situations. I have found the method useful for teaching social work with groups in which students take turns co-facilitating the group process on their own or with me. This occurs either before or during a field experience in working with a practice group. The approach has also served well as the conceptual base for consultation with students who are establishing their first groups in the field. In addition, it has provided a framework for the advanced practitioner's continual professional development through self-study, consultation, supervision, and/or advanced training workshops and seminars.

I want to forewarn the reader about certain unusual aspects of this book. First, there is more repetition than one usually finds in a text. I have done this on purpose. My bias is that repetition is a parent of learning. My assumption is that the more we consider the application of relevant concepts to practice orientation and actions, the more we can integrate them into our knowledge base for practice. The repetition also derives from the book's unique organization around a group process practice model. The approach consistently uses core concepts of group process and group practice such as autonomy, interdependence, empowerment, and mutual aid. These concepts are repeated over and over again in all chapters with the hope that their potential to inform practice is developed with both breadth and depth and with more practical application as the book proceeds.

Second, some chapters in the book exceed the usual length of those found in most texts. This may be especially so in Part I. There is more extensive coverage of perspectives for social work practice with groups in this text. My intent is to ensure more consideration of these perspectives in preparation for practice with groups as well as to promote the importance of such perspectives in all practice. When these are covered in social work texts, they tend to be underdeveloped; thus, faculty and students must seek independent material for fuller coverage. I want to provide the fullest coverage possible within the confines of a single book and to highlight aspects of those perspectives that pertain to the model for practice promoted in this text.

Nevertheless, I expect some readers will be disappointed that other aspects of these foundations are not covered in the lengthy chapters. Still others will be impatient about how the ideas can be translated into practical principles and skills. To the former, I respond that I tried to balance the breadth of knowledge covered in these chapters with the depth of the most relevant application to the "social work with groups" model to which I attend. To the latter, I hope they find that I have succeeded in providing in Part II the concrete practice guidelines that emanate from the abstract frameworks presented in Part I.

Third, I have purposefully used fewer yet fuller practice examples than most recent social work texts. Small tastes of practice samples, which tend to pepper most books on groups, are used less often than examples that depict the flavor of the group process over time. I have selected and used these primarily to demonstrate the fuller application of the principles, concepts, and/or skills that they represent.

I hope that students, faculty, and other readers of this book will appreciate some of these and other less usual profferings. I look forward to feedback about these decisions and their meaning for various readers. Just as we learn practice, I can learn much from what works for readers as well as from my mistakes.

One cannot write a book on groups without having learned from many others. My "many others" are too numerous to name and too significant for me to separate from my current understanding of group process. They include my early mentors, leaders in learning and personal growth groups in which I was a member, fellow members in these groups, and members in my practice and learning groups, who worked so hard on behalf of the group and themselves. In these groups and in my family, I am learning what I consider my greatest lesson: Our thrusts for mutual aid are alive and well, even in a society with alienating, depersonalizing, and dehumanizing counterforces. I hope this book helps others discover this potential for mutual aid.

I especially acknowledge those colleagues who have encouraged and aided me in field testing the substance and organization of this text in classroom and training experiences: Mary Yanisko and Dr. Otha Wright Jr. of Norfolk State University, and Dr. James X. Bembry of the University of Maryland at Baltimore. I also appreciate the contributions of various reviewers to the clarification, refinement, and organization of the ideas in this book:

Paul Abels, California State University at Long Beach

James X. Bembry, University of Maryland

Alice A. Lieberman, University of Kansas

Flavio F. Marsiglia, Arizona State University

Robert M. Ortega, University of Michigan

Steven R. Rose, Louisiana State University

Martha K. Wilson, Boise State University

Dolores Finger Wright, Delaware State University

Special gratitude to George Hoffman for the faith and consultation regarding this text and to Pamela Gordon, Linda Moser, and Jennifer McCaffery for their production assistance.

Finally, I acknowledge my greatest human source of support, encouragement, and inspiration — my partner and wife, Wanda.

chapter 1

Introduction: Basic Premises and Core Concepts

Dominique Moyse Steinberg (1993) was curious about how social workers learned to practice with groups and how this learning affected their practice. So she studied 30 social workers, 15 of whom she classified as educationally prepared through their curriculum in social work with groups, and 15 as educationally underprepared (having had little coursework or practicum experience). The latter tended to gravitate toward increased use of groups in practice, whether through the fiscal priority of "getting more for less" or the identification of the unique value of this practice, or some of both. They most often learned their practice "off the cuff," by "trial and error," through haphazard (even hazardous) supervision, or by trying and applying principles for practice that evolved from theories rooted in other professions and/or based in individual and family treatment knowledge. Steinberg's question: Did these different foundations for practice—from within social work education or outside of it—make a difference in what the practitioners did?

It sure seems like it did.

Those who had an educational foundation for social work *with groups differed from those who did not in three major areas of practice orientation: control, conflict, and stages of group development.*

On control: Social work–educated practitioners conceived of and used control primarily as managing one's self—not the group. They handled their own impulses to control others and the group. They tried to turn their power over to the group. They believed that for a group to develop into a mutual aid system, members must share some real power and responsibility for what happens in and to the group. The practitioners placed this principle in a developmental perspective. They indicated that the shifting and sharing of power, begun in the very first meeting, increases as the group develops its autonomy, responsibility, and interdependent mutual aid potentials.

Those who were undereducated in social work group practice saw control more as using their power to "run the group" and as being necessary when potential confusion (for them or for group members) occurs or could occur. One participant's comment: "If I identify more (i.e., the subject at hand strikes a personal chord for me), then I feel a need to control more; or if there's a high interest in some topic and everyone's talking at once, to reign [sic] them in" (p. 31).

On conflict: Those with a social work education foundation for group practice viewed conflict as an inevitable part of the developing group. Thus, it was an important "system" issue. Conflict, to them, was inherent in difference and in the use of this difference to learn and grow. Because they valued authenticity and consensus, contradictions as an opportunity to learn, and mutual aid dissent as well as assent, they deemed confrontation and resolution of conflict as central to the effective group.

Those without such a foundation saw conflict as an issue of "personality" or "interpersonal power." It threatened group harmony and needed to be prevented or controlled so the group could assume its work. To a member who expressed a difference that raised the tension level of the group, one such "undereducated" participant responded: "Okay, well, no one can help you with that right now. Could we continue?" (p. 33).

On development: The practitioners differed most strikingly in how they saw the group's process as the base upon which they "timed" their "use of self." When asked, those with social work training with groups gave numerous examples about how the needs of the group at a particular stage influenced their responses to group events. Most of those social workers whose group practice foundation came primarily from outside the profession indicated, when asked, that they did not gear their interventions to an assessment of the group's stage of development. In fact, over half of them did not even understand the question!

INTRODUCTION

This book presents social work *through group process*. The model uses the stages of group development as the foremost definition of this process: Preaffiliation (Trust) — Power and Control (Autonomy) — Intimacy (Closeness) — Differentiation (Interdependence) — Separation (Termination). The needs of each stage provide the rationale for the proposed stance, function, and skills of the practitioner. As a group development approach, the model accentuates two fundamental potentialities in practice groups: empowerment and mutual aid.

Social work with groups is a methodology for empowerment of members to improve the quality of their lives. The focus is on members' growth. In this work, the intent is to stimulate their autonomous growth processes through participation in a group process.

The central empowerment process is mutual aid. It emphasizes the member's interactions with others toward achieving common and individual goals; in a word, interdependence. The group becomes a social microcosm for each member — a slice of life in which to integrate the dual needs of autonomy and interdependence. The assumption is that discovering how to live differently and to grow in concert with others *inside* the group can be applied and transferred to living differently and growing *outside* the group. In other words, through mutually beneficial interactions, one helps and receives help to improve the quality of each other's lives.

The process perspective highlights certain developmental elements of the group experience. There are three interrelated forces through which the work gets done: the individual's, the group's, and the helping process. "Process" here connotes a natural progression of gradual changes that lead toward a particular result. It implies forward movement or development in its natural, ideal state — a condition never really existing but only approximated for human process. An understanding of process provides the direction for both the group's and the practitioner's parallel work.

The process model in this text views individual problem situations as immediate obstacles to normal growth and development. The underlying motivation for each group member is growth toward self-actualization. Likewise, group process is developmental. As the group grows toward its own potential as a mutual aid system, members' needs are met in such a way that their individual goals are achieved. They grow. And yet it is not so simple as this.

A recent cartoon depicts two men standing outside their psychiatrist's office. One tells the other, "Dr. Wise says I am not rich enough to have problems . . . I just have troubles." There is more than a semantic difference reflected in the psychiatrist's comments. Many consumers of social work services are not the stereotypical middle-class, articulate, insightful, white females who are seeking a "talking cure" to perceived emotional problems. Rather, they tend to be persons — many of whom may be poor or nonwhite, or both — who are troubled (or "in trouble") by a variety of personal and life conditions and who have sought help, or who have been somehow forced to use help, for improving particular aspects of their personal and social living. The assumption of this text is that certain helping processes are more effective than others in working with these troubled — and often alienated — individuals. They empower more.

BASIC PREMISES

The group process orientation of this text derives from research-supported hypotheses for practice with a variety of service consumers. The basic approach can be adapted to specific group purposes. It generally translates the purpose into group goals through common themes and subthemes. As all members are engaged in shared purposes, goals, and themes and the limited time for their work together, they achieve individual gains.

Even though the work gets done by the members themselves, as it must, the practitioner needs to employ practice theory for enabling group process on behalf of the members. This theory includes three general parts: (1) the philosophical assumptions and theoretical premises about the people to whom practice is directed: the *knowledge* and *values* of individual and group process; (2) the specific theory for instructing the goals and the basic means of influencing these people: the *knowledge* (theory and research) and *values* of the helping process; and (3) procedures and techniques for achieving selected goals with those involved: the *skills* of the helping process. No theory is adequate without all three components. We can know everything we need to know about our goals and plans for intervention, but we must be able to carry it out. We need informed procedures and techniques by which to translate our knowledge and values into action on behalf of those we serve. In short, this theory needs to teach skills.

Group process practice skills provide a way of translating group development knowledge and values into a practice model. These skills meet several criteria deemed significant for teachable group practice (Gill and Barry, 1982):

1. *Generic.* The behavior that constitutes the skill is essential for social workers in *most* settings with *most* group members for enabling the achievement of *most* group practice goals.
2. *Appropriate.* The skill is attributed reasonably to the role and functions of the group practitioner.
3. *Empirically supported.* The skill is consistent with research findings on group practice process and outcomes.
4. *Definable.* The skill is described in terms of operations to perform it.
5. *Observable.* Both experienced and inexperienced observers can identify the skill when it occurs as repeated in like form by different practitioners in different settings.
6. *Measurable.* Objective recording of both the frequency and quality of the skill can occur with a high degree of agreement among observers.
7. *Developmental.* The skill is placed within the context of a progressive relationship with other skills, all contributing to the group's process. Effectiveness of later stage behavior in the helping process depends upon the effectiveness of the skills used at earlier stages.
8. *Group-focused.* The skill attends to the relationship of member(s) to the group. The behavior that constitutes the skill relates most often to the interaction between two or more members and serves to facilitate interaction, to encourage shared responsibility for the group's process, and to invite mutual aid in using the group's resources in decision making and problem solving.

Some generic skill models meet many but not all of these criteria. The models proposed by Lawrence Shulman (1992) in social work and Robert Carkhuff (1989) in human relations training are two examples. Recent frameworks for group practice in social work meet some of these criteria but fall short in defining skills in measurable, observable, and/or developmental terms (Brown, 1991; Garvin, 1987; Glassman and Kates, 1990; Henry, 1992; Northen, 1988; Reid, 1991; Wickham, 1993). Other literature on group counseling and psychotherapy tends to operationalize skills for working with groups more effectively in observable and measurable terms, but it has yet to produce an empirical base (Corey, 1990a) or a developmental perspective (Yalom, 1995) to inform the use of these skills in group practice. The skills addressed in this book are drawn from these cited works, among others, to develop a model that attempts to meet all eight of the above criteria for teachable group practice skills.

The basic premises of this approach are that:

1. Individual development occurs in microcosm through group development.
2. Group process, or group development, transacts with this individual development.
3. Group practice occurs *through* group process.
4. Group process has its own inherent "therapeutic factors." The essence of these factors is the *mutual aid* system that evolves in the empowered group; that is, a group that matures through the stages of group development.
5. Primary needs in group process are interpersonal, related to the growth of autonomy ("I") and interdependence ("We") in relation to the purpose and content ("It") of the group.
6. Natural, evolving group process has these therapeutic factors and the potential for establishing a mutual aid system that empowers autonomy and interdependence for members. It is a slice of life wherein one can learn to live up to the foremost commandment for healthy living; that is, "Love thy neighbor as thyself."
7. The practitioner can either facilitate or obstruct this process.
8. The process in general is a "tacit" dimension of all group experience. In fact, TACIT seems a useful acronym (and perhaps a mnemonic device) for the stages of group development: Trust, Autonomy, Closeness, Interdependence, and Termination. TACIT reflects the major interpersonal themes that are sequential in group process and extends the five-stage model of James Garland, Hubert Jones, and Ralph Kolodny (1973).
9. An understanding of these stages and themes is the basis for the practitioner's use of skills for empowering through group process.
10. This foundation, as supported by existing research on group process and outcomes and the practitioner's functions and skills, provides a framework for effective social work through the group process.

These premises suggest that the core theoretical concepts of group process practice are related to the interpersonal themes in social living. These themes—autonomy and interdependence as integrated in responsibility—are the basis for individual and group process that promotes self-actualization and combats obstacles to this growth.

CORE CONCEPTS

Autonomy

Autonomy and interdependence are significant concepts in social work with groups. In this text, they are the central organizing themes of both the group process and the intervention process. Thus, they are defined and developed more throughout the book. As one reads on, my hope is that the core concepts of autonomy and interdependence will take on more meaning and provide both the framework and the rich texture from which to construct practice models and skill. The intent in this chapter is to introduce them generally as existential givens in being and becoming.

There is the assumption that individual autonomy is a given. At the core of existence each of us is unique, separate, alone, and therefore responsible for our own life choices. We are born with the potential to choose more authentic growth of self. In the group, responsibility must go along with this choice so that members are confronted with the ultimate in freedom: Each person is responsible to himself or herself and cannot escape this responsibility by projecting it onto others.

Individual autonomy here refers to the "I-ness" of my experience, to self-awareness and selfhood (Cohn, 1972). As the individual who is "response-able" for the perception of the outside world emanating to me (I feel good and/or bad about what I receive), I am at the center of my universe. I, in my awareness of you, am still at the center of my universe, although you are now a part of this universe. I am autonomous with regard to you in that I can choose the kind of relationship I want with you and can attempt to create it. You are autonomous in that you can choose to accept, reject, or modify my definition of our relationship. Such individual autonomy relates to self-awareness, self-responsibility, and self-actualization. It involves being captain of one's own ship—one's self. It connotes the acceptance and use of one's personal power and strengths within realistic limits.

Alan Klein (1970) strongly advocated this need for autonomy as a major force in effective social work with groups. His fervor for empowerment through autonomy is encapsulated in the following ideas:

> It is my assumption that much of the power in the members and in the group is locked up and inhibited and that other forces may be misdirected. The members and the group are enabled through unlocking the power.
>
> The major function of the worker and the main concept in this model is to free members. One could say "free them up." . . . This requirement of the model is the most difficult for the worker and the members. For them, freedom of choice is frightening and risky, and they find it difficult to believe that they have that freedom or that they can trust the worker or themselves. If I can find out what you want to achieve, help you to recognize why you are not succeeding in achieving it, help you to eliminate blocks and to develop skills, then I am enabling you to move toward your goals. The strength and power lies with you. (pp. 12–13)

The approach in this book, as it was in Klein's (1970), is predicated on the belief that strength lies in members and in the group. Social work builds upon these strengths. Consequently, our major tasks are *to enable* the group process, to help members accomplish what they want and can within the interdependent well-being of each and all, and to free individual members and the group to use their autonomous strengths and powers on behalf of their needs.

In development, becoming an "I" generally precedes becoming part of a "We." Thus, in group developmental processes, autonomy themes most often evolve before interdependent ones, whereas both are interconnected in life and in group process. Autonomy, underdeveloped, is selfishness — an alienated state of irresponsibility using others for one's own gains. It leads to the manipulation and control of others that we might see in early stages of group development. Autonomy, developed, is the basis for interdependent relationships with others. Consider the aphorism attributed to Rabbi Hillel: "If I am not for myself, who will be? If I am only for myself, what am I?" Self-actualization, then, reflects an integration of autonomy and interdependence. But the ability to "Love thy neighbor as thyself," the basis for interdependence, seems grounded in the power to be one's self — in autonomy.

Interdependence

Although existentially we are separate, we are also connected. John Donne's classic "no man is an island entire of itself; every man is part of the continent, a part of the main/. . . I am involved in all mankind/therefore never seek to know for whom the bell tolls/it tolls for thee . . ." remains a most poetic statement of human connectedness. Interdependence is based on this connectedness; it exists because my autonomy is not sufficient to the satisfaction of all my needs. Lacking others with whom I can get close, I will feel lonely and alienated and many of my most important needs will go unmet. The other does not have to be you. To the extent that I feel *only you* can satisfy my needs, I have exchanged my interdependence for dependency or "co-dependency." There do, however, have to be others.

Interdependence is the basis for the group's potential for mutual aid. The mutual aid concept evolved initially from the work of Petr Kropotkin (1908), who regarded the practice of mutual support and empowerment, not mutual contest and struggle, as the determining factor in both social evolution and social justice. Over the years, the vision of the main task of helping the group develop into a mutual aid system has had many proponents in social work (see Lee and Swenson, 1986). Generally, it refers to enabling the use of people's inherent strengths to seek community; to care about others as well as one's self; to support and challenge others in their being and becoming by actively and genuinely communicating this caring; and to give as well as receive power, resources, and help.

Therefore, autonomy and interdependence are both conceived as existential givens. They can be denied only at the expense of one's fundamental sense of and responsibility toward reality. Their denial is the deep, dark hallway in which powerlessness and alienation lurk. The person who claims helpless and passive dependence in the role of "victim" blots out his or her sense of autonomy and is all alone in a malevolent universe, just as the isolated, alienated, highly mistrustful paranoid is blind to a sense of interdependence. The group approach of this text requires the practitioner throughout the process to provide both the experience and the awareness of autonomy and interdependence of each member in his or her development of responsibility. Such group experiences can enable members to accept the appropriate responsibility that social living and psychological growth entail. In turn, this combats the feelings of powerlessness and alienation that many members bring to our practice groups. It fosters personal, interpersonal, and political empowerment.

Responsibility

Helen Phillips, in a paper published in *The Group* written in 1954, underscored the objective of responsibility development in social work groups when she addressed the question "What is group work skill?" She established that all definitions of social work with groups affirm the "dual aim for the development of individuals and development of the group as a whole toward social usefulness" (p. 3). In more specific terms, she stated the professional objectives of group work as:

1. To help members of a group to value their real selves and to discover, use and develop their strengths through their group association so that they may find a more responsible and satisfying relation to other group members, the worker, agency, and community.
2. To help the group as a whole to develop social interests and activities that will contribute to movement toward a more democratic society. (p. 3)

One can hardly improve on this statement of our aims in practice with groups. This connotes what we now frame as empowerment. To Phillips, empowerment included discovering the personal power of our real selves and building on this strength. It further included responsibility in the use of personal power and in developing it into more democratic interpersonal and political power. Toward these ends, a central task is to empower members and the group to discover and make responsible choices.

The concept of responsibility is central in Irvin Yalom's (1995) interpersonal model of group therapy. To him, developing responsibility in therapeutic groups is a five-step process. Although they are consciously emphasized in interpersonal therapy, these steps appear operative as members interact in any developing group. They mark the interpersonal learning process that contributes to increased personal and social responsibility.

First, members learn how their behavior is viewed by others in the group through feedback and self-observation. Second, they learn how their behavior makes others feel. Third, they learn how their behavior shapes the opinions others have of them (valued, disliked, respected, avoided, exploited, feared, and so on). Fourth, they learn how their behavior influences their opinions of themselves; they evaluate their behavior on the basis of *how they are* as against *what they wish they were to others*. Fifth, they choose, decide, or take responsibility to change this behavior.

Thus, responsibility in group practice considers the members themselves and their process together as the major agents of help. Developing more responsibility outside of the group begins with the encouragement to assume it within by helping each member to be more responsible for the conduct of the group. The practitioner's responsibility is to enable the process by which the group and its members become effective agents of change. This requires acute sensitivity to the location of responsibility in the group, particularly on how much is projected onto the practitioner as perceived "leader" and how much the leader may blindly assume. It also requires that the practitioner understand the stages of group development as they reflect group progress. He or she can then help members to learn about their own process and needs, and can encourage their active choice to progress toward creating the interdependence necessary for meeting their needs and achieving their goals. Among all the skills that can facilitate group process, the underlying strategy is to encourage members to take more responsibility in their lives through learning to take more responsibility for their group process.

The capacity to form responsible relationships with others is a primary index of growth and development. The healthy person engages actively and responds freely in interpersonal transactions. Maintaining one's self-identity and autonomy, this person enjoys close relationships and acknowledges the need for them. She or he belongs to groups and participates in group activities. This person recognizes her or his social responsibilities, or interdependence with others, and is capable of love and compassion.

To some degree, then, an underlying objective of all group practice is to enable the person's capacity to enter into relationships. We help members to become free of the conflicts involving autonomy and interdependence and to assume more responsibility in mutual aid relationships. We primarily facilitate the process through which this can occur by empowering the development of the group to the point that the person is able to risk more closeness with others, to cooperate, and to find more security and power in interpersonal relationships instead of in alienation. Our task is to free this power; the group's task is to direct it.

This help requires the integration of all major points in group process—the members' autonomy, interdependence, and content. In Figure 1.1 on p. 10 these significant elements are labeled the "I-We-It" triangle (Cohn, 1972; Shaffer and Galinsky, 1989, pp. 224–246). This triangle, when placed in the surrounding ecosystem or "globe," depicts the general framework for group process in social work practice.

AUTONOMY AND INTERDEPENDENCE IN GROUP: "I-WE-IT" TRIANGLE IN AN ECOSYSTEM GLOBE

The "I-We-It" triangle represents the significant elements of all interaction, such as in group experience. The "I" reflects each member at any one point in time in terms of needs, feelings, thoughts, and behavior. Without "I's" there would be no group. The "We" reflects the group. "We" is the interrelationships within the group at any one point in time and the awareness of members that they are a distinct, unique

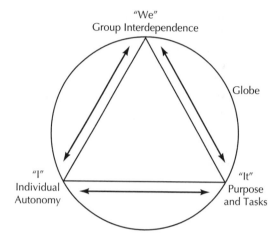

FIGURE 1.1   "I-We-It" triangle/ecosystem "globe"

group with its own particular relationships, interconnections, and concerns. "At any one point in time" denotes that these concepts stand for processes that are changing from moment to moment. Both the "I" and the "We" are developing in transactional and sequential stages throughout the group process. Thus, the "I" aspect of the triangle symbolizes autonomy; the "We" aspect, interdependence.

The "It" point of the triangle reflects the specific group's purpose and function, the individual and common goals that affect content, and the tasks needed to achieve these goals. This is why the group meets. "It" determines much of the group's focus. Whether stated or not, "It" is always present in groups. For instance, the implicit theme of a counseling group in the beginning is often: "I want to feel and function better"; of a personal growth group: "I want to get more in touch with the world inside me and outside me"; of a community action group: "I want more of this community's resources allocated to us." In practice groups, common goals reflect individual goals in the "It" of group purpose. This purpose is clear and shared; over time, it connects more to the "I's" and the "We."

All effective groups balance their attention to all three points of this triangle. Groups become ineffective when one or two points of the triangle are left unattended for too long.

"Content" is a traditional term for much of what is here called "It"; "process," which is often contrasted with "content," is embraced by the "I" and "We." All groups attend to certain of these three points more than to others at times. Often in the early stage of group development, content, or "It," predominates. For example, parents of emotionally disturbed children in a mutual support group might use much of their early time together talking about the difficult parental situations they have in common. Although there is some attention to the "I" in this interaction (as members will likely include a few of their personal thoughts and feelings about the challenges they face at home with their specific children), the "It" may be in the forefront.

Later, "We" aspects may gain salience, as members engage in a discussion of what is happening in the group. For example, a female member of the parents' group might observe that it is the women in the group who participate most; another might wonder whether this is because they, as mothers, feel more closely related to the child; and still another might suggest that the practitioner is a woman and therefore they sense more support in the group. An incipient "I" focus may tinge this "We" at those moments when a member begins to elaborate on her or his personal reactions to the group process. The "I" focus, with minimal attention to the "We" or "It," occurs when an individual member, with little overt reference to either the stated purpose or the other group members, talks about her or his life outside of the group.

In later group process, the content and process often coincide more conspicuously. Members dovetail thematic and interactional motifs in their here-and-now interaction. If "I-We-It" has been balanced earlier in group process and this grooving evolves, the group more effectively assumes responsibility for mutual aid in all members' growth. Let us say, for instance, that in the parents' group Jill describes herself as an overprotective parent. Jack then points out to her that he also sees her playing the "mother-hen" role in the group, trying to protect all other members from harm in any direct confrontation. Several other members agree, and one of them, Nancy, states that this behavior irritates her. At this point Jill begins to talk about her chronic anxiety, which she believes is related to her compulsive concern for the welfare of others. In this segment of the group scenario, the "I" (Jill and her anxious feeling in and out of the group), the "We" (the other members' feedback about her behavior in the group and the feelings this engenders in them), and the "It" (Jill's overly anxious treatment of her child) all intersect. We can sense the power and excitement of what Jill and other members learn through this interaction.

The "I," "We," and "It" are not all-or-none phenomena; they are a matter of more-or-less. For instance, at a point where a mother in the above group talks about the problems of all parents of emotionally disturbed children, her comments are relatively abstract and therefore primarily centered on the "It." Nevertheless, her statements include some inevitable (although diminished) attention to the concrete "I"; it is *her* statement and *her* thought. When she expresses deeper feelings about her particular situation and her child, the "I" focus looms larger and balances more with the "It." When she leaves the content theme altogether and discusses an upsetting experience she had on the way to the group meeting, the "I" focus becomes even larger, whereas the "It" begins to diminish. If, after a few minutes, another member interrupts her in order to express current feelings toward her, the "We" focus, which has thus far remained fairly dormant but has always been there (after all, she is speaking in *this group*), starts to enlarge. In other words, even though one or two of the triangle points may diminish or enlarge, they are all always present to some degree. Figure 1.1 illustrates the interrelationship of these points as they are omnipresent in the triangle of group process.

Additionally, Figure 1.1 places this triangle in a circle. The circle is the "globe" (Cohn, 1972), or the ecosystem, that transacts with the "I," the "We," and the "It." The ecosystem includes the more distant and immediate contexts that constitute the individual member's particular social worlds ("I"), the reasons these members are together ("We"), and of society's, the agency's, and the practitioner's influences on the group's purpose, function, goals, and tasks ("It"). The ecosystem both creates obstacles and provides resources for the group's empowerment possibilities (Balgopal and Vassil, 1983).

The social and physical environments that impinge on social work practice groups is an ecosystem of complex and interpenetrating social organizations (Germain, 1981). The most immediate layer is the member's social networks of family, friends, neighbors, and workmates — all of whom have different functions in relation to each member's personal needs and goals ("I's"). This layer also includes resources such as natural helpers (the members in a mutual aid group — "We") or potentially natural helpers such as landlords, merchants, teachers, physicians, and police (who may, upon entering a group member's or the group's lifespace, represent negatively experienced authority and power and other sources of stress).

Intersecting with this layer are the organizations and institutions that provide services and resources. In social work practice with groups, these include our own agency (which will be a salient presence, for good or ill, in the quality of our group members' lives as well as our own) and the helping process we provide in the group (the "It"). These also include other systems of work, education, welfare, housing, recreation, health care, and the like. These directly shape both the group members' lives and our practice in, with, and through groups.

Finally, the ecosystem entails the societal level. This includes cultural value systems; political and economic structures; and laws, statutes, and policies. The degree of social justice and democratic well-being — or, conversely, oppression and injustices — of this sociopolitical system impacts greatly on the "I," the "We," and the "It."

All these levels demand some attention in understanding the triangle of group process at any point in time. Only through mutual empowerment within the group and in relation to this ecosystem can we achieve our social work purposes through group process.

CONCLUSION

The "I" and the "We" are directly related in the here-and-now of group process. These are the points at which individual developmental themes (the "I") reciprocate and interweave with group developmental themes (the "We"). The practitioner who understands the nature and characteristics of this development is in a position to help integrate these triangular points and the ecosystem "globe" in the group to facilitate members' social learning and growth. Fostering this understanding and its use, as it develops responsibility and combats powerlessness and alienation, is the purpose of this book.

Part I presents the foundation perspectives for social work practice through group process. It considers the group process orientation as it evolved historically (Chapter 2), as part of both generalist (Chapter 3) and multicultural (Chapter 4) social work practice with groups, and in relation to the theory and research of group process and dynamics (Chapter 5). Part II presents the group process practice model. Following an overview of the model (Chapter 6), it covers in detail the stages of Preaffiliation/Trust (Chapter 7), Power and Control/Autonomy (Chapter 8), Intimacy/Closeness (Chapter 9), Differentiation/Interdependence (Chapter 10), and Separation/Termination (Chapter 11). Part III concludes the book, giving special attention to the implications of the model for aspects of direct practice (Chapter 12), task groups (Chapter 13), and practice evaluation research (Chapter 14). The Appendices provide instruments as resources for aiding the learning of particular concepts in this text as well as for studying and evaluating them in practice.

part I

Perspectives

chapter 2

Historical Perspective

When Jane Addams was engaged in social reform and group services work through Hull House, a multiservice settlement house and community center in Chicago, she was recognized in 1900 by the Daughters of the American Revolution (D.A.R.) by election to a lifetime honorary membership. Later, as an ardent activist for racial equality, women's rights, and the peace movement, and as president of the Women's International League for Peace and Freedom, Addams shared the 1931 Nobel Peace Prize with educator Nicholas Murray Butler.

In between, her antiwar stance during World War I and her insistence that even subversives had a right to trial by due process of law caused the D.A.R. to expel her from membership. The story goes that when she heard of her expulsion she commented: "I thought my election was for life. Little did I know I would get time off for good behavior."

INTRODUCTION

Social work with groups has its own unique history, heroes, and heroines, not the least of whom is Jane Addams. This chapter examines its heritage. It especially focuses on how the pivotal concept of group process brought general work with groups into a central, if at times undervalued, part of social work practice. The past sketched in this chapter focuses on social work with groups and its contribution to the model proposed in this text. In this group process approach, significant parts of the past influence present and future conceptions of practice.

Taking a historical perspective allows us to view social work practice, including social work with groups, as inextricably related to its sociohistorical context. That is, the social and economic realities in our North American society, if not in the global community, interweave with ideological and conceptual trends to build an understanding of historical events in the professional evolution of social work. Our history reminds us that as a social profession we are part and parcel of the problems, issues, trends, perspectives, policies, and other realities of the context in which we practice. With raised consciousness regarding their impact on our practice, we may be more proactive in addressing these influences. We may be more empowered to protect and promote the kind of practice we envision to be best (Lee, 1992).

TURN OF THE TWENTIETH CENTURY: ROOTS

Social Reform and Self-Help

Group work sprouted at the turn of the twentieth century. Its beginnings were forged in the sweeping economic, political, and social changes brought on by the Industrial Revolution. With so much change boiling in the cauldron of our society, complete with promises and problems on a grand scale, both the roots of social work as a profession and the attention to group process took hold.

The historical highlights of this period reveal sweltering urbanization, scheming capitalism, and sanctifying imperialism. Masses of immigrants from Europe swarmed into cities in the East and trickled into those in the Midwest. African-American and other immigrants from the South trekked northward to the urban industrial centers. Social class chasms widened. The small number of "haves," those whose power was entrenched through capital gains, exploited the mass of "have-nots" as well as the "have-a-little-and-want-mores." As social problems grew at home, the nation appeared preoccupied with empire building. (Gore Vidal's 1987 historical novel about this era is aptly titled *Empire*.) National heroes included Theodore Roosevelt, who defeated the Spanish at San Juan Hill, and Commodore George Dewey, who defeated the Spanish in the Philippines. Industrialists and politicians sought economic and political power through expansion. Acquisition of resources at home and abroad reflected an attitude of "the more, the better." Charles Darwin's and Herbert Spencer's philosophy of "survival of the fittest" was in ideological vogue and justified this exploitation.

Such a context eroded the social values that fostered democratic mutual aid in neighborhoods, factories, communities, the country, and the world. Groupwork pioneers advanced a different vision — one based on a renewed faith in democratic process and human potential, and geared to self-help and mutual aid.

Jane Addams, the founder of Hull House as a neighborhood center in Chicago, embodied this spirit as she strove both to serve the needs of the poor and disenfranchised and to wrest humane responses to those needs from a reluctant society. Her towering figure cast a large shadow that continues today, especially in the use of the group as a resource for social change and social reform (Lee, 1989).

Addams was an outspoken proponent of democracy and its potential to develop caring communities in the United States and the world. Her legacy to social work encompassed the values of interdependence and mutual aid. She deplored the stratification of North American society and believed that the intermingling of races, religions, and nationalities in the immigrant neighborhoods of the era provided a model for the establishment and maintenance of world peace. Her vision of reform was directed not only toward the relief and prevention of social ills but also toward the "positive idea of raising life to its highest values" (Addams, 1902, p. 32).

Mary Parker Follett's earlier social work with neighborhood centers reflected a similar ideology for social reform. Her plan, put into practice with considerable care and perseverance, was to get people from different social and economic backgrounds and occupations to understand each other's point of view through the "creative experience" of "psychological interpretation" in small groups. She viewed the small group as the cornerstone of the democratic community and social reform. In 1918 she wrote that "group process contains the secret of collective life; it is the key to democracy; it is the master lesson for every individual to learn; it is the chief hope for the political, the social, the international life of the future" (Follet, 1918, p. 3).

Eduard Lindeman also believed that democracy, learned in small group process, was a requisite in the social philosophy significant for social work's response to turbulent social change (Konopka, 1958). He raised serious doubts about the thrusts toward science and technology in the early part of this century and their contribution to centralized, hierarchical, nondemocratic organizational control in North American society. He concluded: "Our neglect with respect to the necessary training for democratic living is the chief factor in our present and shameful dilemma. Democracy becomes a farce, not because it has lost its ideal, but because its devotees are, democratically speaking, illiterate; they do not know how to operate in and through groups" (Lindeman, 1939, p. 6).

This era also brought on the beginnings of social casework. In *Social Diagnosis* (1917), Mary Richmond expressed the theoretical and scientific spirit. She began the systematization of social work practice through her procedures for the study and assessment of individuals and families, and she advanced the professional values of individual autonomy and self-determination. Thus, social work's ideology, responsive to the changes of the Industrial Revolution, was greatly influenced by our early pioneers' visions of fostering both the autonomy of individuals and their interdependence with others. (For an excellent, more personalized historical sketch of the social reform and other movements and their influence on social work with groups, see Wilson, 1976).

Two other major trends of the early twentieth century combined with the strong roots of self-help and social action to form the heritage of social work with groups (Breton, 1990). These were the recreation and progressive education movements.

Recreation

The recreation movement gained visibility in such organizations as the YMCA, YWCA, neighborhood and community "settlement houses," scouting, and Jewish Community Centers. In addition, although less formally organized, a significant use of groups for recreation, developmental socialization, and concrete and emotional mutual aid was evolving in the African-American churches of the era (Martin and Martin, 1985).

The major focus of the recreational group service agencies was on the person as a normal human being. They attended to normal growth and development needs through the use of "leisure-time" activities, regardless of the group members' emotional functioning, race, gender, or economic class. These groups evolved "the non-verbal method" (Middleman, 1968). Members engaged together in activities designed to achieve developmental and pleasurable outcomes. The goal was to help people learn to play together as well as work together.

Pioneers for practice with groups such as Grace Coyle, Neva Boyd, Gertrude Wilson, Gladys Ryland, Wilbur Newstetter, Clara Kaiser, and Helen Phillips were influenced by their experience in this movement. In fact, the first course in group work associated with an education program preparing "social workers" was initiated in 1923 at Western Reserve University in Cleveland, Ohio. Many of the aforementioned were among the original faculty. The curriculum tended to place priority on the "use of program" in work with groups. This connection of the recreation movement to social work with groups continues today in the form of "doing-oriented" activities in practice. (It also continues in libraries using the Dewey decimal system, wherein "social groupwork" shares the same call letters as "recreation" and stands side-by-side on the shelves.)

The recreational trend distinguished group work ideology and practice from the rest of social work by the mid-1930s. During the era when psychoanalytically oriented casework as a method defined most social work, group work advocated a focus on the "nearly normal adjusted individual," or those normal developmental parts of the person, and its use by all strata of society (Coyle, 1935). Hence, group process in essence served an important developmental function: helping members integrate their individual autonomy with interdependent involvement with others. Such small group process also served a social function by providing a laboratory in democracy. Grace Coyle (1935) and others conceived of the group as a place to learn skills for creating the social relations that are so vital to the health of the individual *and* the society. Even when groups were established in the 1930s primarily for problem-focused purposes, the "problems" were defined as of society's and not the individual's making. "Private troubles" were related to "public issues" and were viewed as structural obstacles to normal growth and development.

Progressive Education

The progressive education movement sprung from the work of John Dewey, William Heard Kilpatrick, and others who planted its seeds early in the twentieth century. The progressive education movement aimed to create more autonomous and interdependent ends and means for public education, initially in early childhood experiences. Progressive educators affirmed the natural way children learn through curiosity, experience, and problem solving. Two major principles of the movement were "learning by doing" and "learning through small group democratic problem-solving processes." Generating a debate that continues today, progressive education propounded the function of education not as the acquisition of content determined important by elders to be mastered by the young. Rather, the dual purpose was to maximize individual learning potential and to prepare citizens to live in an interdependent and democratic society.

In a historical aside that may have had more significance than we generally know, John Dewey and his wife, who was a close friend and colleague of Jane Addams, spent time during the earlier part of this century living and working at Hull House. Dewey had already written *Schools and Society* (1899). At Hull House, it seemed that Dewey's concept of the social purpose of education and the place of group process in learning took shape (published in 1916 in his book *Democracy and Education*).

Dewey especially formulated the relationship of individual problem-solving procedures to group problem-solving activities in skillfully facilitated small group process. His original formulation remains today, practically unaltered, for those who posit social work with groups primarily for achieving problem-solving objectives (Kurland and Salmon, 1992; Northen, 1988).

Dewey added his vision of the social purpose in learning through small group democratic problem-solving process to the similar perspectives of Jane Addams, Mary Parker Follet, Eduard Lindeman, Grace Longwell Coyle, and others. Thus, progressive education joined self-help and recreation to contribute to the major historical roots of social work with groups. These roots provide significant grounding for the process model presented in this text. The assumption is that all practice with groups promotes democratic purposes and values and contributes, at least to some degree, to meeting members' normal needs for development and growth.

1930s: EVOLUTION OF PROFESSION AND METHOD

The three major trends in the first three decades of the 1900s mushroomed into a variety of group service–based organizations and a diverse cadre of "group workers." The practitioners and students of small group process variously conceived of work with groups as "a reform movement, a therapeutic tool, an educational method, a field of service, a . . . part of the recreational movement, and a moving spirit in the affairs of many social welfare agencies" (Schwartz, 1959, pp. 119–120). In this same citation, William Schwartz noted two powerful and common convictions in the diverse group services agencies of the period:

> One was their shared belief in the salutory social and personal effects of group association; the other was a tested conviction that the development of sound leadership [and membership] was a central problem and special task in the mobilization of group life in a democracy. (p. 115)

By the 1930s, this legacy of "groupwork" had yet to evolve into method and to fashion its professional identity with social work. In fact, as with many historical developments in social work (and identifiable in many current practice trends and issues), we find the case of a movement searching for a method. The next evolution was toward "social groupwork" as a special concentration in the social work profession. This crystallized in a clear distinction that work with groups in social work was *through group process*. It required principles and skills for facilitating this process regardless of the specific functions for which the group was constituted.

1930–1960: FROM GROUPWORK TO SOCIAL GROUPWORK

The period 1930–1960 brought work on the conceptual and operational definitions of the professional functions and skills of work with groups. This was concomitant with the professionalization of social work. The economic and political context for this trend included such cataclysmic events as the Great Depression, the New Deal social policies and programs, worldwide ethnic genocide, World War II, economic booms, expansive urbanization, the cold war, institutionalized segregation, and the rise of the middle class. The latter created both social mobility and community transience for the more privileged North American families. All these trends and events (as well as others too numerous to note in this brief historical sketch) influenced the rise of professionalism and the increased effort to incorporate diversity into unity in the social work profession. Groupworkers joined others in a "blended family" of professional social workers. The new family experienced many ideological struggles among its various members. It wrestled with how different yet related heritages might fit together with some autonomous yet interdependent contributions to the new family's dreams and goals and its ecosystem's demands and issues.

One significant event in the marriage to come was the National Conference of Social Work in 1946 (Middleman, 1968). By 1946, such schools of social work as Columbia University, the University of Pittsburgh, the University of Minnesota, the University of Pennsylvania, and the University of Denver had initiated and offered group work sequences. However, there was still great debate among group workers and within social work as a profession about whether the group work method was more suited to recreational or to social work objectives. Grace Coyle helped clarify the issue in "Social Group Work in Recreation" (1947). She distinguished that recreation is a *function*, whereas social groupwork is a *method* designed to fulfill many functions, one of which could be recreation. Unlike recreation per se, which attended primarily to program activities or group *content*, social groupwork as a method attended at least as much, if not more, to group *process*.

Coyle elaborated on this distinction and its relationship to social work in a second piece written in the same year. "My own hope is that the emerging definition of social work may define it as involving the *conscious use of social relations* in performing certain community functions such as child welfare, family welfare or health services, recreation, and informal education" (1946, p. 6, emphasis added). Coyle saw the common professional values and norms of caseworkers, group workers, and community organizers as a similar respect for individual autonomy and social interdependence. This respect was carried out in activities that centered on understanding and fostering human relationships.

The year 1946 also marked the initiation of the American Association of Group Workers (AAGW). Most of AAGW's 2,300 members came from the older American Association for the Study of Group Work. They joined Grace Coyle as well as other proponents to advance the mission of developing professional skill in enabling group process on behalf of members in groups with diverse functions and in a variety of organizational contexts. In 1949 the AAGW drafted its official "Definition of the Function of the Group Worker" (Coyle, 1949), which served — unaltered — to clarify the components of social work practice with groups for several decades thereafter. The first sentence of this document emphasized the defining concept of *enabling group process.* "The group worker enables various types of groups to function in a way that both group interaction and program contribute to the growth of the individual and the achievement of desirable goals" (p. 1). The major skill identified to achieve this purpose is stated as "the conscious use of . . . [one's own relationships] . . . to the group, . . . knowledge of program as a tool and understanding of the *individual* and of the *group process*" (p. 3, emphasis added).

Outside of social work, other influences on group work during the period 1940–1950 are particularly noteworthy. The involvement of other mental health professions (e.g., psychiatry, clinical psychology, psychiatric nursing) in responding to the vast numbers of those needing help during and following World War II generated more extensive use and experimentation with group psychotherapy (for a historical review, see Shapiro, 1978). Many branches of contemporary group psychotherapy models came from this period.

In addition, social psychology as a profession boomed and combined with other social sciences to develop theory and empirical research in group process and dynamics. In fact, 1950 symbolizes the "Golden Year of Small Group Dynamics." Many works were published in that year by newly flowering experts on small group dynamics; these include classics by Kurt Lewin (1951), George Homans (1950), and Robert Bales (1950). These works, along with earlier innovative concepts of small group interaction represented by Charles Cooley (1918) and Jacob Moreno (1934), helped to establish the conception of the small group as an entity or social unit worthy of special study and use in the social and behavioral sciences. In sum, the small group was posited as a social system in microcosm, complete with its own boundaries, structure, norms, communication process, and task and socioemotional maintenance functions; as a major medium for reaching, teaching, changing, and developing competence in its members; and as a source of engaging in conflicts concerning power and intimacy — for good or for ill — in social interaction. There was much concern among the early scholars of group process and dynamics about understanding the blind conformity forces in groups. A common ideological stance centered on how the power in the group could be tapped for more responsive individual and social change. This came, of course, on the heels of Adolf Hitler and the Nazi Party's use of small group power to recruit and socialize a nation of youth into wreaking horrors on humanity.

1960–1975: SOCIAL GROUPWORK—METHOD AND MODELS

The earlier ambiguities between groupwork and social work were generally resolved by 1955. The AAGW became one of the major professional associations that joined to form the National Association of Social Workers (NASW) in that year. By 1960, a majority of schools of social work had social groupwork sequences with somewhat equal emphases on the casework and community organization sequences. Bringing faculty experience and expertise and student interest together in such sequences and integrating them officially into NASW pursuits cultivated both the generic aspects of social groupwork method and a variety of models for practice with groups. Group practice, as it evolved during this period, generally bridged the casework and community organization polarities of the "Ruling Triumvirate" of methods (Anderson, 1981). Caseworkers and social groupworkers sought commonalities and differences while learning to use some of each other's methods. Community organizers and groupworkers explored reciprocal contributions to the small group as a resource for environmental change. All were united, to varying degrees, around seeking generic or mainstream components of social work and in sharing work on general systems theory as a conceptual framework for all practice.

This period, began with major contributions to social work practice with groups that appeared in the works of Gisela Konopka (1963), Alan Klein (1970), Helen Phillips (1957), William Schwartz (1961), and Robert Vinter (1967). These works had the following in common: (1) the conceptualization of the generic knowledge, values, and skills for the social groupwork method; (2) the combination of both therapeutic and social goals functions in the use of groups; (3) the application of generic knowledge, values, and skills to the specific functions and contexts of practice; and (4) the central meaning and value of group process as the medium for change and growth at both individual and societal levels in this practice. (Margaret Hartford's *Groups in Social Work*, 1971, epitomized this generic work.)

Another common influence on the social work professionals cited above, perhaps most embodied in Gisela Konopka's work (1951; 1954; 1956; 1963), was personal practice experience in providing group services to children and youth as well as experience in more focused therapeutic practice with adults in mental health settings. By chance or by design, these professionals were in the fortunate position to use their own experiences and scholarship talents to appreciate (1) the natural processes for growth and development in groups that inevitably take on much power in children and youth groups; (2) the structure that promotes more mutual aid in effective problem solving necessary for treatment, counseling, or therapy in groups; and (3) the importance of personal, interpersonal, and political empowerment to varying degrees in all groups. The latter recognition included tapping the power and resources in groups (when necessary) to engage in environmental change, community action, and social justice activity even when the primary focus was on personal and interpersonal therapeutic goals.

During the latter part of the decade 1960–1970 came a professional and social *zeitgeist* of freedom, confrontation of differences, revolutionary movements and concepts, and increased social and political consciousness. (This period also represents significant influences on me personally: I was learning to be a competent social worker, including in my practice with groups. I must confess that the thrusts and upheavals for change were buzzing everywhere for me and were so much a part of me that to stand back, examine, and analyze the historical currents with more clarity and accuracy is likely an impossible task.) It was a time that saw a civil rights movement, a peace movement, a renewed women's movement, much social unrest, and empowerment organization among the poorest families and the most privileged youth in the nation. It was a time of assassinations of important national leaders; a most controversial war; corrupt administrations in state, local, and federal government; youth "free-love" and "flower children" highly critical of their elders; elders accusing each other of exploitation and feeling ambivalent about their own youth; rising power of the military-industrial complex; group violence; an anti-elitism movement in the professions; a human potential movement; and evolving "do-your-own-thing," "tell-it-like-it-is," "let-it-all-hang-out" norms for social interaction. Certainly the evolution of group process both within and outside social work, and as I was learning it, was affected by all these and much more.

By the early 1970s and throughout that decade, there was a significant proliferation of the use of groups as a resource and of models for practice with groups (Middleman and Goldberg, 1987). This proliferation occurred as much or more outside of social work as within. Wherever forged, the models seemed more directly influenced by member-and-group-centeredness, an emphasis on reciprocal and collaborative relationships among members and between members and leaders; a respect for personal choice and authenticity, if not the accompanying expectation of personal responsibility, in their values and norms.

In 1966, Catherine Papell and Beulah Rothman had published an article on the state of the art in social groupwork practice that identified the similarities and differences in the prevailing and evolving models for this practice. Their work, entitled "Social Group Work Models: Possession and Heritage," identified three separate models. These models and their primary developers were:

1. Social Goals: Klein (1973), Konopka (1963), Northern (1969)
2. Reciprocal: Schwartz (1961)
3. Remedial: Vinter (1967)

By 1971, the *Encyclopedia of Social Work* (Morris, 1971) covered "social group work" under separate sections reflecting the work on these three models (with the "reciprocal" renamed as the "interactionalist" approach and the "remedial" as the "prevention and rehabilitation" approach) and an additional one termed "developmental" and formulated almost exclusively in the work of Emanuel Tropp (1972). Subsequent work on the social goals model was primarily associated with the groupwork faculty at Boston University's School of Social Work (Bernstein, 1973); it built on the early work by James Garland, Herbert Jones, and Ralph

Kolodny (1973), which formulated practice with group process primarily through the stages of group development. The interactionist approach was further refined by William Schwartz and his students and colleagues at Columbia University's School of Social Work (Schwartz and Zalba, 1971; Schwartz, 1976). The social treatment approach, originated by Robert Vinter, became known more colloquially as the "Michigan model." Faculty colleagues and students of Vinter's at the University of Michigan's School of Social Work, such as Charles Garvin, Paul Glasser, and Rosemary Sarri (Glasser, Sarri, and Vinter, 1974), made important contributions.

These models were primarily distinguished by their underlying "if-then" intervention hypotheses (Anderson, 1981):

1. Social goals: *If* the practitioner can influence the group and the members to establish a common cause and to convert self-seeking behavior into a social contribution in group process, *then* members will develop their skills for meaningful and responsible social participation;
2. Developmental: *If* the practitioner can influence a group and its members to develop the group's potential for task accomplishment and empathetic interpersonal relationships, *then* the group can achieve its goals, members can increase their interpersonal competence, and individuals can further their self-actualization.
3. Interactional: *If* the practitioner can engage other members with each other and the worker, and establish the group's tasks as autonomous actors in an interdependent mutual aid system, *then* members can accomplish their goals in a manner that increases their skills for mutual aid transactions in the various systems through which they carry on their relationship with society.
4. Social treatment: *If* the practitioner can assess individual members' needs for change and the process for addressing specific treatment goals, *then* members will increase both social functioning in specific areas and their general competence for solving future problems through involvement in interpersonal relationships.

Additional significant work was done on the "behavioral" model by Sheldon Rose (1977) and others. (See Roberts and Northen, 1976, for a comparative review.)

Simultaneous with the growth of these models, the decades of the 1960s and 1970s experienced an explosion in the use of groups as resources and in approaches and models for facilitating group process in areas tangential to or more distant from social work. This trend involved spurts in the theory and use of group psychotherapy; the central place of small group process in the human potential movement and in human relations training (Anderson, 1975); and the use of community action groups, self-help groups, and neighborhood organization groups in the "poverty program." Group psychotherapy developed distinct models such as the psychoanalytic (Scheidlinger, 1980), existential (Goldberg and Goldberg, 1973), and interpersonal (Yalom, 1975). Therapy in a group context grew in reference to the wider use of Gestalt therapy, transactional analysis, rational emotive therapy, reality therapy, and others (Shaffer and Galinsky, 1989). Group counseling methodology gained prominence (Corey, 1979). The cornerstones of much of the human potential movement were encounter groups (Schutz, 1973) and sensory awareness groups (Otto, 1970). Human relations training utilized laboratory training or T-groups (Bradford, 1978) and sensitivity training groups (Blumberg, 1971). Closely related were organizational development approaches via small group process (Pfeiffer and Jones, 1979).

These experiences caused more social workers without specialized training in work through groups to value small group experience as a resource and to develop their skills for such practice. They also underscored the hunger in our society for belonging and for close and more authentic relationships with others. In addition, Morton Lieberman, Irvin Yalom, and Matthew Miles in *Encounter Groups: First Facts* (1973) and others (see *Small Group Behavior* journal issues, 1970–1980) brought empirical research to examine some of the very variables in group structure, group process, and group outcomes that we in social work needed to understand and use on behalf of therapeutic change and growth for members in groups.

1975–1990: TOWARD GENERIC PRACTICE

By the mid-1970s another major issue in our society and in the social work profession impacted on this heritage with continued effect on contemporary group practice. As a society and a profession formally identified with the nation's efforts to eliminate poverty, we were held and held ourselves (often inaccurately) accountable for the failure of the so-called War on Poverty. In response, social work education programs mobilized by reexamining the place of community work in practice. There was more integration of the casework, groupwork, and community organization methods in the preparation of each practitioner. This trend toward "integrated methods," rather than specialized ones, formed the basis of "generalist" practice. In 1974, generalist practice became institutionalized as the objective for preparation for BSW practice. By 1982, it became the requirement in the social work foundation for MSW practice. Many concerns were behind these decisions. The most predominant was that all social workers need to avoid the "law of the instrument" (Kaplan, 1964). This referred to the determination of the needs of those whom we serve primarily on the basis of the intervention methods that are available to use. Thus, if social workers were trained in depth only with individual intervention skills, they tended to define needs as personal problems or pathologies, necessitating individual counseling and psychotherapy.

What resulted was extensive redesigning of social work education curricula and the elimination of methods specialization in favor of generic methods, integrated methods, and/or generalist practice as applied to concentrations in direct services, indirect services, or particular fields of practice. Another result was a watering down of the content, competencies, and heritages for social work with groups (Birnbaum and Auerbach, 1994; Goldberg and Lamont, 1992; Tropp, 1979). Paradoxically this same period saw the rise of group practice in the field, which still booms today in self-help groups, substance abuse groups, support groups, social skills training, parenting groups, socializing groups for the elderly, and so on.

Although this trend may have eroded the skillful preparation for work with groups that had evolved in social work (Birnbaum and Auerbach, 1994; Steinberg, 1993), several important contributions to contemporary practice did begin. These include:

1. Renewed attention to the group as a generic resource (Anderson, 1979) for which social workers needed both treatment skills and task group skills (Toseland and Rivas, 1984);
2. The evolution of structured opportunities with groups and of group psychotherapy, and consideration of their appropriate use in social work practice through attention to what was called "mainstream" in *social work with groups* (Lang, 1979; Papell and Rothman, 1980);
3. The creation of the journal *Social Work with Groups: A Journal of Community and Clinical Groups* in 1978 under the editorship of Catherine Papell and Beulah Rothman as a forum for renewed examination of the important place of social work with groups in all areas of the profession.

Thus, the evolution moved from group work, to social groupwork, to *social work with groups* (Northen, 1969). This latter practice emphasizes the central concepts of *mutual aid* (Gitterman and Schulman, 1988) as the gauge of synergistic social systems and *empowerment* as the primary aim of all social work practice (Parsons, 1991).

The 1980s brought economic recessions and a conservative climate that was not so supportive of social reform. This correlates with more recent work on identifying a "mainstream" model (Fatout, 1992) and with more special focus on clinical social work practice with groups (Reid, 1991).

There are many ways to explain these trends. The hypothesis here is that evolution of a profession like social work, no less than the evolution of society, swings between polarized forces toward an integration of strong differences. Similar to this text's assumption regarding stages of group development, systems evolve in spiral process. Unresolved issues and unattended forces from the past create polarities in current processes toward advancing more balanced integration ("equilibration" in systems terms). According to another source, "[current systems in development] become increasingly differentiated and hierarchically integrated" (Anderson, 1981, p. 97). Historically then, systems such as the social work profession might be expected to follow a pendulum of change between regressive and progressive forces. They maintain enough continuity for survival in the face of change and enough discontinuity to change toward growth in maximizing their strengths and potential.

This historical hypothesis is useful in examining the evolution of social work as a profession, especially in terms of the trends that emerged in the 1980s and greatly affect contemporary practice. The power politics and interest groups within the profession have often differentiated into clinical services and social reform camps, with the camp that is out of power gaining strength to create change moderated toward hierarchial integration through the power of such ideas as generic, generalist, integrated, and "person-in-environment" practice.

With emphasis in direct social work practice, those with casework theory method and skills held power in the profession through the 1940s and 1950s. Social reform through community organization, at the other pole, tended to lose power and appear undervalued in the profession. The 1960s and 1970s reflect dramatic shifts in this power pendulum. Social work's community organizers and policy specialists and those moving more from the direct service camp toward the community-centered one were the vanguard of our profession's involvement in the poverty program. They also increased in power and status to be among the most politically and academically active and influential proponents of generalist practice. Social workers involved in clinical practice were losing power and appearing undervalued in the professional debates to reconceptualize and legislate social work practice (especially via Council on Social Work Education [CSWE] standards for accreditation of BSW and MSW programs).

By 1980 the pendulum again swung, as perceived powerlessness within the profession empowered clinical social workers to organize into regional and national federations, special interest groups within the National Association of Social Workers (NASW), and other associations that lobbied for third-party payments and licensing for their practice (see Dorfman, 1989). This practice was perceived as undervalued not only by the professional thrusts of the prior two decades, but by a country that provided less economic support for our services in an ever-shrinking national economic pie. By the end of the 1980s, clinical social work was well entrenched as a major objective and concentration in preparation for advanced practice in social work education and within the priority issues of the profession addressed collectively through NASW.

What has this "spiral" evolution created for the most ardent proponents of social reform and for social work practice with groups in the 1980–1990 decade? Those most active in the poverty program tend to rue this power shift in the profession, perceiving an abandonment of public social services and commitment to serve the poor and other oppressed and powerless groups (Specht and Courtney, 1993). These voices gain in strength and are being heard even while debated. As a profession and a nation, we need the strength and power of their difference to spark further system evolution and to counter what could become an elitist sphere of clinical social work.

This differentiation, too, has been more or less integrated within the hierarchial structure of the definition and standards for social work practice. By 1989, the official NASW definition of clinical social work practice included the mastery of a generalist foundation. So do CSWE accreditation standards. While emphasizing individual, marital, family, and group psychotherapy and counseling, NASW's definition specifically indicates intervention knowledge and skills for the social contexts of practice through policy analysis, service organizations' accessibility to services and other resources, and community action and development (Northen, 1989).

Those working on developing theory for social work practice with groups (with some exceptions) seem to (1) build on the strengths of those coming into the profession in their motivation to make a difference to clients primarily face-to-face, and (2) expand this strength through an identification with the historical visions and competence that social work with groups has contributed to our profession. This work during the 1980s centered on identification of "mainstream" (or historically central) concepts from which to integrate other approaches — group counseling, group psychotherapy, and support and mutual aid groups — into clinical practice that combines therapeutic and social goals purposes (Lang, 1979; Papell and Rothman, 1980; Schwartz, 1985/86; Middleman and Goldberg, 1987).

THE LAST DECADE: THE SOCIAL WORK
IN GROUP PRACTICE

What are the enduring elements that distinguish social work with groups, both historically and currently? Such components are incorporated in this text's process model. First, the small group is conceived of in a humanistic perspective (Glassman and Kates, 1990), which provides an all-abiding respect for the individual's needs and potentials for both autonomy and interdependence. The model views the human being as having inherent motivation and capacity to use the group as an opportunity for mutual aid, to integrate individual freedom with social responsibility, and to develop the potential for both self-fulfillment and democratic social participation. Hence, the small group experience can be a living, learning resource for empowerment in social functioning and mutual aid.

Second, there is an overriding holistic perspective, which anticipated much of current ecosystems theory and has been refined by it. In this view individuals and groups are understood not only as autonomous entities pitted against each other but also as interdependent parts of a synergistic whole. This "whole" determines the reciprocal processes of common needs, common purposes, common goals, common ground, and the common impetus that drives members toward each other for mutual power, benefit, and growth. Likewise, the group and the wider ecological environment share a common gestalt, requiring balanced attention in practice. This perspective reflects the central principle of *integration* in such aspects as individual change and collective action; task and process; talk and action; rational and creative activity; structure and spontaneity; power and mutuality; practitioner purpose and group autonomy; and social role and authenticity (Papell and Rothman, 1980).

Third, within these humanistic and holistic traditions, the practice group approximates the natural group as closely as possible. As Norma Lang (1979) states:

> The group interaction process ranges freely, naturally and spontaneously both with respect to how people communicate, to what substantive content is addressed and how, and the variety of means and routes the group may use to process its goals. The process is similar to that found in natural groups in society. (pp. 210–211)

Fourth, there is a crucial collaborative practitioner stance and function in relation to empowering group process to develop its potential as a mutual aid system. Schwartz (1985/86) describes the traditional worker-member relationship as "co-active, reciprocal, functional, first-among-equals, mentoring and collaboration in the pursuit of group tasks" (p. 20). In this stance the practitioner is the expert on the group helping process, the "guardian of method," rather than the authoritative expert on the lives of members or their needs within and outside the group. Papell and Rothman (1980) describe this style as purposeful, warm, informal, authentic, and forthright. As much as possible, in social work groups the practitioner enables both autonomy and interdependence through establishing shared power and responsibility. This egalitarian collaboration combines with the practitioner's stance as a fellow human being whose function is to mediate the processes through which individual group members connect mutual needs and purposes. Thus, the practitioner models both purpose and reciprocity in interpersonal relationships and encourages members to relate with mutuality and purpose to use the group's power and resources on behalf of themselves and others.

Ruth Middleman and Gale Goldberg, writing the section entitled "Social Work Practice with Groups" for the 1987 edition of the *Encyclopedia of Social Work*, incorporated these concepts into four criteria proposed to qualify work through group process as *social work* with groups. These represent what they call the "mainstream model" and include:

1. Attention to the group as a whole and its process;
2. Focus on helping members develop a system of mutual aid;
3. An attitudinal set that promotes members' and the group's autonomy and interdependence. In Middleman and Goldberg's words: "From the first group meeting, the [practitioner] thinks about working herself or himself out of a job. That is, the [practitioner] tries to enable the group to increase its autonomy so that it can continue as a self-help and mutual support group. This does not hold for groups of children or severely limited adults. In these instances, the [practitioner] helps groups become as autonomous as possible" (p. 721); and
4. The special attention to members' re-experiencing their "groupness" at the point of termination (pp. 721–722).

CONCLUSION

As the pendulum swung and cycles of forces spiraled in the evolution of social work practice with groups, the enduring trends have been periodically re-discovered and re-committed. The past informs the common base of diverse uses of group process in present and future practice.

The model in this text illuminates the importance of enabling both autonomy and interdependence in the stages of development as these mark therapeutic group process. It emphasizes the functions and skills that empower individuals and groups in mutual aid systems. It combines strength-oriented and problem-solving aims for group process and outcomes. It values the group process as a "slice of life" wherein natural processes and purposeful work contribute both to normal growth and development and increased skills in problem solving. It conceives of problem solving as empowerment at personal, interpersonal, and/or political levels. Its intent is to build on the strengths of today's social work practitioners and social work practitioners-in-training to use the self for therapeutic aims in personal and professional relationships. It adds increased competence and skill in using a variety of group service resources to "raise life to its highest value" (Addams, 1902) and to promote "hope for the political, the social, the international life of the future" (Follet, 1918). It imbues our professional power with the strength of this historical vision.

chapter 3

Generalist Perspective and Practice

A physician, an attorney, and a social worker were engaged in a lively debate about which of their three professions — medicine, law, or social work — was the noblest. They had decided that the oldest of these was the most noble, and the debate began.

The physician started with this statement: "If we go to the Bible, we read in Genesis that Eve was created from Adam's rib. Now for that operation to have occurred, there must have been a surgeon present. Hence, medicine is the oldest and noblest profession."

Upon hearing this, the attorney deliberated for several minutes and then retorted: "If I recall, before the Adam and Eve story, we learn in Genesis that order was created from chaos. Now for order to come about in society, there must have been a lawyer present. Ergo: Law is clearly the oldest and therefore noblest profession. I rest my case."

At that point, the social worker quickly ended the debate by asking, "But who do you think created the chaos?"

INTRODUCTION

The ambiguities that have plagued our profession in the past, during the present, and perhaps even into the future, stem to a large degree from two facts suggested in the last chapter: Social work is an ideological profession, and its practices are very diverse. Webster defines ideology as "visionary theorizing." As an ideological profession, social work has grappled with developing approaches and models that combine philosophical and theoretical underpinnings, vision with practice. What we face now and in the twenty-first century is a renewed effort to develop such approaches and models for informing practice. The call is for "re-vision."

As a diverse profession, we wrestle with seeking unity within diversity. In addition to ideological clarity, work on the common elements among diverse practices ("generic" or "mainstream" approaches) marks the evolution of both social work as a profession and our practice with groups. These historical trends flow into the streams of contemporary and future practice. This chapter examines these currents as related to small group practice and the process model of this text.

VISION AND PRACTICE: CAUSE AND FUNCTION

The stuggle to combine vision and practice can be examined historically in relation to the cause and function debates. In 1905, less than a decade after jolting the medical profession by recommending a common educational foundation, Abraham Flexner took the podium at the National Conference of Charities and Corrections to address the question, "Is Social Work a Profession?" As the audience of social work pioneers waited in hopeful anticipation of his answer, Flexner studiously applied his six criteria of professional activity to social work. He both disappointed and challenged participants with his verdict that social work was *not* a bona fide profession (Flexner, 1905).

Most social workers remember Flexner's final verdict. Many recall how he found us wanting. Flexner's opinion was that social work had no teachable technique of its own, but only mediated between people with needs and formal resources to meet those needs. Few social workers, however, may realize how he concluded his classic presentation. His final words were: "The unselfish devotion of those who have chosen to give themselves to making the world a better place to live in can fill social work with professional spirit and thus to some extent, lift it above all the distinctions which I have at [*sic*] such pains to make" (p. 590).

Flexner credited our vision, or cause. That social work was a profession with the ideology of "those who have chosen to give themselves to making the world a better place to live in" was our strength. He challenged us to work on our function, or the teachable principles and skills deemed effective to address our cause.

We now face the changes and challenges of life in post-industrial society, to use Daniel Bell's (1973) label — or what Alvin Toffler (1970) calls the "information society" of the post-modern future, and Robert Naisbitt (1984) deems the "time of parenthesis" or the time between eras, the time of change and questioning. We are an important profession in an era of swift social change — provided we find a way to combine our past identity with present trends and future vision. This seems no less so for social work with groups.

Current definitions and standards for social work practice emphasize several points: a generalist perspective, multicultural sensitivity, conscious use of skills, and empirical support (Council on Social Work Education, 1994). This chapter places the group process model in the generalist perspective. Indeed, the generalist perspective and approach (Sheafor and Landon, 1987) defines the foundation for all practice (CSWE, 1994). The implications of this model for this practice especially attend to the empowerment processes in group practice to inform the teachable functions and skills for which Flexner called.

THE SMALL GROUP IN GENERALIST PRACTICE

The small group is at the heart of generalist practice. Research by Mona Schatz, Lowell Jenkins, and Bradford Sheafor (1990) defines current conceptions of the generalist perspective through four components: (1) the practice is client-centered and problem-focused; (2) it evokes direct and indirect intervention; (3) it envisions democratic, humanizing, and empowering transactions between people and their environments; and (4) it uses research-based knowledge to inform the practice principles and skills.

Thus, conceptions of generalist practice depend significantly on the development of methodology that bridges individuals and the community. Practice through group process is an important resource for such intervention. This is especially so when group process facilitation aims for empowerment in both personal growth and community development.

Figure 3.1 depicts a generalist framework for this practice. The framework describes generalist practice primarily in terms of its unit of focus and its particular change objectives. The two units of focus are client systems or resource systems. The two change objectives are in problem situations or resource systems. Such a classification generates four major areas of work. Quadrant A depicts direct work with microclient systems in their own behalf (direct intervention). The practice methods and procedures here target primarily on individuals, families, and small groups (conceived as interpersonal problem-solving systems). Quadrant B depicts work with people within resource systems in behalf of particular client systems' problem situations. The primary target for these generalist practice tasks is the connection or transaction between particular client systems and particular resource systems. This is the other side of direct, microlevel work.

Quadrants C and D constitute the more indirect, macrolevel aspects of generalist practice (indirect intervention). In Quadrant C, the work focuses on resource systems to change the nature of these resources in behalf of particular client systems. The target is the formal and informal organizational context as a resource for or obstacle to effective service delivery. Quadrant D extends generalist practice to the community. The work is with resource systems to change the nature of resources in behalf of current, known clients and future, unknown clients and others. The emphasis is on community or social change to increase maintenance, restoration, prevention, or enhancement resources for all who need them.

In the center of this practice, which potentially involves work in all four quadrants, is the small group. With empowerment principles and skills informing this practice, the small group is a central resource for generalist practice that bridges the four quadrants. It spans the work with both client and resource systems for both problem situation and resource system change.

UNIT OF FOCUS

	CLIENT SYSTEM	RESOURCE SYSTEM	
PROBLEM SITUATIONS	A. Work with client systems in their own behalf.	B. Work with resource systems in behalf of particular problem situations.	**DIRECT MICROLEVEL**
CHANGE OBJECTIVES Maintenance/ Restoration/ Prevention/ Enhancement	TARGET: "CASE" Individuals, families, small groups (interpersonal systems) METHODS: e.g., interviewing, interpersonal helping, psychological treatment counseling, skill training	TARGET: "CONNECTION" Client system/resource system transaction METHODS: e.g., case management, case consultation, networking, linkage	
	C. Work with resource systems to change nature of resources in behalf of particular client systems.	D. Work with resource systems to change nature of resources in behalf of clients and unknown others.	
RESOURCE SYSTEMS	TARGET: "CONTEXT" Organizations (formal and informal) METHODS: e.g., environmental modification, organizational development (O.D.), "case" advocacy, management, supervision	TARGET: "CAUSE" Communities. METHODS: e.g., prevention, "cause" advocacy, political action, community organization, policy and/or program development	**INDIRECT MACROLEVEL**

*(center spanning text: **SMALL GROUPS**)*

FIGURE 3.1   Generalist framework

EMPOWERMENT

Empowerment as the major aim in generalist practice with small groups attends especially to the development of both autonomy and interdependence through group process. Lorraine Gutierrez (1990, p. 149) defines empowerment as "a process of increasing personal, interpersonal, or political power so that individuals can take action to improve their life situations." Thus, it can include work at many levels: (1) gaining personal power and control over problem situations; (2) raising critical consciousness regarding the sociopolitical context of powerlessness; (3) sharing power by engaging in interpersonal mutual aid; and (4) establishing power coalitions and managing power conflicts with others for political action to change social institutions and promote socially just and humane communities (Lee, 1995; Miley, O'Melia, and DuBois, 1995; Parsons, 1991). This definition of empowerment combines the personal and political, the micro and macro, in generalist social work practice.

AUTONOMY AS EMPOWERMENT

At the micro or personal level, empowerment has come to reflect the development of increased self-autonomy, or personal power and control over one's life (Pernell, 1985; Pinderhuges, 1983; Rappaport, 1986; Simmons and Parsons, 1983). Julian Rappaport (1986) describes this psychological empowerment:

> It suggests a sense of control over one's life in personality, cognition, and motivation. It expresses itself at the level of feelings, at the level of ideas about self-worth, and at the level of being able to make a difference in the world around us, and even at the spiritual level. It is an ability we all have, but that needs to be released, much the way our bodies can be self-healing when endorphins are released. We all have the potential. It does not need to be purchased, nor is it a scarce commodity. (pp. 69–70)

Empowerment, conceived of as the development of autonomy, evolves from the assumption that self-determination or choice is a natural thrust and inherent potential of human beings. The literature promoting such personal empowerment focuses on the psychological outcomes of increasing self-efficacy and perceived competence (Gutierrez, 1990; Simmons and Parsons, 1983); reducing self-blame and increasing self-esteem (Pinderhuges, 1983; Solomon, 1976); and increasing an internal locus of control, where appropriate, and assuming personal responsibility for change (Gutierrez, 1990; Pinderhuges, 1989; Rappaport, 1986).

The opposite of this sense of self-autonomy appears as dehumanization, or a sense of personal alienation (Anderson, 1976). Alienation manifests itself in feelings of powerlessness, meaninglessness, normlessness, isolation, and self-estrangement (Seeman, 1985). Powerlessness is experienced when people feel they cannot achieve desired goals by their own efforts. Meaninglessness is experienced when one does not understand and cannot predict the outcome of one's own efforts. Normlessness is the perception that goals are more likely achieved, if at all, by actions that are disapproved of by the dominant society. Isolation is disintegration from and noncommitment to the goals and norms of a community that is perceived as not working for one's own interest. Self-estrangement is the perception of self and others as objects to be exploited and manipulated rather than valued as significant human beings.

In practice, this personal empowerment perspective combats alienation by promoting autonomy. Direct intervention relies on a balance of power in helping transactions. There is encouragement of self-help and client-centered decision making. The work begins with accepting the client system's definition of the problem situation. It presumes that the solution to the client system's issues does not lie in the social worker but in the client system's strengths to resolve the situation. This strength evolves through a helping relationship based on collaboration, trust, and the sharing of power (Gutierrez, 1990).

Generally, a balance of power in direct intervention assumes that problem situations initially have power over client systems. This imbalance requires a counterinfluence wherein the collaborative power of the practitioner and the client system begin to supersede the power of the problem situation. Then, the power of the client system might shift to a critical analysis of the power structure and to the client's sharing of power through interdependence with others (Lee, 1995; Seitz, 1985).

INTERDEPENDENCE AS EMPOWERMENT

In this development, empowerment initiates in personal autonomy and competence and moves toward interdependence, or the sense of community. Such empowering through interdependent mutual aid and self-help was noted by Bertha Reynolds (1941) over a half-century ago:

> Help must be connected with increase . . . of self-respect, and it must imply the possibility of a reciprocal relationship of sharing within a group to which both giver and receiver belong. . . . It is not hard to take help in a circle in which one feels sure of belonging. It hurts to feel doubtful on being able to repay at all, and by that means to be again in full status as a giving, as well as receiving, member of the group. (pp. 24–25, 162)

Those who address empowerment as a sociopolitical process also posit a general pattern of movement from autonomy to interdependence (Kieffer, 1984; Rappaport, 1986). This evolution of mutual aid appears to be a powerful resource for grassroots community and political action. Those in community organization (Katz, 1989; Kieffer, 1984), adult education (Schmitt and Weaver, 1979), the feminist movement (Albrecht and Brewer, 1990), and populist politics (Boyte and Reissman, 1986) all tend to identify three general stages of transforming mutual aid, self-help processes into political movements. They suggest that:

1. The very process of mutual aid, marked by personal autonomy and interdependence, combines the empowerment of people feeling able to control some aspects of their lives with actual competencies for working together and sharing. This self-efficacy motivation and competence for interdependent actions increase confidence in addressing larger issues.
2. A critical consciousness and advocacy focus can appear as people engaged in mutual help discover together the external causes of their problems. Underlying this critical consciousness is the self-help ethos that emphasizes the indigenous strengths of the people involved and a self-determined proactive stance for advocacy. This contrasts with a reliance on external, elite experts who lobby as advocates for constituents who remain basically passive, inactive, and without a personal sense of empowerment.
3. From these more "pre-political" forms there can emerge a consciousness of the interconnections of issues and the extension of motivation and competency into interdependent actions to increase opportunities for political action and change. Such new populism creates political

movements based on empowerment — or the demand of a variety of groups and movements for more control over their lives.

In sum, empowerment fosters both autonomy and interdependence. The development of empowerment requires beliefs about one's competency and efficacy as well as one's involvement in activities for exerting control in the sociopolitical environment. There is a proactive approach to life, a psychological sense of competence and control, sociopolitical activity, and organizational involvement. Developed empowerment, then, is how people integrate themselves into their community so it is experienced as working for them and not on them.

EMPOWERMENT THROUGH GROUP PROCESS

As Ruth Parsons (1991) has recently proposed, empowerment is a powerful concept to explicate the underlying aim and the change principles for generalist social work practice through group process. The empowerment theme is particularly relevant in practice that targets populations at risk in the development of multicultural communities. The antithesis of multiculturalism is seen in communities marked by both cultural and structural inequalities rather than by cultural and structural pluralism (Anderson, 1991). In the face of such social injustices as discrimination and oppression, the poor, people of color, women, the elderly, and people who are physically or mentally challenged are particularly vulnerable to actual and perceived powerlessness. As William Ryan (1972) and Barbara Solomon (1976) originally proposed in their separate seminal works, and as more recent research (Kieffer, 1984) has supported, this powerlessness is both (1) *perceived* from the basis of negative self-evaluation and internalized self-blame, and (2) *actual* in the experiences of intergroup interactions and the larger sociopolitical context.

The relationship of small group process to empowerment with populations-at-risk has led Gutierrez (1990) — in addressing social work practice with women of color — to conclude:

> Small group work is . . . the ideal modality for empowerment interventions . . . whether the goal is empowering individuals or changing institutions. . . . The groups facilitate empowerment by creating a basis of social support . . . , a format for providing concrete assistance or opportunity to learn new skills . . . and a potential power base for future action. . . . They also can provide the context for developing group consciousness, by involving clients in dialogue with others who share their problems. (p. 151)

In subsequent research Gutierrez, along with Robert Ortega (Gutierrez and Ortega, 1991), generally found support for the importance of small groups for empowering members through social support, concrete assistance, learning new skills, and, especially, increasing critical consciousness and commitment to action. Their study of Latino students in a large midwestern university compared ethnic identity and consciousness-raising groups with no-treatment control groups with respect to particular empowerment outcomes. The ethnic identity and consciousness-raising groups were statistically significant in increasing members' commitment to take action on behalf of themselves and in concert with others in situations of oppression. The consciousness-raising group was especially important in its increasing of both personal autonomy and members' plans to take action interdependently with others in promoting institutional change.

The principles for this empowerment in generalist practice indicate the need for practitioners to move beyond work with individual clients and problem situations to think of ways to engage clients together in group efforts toward both individual and community change. Hence, groups have therapeutic and community empowerment objectives. Those who have studied the linking of personal, interpersonal, and political empowerment based on both personal growth and grassroots community action propose remarkably consistent components. These are:

- Positive perceptions of personal worth, efficacy, and one's sense of autonomy, which manifest themselves as achievement of self-determined goals through the use of personal resource and skill.

- Recognition, by both self and others, that some of one's perceptions about one's self and the surrounding world are indeed valid and therefore legitimate to voice.

- The ability to move from individual needs and goals to mutual aid needs and goals and to develop and share the power of knowledge, caring, and action to achieve group goals.

- The ability to think critically about macrolevel social, political, and economic systems and their effect on one's sense of dignity and worth and capacity to meet needs.

- Knowledge and skills necessary to develop action strategies and cultivate resources to influence micro, mediating, and macro systems for attainment of one's own goals and the goals of those one cares about.

- The ability to act in a reflective and efficacious manner in concert with others to define and attain collective goals and achieve better balanced power relations in responsible social change.

PRACTICE EXAMPLE

Ruth Parsons (1991, pp. 14–19) presents an especially relevant practice example of generalist empowerment through a group process approach to social work with groups.[1] The supervisor of a social worker assigned to a Head Start

---

[1] This case study is slightly adapted from R.J. Parsons, Empowerment: Purpose and practice principles in social work. *Social Work with Groups*, 14 (1991), 7–21. Adapted with the permission of The Haworth Press.

agency in an inner-city housing project asked her to intervene with the mothers of specific children in the Head Start program. The supervisor identified the mothers as all having children who were experiencing difficulty in school. Head Start staff indicated they were all single parents who seemed to have problems disciplining their children. This lack of discipline presented problems in the Head Start classroom and was of concern to the teachers.

The Approach

The practitioner approached each woman individually to discuss her child, parenting issues, and any identified concerns regarding discipline. Although some women identified the disciplining of their children as a specific problem for them, others seemed to take parenting in stride along with other stress-producing situations. They particularly noted environmental conditions that contributed not only to parenting issues but to concerns in their lives in general. The practitioner did not identify each woman as having a discipline problem with her child. Instead, she asked each woman if she would like to be a part of a group of women like herself who had children in the Head Start center. The practitioner said the purpose of the group would be to share parenting hassles and solutions (mutual aid support). Seven women agreed to come to the group and try it out.

The Group Members

The practitioner was Anglo, 29 years old, with no children of her own; she had had training in social work with groups during her BSW and MSW education. She had three years of pre-MSW degree experience working with AFDC (Aid to Families with Dependent Children) mothers in Hispanic communities and two years of post-MSW experience, including social work with groups.

Initially the group's seven members were all Hispanic but for two. One was an Anglo woman who was severely scarred from multiple birth defects and subsequent surgeries. Another Anglo woman was illiterate. Their ages ranged from 30 to 45. All were basically single parents. Two experienced intermittent involvement with the father of their children (he was in and out of the house). All were low income, living either on AFDC or at a similar subsistence level. All lived in a public housing project in the same neighborhood. Another Hispanic woman, Lupe, who was a teacher aide in Head Start, joined the group also. She identified with the other women as single parents living at a low level of economic security, as she had been in a similar situation. She also suggested that including her as a group would encourage the other women to participate in the group. It did.

The Contract

The practitioner began the group by supporting all the woman for being a part of the support group wherein "we could share common problems and common solutions about parenting." The practitioner clarified her expectations for the group and promoted the group's autonomous development by members. She indicated that the group would set its own goals and the activities for achieving them.

The practitioner then reached for the commonality of group members, including (but not exclusively) the parenting concerns. While members shared these, they also voiced many other concerns very early in the group. These issues included the stresses associated with single parenthood such as low incomes; housing problems (especially those in the housing project itself); ex-husbands, boyfriends, and relationships with men in general; and feelings of anger about their lives. The anger seemed to stem from being left by the men to raise children by themselves with little or no support or economic base to do so. Quickly the group became a resource for venting and sharing these more intense and common needs, and group goals combined to create a group culture with therapeutic norms for validating and supporting their feelings and perceptions.

The practitioner reinforced these evolving norms to facilitate the supportive and validating environment of the group. The members quickly perceived themselves to have common feelings, problems, and experiences. They experienced other members and the practitioner as hearing and validating their feelings regarding their circumstances. The contracted goals for the group expanded beyond dealing with parenting to supporting each other in dealing with the stresses of being poor and being a single parent.

The Group Process

Initially members were reluctant to trust one another with confidentiality owing to their close living proximity. They also were reluctant to trust the practitioner, who represented a different ethnic group, social class, and lifestyle. Lupe helped allay some of this mistrust in the beginning, serving as a bridge between the practitioner and the group. However, the group had to deal (both directly through expressed concerns and less directly through "testing out") with the practitioner's stake in them and in the group. As trust began to form and members felt supported by one another, they expressed more of their feelings about their situations and experienced being heard. When they resolved the initial trust issues, they were ready to assert more autonomy regarding what they wanted in *their* group and moved on to learning more specifically about the context of their situations and about solutions.

The practitioner collaborated in this work, sharing some of her expertise regarding income and other resources, knowledge about the housing project, and information about parenting techniques. As members developed more closeness in their shared support, understanding, and work, they voiced and focused on common problems. They targeted specific problems for work, and together with the practitioner they shared knowledge and skills about resolving these problems.

Mutual Aid Empowerment

As group members began to share both problems and expertise in an evolving mutual aid process, they identified many environmental conditions that were common to all of them. These involved a teacher in the local neighborhood school whose racist attitudes were a source of frustration and anger to their children and to them, the local grocery store owner who charged an exorbitant fee to cash monthly checks, the local city recreation center director who dealt drugs at the center, broken-down equipment on the playground, poor lighting in the projects that made it unsafe for women and young girls to walk at night for fear of sexual assault, and the housing manager who dealt unfairly and capriciously with the many residents in the project. All these issues were integral to parenting. They constituted the ecosystem of the women's single parenthood with major consequences for them, including issues of disciplining their children.

One by one the group put these problems on the agenda. With much interdependence, group members and the practitioner educated each other about the issues. Interdependently, too, they developed action strategies to address them and became more convinced that they could take effective action and control in regard to the problems that now controlled their daily lives.

The group did indeed intervene in the school system regarding the racist teacher. They intervened with the city regarding the recreation center director. They were able to confront the housing manager about his behavior. The housing office appointed a liaison to work directly with community residents to ensure more responsiveness to their concerns. When the local grocery store owner refused to lower his check-cashing fees, the women led a boycott against the store and organized transportation to a supermarket where they could buy groceries at a lower price and cash checks for free.

As they experienced success and some failure, the group members began to observe that there were other groups and organizations, resources both within and outside of the community, concerned with the same issues as theirs. They began to join forces. For example, they joined the local community interagency citizens action council, which was concerned with the whole of the community. Through that council they became members of task forces working on specific community projects. They were able to get the community council to engage in grant writing for playground equipment and lighting for the community. They joined with the community council to get a stoplight at the corner for protection of the children for crossing. They eventually began to serve on citywide task forces, as representatives from the community action council.

Although the group experienced success in working collaboratively with other community groups, they desired to continue their group for support and for discussion of such personal and interpersonal concerns as parenting and their relationships with men. For specific community projects, they worked as a subgroup of the community action council. One such project was to raise the awareness of counselors at the local community mental health center regarding the community. As a group they were concerned about the large number of depressed women, some suicidal and abusive to their children. They observed that when these women went to the community mental health center for help, they rarely went back a second time. Thus, they decided to intervene with the center itself. They asked counselors to come to the women's homes and to alter the services to fit the culture and needs of the community. They served as liaisons for the community mental health center, setting up meetings between specific women and center counselors.

Overall, the group's life was approximately three years in duration. Membership changed, but a core remained active throughout. Discipline of children was a running theme in the group's discussions. However, it was never viewed as a problem internal to the members. It was consistently viewed holistically in its ecosystem context and as being related to many other parts of the group members' lives. The women's self-esteem, not only as parents and as partners in relationships with men, improved remarkably. Consequently, so did their parenting skills!

This example richly depicts how a group process approach that utilizes the principles of empowerment can inform generalist practice. Such practice follows the intervention tasks that evolve in the group to address problem situations with various change objectives through focus on different units at different times. In this example we see a case of the small group in the center of practice that attends to targeted intervention in all four quadrants of the generalist framework presented in Figure 3.1.

In addition, the model informs more use of the group process in applying the wide range of approaches and models available for generalist practice with groups. The next section explores this contribution for contemporary practice.

APPROACHES FOR GENERALIST PRACTICE WITH GROUPS

Generalist practice requires generic competence in facilitating group process. It also includes some application of generic competence to specific approaches designed to achieve different objectives and to focus on different intervention levels. Table 3.1 organizes the diverse practices currently available for generalist practice with groups. It demonstrates, too, the relationship of these approaches to the group process model. It suggests how its incorporation can ensure that this work with groups occurs *through group process* as much as possible.

The two main dimensions for conceptually consolidating and distinguishing current groups in generalist social work practice are the "primary intervention purpose" and the "primary intervention focus." The three practice purposes of groups are preventive/developmental, problem-solving, or remedial. These reflect a continuum. Thus, as shown in Table 3.1, there are arrows for overlaps. Developmental groups focus on education or enhancement activities designed to strengthen particular systems and prevent possible dysfunctions. Problem-solving groups emphasize the amelioration of particular problems with the assumption that their resolution returns the system to a functional state. Remedial groups aim for reconstruction of systems considered dysfunctional.

The primary intervention focus for the group can be one of four: the individual member, the group itself, the organization, or the community. These are the systems that practitioners, and presumably members, want to influence most in order to meet service needs and goals. These targets relate to the intervention purpose; they are the unit of attention, or focus, through which the practitioner achieves the preventive/developmental, problem-solving, or remedial objectives.

This purpose/focus matrix structures further into whether the group approach attempts the accomplishment of primarily personal or task goals. Most group practice models accent more-or-less (rather than either-or) influence on personal ("I-We") or task ("It") processes and goals. Few advance equal intervention efforts at each. Table 3.1 represents this boundary with arrows. This indicates that the personal- or task-orientation is permeable and not so rigidly separated in most groups.

The dimensions on Table 3.1 consolidate into twenty-four cells. The group "approaches" that are representative of each cell (literally, come "nearer" to particular cells — or "approach"), exemplify the horizon of broad-based generalist group practice. To illustrate the volume of practice models available, the matrix includes examples ("Eg. Models") under each group approach.

The matrix indicates that the small group is a vital resource in generalist practice. Mobilizing this resource appears to require an exceptional repertoire of knowledge and skills, even in a limited range such as practice with individuals, groups, and organizations for developmental and problem-solving purposes. The process model in this book provides a more generic base for such work. It also helps to incorporate more of the empowerment principles into small group approaches. It ensures some attention to "I," the "We," and the "It" points of group process in social work group practice.

When groups serve developmental, problem-solving, and remedial purposes primarily for individuals (the first horizontal row in Table 3.1), the "I-It" tends to receive foremost attention while the group structure and process ("We") tends to recede into the background. This gestalt is traditional to personal growth groups, life skill development groups, individual problem-solving groups with either a personal- or task-orientation, and personality change or rehabilitation groups. The approaches subsume such models as awareness, action-oriented (e.g., dance and art "therapy" workshops), human relations skills training, Gestalt, transactional analysis, psychodrama, psychoanalytic and existential (Shaffer and Galinsky, 1989), and remedial social skills groups (Shean, 1985) as well as such social work models as task-centered (Garvin, 1985, 1992), social treatment (Sundel et al., 1985), cognitive-behavioral (Rose, 1990), and problem-solving skills training (Priestley et al., 1979). Although they differ in purposes and goal orientations, they share the common target of "individual change through small groups" (Sundel et al., 1985). Here, the process model directs the practitioner to develop the group's total process ("I-We-It"). Hence, the group process (especially the "We") is challenged as an obstacle and tapped as a resource for a more empowering and mutual aid experience in actualizing the group's purpose and goals.

In the second horizontal row in Table 3.1, wherein the group is the primary focus, the approaches promote attention to interpersonal group dynamics ("I-We") and/or the group's development of common tasks and goals ("We-It"). These include interpersonal growth, learning, interpersonal problem solving, interpersonal skills training, relationship change, and rehabilitation approaches. The approaches reflect such models as T-groups; sensitivity training; encounter; relationship enhancement; group counseling; support groups for both emotional support and coping; couples communication therapy; other, more interpersonal forms of group psychotherapy (Levine, 1979; Whitaker and Lieberman, 1965; and Yalom, 1995); reality

TABLE 3.1 Matrix of group resources in generalist practice

Primary Intervention Focus	Primary Intervention Purpose					
	Preventive/Developmental		*Problem-Solving*		*Remedial*	
Goal Orientation	PERSONAL	TASK	PERSONAL	TASK	PERSONAL	TASK
INDIVIDUAL						
Approach	Personal growth groups	Life skill development	Individual problem solving	Individual problem-solving skills	Personality change	Rehabilitation
Eg. Models	Awareness, action-oriented (dance therapy, art therapy, etc.)	Life themes, human relations, skills training	Gestalt, transactional analysis, psychodrama	Task-centered, social treatment, cognitive-behavioral, problem-solving skills training	Psychoanalytic and existential psychotherapy	Remedial social skills training
GROUP						
Approach	Interpersonal growth	Learning	Interpersonal problem solving	Interpersonal skills training,	Relationship change	Resocialization

46

Eg. Models	T-groups, sensitivity training encounter	Relationship enhancement	Mainstream counseling, developmental social goals, interactional, emotional, support/coping	Couples communication, mediation/conflict resolution	Interpersonal psychotherapy, reality therapy, group analytic therapy, behavioral group therapy	Residential, confrontation, guided group interaction, positive peer culture, behavioral treatment
ORGANIZATION						
Approach	Management development	Organizational development (O.D.)	Employee problem solving	Organizational problem solving	Employee change	Organizational change
Eg. Models	Leadership training, team development	Quality circles, O.D. T-groups	Employee assistance	Ad hoc problem solving and discussion	Stress management	Social climate
COMMUNITY						
Approach	Primary prevention	Community development	Social supports	Social networks	Secondary/tertiary prevention	Community change
Eg. Models	Life transition	Community planning	Support, mutual aid/help	Networking volunteers	Self-help, Alcoholics Anonymous	Community action

therapy groups (Anderson, 1984); confrontational groups of the Synanon genre; "guided group interaction" (Pillnick, 1971); and "positive peer culture" (Vorrath and Brendtro, 1985) as well as the more traditional social work models: developmental (Tropp, 1977), interactional (Schwartz, 1977), and social goals (Klein, 1973). When adapted within these, the process model accents the inclusion of "I's" and the relationship of the group to its ecosystem to foster more personal and political power.

In organizational groups (the third horizontal row in Table 3.1), the social worker using more of the group process approach supplements the members' attention to the "I-It," the "We-It," and the immediate ecosystem (organization), with appropriate focus on the "I-We" (or human relations agenda) in the group process. Thus, in management development, organizational development, and employee change groups, this practice enhances the traditional models (e.g., team development, "quality circles" employee assistance groups, ad hoc problem-solving and discussion groups, stress management groups, and social climate groups). These more task-oriented groups can develop their potential to share power interdependently through mobilizing the members' consideration of their process, or their here-and-now human relations agenda (the "I-We").

Community groups (the fourth horizontal row in Table 3.1) also tend to emphasize the "I-It," or especially the "We-It" and the ecosystem, with some expense (if not benign neglect) of the "I-We." In primary prevention, community development, social support and social networking, secondary/tertiary prevention, and community change groups through such practice models as life transition, planning, support, networking, self-help, and community action groups, the group process model suggests here-and-now, "I-We" attention on behalf of both task completion and the group's process.

CONCLUSION

A group process model is most useful in conducting a vast array of groups in generalist social work practice. As a generic approach that is consistent with many of social work's empowerment principles and concepts, it can provide a vital and manageable tool in the practitioner's repertoire for enabling group process for a wide range of purposes and goals.

chapter 4

Multicultural Perspective

In Malaysia, a daughter from an upper-class family fell in love with the son of a lower-class family. The son went to his parents to tell them he wanted to marry. His mother said she would approach the young woman's family to seek approval. She made an appointment with the woman's mother and went to the home on the proper day. The mother greeted her and escorted her into the sitting room. She served her tea and bananas. The two talked about the weather and other topics, not once mentioning their children. After an appropriate period of time, the young man's mother thanked her hostess politely and left. Upon returning home, she told her son the marriage was unacceptable and, therefore, not possible. (Story told to me by a Singaporean Malay to indicate differences in Eastern communication styles that are difficult for Westerners to understand.)

INTRODUCTION

Social workers and members alike hear many different voices, longing to be heard and validated, in groups. Understanding and appreciating cultural and other human diversity becomes not only an important challenge for practitioners but a crucial task for members in today's and tomorrow's social work groups. This chapter examines the knowledge, competencies, and tools for the practitioner's understanding and appreciating of diversity in multicultural practice. The focus is on how the practitioner can use this perspective in preparation for group practice, especially in assessing prospective members' needs and expectations, in preparing members for the therapeutic culture that evolves in social work practice through group process, and in composing groups with sensitivity to significant issues of diversity (Chau, 1992). It also considers guidelines for practice when these issues

49

become salient for group members and thus for the group as a whole. The chapter then turns to ideas for challenging obstacles to and building bridges for cross-cultural relationships on behalf of the group's purpose and work. The chapter attends primarily to the diversity of ethnicity/race and gives less attention to gender and class.

ETHNOCULTURAL FRAMEWORKS FOR PRACTICE

It is useful to place a focus on ethnocultural differences in a more holistic context. Therefore, it is pertinent to remember that every human being:

1. Is like no other in one's uniqueness;
2. Is like some others in one's cultural and other group influences; and
3. Is like all others in one's common human needs.

At one level we are as unique as our DNA. At another level we all have similar potential, limits, and survival and growth needs. The level of what we have in common with some, rather than all, others makes cultural influences more salient in practice.

This area is especially vital to the definition of self and the understanding of self for the ethnocultural groups whose differences from the dominant sociocultural group are marked by skin color, language, and/or lifestyles. These populations hope to be understood more within their cultural differences in our social work groups. Instead, they sometimes experience negative stereotyping, misunderstandings, powerlessness, and alienation from practitioners and members in groups dominated by representatives of Eurocentric American cultures.

Building bridges of dialogue and understanding requires more knowledge of culture and its influences on ourselves and those with different backgrounds. Some understanding, when actively demonstrated in practice, comes from our sensitizing (rather than stereotyping) use of the knowledge of different groups' ethnocultures. This refers to the "etic" knowledge of group diversities. Additional understanding evolves in the process of cross-cultural experiences when we put aside what we have learned about the ethnic "culture in the group" in order to learn more about the "culture in the person" from people themselves (Pedersen, 1988). This is the "emic" knowledge garnered through an ethnographic stance and skills for understanding relevant cultural differences.

This chapter provides some frameworks for the application of etic and emic knowledge to practice. It selects and presents those frameworks deemed most fruitful for multicultural competence in preparing for practice through group process. The frameworks increase the odds for social workers to enable groups to achieve their powerful potential as a resource to create a more mosaic microcosm. In such a process, both the autonomy of difference and the interdependence of common concerns and commitments constitute the utmost of mutual aid.

CULTURE AS WORLD VIEW

Perhaps the most serviceable conception of culture for social work with groups is one that emphasizes culture as "world view" (Anderson, 1992; Chau, 1992). World view is a lens through which to focus on significant aspects of one's personal and social experiences, to bring meaning to them, and to determine appropriate ways of dealing with them (e.g., problem-solving activities). Cultural world views emanate from the collective wisdom and heritage of particular groups. Through values and norms, cultures sanction actions for survival and for adaptations to environmental contexts. These cultural world views are so much a part of ourselves, others, and our contexts that we take their assumptions for granted—that is, unless we spend time in a different world and experience the "culture shock" of views that are very different from our own (Adler, 1975). Not only are we generally unaware of how much our culture affects our perceptions and transactions, but we often learn this world view as a "Truth." That is, we internalize it as the best philosophy for survival and growth. But this causes it to become an obstacle to our realizing its relativity to our particular cultural heritage and our acceptance of the validity of other, different, cultural world views.

The cultural world view can be viewed as a configuration of major components (Dana, 1993). The components are identified in this chapter as group identity, individual identity, values, beliefs, norms, and language. Separately and together, they affect perceptions of reality—including what group members will expect and, to a great extent, experience in our practice groups. Figure 4.1 presents a format of these world-view components.

Group Identity

People develop both group and individual (or personal) identities. Group identity relates to one's cultural heritage and the nature of experience in bicultural or multicultural transactions. Cultural heritage advances a predominant or ideal model; this has been identified as "national character" (DeVos, 1968). It refers to the cultural consciousness of what especially makes one an American, African American, Hispanic American, Asian American, Italian American, Dakota Sioux, Native American, and so on. Ethnic identity in the United States involves placing one's group identity in the context of its image for one's group and for the dominant Anglo/European American culture. Group identities of those with socially ascribed ethnic minority status account in part for their difference from the dominant culture. Thus, the nature of bicultural and multicultural experiences has considerable influence on ethnic identity.

Group identities for those who are ethnically different from the dominant culture often develop in four general forms: traditional, nontraditional, marginal, or bicultural (Dana, 1993). Traditional identity affirms the heritage of difference and the strength of this heritage. For instance, this is the thrust of the Afrocentric identification, the Latino perspective, and the American Indian Movement (AIM). Nontraditional individuals do not share this traditional identity. They tend to reject being defined on the basis of their original cultural group; they identify more strongly with the dominant culture. Marginal identities describe those who reject both the original and the dominant

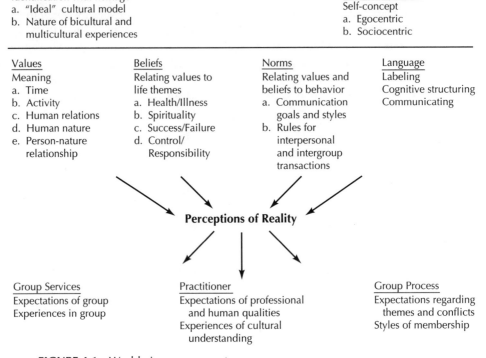

Group Identity
Identification with heritage
a. "Ideal" cultural model
b. Nature of bicultural and
   multicultural experiences

Individual Identity
Self-concept
a. Egocentric
b. Sociocentric

Values
Meaning
a. Time
b. Activity
c. Human relations
d. Human nature
e. Person-nature
   relationship

Beliefs
Relating values to
life themes
a. Health/Illness
b. Spirituality
c. Success/Failure
d. Control/
   Responsibility

Norms
Relating values and
beliefs to behavior
a. Communication
   goals and styles
b. Rules for
   interpersonal
   and intergroup
   transactions

Language
Labeling
Cognitive structuring
Communicating

Perceptions of Reality

Group Services
Expectations of group
Experiences in group

Practitioner
Expectations of professional
   and human qualities
Experiences of cultural
   understanding

Group Process
Expectations regarding
   themes and conflicts
Styles of membership

FIGURE 4.1   World-view components

culture. In the absence of strong group identities, they face a stronger sense of alien-ation and its accompanying attitudes and behavior. Persons with more bicultural or multicultural (Ramirez, 1991) identities incorporate, at least, aspects of both their orig-inal and the dominant culture. They prefer shifting world views and behaviors to sur-vive and adapt in contexts that are primarily influenced by original cultural or domi-nant cultural definitions of reality. These interact, of course, with other influences on group identity such as class, religion, and geography.

In our practice with groups, our initial and ongoing assessments of prospective members' needs and goals benefit from our understanding of the nature of particular members' group identities. We need to develop ways to "tune in" to what others tell us indirectly about their identifications with ethnocultural influences, to reach for more direct communication of these indirect cues, and to let prospective members define their group-based identities for us.

Individual Identity

Individual or personal identity often constitutes the self-concept. It refers to how one lives up to one's self-ideal. It includes one's self-esteem and one's sense of au-tonomy in defining who one is and who one wants to be. In Anglo/European American culture, which has been traditionally male-dominated, the definition of self-concept is largely egocentric (Sampson, 1985, 1988). This dominant culture sees self-concept and self-esteem as comprised of firm boundaries, a self-contained sense of individualism, autonomous control and power to take action in one's life situation, and a sense of a unique self that is separate from others. Research instruments currently used to measure self-concept assume these constructs. Thus, on such instruments people from other cultures often receive low self-esteem scores (Dana, 1993).

In contrast, cultures of non-European origins tend to promote a strong self-concept that is more sociocentric than egocentric (Triandis, 1988). They consider primarily a connected, extended, or interdependent self. This self is distinguished via its responsibility and obligation to a variety of other persons. The self-concept forms through group memberships. An individual's actions cannot be considered in isolation from other persons affected in one's decision-making and problem-solving situations.

When members enter our social work groups, we build on these differing individual and group identities to promote both autonomy and interdependence. We need to tune in to the way they combine in the personal identities of different members and promote a culturally appropriate blending of members' preferences for one or the other as foremost in their core self-concepts.

For example, Leon Chestang (1982) in social work and Shelby Steele in his controversial best-seller, *The Content of Our Character* (1990), note conflicts for African Americans as related to an ethnic group identity that can create obstacles to a personal or individual identity. They indicate that a racial identity that restricts individualism — for example, in the judgments that some brothers and sisters aren't "black" enough in their cultural identifications — thwarts self-actualization. They suggest that the sense of self arising from individual achievement and self-realization increases self-esteem apart from race. This more personal power can enhance racial identity, as race no longer holds some of its meaning to protect one against the fears of inferiority introjected from a racist society. Such notions place identity in the context of holism (wherein the unique, separate self has its place) and biculturalism (wherein there is some functional integration of both egocentric and sociocentric self-concepts). Members of our groups who are in the process of creating their own individual identities apart from and as part of group identities can feel especially misunderstood if overly defined on the basis of their race. This will be the case whether whites or other members of their ethnic/racial group are doing the defining. By skillfully helping members define who they are and who they are becoming (their personal identities), as well as by understanding their group identities, we can aid in the resolution of conflicts for such members and others in the group.

Values

Value orientations can sensitize us to certain significant ethnocultural differences (Anderson, 1991). Value orientations are distinguished from concrete values by their levels of generality: "A value orientation is a generalized and organized conception, influencing behavior of time, of nature, of [a person's] place in it, or [a person's] relation to [other people], and of the desirable and undesirable aspects of people-environment and inter-human transactions" (Kluckhohn, 1961, p. 14).

Value orientations have three significant qualities. They are (1) directional — they provide a program for selecting behaviors between more or less favored alternatives; (2) cognitive — they provide a conceptual world view through which people filter their understanding of the nature of the world and human affairs; and (3) affective — they are invested with strong feelings (never taken lightly; people are ready to bleed and die for them), and they are among the major reasons people and cultural systems are so resistant to change.

These value orientations can sensitize us to ethnic differences based on the following propositions (Kluckhohn, 1954):

1. There are a limited number of common human problems for which all people in all places must find solutions. These are:
   a. Time — the temporal focus of human life
   b. Activity — the preferred pattern of action in interpersonal relations
   c. Human Relations — the preferred way of relating in groups
   d. Person(s)-Nature Relationship — the way people relate to the natural or supernatural environments
   e. Basic Nature of Human Beings — the attitudes held about the innate good or evil in human nature and behavior
2. Although there is variability in the solutions to these problems, this diversity is neither limitless nor random but occurs within a range of three possible solutions, or general value orientations, for each of the problems:
   a. Time — past, present, future
   b. Activity — doing, being, becoming
   c. Human Relations — autonomy, interdependence, hierarchy
   d. Person-Nature — harmony, mastery, subjugation
   e. Basic Nature of Human Beings — neutral or mixed, good, evil
3. All possible solutions are present in varying degrees in the total structure of every culture, and every culture will be characterized not only by a dominant profile of first-order choices but also by substitute second- and third-order choices. Differences among cultures are based on the pattern of preferences for each of these solutions in a dominant-substitute profile of values.

Table 4.1 summarizes general value orientation profiles for a select group of ethnics in the United States. More refined concepts evolve from a constellation of these profiles with such variables as socioeconomic class, generation, religion, and geographical location. Also, although these profiles sensitize generally to differences, it is important to note that there are a variety of discrete group profiles subsumed under the general classifications. For instance, one finds differences among those who identify as West Indian blacks and African-American blacks; among Japanese, Korean, Chinese, and Pacific Asian Americans; among Puerto Rican and Mexican American Hispanics; as well as among diverse Caucasian ethnics.

TABLE 4.1 Comparison of selected ethnic value orientations profiles*

	Dominant Caucasian American Middle Class	African Americans	Hispanic Americans	Asian Americans	Process Model
Time	Future > Present > Past	Present > Past > Future	Past > Present > Future	Past > Future > Present	Present > Future > Past
Activity	Doing > Becoming > Being	Being > Doing > Becoming	Being > Becoming > Doing	Doing > Becoming > Being	Being/Becoming/Doing
Human Relations	Autonomy > Interdependency > Hierarchy	Interdependency > Hierarchy > Autonomy	Interdependency > Hierarchy > Autonomy	Hierarchy > Interdependency > Autonomy	Autonomy > Interdependency > Hierarchy
Person-Nature Relationship	Mastery > Subjugation > Harmony	Harmony > Subjugation > Mastery	Harmony > Subjugation > Mastery	Harmony > Subjugation > Mastery	Harmony > Subjugation > Mastery
Basic Nature of Human Beings	Neutral > Evil > Good	Good > Evil > Mixed	Good > Evil > Mixed	Mixed > Good > Evil	Good > Mixed > Evil

*For a different reflection of some of these groups, see Ho (1987); for a classification of selected Caucasian ethnic groups, see Spiegel (1982).

SOURCE: Sources here are primarily McGoldrick, Pearce, and Giordano (1982); Chunn, Dunston, and Ross-Sheriff (1983); Minahan (1977); Sue and Sue (1990); and Dana (1993).

The last column in Table 4.1 depicts the value orientations that are integral to the process model of this text. Here, we find a time orientation of present > future > past. This emphasizes change and growth initiated in experiencing where one is and what one wants in the present situation. The present serves as leverage for actions toward future-oriented goals. These goals often are achieved through examination of how strengths and obstacles in past patterns work to accomplish such self-determined goals.

The process model values being/becoming/doing synonymously in the activity dimension. Similar to the time orientation, the first step involves learning from experience in the present (being). The group experience generates future goals with more awareness of one's needs for growth toward self-actualization (becoming). Generally, then, the model values and empowers acting (doing) in the group and outside on behalf of both one's being and becoming.

The model places greatest value on the synergistic combination of autonomy and interdependence in human relations. Although it conceives of autonomy themes and growth as generally preceding interdependence in the stages of group development (at least in Western society), it assumes and values members' common developmental needs as the integration and not the separation of autonomy/interdependence. Hierarchy per se is less valued and in most groups is deemed an obstacle to development of the potential for autonomy/interdependence. It is recognized, however, that cultural norms strongly influence the conception of hierarchy in relation to autonomy/interdependence. For instance, Asian/Pacific American groups will find ways of blending autonomy with their very strong value orientation toward hierarchy and interdependence. In practice with Asian groups, I have consistently found the initiation of autonomy directed toward me as the "leader" in questions or comments designed to discover how individual members' wants "fit" in their interdependence with other members. Thus, the hierarchical structure served as the channel for communication to address the autonomy themes among members of the group and to limit this autonomy to areas where one's own needs were interdependently connected to others in the group.

In its conception of group process as a natural evolution, the process model values harmony in the person-nature relationship. It balances individual and group process needs. There follows a strong emphasis on not manipulating or controlling this process. Rather, there is subjugation of the need to control to trusting in the underlying process, given an empowering or enabling facilitation that supports and challenges the members and the group to evolve as naturally as possible. Mastery is an outcome of the process, but this primarily refers to increased competence in meeting one's needs with more integration of autonomy and interdependence both within and outside of the group. The more natural group process promotes controlling one's needs to "master" others while mastering one's ability to control behavior that meets one's needs more autonomously and interdependently.

The model assumes the basic nature of human beings as primarily good. We are endowed with the seeds of development toward the autonomy of meeting our needs in a manner that is responsible and "response-able" to the interdependent needs of others. The mixed potential for both good and evil, however, marks our underlying existential nature as human beings and makes our moral development toward responsible choices regarding our selves and others crucial to tapping our potential for good. In most of us the evolution of the potential for evil is overpowered by the desire for good, but it can arise in those whose life experiences have been marked by alienation and personally disempowering or nonempowering human relations. To the degree that we experience humanizing relationships, we discover the good in our human nature. Thus, groups are humanizing experiences that pitch to our underlying strengths to value and live by principles of love, justice, and goodness.

As noted, the value orientation profiles presented in Table 4.1 are subject to extreme within-group variations. Values and value changes are associated with such variables as identity, age, socioeconomic status, generation in this country, urban-rural residence, other geographical factors, and religion. Hence, value orientation theory suggests illustrative guidelines that can only *sensitize* us to potential value differences and conflicts in our groups.

Perhaps foremost in this sensitivity to value orientations and differences is its conscious use in preparing for our groups. Social work practice groups have implicit and explicit value orientations that differ to some degree from the cultural orientations of most members, including those from the dominant culture. In fact, all small group practice — indeed, all helping and therapy — is to some degree a culture-blending and culture-building experience. Our groups propound values and norms for establishing a *therapeutic culture*. If this therapeutic culture is to be helpful to members, it must blend enough with their cultural values and norms and, to some degree, require all to "stretch" values, norms, and behaviors toward those most functional for achieving therapeutic purposes and goals. When we are sensitized to these differences and their potential conflicts in what may even be conceived of as the "counterculture" that we encourage in our groups, we are in a better position to promote members' *choices* to blend, stretch, or change the meaning of their cultural values and norms. Such change promotes functional competence in various contexts. It also can enhance members' personal and group identities.

This choice needs to be as informed as possible. For instance, we need to find ways of informing prospective members of our groups of the meaning and expectations of such values as trust, autonomy, closeness, interdependence, mutual aid, self-disclosure, respect, honesty, feedback, and difference. This information needs to be "up front" in relation to how we perceive the group's purpose and how we plan to shape the evolution of therapeutic values and norms in the group's process. Prospective members need to know our vision for the group's process and whether we plan to encourage, invite, demand, impose, manipulate, withdraw, or otherwise use our influence to promote the development of a therapeutic culture. The process model suggests that we share our vision that members will have considerable autonomy and choice in determining what they consider culturally appropriate. Yet we expect them to examine how these choices meet their own individual needs, wants, and goals; the group's needs and purpose; and their ability to maximize the mutual aid potential that is the basic therapeutic power of the group. Thus, there is an assessment of the evolving culture and the encouragement to create it in reference to the underlying aim of empowerment for all members.

Beliefs

Value orientations are central components of cultural belief systems. Beliefs constitute the philosophy derived from applying values to particular life themes. These shared beliefs affect both individual and group aspects of identity. They structure shared values, common language, and similar life experiences. They direct how to apply values and norms to such themes as health and illness, spirituality, the extent of personal responsibility and control over personal well-being, and what is considered success or failure within cultural norm regulations.

For instance, illness as disease and health as the absence of disease are beliefs in the germ theory of Anglo/European Americans. Groups of non-Europeans may hold beliefs that disease is an imbalance or disharmony. For them, health in more holistic terms is a balance or harmony maintained by certain rituals. Thus, a variety of natural influences including spirits, magic, dreams, and other malevolent forces in nature are seen to cause illness and need to be addressed in more holistic healing toward health. These beliefs also might see mental health and physical health as inseparable. All aspects of health and spirituality might be combined under the same rubric of beliefs.

If our groups operate with a belief system that does not allow room for contrary views, we deny members of non-European cultures an opportunity to share a most meaningful part of themselves — their own cultural beliefs. We also deny all members, regardless of cultural background, the opportunity to learn from each other in a way that can enable the expansion of culturally encapsulated beliefs toward the creation of personal meaning most functional to the health and well-being of each.

A very important aspect of cultural belief systems in relation to social work practice through group process is their configuration of "locus of control" and "locus of responsibility" (Sue, 1978). The therapeutic culture in such group practice promotes individual and group autonomy as a basis for interdependence or mutual aid. This implies that a clarification of the concept of "locus of control" (which most theory and research tends to assume as synonymous with autonomy) as related to "locus of responsibility" can inform our cultural sensitivity in our groups.

"Locus of control" connotes people's beliefs regarding the consequences of their behavior (Rotter, 1966). An *internal* locus of control (IC) views consequences as a result of one's personal choices and actions. One believes we are the master of our fate. An *external* locus of control (EC) views consequences as independent of one's choices and actions. Fate, luck, or chance is the determining factor.

Derald Sue (1978) adds the construct of "locus of responsibility," derived from social attribution theory (Heider, 1958), to Julian Rotter's (1966) notion of "locus of control." Locus of responsibility indicates beliefs about the causes of behavior. These causes are generally seen as person-based (*internal* locus of responsibility, or IR) or as system-based (*external* locus of responsibility, or ER). IR or ER beliefs attribute "responsibility," "blame," "credit," "cause," and/or "explanations" for one's own and others' situations and behaviors.

Sue hypothesizes that "locus of control" and "locus of responsibility" are independent yet related variables in understanding cultural world views. For example, the way they combine affects group members' values, beliefs, and norms regarding personal and group autonomy. These variations are depicted in Figure 4.2 (Sue, 1978, p. 422).

High IC-IR in Quadrant I reflects the dominant society's construct of autonomy. Autonomy here refers to individual responsibility, personal powers, and self-determining actions. This strongly defines autonomy as independence (the "rugged individualism" ethos) and pits it against interdependence. In groups, those with high IC-IR beliefs need to develop their connective "response-ability" to others as well as to self.

High EC-IR in Quadrant II reflects beliefs most associated with marginal individuals in economically or socially oppressed groups or in otherwise-perceived powerless situations (e.g., substance abusers and other addictive situations). They define autonomy similar to the dominant culture's definition, that is, in terms of self-responsibility. They tend to feel responsible for their "problems" but not for the "solutions." They perceive very little autonomy or control over how they are defined by others. Paulo Freire (1990), on the basis of his empowerment group practice with oppressed populations, suggests that in "dialogue" groups of collaborative (not dominate-subordinate) relationships, marginality subsides with the autonomous choice to confront oppressors. This increases both personal and group autonomy *and* interdependence. Members move more toward the IC-ER world view of Quadrant IV.

Those who tend to fall in Quadrant III (high EC-ER beliefs) feel especially powerless in the face of oppression, leading in the extreme to "learned helplessness" (Seligman, 1982). They perceive what little autonomy they have as limited. They cannot control the suffering from their inequities. They might reflect normative behavior that placates and defers to those in the dominant culture. They would especially be thrown with expectations of autonomy in groups, unless these were couched in terms of validating them as human beings, learning new survival and coping skills, and experiencing the power of a group autonomous enough to form collaborative, shared power relationships with each other and the practitioner.

FIGURE 4.2 Dimensions of world-view beliefs

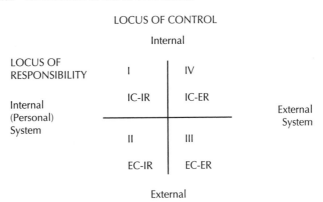

SOURCE: D.W. Sue, Eliminating cultural oppression in counseling: Toward a general theory. *Journal of Counseling Psychology*, 25, p. 422. Copyright © 1978 by the American Psychological Association. Reprinted with permission.

High IC-ER people of Quadrant IV believe in their autonomous ability to shape events in their own lives, given the same opportunities, privileges, and rights by those systems that currently discriminate. Although not feeling responsible for their "problems," they do feel responsible for the "solutions." To combat racism and other elitist obstacles to egalitarianism, they identify with norms for both individual and group autonomy. They also value interdependence within their ethnocultural group and can support the ideal of mutual aid in social systems. Groups in which personal, interpersonal, and political power is promoted appear most congruent with their beliefs regarding autonomy and interdependence. For example, because they see abuses in discriminating systems, they do not expect the dominant white culture to address racism and its institutional disempowering. Rather, there is a strong preference for autonomy and interdependence within their own cultural group before transactions in mixed groups.

These four belief systems can create many misunderstandings between diverse members in our groups. A significant obstacle is what Thomas Pettigrew (1979) calls "ultimate attribution error." Research indicates a strong tendency for attributing internal and external control and responsibilities for behavior through our in-group identification and prejudices (Hewstone and Brown, 1986; Pettigrew, 1978). In summary, we are more likely to attribute appropriate behavior in our own in-group as internally, or personally, caused (IC-IR) and inappropriate behavior as externally, or environmentally, caused (EC-ER). For out-group members' behavior, there is the opposite tendency to attribute "negative" behavior to personal dispositions (IC-IR) and "positive" behavior to environmental situations (EC-ER) and to treat these positive behaviors as "exceptions to the rule." Similarly, for in-group members we credit both members and our group for responsible behavior and blame the environment for irresponsible behavior. For out-group members we credit the dominant system for responsible behavior and blame the individual and his/her ethnocultural group for irresponsible behavior.

In white-nonwhite transactions in our groups, members of different ethnic groups will have cultural norms for attributions that may reflect the biases of this "ultimate attribution error." In forming groups and in facilitating them, it is most helpful to discover from others their *own world views*. This includes their beliefs regarding locus of control and locus of responsibility, and how these beliefs are applied to their interpretations of their own and others' behavior.

Norms and Communication Styles

Cultural norm dispositions operationalize values and beliefs in behavior. They are the implicit and explicit standards and rules for how to behave in a manner that is consistent with cultural values and beliefs. These unwritten rules direct rituals and other patterns of behavior. They particularly influence communication styles and their meaning within the culture, as well as the rules for interaction in interpersonal (or intimate relationships) and inter-group (or less intimate, more instrumental) relationships with members outside of one's culture.

Cross-cultural misunderstanding arises not so much from differences in values (e.g., respect) as from differences in norms and communication styles (e.g., how respect is to be expressed and tends to be expressed within the cultural group).

One important way in which cultures differ is by placing priority on either collectivism or individualism. Collectivistic cultures regard the development of the group as the value-end and the individual valued as he/she serves to protect and enhance the group's development. Individualistic cultures reverse this priority, regarding the development of each individual as the value-end and the group valued to the extent that it maximizes individual development.

Edward Hall (1976), a cultural anthropologist, and others (Erlahaus, 1983; Tannen, 1990; Ting-Toomey, 1988) relate this collectivistic/individualistic dichotomy to norms, communication styles, and ways of interpreting behavior. In collectivistic cultures there is a "high context" standard for norms and the interpretations of behavior. Thus, communication is much more indirect in relation to words and messages and much more embedded in the nonverbal and situational symbols of the context. The story of the Malay families cited at the beginning of this chapter is an example of a collectivistic – high context – indirect communication style culture. In Malaysia, one does not serve bananas with tea. The daughter's mother indirectly (in a way that "saved face" and was deemed as maintaining relationship harmony) communicated through the context that she did not see her daughter and the other mother's son belonging together. The son's mother understood the message immediately. She graciously left to inform her son of the meaning. Its subtleness, easily understood by these two women, inevitably puzzles us Westerners.

Individualistic cultures are "low context" and socialize toward more direct communication styles. They place primary meaning on the verbal aspects of communication and on the psychological factors reflected in paralanguage (e.g., tone of voice, pacing of words, etc., which we interpret as messages about how others feel toward us and how they are defining their relationship to us).

Research on conflict resolution styles within cultures and in cross-cultural relationships demonstrates misunderstandings of these normative dispositions and styles (Kochman, 1981; Tannen, 1990; Ting-Toomey, 1988). Figure 4.3 represents some current results of this research.

In the individualistic – low context – direct communication culture of Anglo/European Americans, norms define conflict most appropriately as instrumental. Solutions are goal-directed. The goal is to resolve the conflict through a rational solution. The best solution avoids interpersonal differences (the expressive components) to focus on the best idea and the rational support for this idea. On the other hand, African Americans, although sharing the individualistic – direct communication – low context configuration (*among peers* especially; this can be very different in relation to differing with elders), see conflict as relationship-directed. This expressive perspective on conflict for African Americans supports norms that contend more with the person debating the idea. There is a belief that if all state their opinions strongly, these "truths," taken together, might maximize the best conflict resolutions for the group.

NORMS FOR CONFLICT

		Instrumental	Expressive	
	Direct (Low Context)	Caucasian Anglo- European Americans	African Americans	Individualistic Cultural Values
NORMS FOR APPROPRIATE COMMUNICATION	Indirect (High Context)	Asian Americans & Pacific Islanders	Hispanic Americans & Native Americans	Collectivistic Cultural Values

FIGURE 4.3   Conflict resolution cultural styles

Thomas Kochman (1981) examines this difference in *Black and White: Styles in Conflict*. He reveals numerous misunderstandings that occur when blacks and whites are involved in conflict—especially in his classroom debate groups. He hypothesizes:

> The modes of behavior that blacks and whites consider appropriate for engaging in . . . debate . . . differ in their stance and the level of spiritual intensity. The black mode—that of black community people—is high-keyed, animated, interpersonal and confrontational. The white mode—that of the middle class—is relatively low-keyed, dispassionate, impersonal, and non-challenging. The first is characteristic of involvement [expressive norms]; it is heated, loud, and generates affect. The second is characteristic of detachment [instrumental norms] and is cool, quiet, and without affect. (p. 41)

In Kochman's groups, these different styles led to many misinterpretations and misunderstandings for both Caucasian and African-American members in their intergroup (stereotype-to-stereotype) relations and created obstacles to interpersonal (person-to-person) relating. When African Americans asserted their messages with strong affect, Caucasians would respond with even more dispassionate and impersonal ideas (e.g., "I read in a book that . . . "). This would lead the African Americans to turn up the heat of their expressions, which the Caucasians in turn read as a personal argument marked by anger and hostility. They were intimidated by this "passion" and tended to withdraw. As a result, the Caucasians often concluded that the African Americans were not sincere about their ideas and were hiding this insincerity behind the assertion of strong affect. The African Americans, often concluded that the Caucasians were not sincere about their ideas or would have invested more earnestness in their communication and certainly would not have withdrawn from the debate. Interventions to build a bridge for conflict resolution at this point succeeded in toning down the assertiveness of the most energetic, confident, and skillful-in-debate African-American members but were not able to increase the assertiveness of the Caucasians, who decided to withhold all opinions and sit in silence.

Asian Americans and Pacific Islanders (reflected in the Malaysian tale at the beginning of this chapter) hold strong norms for indirect, high-context, and collectivistic conflict resolution. In fact, the prevention of any escalation of conflict that might cause the "loss of face" predominates. In groups, these individuals expect the authority or "expert"—the practitioner—to intervene to buffer conflict and present resolutions that maintain a sense of harmony.

Hispanics and Native Americans are distinct from other ethnic groups in that they emphasize indirect expressive norms within their more collectivistic-high context cultures. In treating conflict, there is strong emphasis on maintaining close, intimate, warm relationships that respect the social structure of the family, "tribe," and/or community. The wise person in these groups is not the most intelligent in terms of formal learning. It is the person who is an expert in human and/or spiritual relationships. Conflict resolution involves the contextual expression of strong feelings of warmth through such media as sharing food or pipe, dancing together, music, and play. It may also include the use of humor to defuse situations.

In multicultural groups, the conceptual model developed here can help us tune in to what may be major misunderstandings related to the members' interactional and communication norms and styles. In general, members of low-context, individually referenced cultures do not adequately emphasize situational factors when interpreting the behavior and message of members of high-context, collectively referenced cultures. In contrast, collectivistic cultures tend to de-emphasize factors internal to the individual to explain the behavior of members of low-context cultures. In addition, styles of communication and speech patterns differ in directness.

For effective cross-cultural communication to occur, someone involved needs to be aware of the different styles, work to interpret the other person's message more from his/her cultural perceptions, and accommodate through some shift in his/her communication style (Gudykunst, 1991). In practice groups, this is our professional responsibility. Our competence for such understanding and accommodation is vital in assessing prospective members' needs for the group, in preparing them for joining the group, and in helping them to learn from and accommodate more in their interdependence in the group. This suggests an ethnographic stance to understanding the meaning of culture in our group members.

THE ETHNOGRAPHIC STANCE FOR
CULTURAL UNDERSTANDING

When we are alert to and yet do not understand the cultural features of the client's background that seem to influence the process and outcomes of our group work, we need to discover them. The best sources are either the client or another cultural consultant. This ethnographic stance places us in the role of the learner and the client or group member in the role of the authority. John Lofland (1971) defines the ethnographic interview (a central tool in the ethnographic stance) as a process of discovery by which the interviewer proposes to ask focusing questions designed to channel his or her learning and the interviewee serves as the expert to guide the learner through his or her culture. James Spradley (1979) suggests that the ethnographic interview be thought of as a "friendly conversation" in which the interviewer clarifies the learning focus and offers procedural explanations during the process as to the ethnographic importance of the information sought. To Lofland and Spradley, ethnographic interviewing is a qualitative research tool designed to discover the meaning of the culture as the interviewee sees it and has internalized it in his or her own belief systems, cognitive and communication styles, and behaviors.

In this ethnographic stance to communication we avoid assumptions, seek relevant data, ask questions before drawing conclusions, and share our conclusions with clients or group members to "check out" our understanding. We learn about the nature of the community in which the person lives and about the person's ways of perceiving, thinking, and acting. We learn what differences appear to make the most difference to the client from his or her perspective. For the moment, in using an ethnographic approach, the learning is not necessarily focused on the person's problems or immediate goal. The underlying motive for the dialogue is to achieve a better understanding of the member's ethnographic perspective.

The specific techniques for this are to ask persons to talk in their own terms, use their own language, and permit the asking of questions about the meaning of these terms. For example, ask if the explanations a person gives are the same ones he or she would give to a friend (Austin, Kopp, and Smith, 1986). If not, ask them to use the same terms that they would use with friends. This encourages them to explain how they would really experience different aspects of their lives. It also highlights what aspects of this difference actually make a difference, especially in their cross-cultural encounter with the practitioner and possibly with other members in the group.

Such ethnographic interviewing can especially help bridge the gaps from lack of shared language, shared meanings, shared jargon, or shared understandings. The language we learn through the interview will include the meaning of concepts in the other's culture and how similar or different they are from our own. It will also include aspects of cultural communication style (Kochman, 1981). The pace of talking, the expressiveness, the timing of questions and answers, the nonverbal behaviors, the attention to context — all are relevant to learning the cultural language and context of another in an ethnographic interview. The learning comes from sensitive listening with both the eyes and ears.

William Gudykunst (1991) suggests four important communication skills that are pertinent to ethnographic interviewing and learning: (1) separating description, interpretation, and evaluation; (2) using feedback; (3) dialogic listening; and (4) metacommunicating. The skill of consciously *separating description, interpretation, and evaluation* requires that we first label and focus on data empirically (i.e., what we see, hear, feel, touch, and taste). Next, we must consider as many interpretations of the meaning and intent of empirical data as possible. We then use our current understanding of psychological, cultural, and/or sociological data to make an "educated guess" in evaluating the meaning. *Using feedback* involves sharing our observations and evaluations with others and asking them whether we have understood correctly. *Dialogic listening* is another form of feedback, designed to discover whether mutual understanding is or is not occurring. John Stewart and Milton Thomas (1990) see active and empathetic listening as the focus on understanding. They add dialogic listening as a tool to determine whether the communication itself is working effectively. For them, it helps to develop ideas, tease out nuances, and clarify incomplete messages. Primary techniques include asking for clarification and elaboration when we are unsure of what others mean (e.g., "Say more"), initiating paraphrasing, and requesting restatements (e.g., "Repeat in your own words what was just heard.") *Metacommunicating* involves communicating about the communication. It reflects how we intend our messages (e.g., questions) to be understood. It tells the other why we sent the message, how we want them to see it, and/or what we want them to do. To set a stance for authentic learning via the ethnographic interview, we need to do a great deal of honest meta-communicating (e.g., "I ask this because I don't know and want to learn more"; "I am not responding because I am making judgments on what you've just told me. I am just letting it sink in so I'm sure I'll understand it better.")

The outcomes of effective ethnographic interviewing are (1) more shared understanding of what differences will make a difference in the group; (2) less uncertainty and ambiguity for oneself and the other; (3) more empathy regarding how the person is like no other person, like some other people, and like all human beings; and (4) more ability to adapt communication skills appropriately to the person's cultural context. Practitioners might hear the person's voice much more directly and their own voice much less as they proceed from this base in the work together.

The ethnographic, or emic, stance for learning about relevant cultural differences is basic to more recently developed cross-cultural group techniques. These aim to accentuate and understand cultural themes for group members and help them decide whether and in what ways they might want to blend this with the therapeutic culture of the group. This can include discovering what cultural dispositions seem dysfunctional for accomplishing goals in less culturally congruent contexts.

For instance, Gerald Corey et al. (1992) suggest the following techniques to "highlight cultural material as it emerges in a group session by providing individuals with an invitation to identify relevant discussions of their culture":

"Tell us something about your culture and how you think it may influence your participation in this group."

"If you think many members of this group might have a certain cultural perspective different from your own, would you pick out some people here and tell each of them about some of the things that you are likely to see differently?"

"Could you pretend for a moment that you're back home among members of your ethnic group? Try to explain to them what this group is all about. What would you say?"

(To a specific member): "I'm aware that many of us in this group are from a culture different from yours. Would you be interested in some of us expressing some of our assumptions or stereotypes about your culture? You can then react to what you hear, which could be a means for us to find out more from you about how we could reconsider some of our conclusions." (p. 9)

All these ethnographic techniques bring more of the "culture in the person" to the group's service. Potential conflicts and misunderstandings can be dealt with more openly. If cultural themes and potential issues of diversity remain latent, mistrust and lack of cohesion can result from unspoken thoughts and unexpressed reactions. On the other hand, a group that addresses difference is an ideal place for members to learn how to understand, appreciate, and respect their cultural differences simultaneous with the discovery of the ways they are bound by universal human concerns and common needs and goals.

RACE AND THERAPEUTIC GROUPS

African Americans and other ethnic minorities oppressed by racism enter groups with more awareness of the very issue of which Caucasians are least conscious regarding their status — white privilege. "White privilege" refers to the unearned, taken-for-granted, social ascription of choice, power, and other privileges given to whites because of the accident of their skin color at birth (McIntosh, 1989). African Americans and other nonwhites do not experience these same rights, opportunities, and privileges.

For instance, in the beginning of a mixed group, African Americans do not expect that they will have as much opportunity as Caucasians to define themselves through ongoing self-disclosure. They "know" their very presence has already been taken by whites as a disclosure and they likely have been already primarily defined on the basis of their skin color and the racial stereotypes this activates. They expect there is a high likelihood that this "self-disclosure" will be misunderstood; they will be placed and treated in a "box" labeled "race." Essentially, this privilege differential is experienced as a power differential. In brief, nonwhites in mixed groups often feel less power to influence their being known and understood in early group process.

This socially ascribed status and power differential is what defines "minority." As power is a most central dynamic in all groups, the privilege, power, and status issue is highly salient in mixed racial groups. Research reflects how white privilege creates obstacles in group process. Nonwhites mistrust. Whites blindly operate from the base of white privilege rather than from earned status and shared power in the group. This sense of white privilege is behind the comments of African Americans that they have to work twice as hard to get just as far as whites — a comment that some whites may understand but still not see in the context of their own unearned privileges. African Americans and other nonwhites in our mixed groups might experience their goals and participation as affected by this perception of the privilege differential, which in turn may not be appreciated or understood by the Caucasian members.

Larry Davis and Enola Proctor (1989) provide an excellent and invaluable review of the theory and research on ethnicity and race and group treatment, especially as applicable to social work with groups. Incorporating their major findings[1] with others reveals the following:

---

[1] Much of this section, as well as the following on gender and class, is adapted from L.E. Davis and E.K. Proctor, *Race, gender, and class: Guidelines for practice with individuals, families, and groups.* Copyright © 1989. All rights reserved. Adapted by permission of Allyn & Bacon.

1. African Americans tend to prefer a 50-50 percent membership in mixed groups.
2. Caucasians prefer an 80-20 percent mix in which they are the numerical majority.
3. The less formal and more potentially intimate the group, the more these different preferences arise.
4. Groups with all ethnic minority members can experience special difficulties in deepening their cohesiveness over time because members' cultural identities and cultural dimensions differ. Groups such as Asian American and Hispanic are not monolithic.
5. African Americans in treatment groups tend to prefer African-American leaders even though they generally expect to be in groups with leaders who are not African American. These preferences appear to be influenced by other group leader variables (especially the extent and quality of the leader's prior experience with African Americans).
6. Interracial groups formed for the purpose of reducing prejudice and enhancing racial harmony (Williams, 1977; Cobbs, 1972; Pinderhuges, 1989) seem most effective when the composition is 50-50 and members share similar socioeconomic and other statuses. When these groups tip toward a numerical majority of white ethnics, African Americans in the group tend to speak predominantly for their race as a whole rather than as individuals.
7. Same-ethnicity groups with same-ethnicity leaders can better achieve the purpose of enhancing ethnic identity (Gutierrez and Ortega, 1991). These groups appear to be more empowering through members' more honest expression of the experienced positives and negatives regarding their ethnicity.
8. In general, practitioners in treatment groups with ethnic minority members, regardless of the leader's ethnicity, do not alter their leadership styles to accommodate for differences. However, a style that is informal and relaxed, yet not lacking in courtesy and respect, and active in self-disclosure and expression of surface (not intense) feelings appears more effective in the research to date. This is especially so for Hispanic Americans in therapeutic groups (Verdi and Wheelan, 1992).
9. The only leader personality variable found significant thus far in the research is "biculturality." Leaders who are biculturally oriented appear more comfortable and assertive in the face of group mistrusts and members' expressed concerns regarding leadership in the group. This correlates with higher member outcomes.
10. Many concerns regarding leadership tend to go unexpressed in the group. This includes white ethnic members with conservative racial attitudes judging nonwhite leaders more harshly. In turn, when whites are a numerical minority and the leader is white, they judge the leader's performance more favorably.
11. Group dynamics and group processes are affected by group intimacy, size, and racial balance:

a. When racial members are a minority in number, there is likely to be more subgrouping and less vying or competing for leadership;

b. When group membership exceeds 20 percent of African-American members, white ethnics tend to experience themselves as a "psychosocial minority" and assert less power. When African Americans approach 50 percent of membership, they experience a "psychosocial majority" and assert more power. Racially balanced groups, therefore, tend to throw all members psychologically off balance with shifts in power and status.

c. Related research indicates that the result of these power shifts depends on the purpose, goals, and norms in the group. Cooperative ones increase reduction in interracial prejudice. Competitive ones increase the "ultimate attribution error" wherein those not performing to norms are judged more harshly and with existing prejudicial stereotypes. When helping behavior and mutual aid norms are established, these judgments appear to change significantly.

12. More racial balance in groups has been found to correlate with:

a. African Americans increasing in honest communication;

b. Hispanic Americans tending toward more member-member and less member-leader communication, especially when expressing negative feelings and evaluations;

c. Asian Americans appearing less inclined to disclose personal problems and being more bound by cultural norms that deem these expressions as lacking will-power, too egocentric, and potentially confrontational;

d. Whites and Asian Americans perceiving confrontation as interpersonal conflict and establishing norms to avoid such confrontation. African Americans tend to view confrontation as a cooperative challenge of opposing positions and viewpoints, not as interpersonal conflict.

13. Outcome research suggests that the group is a powerful resource for ethnic minorities. All ethnic minority cultural groups tend to identify strongly with the values of interdependent mutual aid and especially benefit from groups that promote these processes. Hispanic and Asian Americans expect this mutual aid to evolve harmonically rather than with much conflict, and they benefit more when these norms mark the group's process. Same-ethnicity groups especially increase outcomes in members' self-concept and self-esteem. Mixed groups reflect more group productivity and increase in members' perceived and actual competencies. The effectiveness of treatment groups for ethnic minorities has yet to be related to the group leader's ethnicity. More research is needed in all these areas.

GENDER AND THERAPEUTIC GROUPS

Theory and research has only recently attended to gender variables in group treatment. Davis and Proctor (1989) review and critically evaluate this work. Among their findings, as well as more recent research, are the following:

1. Men prefer mixed gender groups.
2. Women prefer mixed gender groups only if they are large.
3. There is a tendency for leaders to prefer and compose all-women groups. They assess that these groups appear to engage in greater trust and mutual aid (Brody, 1987).
4. More recently and less frequently, male leaders are promoting all-male groups for their trust and mutual aid potential.
5. Same-gender groups appear to address issues of sexual identity and gender roles more than do mixed-gender groups.
6. Group dynamics and group processes can be significantly affected by gender composition.
    a. There are more favorable responses to the group between genders when they are approximately equal (50 – 50) in number.
    b. All-women groups and mixed groups appear more expressive than all-male groups. This is especially so for men in mixed groups.
    c. Women appear more cooperative and men more competitive (in general) in group process.
    d. Men tend to be less conforming and more risk-taking in groups in which they are the numerical gender majority.
    e. Mixed groups tend to be more successful when both men and women learn to accept and make some accommodation to different communication styles (Tannen, 1990).
    f. When there are only one or two men or women in mixed groups, members tend to project more gender stereotypes onto them (Gemmill and Schaible, 1991).
7. Ascribed gender status does affect stereotypes among members in treatment groups but has yet to be correlated with leadership styles.
    a. Some findings suggest that leaders' styles assume more characteristics of the opposite gender as the number of these members increases in the group.
    b. Male members appear more tolerant toward the mistakes of male leadership than of female leadership.
    c. Both males and females tend to like other members more when the leadership is more informal.
    d. There appears to be an interaction of leader's personality style (masculine, feminine, or androgynous) and members' gender attitudes (traditional vs. liberal) that influences the perception and evaluation of group leaders *in the early stages of the group.*
    e. Women's leadership tends to be less frequently responded to and positively evaluated by both male and female members, even when identical to the male's — suggesting that society's "status incongruency" is at work in treatment groups.
    f. Mixed male-female co-leadership shows mixed views. There is some evidence that it can model nonsexist interaction, but more groups studied tended to perceive a male/leader and woman/helper dichotomy.

8. Different outcomes appear to relate to the gender composition in groups:
   a. Women in same-gender groups tend to increase more in their self-esteem and sense of identity.
   b. Mixed-gender groups correlate with more favorable evaluations by women members and with higher outcomes in interpersonal competencies and wanted behavioral changes.
   c. The groups most effective in treating gender-related concerns from both men and women clients in the research to date are consciousness-raising and self-help groups. These focus on growth rather than pathology, are less formal and hierarchical, and promote mutual aid and collaboration, or the sharing of power.

CLASS AND THERAPEUTIC GROUPS

Class often interacts with race and gender in the diversity that members bring to social work groups. The impact of class in group process and outcomes is much less developed separately in both theory and research. Davis and Proctor (1989) found they needed to extrapolate from the empirical studies on practice with individuals to develop guidelines for addressing class variables in practice with treatment groups. Research currently suggests the following:

1. Middle-class members prefer same-class groups; low-income members prefer mixed-class groups if they are not alone in the group (i.e., they perceive at least one other member who is also low-income).
2. Interactions and communications tend to occur more often within than between "class" members in groups.
3. Practitioners high on "external locus of control" appear more effective in engaging low-income members in the early stage of the group. Those with an "internal locus of control" are more effective with middle-class group members.
4. The level of the group leader's experience and the possession of a democratic attitude appear beneficial in working with low-income group members, especially when this is combined with a more active and directive style in terms of accomplishing necessary group tasks.
5. Most theorists advocate for the poor a practice theory for short-term, open-ended, directive groups with a crisis orientation—yet there appears no empirical evidence to support this approach over any other group model.

SEXUAL ORIENTATION AND THERAPEUTIC GROUPS

The multicultural perspective can be useful to increase our understanding of some of the effects of sexual orientation in our practice groups (Lukes and Land, 1990). As do other populations at risk of prejudice and/or power differentials that are institutionalized in forms of oppression and discrimination (e.g., people of color and women), gay, lesbian, and bisexual members of practice groups are especially attuned to issues and dynamics of power, status, and privilege. In predominately heterosexual groups, as in transactions in their social worlds, they expect stigmatized judgments and discriminatory treatment by those with heterosexual orientations. Simultaneously, they need and want their difference to be validated and accepted as a significant part (not the whole) of their being and identity. Their universal autonomy and interdependence needs, as other members' needs, seek an appreciation of how their uniqueness and differences can contribute to and evolve from the common ground that forms the group.

Much current social work practice appears to place gay, lesbian, and bisexual persons together in groups that exclude heterosexual members (Ball, 1994; Lee, 1994; Morrow, 1993; Robinson, 1991). This practice emphasizes the group as a resource for support, mutual aid, and/or empowerment. The prevailing view considers members' sexual orientations as interconnected with such developmental variables as health, age, level of mental health functioning, and stages of the "coming-out" process, as well as such multicultural variables as class, ethnicity, rural or urban background, religion and social supports (Shernoff, 1995; Woodman, 1995). Within this diversity, however, the group — whether composed of only gay men, only lesbian women, or a mix of gay, lesbian, and bisexual persons — constitutes a common ground of strengths and issues in promoting well-being in transactions with a stigmatizing homophobic social structure.

A number of general propositions, yet to be empirically tested, derive from the practice. These are as follows:

1. Group leaders need to be knowledgeable regarding homosexuality and critically conscious of the degree of homophobia and heterosexist bias in one's self and the sociopolitical context (O'Hare, Williams, and Ezoviski, 1996; Morrow, 1993). Generally, there is a strong preference for leaders with gay or lesbian sexual orientations who are comfortable with their sexual identity.

2. Gay and lesbian adolescents and others in the identity formation stage of the "coming-out" process are best served by support groups that can promote mutual aid processes (Ball, 1994; Morrow, 1993; Robinson, 1991). Such groups may evolve over time toward more empowerment purposes and activities targeted on oppressive and discriminatory social structures and practices (Lee, 1994). The rationale for this practice asserts that gay, lesbian, and bisexual persons, dissimilar to other stigmatized and oppressed populations-at-risk, likely experience growing up in heterosexually oriented families who socialize them with cultural values, norms, and beliefs that are opposed to their homosexual identity. Thus, they need special validation by those with similar sexual orientations.

3. The group, then, serves as a resource for integration of gay, lesbian, or bisexual identity with individual identity. Judith Lee (1994) has expressed this objective: "[It] . . . involves a synthesis of gayness into an overall

sense of identity, a full self-acceptance and self-definition, and a reintegration of being gay with all other aspects of one's life. It is one more identity peg, . . . not overshadow[ing] all the unique aspects of a person's being" (p. 97).

4. Same or similar sexually oriented groups provide the opportunity for members to affirm their different sexual orientation and to help each other deal with the consequences for them of stigmatized identities. Also, members may experience and accept more the "totality of their being" as they discover a variety of differences and similarities in themselves and others in the group.

5. Finally, these groups can promote political empowerment through "externalization of the oppressor" in development of more critical consciousness. Members in such groups, or as a result of them, can network and organize for social and political action that focuses on such common issues as gay and lesbian rights (Lee, 1994).

In contrast to this recent work on behalf of gay and lesbian members in groups, there appears a dearth of attention to practice with gay and lesbian members and heterosexual persons when their differences become an issue in predominately heterosexual groups. Yet the reality in practice is that social work groups formed, for example, around identified common service purposes (e.g., substance abuse, truancy, health concerns, AIDS, unemployment) often entail diversity in all its forms— including sexual orientation. The multicultural frameworks presented in this chapter, especially the ethnographic stance and techniques, do have some implications for understanding and addressing this dynamic of difference when sexual identities become an issue in practice groups.

This chapter suggests that cultural and other world views transact with the therapeutic culture that evolves in practice groups. The meaning of these differences and how they might be approached relate to the negotiation of therapeutic norms in the group's process. All members bring their sociopolitical cultural context with them and expect acceptance of this part of themselves. This includes those who identify strongly with the privileges, power, and statuses granted to them from existing social structures as well as those who identify the more sociopolitically privileged as representing their oppressors. They, too, expect acceptance of their opposing world view. The questions become: How can the group evolve norms of mutual acceptance when there are very different world views among members (especially in issues regarding color; men and women; heterosexual and gay and lesbian persons)? How do groups accept differences that are particularly polarized and central to separate world-view values and beliefs? Or, more generally and directly: Can democracy work in practice groups?

To the degree that this is possible, members need to agree to some therapeutic norms in the group that promote the possibility for change in their interactions in the face of difference. These include norms that mediate the constructive resolution of conflict; that advance the collaborating work of the group inherent in its particular purpose and function in the lives of its members; that determine the nature of risk, honesty, and exploration, which blend members' goals and cultural values and norms with the group's purpose and goals and with the leader's consultation on how desired outcomes can be achieved in this context; and that operationalize our social work purpose of fostering both personal well-being and social justice. All these norms (i.e., "unwritten rules" for appropriate and inappropriate behavior in the group) must combine expectations that members can be who they are (autonomy) in the context of the group with the group's resources to work to change patterns that they discover as obstacles to their own and others' well-being (interdependence). These include norms that permit and encourage examination of how social constructions of power affect the growth and well-being of both the privileged and the less privileged.

Such norms suggest that we influence efforts at honesty and mutual understanding with a focus on the themes that are appropriate for the particular group's purpose, function, and goals. These must be shaped as prerequisite to and in conjunction with norms that guide work to discover a common ground in differences (however polarized and conflict-creating) and to examine and choose actions that members determine as being more functional to one's own and others' well-being. This honesty and mutual understanding begins in the leader's acceptance that the social context *in us all* includes prejudices, stereotypes, biases, and values that we bring with some degree of consciousness into any group. It also begins in the leader's vision and values that personal well-being requires work in ourselves and in society to purge the injustices created by our actions (and nonactions) from these learned prejudices. In terms of sexual orientation, our mixed practice groups can be resources (1) for change toward more collaborative attitudes and actions between heterosexual and gay and lesbian persons, and (2) for more collaborative attitudes and actions between social workers and group members toward increased commitment to social justice.

In operational terms, this position suggests that we help all members to bring out, voice, clarify, and acknowledge each other's similarities and differences and assess them as resources and/or obstacles to achieving the group's purpose and accomplishing members' common and individual goals. Thus, we need to initiate a message regarding "secret," "taboo," or "politically incorrect" themes: We must indicate that we are ready to address them as possible dynamics related to the group's work when the members themselves are ready. This stance does not mean that we ask members to bare their souls and expose all. Rather, it proposes that we are not blind to color, gender, or sexual orientation in our responses to any members.

This practice evolves from our ethnographic stance. We can ask members to teach us what multicultural perspectives we require in order to understand their context in them. We can ask members to share their awareness of the aspects of their contexts that are relevant for them to the group: "How does how you define yourself sexually, ethnically, religiously, etc., relate to the goals you have stated?" "How does your feeling misunderstood, as you've just shared with us, relate to how you see major differences between yourself or me, or any particular other member of this group?"

We can also help members teach us more about the differences that make a difference for them by asking if we can inquire about them in order to understand them more. If they agree, we can clarify how they see and experience their differences. This dialogue models norms for members to permit and inform learning about each other's differences as an important step in their potential learning from each other's differences. For those whose sexual orientations are different, this dialogue can help us begin to understand what part this difference holds in their current identity process as well as its place in their individual and integrated identity.

When members themselves initiate such assertions of differences, we often can best begin with discovering more from them what they expected and wanted from the disclosures. Frequently, they somehow reveal that they expect to feel "freer" in their being in the group and mixed reactions simultaneously from other members. They tend to want honesty regarding these reactions with authentic acceptance of their identified difference. This clarification and understanding of the meaning of self-disclosed differences in terms of the intent for the member of the group opens the possibility of further clarification before other members might react. Especially useful are questions designed to relate the disclosure to the group's process and, in turn, to the group's purpose. Then, we can engage all members in deciding whether they assess the disclosure as a relevant theme in the group and how they wish to address the member and the theme at this point.

For instance, a single gay young adult in a substance abuse therapy group in a residential treatment center disclosed and (with leader questions) clarified that he just wanted to "come out" to the group, expected the other men in the group to reject him, and hoped members would accept him, including his different sexual orientation. The leader then asked: "What do you believe would help us get to know you and understand you best, as well as perhaps help you get to know and understand other members better at this point — discovering first what acceptance may be here, or what might be less-accepting reactions to what your coming-out here has meant?" After clarification has been given (in this case, the belief that he would benefit most from both), starting with the parts of this revelation that "turn you off," the leader asks the group: "How relevant do you believe this request is for this group at this time? How willing are you to stay with this now and respond to this request?"

Throughout group process, practitioners using a multicultural perspective can continually focus on the meaning of potentially stigmatizing and polarizing differences at all levels of the group's process. These include their effect on the individual members (or "I"s); the patterned relationships among members ("We"); the group's purpose, goals, and tasks, ("It"); and the way in which the world-at-large in microcosm affects the group and the way in which the group can affect change in injustices and dysfunctions in the world-at-large (the "Globe"). This is done in such a way that all members have a "voice" to be heard and that there is a common ground of mutual aid expectations for the dialogue of differences. Such mutual aid processes, as they evolve, simultaneously serve members' needs for autonomy and interdependence within the group and in a more just society. Our practice groups, then, can advance social work purposes: enhancing well-being and contributing to the elimination of the causes and consequences of discrimination, oppression, and other social injustices.

CONCLUSION

Appendix A provides a Diversity Awareness Inventory (adapted by Mary Yanisko and Brenda Exum) to assess members' needs and issues regarding diversity in mixed groups. This tool can be useful to sensitize members and practitioners to these needs and issues prior to the group's initiation. Appendix B includes a Value Orientation Inventory, which also might aid this assessment.

Following are useful guidelines for cross-cultural practice proposed by Nancy Brown Miller (1982):

1. Consider all clients as individuals first, as members of minority status, and then as members of a specific ethnic [or other minority] group.
2. Never assume that a person's ethnic [or minority group] identity tells you anything about his or her cultural values or patterns of behavior.
3. Treat all "facts" you have ever heard or read about cultural values and traits as hypotheses, to be tested anew with each client. . . .
4. Remember that all [ethnic] minority group people in this society are bicultural, at least. The percentage may be 90–10 in either direction, but they still have had the task of integrating two value systems that are often in conflict. . . .
5. Some aspects of a client's cultural history, values, and lifestyle are relevant to your work with the client. Others may be simply interesting to you as a professional. Do not prejudge what areas are relevant.
6. Identify strengths in the client's cultural orientation which can be built upon.
7. Know your own attitudes about cultural pluralism, and whether you tend to promote assimilation into the dominant society values or to stress the maintenance of traditional cultural beliefs and practices [or some of both].
8. Engage your client actively in the process of learning what cultural content should be considered.
9. Keep in mind that there are no substitutes for good clinical skills: empathy, caring, and a sense of humor. (p. 182)

chapter 5

Small Group
Dynamics Perspective

One bright winter morning, Piglet came upon Pooh Bear in the snowy woods. Piglet's curiosity peaked as he watched Pooh Bear walking around a spinnet bush with his head down, staring intently at the snow. "What are you doing, Pooh Bear?" Piglet asked. "Tracking," replied Pooh Bear. "Tracking what?" retorted Piglet. "I don't really know," said Pooh Bear. "You can't always tell with paw marks."

So Piglet joined him since he didn't have anything else to do until Friday anyway. The paw marks they were following continued to lead around the spinnet bush. "I wonder if this creature we're tracking might be a Woozle or a Wizzle," mused Piglet with a tremor of fear in his voice. "I don't know," whispered Pooh Bear; "But look!" Suddenly it appeared that whatever it was had been joined by another Woozle or Wizzle. And to their mounting astonishment they found as they continued that they were evidently pursuing more and more Woozles and Wizzles!

In fact, Piglet became so befuddled that judging the time to be twelve o'clock, he was suddenly moved to recall he had something to do between the hours of twelve and five past twelve. So he left Pooh Bear to his tracking, sizing up the situation as: "He who tracks and runs away will live to track another day."

And so it was Pooh who made the great discovery. After a while he stopped going around the spinnet bush and looked closely at all the tracks made by the Woozles and Wizzles. Now he looked at them for a very long while, as he was a bear of big heart but very small brain. Then, he carefully placed his own paw snugly down into one of the Woozle tracks! And when Pooh Bear did that he did a very remarkable thing from which he learned a very important lesson. Pooh Bear got wise to himself. (Adapted from Milne, 1954)

INTRODUCTION

Small group theory and research resembles Pooh Bear's trek around the spinnet bush. We all have made tracks in and know something about groups. When we add our ideas to those who examine the paw marks of small group dynamics, we might find a herd of Woozles and Wizzles. Hence, we often do best to try on these concepts ourselves to see what fits our own experiences and observations. One hopes they can illuminate us toward more knowledge (if not "wisdom") in our search to understand our practice groups. This chapter selects from the volumes of small group theory and research those concepts that appear to fit best with informing social work practice through group process.

Groups epitomize our basic interdependence as human beings. The concept of the small group arises from the fact that we share a sense of membership and interdependent outcome with others in face-to-face interactions during a particular interval. A number of people interacting becomes most like a small group when an event that affects one member affects all. This interdependent influence has marked most definitions of small groups ever since Kurt Lewin (1951) first postulated such a central defining concept (for review, see Shaw, 1981).

The classic example of the distinguishing dynamic between an aggregate of people and a small group is the elevator story. Seven people enter an express elevator to the top floor in the lobby of an office building. It is likely that several surreptitiously take notice of the others. When the doors close, they experience the boundary of being together with each other and no one else, even if for the briefest time and even if not face-to-face. Some might smile at a few others; some might even chat. Now the elevator gets stuck somewhere between the fifteenth and sixteenth floors. The people suddenly share a common fate and task. They might begin to move from their current collectivity toward what resembles a group. Now the elevator has not moved for ten minutes, and its emergency phone is not working. At this point the seven individuals' common fate and tasks may now affect their perception of themselves in relation to the others. They likely perceive themselves more as members of a group in a stuck elevator facing discomfort—if not outright disaster—and needing to take action to change their situation. Their interactional patterns may also change. They might increase face-to-face communications for the purpose of accomplishing something together. So might they alter their actions. Their behavior may begin to take into account how what they and others do affect them all—their interdependence. At this point they are developing into a small group. If they remain stuck without help for an hour and a half, almost certainly a small group will evolve—which will reflect many of the variables that constitute group process and dynamics.

Concepts of group process and dynamics, therefore, pertain primarily to experiences that constitute interdependent (and potentially "mutual aid") groups. Neither the concepts covered in this chapter nor the group process model of this text suggest much applicability to other collectivities. When conditions are such that the people we bring together face-to-face have the potential to evolve interdependent influence, or mutual aid, we form practice *groups*. Other arrangements in practice are more accurately defined as a "collectivity" as opposed to a "group" (Lang, 1987; Young, 1987). As James Satterley (1995) argues persuasively, such collectivities require a special practice theory base that is currently only in initial development.

Interdependence, as the defining element of a small group, implies that all the forces that influence interactions are connected. They simultaneously affect individual members, interpersonal relationships, and the group system (or group-as-a-whole). Similarly, variables of group dynamics transact. They mutually influence each other. To classify and review them separately, as I do in this chapter, is a necessity of exposition. In metaphor, the dynamic forces in groups are not a row of toy soldiers but a dance whose choreography is co-created by the dancers.

GROUP DYNAMICS

Most often, social work scholars who focus on the small group use the concepts of group theory, group dynamics, and group process interchangeably (Hartford, 1971; Heap, 1977; Toseland and Rivas, 1995; Zastrow, 1985). Small group experts in cognate social science disciplines generally use "group dynamics" as the umbrella term under which they place all the complex properties and forces that affect what individual members and groups as social systems do or do not do (Knowles and Knowles, 1972; Napier and Gershenfeld, 1981; Nixon, 1979; Shaw, 1981).

This chapter considers group dynamics as encompassing concepts that affect the "I," the "We," and the "It" as the triangular parts of group process. "Group process," on the other hand, refers to how the dynamics of each of the parts interweave during the evolution of the group. As elaborated in the next section, this text conceptualizes group process as the sequential themes or common threads that evolve during the stages of development in small groups. The "I-We-It" group dynamics discussed in this chapter are those (1) deemed significant in practice theories concerning small groups, and (2) operationalized to some degree as variables in research on practice groups in a variety of professions. They are outlined as follows:

Outline of Group Dynamics

    I. "I" Group Dynamics
        A. Member orientations
        B. Composition
        C. Therapeutic factors
   II. "We" Group Dynamics
        A. Group Structure
            1. Positions
            2. Status
            3. Roles
            4. Norms
            5. Goals

GROUP PROCESS

The concepts of group dynamics and group process are intimately related. In this book, however, they are not synonymous. Group dynamics encompasses all the forces that shape and change what members do in groups and how groups influence members—*for good or for ill*. Group process, rather, describes and explains how these forces result in change that is progressive. Process, here, connotes movement toward maximizing the group's potential as a resource to meet members' needs and achieve desired individual and group outcomes. Thus, *group process means the stages of group development*. It is defined via the themes that integrate growth in the "I," the "We," and the "It."

These stages and themes of members and the group-as-a-whole reciprocate. They constantly transact with group dynamics variables in the developmental process. Understanding of, respect for, and skill to facilitate this process increase the odds that the practice group ("It") develops these dynamics for the benefit of each member ("I") and the group itself ("We").

Group process, which represents qualitative movements in the group-as-a-whole, differs from "process in groups." The foremost proponent of attending to process in therapeutic groups is Irvin Yalom (1995), whose seminal text on group psychotherapy is now in a third edition. When Yalom addresses process in groups, he applies an interpersonal (not a group system) perspective and model. Although he recognizes that what happens between and among members affects all (i.e., relates to the group system), the process to which he attends involves the patterns in interpersonal relationships represented by the present interactions in the group (the "here-and-now"). Process, to Yalom, connotes the nature of relationships between and among members. He deems it the primary context in which to understand the meaning of individual members' and the group's content. In this interpersonal perspective, Yalom views the members' content as symbolizing their current level of awareness about the nature of their relationships with other members and/or statements regarding how they want these relationships to be. This is very similar to what family therapists mean by "family process." Interactions are seen as a social microcosm. They are snapshots that reflect how family or group members normally function (for good or for ill) to negotiate getting their needs met by or with others.

Yalom's (1995) concept of process in groups is an informative way to understand here-and-now events and members' needs and content in practice groups. Therefore, I incorporate many of his ideas in the group process model of this text. However, the primary unit of attention is the group-as-a-whole (the particular stage configuration of the "I-We-It"). The assumption is that individual, interpersonal, and group process grow synergistically. They develop in mutual enhancement toward their more ideal state. We can focus on any of these units of attention in the group to discover developmental needs and potentials. Likewise, enabling the growth of any of the three dynamics affects the others. The group process model posits that the most growth from the least effort and intrusion occurs when we work to empower the development of the group-as-a-whole. Especially vital to social work practice, this focus increases the possibilities that members help to promote more synergy processes in their social contexts (their real-world "Globe"). Trust in and facilitation of the stages of development in our practice groups constitute social work through group process.

"I" GROUP DYNAMICS

"I" group dynamics (individual variables) relate to the theory and research on pre-group members. This work includes: (1) what the particular "I's" initially bring to the group ("member orientations"); (2) how the collection of "I's" might work to achieve their individual and group goals ("composition principles"); and (3) what resources in practice groups meet individual members' needs and goals ("therapeutic factors").

Member Orientations

Some theory and research relate to what the "I's" bring to practice groups and how these variables relate to outcomes. Current knowledge suggests that some potential members have more chances for positive outcomes in intensive small group experiences than do others (Abramowitz and Abramowitz, 1974; Bednar, Melnick, and Kaul, 1974; Bostwick, 1987; Bugen, 1978; Grotjohn, 1972; Kaul and Bednar, 1986; Lee and Bednar, 1971; Lieberman, Yalom, and Miles, 1973; Melnick and Rose, 1979; Melnick and Woods, 1976; Rosenzweig and Folman, 1974; Schopler and Galinsky, 1981; Schutz, 1958; Slavson, 1964; Van Dyck, 1980; Yalom, 1995).

The characteristics of those most likely to benefit from intensive small group experiences are as follows:

1. They have some awareness of and can articulate to some degree what they want for themselves from joining the group. That is, they have some consciousness of their personal goals. When these initially desired outcomes are fairly realistic and include some recognition of how they might be framed and achieved—at least in part in terms of interpersonal changes—the chances for positive outcomes appear higher. The theory and research do not suggest that these goals are fully formulated or unchangeable. In fact,

individual goals — especially in therapeutic groups, including those of a short-term, four-to-six meeting duration — appear to change over time in the group. They shift toward more clarity, more relevance to the group's purpose and perceived resources, and more consequence for members' interpersonal contexts and needs outside of the group (Anderson and Paik, 1994).

2. They have enough sense of personal identity that they are willing to venture change. They will make some initial investment in this change. They will risk exposure of their current sense of self in the challenge of learning more about this self through experimentation with others. They express both fears *and* wishes for becoming more aware of who one is, and can be, with others. The sense of self is in flux, and the person is at least dimly aware of this process within. In brief, the person experiences and demonstrates some openness to know and understand his or her self better and to form it more.

3. They suggest some need to get closer to others. There is a need for belongingness and acceptance, which is reflected in some behavior that reaches out to others, discloses, and seeks feedback. "Some" here indicates more than "none." The point is that at least the beginning of the need for others is represented in these individuals' current orientations toward people. (Some potential members defend against experiencing this universal human need so strongly that they verge on autistic relationships with others. They are not good candidates for constructive group experiences.) These affiliative needs, or "social hunger" (especially when combined with a sense of personal autonomy), strongly affect positive group process and outcomes (Anderson, 1979; Schutz, 1958; Slavson, 1964; Yalom, 1995). Such potential group members reach out to others, want to be with others more and feel less alienated, and offer enough fidelity to connect with group members through their communication. They appear to desire to learn more not only about themselves but also about others and people in general.

4. They have expectations that appear realistic. In fact, their expectations are so reality-oriented from their past experiences that they generally expect less than what they usually get. Their major compatible expectation is that the group can be a medium through which they can learn to improve certain aspect(s) of their lives and aspects of their relationship to others. The group is not at first perceived as real "living" but as a place to experiment with and learn how to relate and live differently in the social world. In addition, post hoc research on high achievers of outcomes in groups invariably show members noting a world of learning experiences that exceeded their original expectations. They especially report events in which they learned to perceive and conceive of themselves and others differently; received honest feedback coming from good intentions; functioned in an interdependent "community" with others; were held to and took responsibility directly for themselves; expressed strong feelings

and experienced others' acceptance and understanding of these; increased confidence in their own competence; felt their more authentic selves accepted; and experienced the sheer pleasure of being close to others, caring for others, and being cared for by them. (For an earlier review, see Hill, 1975; for a recent review, see Yalom, 1995.)

5. Those who join groups and have the potential to be harmed by them reflect initial and continued unrealistic expectations. These expectations tend to be fed by the leader, who coerces the member to meet them. When the member fails to achieve the expected, he or she is often relegated to a deviant, nonviable role by the leader, by other members, and in terms of self-acceptance. Research suggests that many of these expectations involve the immediate expression of intense, innermost feelings in the group (Lieberman, Yalom, and Miles 1973; Schopler and Galinsky, 1981). The member wishes and expects to break through schizoid-like straightjackets to get in touch with feelings, while at the same time fearing aspects of self-revelation. In this bind, an attack by a powerful and aggressive leader, rejection by a power clique in the group, or over-stimulation almost guarantees some injury to these members.

Studies of dropouts from groups reveal a similar dynamic and suggest that many of them may be casualties (Bostwick, 1987; Schopler and Galinsky, 1981; Rosenzweig and Folman, 1974). Such persons tend to fear their own anger and intimacy and mask these fears in the unrealistic expectation of instant intimacy in the group. This strong need may be mixed with an extreme concern about the group's attack, anger, or rejection.

Prevention of such injury requires first that the expectations members have for the group be realistic, clarified, and mutual. Pregroup interviews for this purpose are helpful (DeJulio, Bentley, and Cockayne, 1972; Manor, 1986). Contracting is essential. Early forays into the group by members need to be supported (at least by practitioners) and need to invite the trust that each member can explore each other and the group at arm's length before risking deeper levels of self-assertion and self-disclosure.

Composition Principles

We actually know very little about how to compose groups, even though a great deal of research has been devoted to this issue (Slavson, 1964; Stava and Bednar, 1979; Woods and Melnick, 1979; Van Dyck, 1980; Yalom, 1995). The general principle that has evolved is that groups should be composed homogeneously in regard to objective criteria (age, sex, socioeconomic status, disease, and so on) but heterogeneously in regard to behavioral characteristics (Bertcher and Maple, 1977). There is recognition that the range of these behavioral characteristics not be *too* wide, but there is no clear direction for where to draw the line. The most consistent findings suggest that it pays to compose the group in such a manner that each member is compatible with at least one other member (Anderson, J.D., 1984; Stava and Bednar,

1979). This position seems to prevent the evolution of neglected isolates or scapegoats in the group. Members may not always experience the supportive dynamic of "we are all in the same boat," but they may at least experience the sense that they are not all alone — a great source of support in itself. In social work theory this has been called pairing (Anderson, J., 1984) or the Noah's Ark principle (Reid, 1991).

Therapeutic Factors

The essence of group process on behalf of members is mutual aid. All the extensive research done to date on the perceived "therapeutic factors" in groups attests to this singular quality of mutual aid as it develops in group process for influencing positive outcomes for members. (For a review, see Yalom, 1995.) A closer inspection of these factors, as identified by members and group leaders, can inform our choice of the group as the method for delivering services and our criteria for composing groups. These factors suggest the presenting service needs wherein the group might be the more effective method-of-choice in providing needed services. These "therapeutic factors" are the following:

1. *Instillation of Hope:* Members perceive the potential of the group and the practitioner to meet particular felt needs that are necessary for lessening currently painful experiences and increasing fulfillment and growth;
2. *Universality:* Members experience some commonness and connection with others in similar life situations and with similar reactions to these situations. They feel less apart from others and more a part of humanity;
3. *Imparting of Information:* Members receive ideas and advice designed to understand and act differently in relation to their life situations;
4. *Imitative Behavior:* Members learn through the various models in the group, especially as they work on representative themes, concerns, and issues that are similar to or closely related to one's own.
5. *Interpersonal Learning:* Members discover their interactional and communication patterns through experience with and feedback from other members in the group, evaluate how these work or do not work to meet one's needs, and experiment with new interpersonal behaviors;
6. *Altruism:* Members engage in cooperative mutual aid, a give-and-take, to support and challenge each other's change and growth;
7. *Family Recapitulation:* Members discover the unfinished issues from the first interpersonal and group system — their family — and how these issues transfer, affect, and often distort the meeting of one's current needs in interpersonal relationships and other social systems;
8. *Catharsis/"Corrective Emotional Experience":* Members risk expressing strong interpersonal emotions that are often denied or unexpressed; find the group supportive of this risk; test the reality of these within the consensual validation of the effect on other members and the self; and change feelings, behavior, or both to facilitate opportunity for more close, honest interactions with others;

9. *Cohesiveness:* Members develop their potential for human bonding, which includes more caring for the group, other members, and the self. Each member feels more connection and closeness and less isolation and alienation;

10. *Socializing Techniques:* Members develop more competence and social skills for establishing effective and satisfying interpersonal relationships;

11. *Existential Factors:* Members increasingly recognize that one is both a separate and a connected self. There is more sense of responsibility to one's self and for one's life. One perceives more choices about how to live one's life before one's death more authentically and honestly, even in the face of pain and suffering.

These factors indicate that the foremost criterion for composing groups is the concept of a common purpose. In groups whose members share a purpose, the therapeutic factors of altruism, cohesiveness, universality, interpersonal learning, instillation of hope, and social learning are more likely to occur. If we look beyond potential "I's" to a potential "We," we can discover how similar needs and goals might generate a common purpose. The group is especially a resource when it evolves group goals that include members' increased competencies and empowerment within the group and in their lives outside.

"WE" GROUP DYNAMICS

"We" involves what most theory and research identify as group dynamics. These include the concepts of group structure, group climate, group cohesion, and group communication.

Group Structure

Position.   Position is one's place in the group, as perceived by oneself and by others. Members experience their position (and researchers measure it) by how "in" or "out" of the group they perceive themselves to be. Basically there are central, peripheral, and outside positions in groups. These affect (1) where members stand in reference to the group, and (2) the quantity and quality of their interactions within the group (Leavitt, 1951; Middleman, 1978). Those in the center have access to the group's resources for interpersonal satisfaction and task accomplishment. Those on the immediate periphery and outermost edges increase access as they move more into the group. Those on the outside who do not enter more become structurally stuck in positions of neglected "isolate" or rejected "scapegoat." The former receives little attention in interaction; the latter at least gets some attention through group pressure to change. Neither has access to the group's resources. If they are not brought "in," their chances of positive outcomes are low and of injury high.

Status. Status relates to position but refers specifically to the rank one assigns oneself and is assigned by other members. This status is experienced (and measured) by a hierarchical ranking of members. One decides, in order, who stands first, second, and so on in the group; or who appears most important, next in importance, and so on. In general, there can be high-status, middle-status, and low-status members. One's status often closely correlates with one's position and roles and the values and norms in the group (Balgopal and Vassil, 1983; Ephross and Vassil, 1988; Toseland and Rivas, 1995). At least in early group dynamics, members allocate status from the perspective of the sociopolitical context and their socialized cultural values and norms. Our society's socially ascribed statuses tend to follow members into small groups and to some degree influence how members evaluate each other's social value. Over time, as members assume positions and roles that promote and establish group norms, they attain more particular statuses in the group.

High-status members generally experience high self-esteem in reference to the group; low-status members experience painful self-doubts. Casualty often occurs when members with high self-esteem needs have low status. This is extremely threatening to their self-confidence and feelings of worth. Members seem to benefit most who learn that everyone, including themselves, can get higher and more equal status by assuming mutual aid roles, coming "in" or involving themselves in the group, and living up to the group's norms. If any member has both a very low status and an outside position for some time, the odds are very high that he or she will drop out, be hurt, and feel a failure (Lieberman, Yalom, and Miles, 1973; Schopler and Galinsky, 1981). Research implies that members of practice groups are more sensitively and accurately aware of who is ranked where, who is valued more or less, and who is most vulnerable than are group practitioners. We can prevent many of the destructive consequences of status allocation in our groups by helping members to periodically examine this aspect of current group structure for themselves and for us. It is especially important when the "We" variable begins to evolve in our groups. Otherwise, a combination of positions, statuses, and roles of power can become entrenched for the benefit of some members at the expense of others.

Roles. Roles are the behavioral expectations we have for ourselves and perceive that others have for us in conjunction with particular positions and statuses (Cartwright, 1951). Role concepts evolve from the social systems theory of Talcott Parsons (1951), who proposed that all social systems develop and maintain themselves through two functions: instrumental and expressive. Instrumental functions are necessary to accomplish the tasks pertinent to the achievement of the system's goals. Expressive functions are necessary to ensure that members' personal and interpersonal relationship needs are met enough for them to remain in and work on behalf of the system and its goals. In this theory, all social systems develop a set of instrumental and expressive role expectations to keep the system functioning. These roles are like a variety of types and sizes of shoes that a system provides and that members must wear regardless of how well they fit. To Parsons, roles are functional to the system; members must function within the expected instrumental and expressive roles in order to promote systems maintenance and adaptability.

Robert Bales (1950) applied this construct in his theory and research of small groups. He studied roles in groups and their effects on members as task (instrumental) and/or socioemotional (expressive) maintenance. Subsequent work on group roles has identified a cluster of behaviors that represent task, maintenance (socioemotional), or self intentions. That is, some behaviors primarily function to assist the group in the accomplishment of its purpose and goals. These expected behaviors structure task roles. Some function to create or maintain harmonic feelings and working intermember relations. These organize into maintenance roles. Some, however, are intended to draw attention to "oneself" in order to meet personal and/or group needs. These constitute personal (self) roles. Within each are behaviors and roles that are more or less functional for the group. Dysfunctional roles do not imply pathologies within individual members. Dysfunction is a systems concept, not a personality variable in small group theory. People enact dysfunctional roles when their behaviors serve to obstruct or detract from the group's attaining its goals and meeting members' needs. Usually, then, dysfunctional roles fall within the "personal" category and indicate behaviors that bring attention to oneself to meet one's personal needs in ways that can restrict the group from meeting its instrumental and expressive needs. The following list provides a sample of the roles and behaviors that seem most representative and functional in practice groups.

Examples of Task, Maintenance, and Self Roles and Behaviors

Task Roles and Behavior:
Any behavior that assists in accomplishing the task or purpose of a group.

1. Task Orientor: Defining the task	Identifying the group task, purpose, or objective, including related outcomes.
2. Task Analyzer: Suggesting subgoals	Suggesting subgoals and methods to help accomplish the group task.
3. Idea Generator: Giving/asking for direction	Expressing or requesting ideas to resolve questions about how to proceed.
4. Decision Organizer: Deciding on group procedures	Deciding how to make group decisions and solve group problems.
5. Initiator: Initiating	Offering comments or ideas to initiate action, discussion, or decisions.
6. Data Provider: Giving/asking for information or opinions	Expressing or requesting relevant information, ideas, or opinions needed to help group discussion or decisions.
7. Communication Clarifier: Giving/asking for paraphrase	Paraphrasing or requesting a paraphrase of particular comments to clarify or promote understanding.
8. Summarizer: Summarizing	Summarizing ideas, suggestions, or group performance to help clarify or understand.

9. Idea Evaluator: Evaluating ideas or solutions — Evaluating ideas and suggested solutions against group goals or standards of practicality or workability.

10. Catalyzer: Enthusing group members — Stimulating group members toward more productive and higher quality work or decisions.

11. Performance Evaluator: Evaluating group performance — Comparing group performance with standards or goals established by the group.

Maintenance Roles and Behavior:
Any behavior that assists in creating or maintaining good feelings and working relationships within a group.

1. Norm Setter: Setting norms — Helping to establish or remind the group of important norms or guidelines for acceptable behavior.

2. Gate Keeper: Involving others — Inviting quiet group members into conversations or soliciting their ideas to involve them in the interaction.

3. Supporter: Encouraging or supporting others — Encouraging, commending, praising, supporting, or agreeing with the contributions of others.

4. Obstacle Identifier: Recognizing relationship problems — Drawing attention to difficulties with the relationships or feelings within the group.

5. Assessor: Diagnosing relationship problems — Attempting to determine the source of or reasons for difficulties with the relationships or feelings within the group.

6. Feeling Clarifier: Giving/asking for paraphrase — Paraphrasing or requesting a paraphrase of expressed feelings to clarify or promote understanding.

7. Tension Reliever: Relieving tension — Engaging in any behavior to reduce tension within the group.

8. Harmonizer: Harmonizing, compromising or resolving — Avoiding or reducing conflict by promoting compromise between group members or by helping to resolve differences.

9. Obstructor (functional): Blocking misbehavior — Stopping or helping to stop unethical, harmful, or other inappropriate behavior.

10. Responder: Giving feedback — Sharing one's personal reaction to the behavior of another group member.

11. Processor: Observing and debriefing	Observing, sharing, and discussing observations of group behavior, feelings, or relationships.

Personal (Self) Roles and Behavior:
Any behavior that draws attention to oneself in order to meet personal and/or group needs.

1. Asserter: Asserting oneself	Expressing one's own desires or opinions with confidence and without excuse.
2. Emoter: Sharing spontaneous feelings	Openly sharing personal feelings as they occur, without premeditation.
3. Discloser: Disclosing oneself	Sharing information about oneself to enlighten or help others understand one's behaviors, feelings, or motivations.
4. Personalizer: Using personal examples	Using personal examples to illustrate an idea or to instruct members of the group.
5. Reflector: Exploring oneself	Thinking out loud about one's behaviors, feelings, or motivations for the purpose of personal discovery, learning, or insight.
6. Requester: Responding to feedback	Acknowledging or reacting to other members' observations or feelings about one's behavior.
8. Receiver: Seeking help	Requesting assistance from others with understanding or changing one's behavior, feelings, or circumstances.
9. Joker: Being playful	Joking or playing around to reduce personal rather than group tension or boredom.
10. Container: Remaining silent	Remaining quiet or otherwise not participating outwardly in the group interaction.
11. Attention Seeker: Seeking recognition	Seeking recognition for one's achievements or behavior in the group.
12. Soap Boxer: Promoting special interests	Taking advantage of opportunities in the conversation to promote groups or topics of special interest to oneself.

We can also conceive of opposing roles in small groups in terms of active-passive, leader-follower, and influencer-deviant (Ohlsen and Pearson, 1965). In such theory and research, assuming roles that both meet one's own "I" needs and contribute to "We" goals creates the deepest sense of belonging in the group (Getzels and Thelen, 1960). Earlier practice group research found that highly positive change was significantly related to members' sharing roles that actively supported group norms, influenced the group's work, and permitted spontaneous authentic, flexible, and frequent activity (Lieberman, Yalom, and Miles, 1973). In other words, for positive outcomes to occur, all members need at times to assume active, leader, goal-influencing roles and receive other members' support and challenge for these. Those entrenched by members' expectations in passive, follower, and/or deviant roles are low changers or casualties. They do not experience belongingness in the group. The research indicates that high changers actually increase their active, leader, influencer roles during the group experience; negative changers and casualties decrease in these areas. The role variable that appears most predictive of failure for a member in an evolving group is a combination of deviance and a low sense of belongingness. To be treated and to perceive oneself as a "nobody" in a group of "somebodies" is a personally devastating experience, which practitioners must prevent in every possible way.

Norms.   Norms are the shared expectations of appropriate behavior in a particular social system. In groups, norms entail members' consensus regarding how to promote their wishes and to protect their fears while regulating acts that are pertinent to the attainment of goals (Psathas and Hardert, 1966). In operation, norms are like a group "program," akin to a computer program. They explicitly or (most often) implicitly direct the operations deemed necessary for group maintenance and change. Members' assumptions regarding the norms do "program" their behaviors within the group to a great extent. Researchers usually measure norms by asking individual members about their assumptions. Norms, then, are the proportion (such as two-thirds) of members' agreement on what "do's" and "don't's" are "in force" in the group.

For instance, Gary Bond (1983, 1984) studied the norms generally found in therapeutic groups. He discovered that such norms have two components that prescribe certain behaviors and restrict other behaviors. The first is members' assumptions regarding what the group considers acceptable or not. This is the *evaluation* component. The second is members' beliefs regarding whether particular behaviors (whether acceptable or not) are likely to occur in the group. This is the *expectation* component. Measuring and comparing the degree of consensus in reference to these two norm dimensions, Bond (1983) discovered five major types of norms in therapeutic practice groups: (1) *positive norm regulation*, or members' consensus that the behaviors are both likely to occur and acceptable to the group; (2) *negative norm regulation*, or beliefs that behaviors are both unlikely to occur and unacceptable to the group if they do; (3) *risky norms*, or beliefs about behaviors that would be acceptable but currently are assumed as unlikely to occur; (4) *deviant norms*, or beliefs that particular behaviors are likely to occur and would be considered unacceptable; (5) *unregulated areas*, or behaviors currently not fully covered in the group's norms. The latter type involves a lack of consensus on either the evaluation (acceptable/unacceptable) or expectation (likely/not likely) components, or on both (totally unregulated).

Norms interact with the variables of positions, statuses, and roles in small groups. Leaders and high-status members tend to embody the more significant group norms in their behavior. In effective practice groups, all members help shape the norms. This reflects their more central positions, equal statuses, and active leadership roles. It evolves from and reciprocates more the development of norms that support the equal-opportunity structure.

Consistent empirical evidence correlates group norms to member position and negative outcomes (Bond, 1983; DeJulio, Bentley, and Cockayne, 1979; Hall and Watson, 1970; Lieberman, Yalom, and Miles, 1973; Psathas and Hardert, 1966). As stated in the conclusion to one of the most extensive research projects on practice group dynamics and outcomes, "Norms *do* make a difference in the prediction of outcomes — a condition at least as powerful as that of specific leader behavior" (Lieberman et al., 1973, p. 270). Group norms appear to relate to outcomes in very interesting ways. Groups that have a higher yield in desired outcomes have loose boundaries about content (almost anything can be talked about without rejection); have norms that favor peer control of participation (wherein members themselves consider domination and withdrawal as equally unacceptable); and have a large number of norms (regardless of the specific content).

Groups that have hurt members tend to lack peer control norms. Often, these are groups in which members permit leaders to establish norms primarily aimed at here-and-now disclosure and confrontation as the most appropriate behavior in the group. In these groups, it seems that some members work at becoming the "good" members that the leader expects. They dominate the group while others withdraw or become indifferent. It appears, then, that helping groups to develop peer-oriented norms that prohibit manipulation and domination and discourage withdrawal and indifference may well be needed to protect members against negative outcomes.

The research on norms tends to confirm two other hypotheses. First, the actual norms in the group are closely related to the initial expectations of members. If these member expectations match those of the leaders, they generally become actual group norms and influence higher-level outcomes. And these are generated to a great extent from members' cultural values and beliefs. Leader influence on group norms seems largely restricted to strengthening existing expectations (e.g., negotiating "ground rules") or to converting uncertain expectations into decisive norms (Bond, 1983). Here we have another case for pregroup clarification of expectations and for mutuality in contracting early in the group's work.

Second, group norms are the strongest variable now known to relate systematically to outcomes of actual behavior change. If changes in particular behaviors are among our outcomes in groups, we would do well to help the group establish norms that support and challenge experimentation with these behaviors in the group.

Goals.   Concepts of goals in groups are complex (Garvin, 1987). Goals affect the transactions and the structured patterns among all points of the "I-We-It" group process configuration. Thus, there are individual goals ("I's"); group process goals ("We"); and group practice goals ("It"). These goals are generally defined as "expected consequences," "intentions," or "desired outcomes." The goals at each of these points can be compatible or not. Further, they can occur at both conscious and unconscious levels. When conscious, they may be stated or unavowed. When stated, they may be clear or vague, direct or indirect, and so on. Nevertheless, the expression and negotiation of more or less explicit goals determine how members develop and experience group structure.

A significant mark of mutual aid in the group is the existence of compatible "I-We-It" goals. Congruence among individual goals and group process and outcome goals is concomitant with changes in the earlier group structure. Members retain and strengthen positions, statuses, roles, and norms that are functional to mutual aid work. They change those that serve as obstacles to such interdependence. Together, then, members in an evolving practice group co-create a group structure and culture that appears most necessary for both individual member and group well-being and growth.

Practitioners enable this process through their continuous efforts to educe the goals that are at work in the group. From the very first meeting, they find ways of discovering what individual members want for themselves, other members, and the group; what is shared in these desires; and how the group's current and possible structure and functioning facilitates and/or obstructs these outcomes. Members of a developing group periodically review these questions in the context of more realistic knowledge from their experiences of the specific group's resources. This strengthens goals in operation at the "I," the "We," and the "It" dimensions. An important point of this process perspective is that early individual and group goals, while formulated as clearly and consciously as possible (especially in shorter-term groups; Yalom and Yalom, 1990), are expected to change in correlation with the other changes in group structure over time. That is, the structural variables of groups illuminate aspects of group process that, in assessment, functions as a gauge for determining aspects of the stages of group development. We will most likely see substantive and qualitatively different changes in goals — as well as in positions, statuses, roles, and norms — as we empower our practice groups toward their mutual aid potential.

Group Climate

Group climate is an elusive concept. Yet all of us who have experienced groups, and some who have studied them, can attest that atmosphere-like variables such as warm/cold/frigid or light/heavy or calm/stormy can indeed affect groups and their members. We appear to have a built-in barometer to assess the climates of groups differentially. This section presents three such concepts that have been used in practice group research to study group climate variables and their effects on outcomes. These are involvement, intensity, and harmony.

Involvement.   Involvement refers to members' investment in the group. It reflects their commitment to membership and their sense of belonging. A group in which most or all members have a high involvement is a group that takes on significance for members. It therefore becomes a more potent resource for influencing them (Bassin, 1962; Mezzano, 1967). The climate for growth or for painful rejection increases.

If this involvement builds a climate for acceptance and belonging, members tend to take more risks that they identify with their own growth (Scheidlinger, 1966). Although the sense of belonging through involvement does not appear to guarantee successful outcomes for members in practice groups, its lack correlates with low outcomes, negative outcomes, and casualties (Lieberman, Yalom, and Miles, 1973).

Intensity.   Intensity is a climate variable that generally connotes the level of emotional expressiveness in groups (Snortum and Myers, 1971). High-intensity groups ignite spontaneous interchange of anger, fear, pain, grief, love, and joy. Low-intensity groups express only surface feelings, if any at all.

A certain level of intensity appears to promote change and growth in practice groups. Too little intensity reinforces current levels of functioning rather than challenging the strengths to increase competence. Boredom closely follows. Too much, especially early, churns and excites but also scares and can hurt members, preventing initial trust. Intensity best creates a climate for change when it increases during group process. There is initial stability and trust, some challenge for engaging in "corrective emotional experiences" (Yalom, 1995), and enough security to risk change and growth in interaction. Once a more solid, cohesive group evolves, with accepting responses to more intense feelings likely, this intensity seems a necessary variable in the climate for change (Levine, 1971; Lieberman, Yalom, and Miles, 1973).

Harmony.   Harmony is the experience of warmth in the atmosphere of group member relationships (Zimpfer, 1967). It reflects a mutual regard among members as well as such factors as congeniality, fellowship, friendship, and cooperation. This variable relates closely to group cohesion; it includes the sense of group bond and consensus. Although harmony entails cooperation, it does not imply lack of conflict. After all, conflict is inherent in human difference. It appears inevitable, whether overt or covert, in group process. Harmony as a cooperative atmosphere does, though, include an underlying agreement to disagree. The consensus is to face conflicts and resolve them in a way that keeps the group together and benefits all parties involved as well as the group (as much as possible). Research on groups in practice reveals that when members express anger early in the process and it lessens over time, harmony develops. Such groups tend to yield higher outcomes. Conversely, sustained intense conflict and anger correlate with low harmony and low group yield.

Group Cohesion

Group cohesion receives special attention in theory and research on group dynamics. The strong sense of "We" that symbolizes group cohesion is a central concept for group dynamics experts (Cartwright, 1968; Napier and Gershenfeld, 1981; Nixon, 1979; Shaw, 1981) as well as for social work authors who discuss group dynamics in practice (Anderson, J., 1984; Garvin, 1987; Hartford, 1971; Toseland and Rivas, 1995; Zastrow, 1985). The research on groups in a variety of practices proposes group cohesiveness as a major variable in relation to outcomes.

Cohesiveness refers to members' feelings about the group — in particular, the group's specialness as compared to other groups and members' attraction to it. It is the glue that binds members to the group. Individuals want to remain members and thus invest in membership requirements in highly cohesive groups. Less cohesive groups include members who are much more ambivalent about committing themselves to the group and its membership requirements. Such cohesiveness in practice with groups offers leverage for change, seen as analogous to the helping relationship in practice with individuals (J. Anderson, 1984; Garvin, 1987; Toseland and Rivas, 1995; Yalom, 1995). Research on cohesiveness does find it to be a significant variable in relation to therapeutic outcomes (Anderson, 1978; Bednar and Lawlis, 1971; Evans and Jarvis, 1980; Evans and Dion, 1991; Lieberman, Yalom, and Miles, 1973). Yalom (1995), for instance, correlates cohesiveness to such process and outcome variables as increased self-esteem and self-confidence, more willingness to listen to others (including feedback from other members), freer expression of feelings, and improved reality testing.

Researchers define and operationalize cohesiveness in several ways (Evans and Dion, 1991). Most often, following Dorwin Cartwright's (1968) work, they develop an aggregate score of individual members' attraction measures. These involve four sets of transacting variables: (1) affiliation needs; (2) perceived group resources; (3) a cost/benefit analysis of membership; and (4) a comparison to other similar groups. In practice groups, a most important variable is the belief that members want to benefit both themselves and others through being together. (See Appendix K for one such cohesiveness scale.) In sum, cohesiveness describes members' feelings that they are in a very special group — one in which "We" have common goals as well as a common commitment to these goals and to a desire to understand and help each other.

Research suggests that cohesiveness is strongest when it develops over time. The movement from lower to higher cohesiveness during group development increases outcome achievement. Low-cohesiveness groups, or groups that begin with relatively high cohesiveness that drops sharply during the process, tend to produce negative change and casualties. The latter appears especially so for practice groups wherein the practitioner plans exercises to promote "We" feelings early in the group and continues to lead the group through such programming (Anderson, 1978; Levin and Kurtz, 1974; Stockton, Rhode, and Haughey, 1992; Yalom, 1995).

Some research indicates that cohesiveness affects outcomes independent of the practitioner's methodology or leadership style (Anderson, 1978; Evans and Dion,

1991; Lieberman, Yalom, and Miles, 1973). This suggests that the best protection from ineffective or potentially harmful practitioners is the group's development of its own cohesiveness. One study (Anderson, 1978) found cohesiveness to be very highly correlated with members' feelings of being understood by other members. In fact, it did not matter whether members were actually accurately perceived. What mattered most and correlated greatly with both cohesiveness and positive outcomes was that they *felt* understood — they believed that other members were capable of understanding them. It appears that only in cohesive groups does this dynamic of trust and closeness occur and provide the catalyst for risking and experimenting with change and potential growth.

All the relevant research avers that this cohesiveness is strongly, significantly, and independently related to group results. It could be that one of the greatest practitioner skills is the ability to enable the group to develop its processes toward cohesiveness. Also, such cohesiveness corresponds greatly with the development of intermember empathy (Anderson, 1978) and member "altruism" or mutual aid (Hill, 1975; Yalom, 1995). Cohesiveness, then, is a dynamic that establishes the group's resources to combine support and challenge for member growth.

Group Communication

The dynamics of communication in groups includes a plethora of concepts. These range from the components of communication generally, through the effect of structural variables on communication patterns, to how the meanings of communication relate to such universal needs and themes as "power" and "intimacy" (Bennis and Shepard, 1956; Shaw, 1984; Toseland and Rivas, 1995). This section considers two communication dynamics that appear to be fundamental to practice group process and outcome: self-disclosure and feedback.

Self-Disclosure.   At some level, to whatever degree explicit or implied, all communication involves exchanges of self-disclosure and feedback. A dynamic in small groups, especially in many practice groups, is a deeper level of and more explicit and direct self-disclosures and feedback. These mark much of communication and its interpretation.

Self-disclosure generally encompasses the expression of intense, honest, deep, risky, and/or immediate feelings and material in the group. Research on the self-disclosure variable does not yet indicate that it is independently related to outcomes (Anchor, 1979; Bean and Houston, 1978; Leiberman, Yalom, and Miles, 1973; Yalom, 1995). For instance, according to some post hoc reports, members feel better about themselves if they express intense personal feelings and attribute this dynamic to their change. Yet it does not appear to be related to the more objective measurements of outcomes (Lieberman et al., 1973; Yalom, 1995). Rather, the expression of feelings seems more accurately a clearing of the underbrush that opens a path for growth. The feelings likely need responses that constitute a "corrective emotional experience" (Yalom, 1995), which garners new insight into the self and others. *Work* is needed to travel this opened path for new understanding.

Likewise, outcomes of self-disclosure depend on the interpersonal context in which it occurs. Others need to understand, appreciate, and accurately interpret it. Then it becomes dialogue. Such dialogue promotes the new cognitive insight that is concomitant with effective self-disclosure in groups.

Also, effective self-disclosure relates to autonomy. As members develop their autonomy in the group and begin to experience their own personal power to master their lives within and outside, they are more likely to engage in the self-disclosure that increases their interpersonal competence (Anderson, 1978, 1984; Diamond and Shapiro, 1973; Bean and Houston, 1978). Increased awareness and insight regarding choice and responsibility accompany more autonomous disclosures. This choice is based in one's will to grow.

Generally, intense self-disclosure from early dependency rather than autonomy appears especially harmful to members (Anchor, 1979). It can lead to embarrassment, shame, doubt, and self-effacing without the group being ready to understand, appreciate, and empathize with these feelings. It almost ensures a group casualty. Practitioners would do well to prevent or deflect this early extreme exposure of members rather than to encourage it. Reinforcing of such disclosures often arises from a misguided belief that the intense emotional expression serves as a necessary "catharsis" for the individual and the group. However, the sparks that such inappropriate early disclosure create may heat up the group momentarily, only to burn forever in the pain of those left exposed and not understood.

Feedback. Feedback generally involves giving information to others about one's perception of them and receiving such data about oneself (Jacobs, 1974). Research on feedback in group communication has focused primarily on the receiving end of this transaction, on getting information that the receiver considers important and useful (Yalom, 1995). Many participants in intensive practice groups rank feedback (in conjunction with cathartic self-disclosure) *high* (second only to cohesiveness) in their assessment of helping mechanisms in their group (Yalom, 1995). This feedback includes information that is positive, negative, or mostly neutral (as in advice or cognitive data).

Research has not directly identified feedback as a dynamic for specific outcomes (Lieberman, Yalom, and Miles, 1973; Martin and Jacobs, 1980). There is a trend toward high changers receiving a mixture of positive and negative feedback and low or negative changers receiving mostly negative feedback, if any. Feedback also appears to be more of a change dynamic when it follows self-disclosure. This finding probably indicates that using one's own autonomy to increase self-understanding is a different and more empowering experience than initiating it from others' feedback. Further, self-disclosure indicates that one may be more ready to use feedback. To enable the communication dynamic of exchanging self-disclosure and feedback, practitioners should reach for the feedback in the group when the members self-disclose.

"IT" GROUP DYNAMICS

There is no question that "It" dynamics such as types of groups and leaders can influence groups greatly, for good or for ill. This section reports primarily on the leadership variable. It addresses theory and research on leadership functions and styles and their influence on outcomes in various practice groups (Anderson, J., 1984; Ashkenas and Tandon, 1979; Hurst et al., 1978; Lieberman, Yalom, and Miles, 1973; Lungren, 1977; Scheidlinger, 1980; Sibergeld, Thune, and Manderscheid, 1979; Wogan et al., 1977).

Leadership Functions

Research on leader behavior has identified particular leadership behaviors in reference to practice groups. Practitioner actions tend to cluster into four basic functions:

1. *Providing:* This involves provider roles of relationship- and climate-setting through such skills as support, affection, praise, protection, warmth, acceptance, genuineness, and concern.
2. *Processing:* This involves processor roles of illuminating the meaning of the process through such skills as explaining, clarifying, interpreting, and providing a cognitive framework for change, or translating feelings and experiences into ideas.
3. *Catalyzing:* This involves catalyzer roles of stimulating interaction and emotional expression through such skills as reaching for feelings, challenging, confronting, and suggesting; using program activities such as structured experiences; and modeling.
4. *Directing:* This involves director roles through such skills as setting limits, roles, norms, and goals; managing time; pacing; stopping; interceding; and suggesting procedures.

These four functions appear to have a clear and striking relationship to outcomes when carried by leaders in intensive small group experiences (Lieberman, Yalom, and Miles, 1973). Providing and processing have a linear relationship to outcomes: the higher the providing (or caring) and the higher the processing (or illuminating the meaning of events), the higher the positive outcome. The other two functions — catalyzing (or emotional stimulation) and directing — have a curvilinear relationship to outcomes; that is, too much or too little catalyzing or directing results in lower positive outcomes. This finding suggests that leaders who do not catalyze at times will have unenergetic, devitalized groups. On the other hand, too much catalyzing (especially with insufficient focus via processing) results in a highly emotionally charged climate, with the leader pressing for more emotional interaction than the members can integrate (or "process" into their own experience). Too little directing — a laissez-faire style — results in a bewildered, floundering group. Too much directing creates a highly structured, authoritarian group whose interaction process will be stilted and not freely flowing, and whose members will fail to develop a sense of self-autonomy.

Leadership Styles

Effective leadership styles appear to help more. Leaders especially empower the group to become the agent of change by functioning moderately as catalyst and director and highly as provider and processor. Both providing and processing are critical. Neither, by itself, seems sufficient to increase the possibilities of success. Providing, or actively caring, establishes the climate and *support* for growth; but this change requires members to work. And work requires the *challenge* of processing and some catalyzing and directing. This reflects the enabler style, as contrasted with others in the research findings to date on leader styles and outcomes. Table 5.1 depicts these findings.

GROUP PROCESS

Social work with groups has long considered group process primarily in terms of stages of group development (for comparative historical models, see Hartford, 1971; Northen, 1988). The most developed model is proposed by James Garland, Hubert Jones, and Ralph Kolodny (1973). Their model provides the basis for recent work on empowerment through groups (Berman-Rossi, 1992), the practitioner's differential tasks and skills (Berman-Rossi, 1993; Glassman and Kates, 1990), and specific interventions in treatment groups (Wickham, 1993). Their stages and their central concerns are organized around the following sequence: (1) Preaffiliation, (2) Power and Control, (3) Intimacy, (4) Differentiation, and (5) Separation. (For a comparison of this and other five-stage models, see Appendix C.)

This section adds TACIT themes (Anderson, J., 1984) to the earlier model. It uses additional data from empirical research on stages of group development (most of which to date has evolved outside of social work). And it incorporates aspects of other models derived through the experience of a variety of professions and disciplines in the work and study of small group therapeutic process (Banet, 1976; Bennis and Shepard, 1956; Bion, 1959; Bonney, 1974; Cohen and Smith, 1976; Kellerman, 1979; Lacoursiere, 1980; Levine, 1979; Lungren, 1977; Rogers, 1970; Tuckman, 1973; Tuckman and Jensen, 1977).

TABLE 5.1 Leadership styles by order of effectiveness

Style	Processing	Providing	Catalyzing	Directing	Degree of Change	Degree of Casualty
Enablers	H	H	M	M	H	L
Social engineers	H	L	L	M	M	M
Energizers	L	H	H	H	M	H
Laissez-faires	M	L	L	L	L	L
Impersonals	L	L	H	L	L	M
Managers	L	L	H	H	L	H

H stands for High; M for Moderate; and L for Low.

Special focus is on the themes that integrate aspects of individual, interpersonal, and group development. This reflects the assumption that one explanation for the stages of group development is that the developmental needs of individuals, interpersonal relationships, and groups are synergistically related. Thus, individual models such as those proposed by Erik Erikson (1950) and Abraham Maslow (1970) also suggest the themes we might expect to find in some salient sequence in groups. These appear as Trust, Autonomy, Closeness, Interdependence, and Termination — or TACIT.

Development is based on the hypothesis that the individual is born into the world with inherent thrusts for growth. These thrusts guide the individual's creative interaction with the environment in personally meaningful ways. Such a perspective is consistent with Abraham Maslow's (1970) model of self-actualization. Present from the first day in the life of the individual, the self-actualizing motivation is primary when the lower-level needs are met. These foundational needs — in order — are: physiological, safety and security, love and belongingness, and self-esteem or self-respect. Individuals in the group can be perceived as manifesting behavior that attempts to meet these needs and extends the resources for self-actualization. Often, as in any new situation we experience, these needs can emerge in a similar sequence in the group.

The fountain of group process is each member's self-generative characteristics — the thrusts for growth — that propel development toward self-actualization. As members build a social system in the group that meets safety and security needs, they tend — by their own growth thrusts — to revise the system to meet their higher-level needs of belongingness, love, self-respect, and self-actualization. For them to grow, the system they create together must be growing.

SPIRAL STAGES

The actual process of individual development is as unique as one's thumbprint. We come into the world with unique potentialities. Each of us experiences an individualized interaction with our particular context — this is basic to the stunting or flowering of our potentials into actuals at every point in our development. Yet just as people's thumbs may be more similar than their prints, when individual development is viewed overall, there are some common stages. These underlying, natural stages are the results of the evolution of particular themes and their recurrent crises for the individual.

The model of group development presented here proposes a principle similar to the "tacit" (i.e., natural, or known at a level beyond words) dimension of group development. "TACIT" also serves as a useful acronym for the themes that mark the stages of this development. It reflects the interpersonal themes that are often sequential in human development. Indeed, as one moves toward discovering and getting close to more of one's self (an "I") in trust and autonomy, one can become connected with others in closeness and interdependence (the "We"). To use Karen Horney's (1951) metaphor, the "acorn" develops the "roots" of initial trust and self-autonomy before growing into the strong and sturdy "oak tree" of close, interdependent, mutual aid relationships with others.

Individual and group development can be mapped out by signposts of themes and crises that reflect sequential stages. However, this is not a simple step ladder. Individual members may be at different stages (Tucker, 1973). There is both progress and regress to recurrent themes as each new critical period is faced. Thus, development is best conceived of as a spiral. The spiral concept of development, presented in Figure 5.1, more accurately represents group process. First, the loops overlap and spring from each other, indicating developmental continuity between stages. Second, the loops form qualitatively separate and higher-level configurations, indicating developmental discontinuity. The continuity supports stability or security. The discontinuity creates change or growth. Third, the loops demonstrate that very often the first step toward progress is regress. That is, progress tends to include regress—an equilibrium (or a "steady state") in the present stage and enough disequilibrium (or "tension") to anticipate a future state.

Spiral stages of group development subsume elements of both "phases" and "trends." The premise is that the group process does flow through inexorable stages that cannot be artificially manufactured or pushed. When the group returns to earlier themes in transitional or impasse "phases," it does not face the issues in the same way as when they were first encountered. In a new state, discontinuous from the earlier one, the group confronts the continuous themes from a sequentially evolved "stage" that is different from prior ones. Therefore, the group is more adept at resolving the recurring crises. This ability to deal with both emerging and unresolved recurring themes, as in individual development, reflects the group's level of maturity in its own process.

FIGURE 5.1   Spiral tacit development

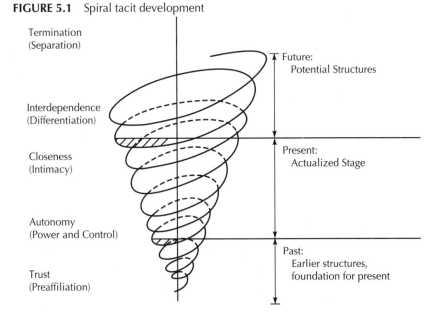

A more concrete metaphor may help here. The evolving of stages is analogous to changing tires on a car. Each bolt is loosely in place to begin with. Then there is the sequential tightening of the bolts. In order, each one is more secure before moving around the hub.

There are, of course, complex variations to the stages. These are due to special characteristics such as group purpose, size (Wheelan and McKeage, 1993), structure (Brower 1989), setting (Wogan et al., 1977), composition (Alissi and Casper, 1985), leader directiveness (Anderson, J.D., 1984), and length of time (Galinsky and Schopler, 1989). These and other variables cause alterations and uniqueness in overall flow. A comparison of studies, however, indicates the remarkable fact that in a wide variety of groups, conceived by an equally wide variety of models, the stages of group development are much more similar than different (for a more recent review, see Mennecke, Hoffer, and Wynne, 1992).

This text assumes that the similarity comes to a great extent from the existential givens in all group life: autonomy and interdependence. Our struggle to be true to the self and to appreciate our unity with others is at the very core of our existence as human beings. Therefore, autonomy and interdependence themes are often the areas in which we are most conflicted, most anxious, and most unaware. We build our groups to map a way to resolve these conflicts, among the greatest sources of our wishes and fears, on the basis of where we are in our own individual development. In the group, then, a particular stage of development is the existing balance of all the forces impinging on events to deal with autonomy and interdependence, the "I" and the "We." As anxieties are increased when these needs arise, members use their autonomy to seek power and structure and to protect themselves from premature closeness. Then they can use more of their autonomy to seek the freedom to be more of themselves in relation to others. When the autonomous "I" needs are met more fully in negotiating the "We," the "We" needs are responsibly sought and the group process is developed more for closeness and interdependence. The following summary of the stages of development in practice groups reflects this process.

STAGES OF GROUP DEVELOPMENT

Preaffiliation/Trust

Trust issues accompany unpredictability. The unknowns abound at the beginning of any group. All that members bring and know are their individual orientations, experiences, and norms regarding trust. The work of the group is yet unknown; the focus is ambiguous. There is not yet a structure to provide a secure anchor against fears and vulnerabilities. The nature of this group, especially its structure and norms, may or may not benefit the member; the odds are just as high that one will lose as gain in one's current sense of integrity. All this depends at least as much on who others are and what others do as on oneself. An atmosphere of mistrust seeking more security and trust marks the "I-We-It" of the beginning group.

A major process theme in relation to trust is that of involvement before choices of investment and commitment can be made. The search by members is for the potential of resources within the group to meet trust and security needs. The major questions to be answered by them before involvement are: "How is this going to benefit me? What does all this have to do with me?" These questions pepper discussions, often creating confusion about personal and group goals. At the same time, members are sizing up one another and the group through an arm's-length exploration process. They search for a viable role for themselves, quite often predisposed toward their familiar roles. These seem to provide security from too much closeness and commitment as well as some power to influence the group system's actual goals and norms.

Members are ostensibly together because of their interest in the common purpose of the group and will ultimately build trust around their mutual commitment to this purpose. However, the initial social forces are at work toward much investment of their energy in the establishment of *initial trust*. This most often entails the search for approval, acceptance, respect, or domination. Members seek this especially in finding a place in the group's evolving structure. They use approach/avoidance behavior to explore answers to the question of what membership entails: "What are the admission requirements, the price of the ticket to belong? How much must I give or reveal of my prized individuality? Should I involve myself for the gratification promised, or remain lonely and left out? Will I feel more hurt if involved, and who may hurt me? Can my needs be met better through investment somewhere else?" At a nearly conscious level they seek answers to wish/fear questions like these and maintain a constant, often subtle, vigilance for the types of behavior that the group expects and approves. They scan what this behavior implies about the system's goals and norms in relation to their own needs. Thus, they tentatively and more cautiously explore the "I," the "We," and the "It."

Even though the group in the trust stage is often puzzled, testing, and hesitant, it is also dependent. In practice groups, the members overtly and covertly look to "leaders" (especially the practitioner) for a safe and more familiar structure, as well as for approval and acceptance. There is the underlying hope that "If leaders, these powerful significant others, see me as belonging and O.K., then I am O.K. in this group." Much of the initial communication is directed toward the practitioner. He or she is carefully studied for rewards, as members manifest behavior that has gained approval and acceptance from authorities in the past.

Through this interaction, members discover similarities and differences and begin to build the group norms for security. There is a strong tendency to accommodate "I" needs—to go along to get along. This climate builds a base for closeness and cohesiveness. Such buds for connection are needed before members can risk their more authentic differences and invest in their growth without fears of severe rejection or judgment by other members, especially more powerful ones. The climate also creates the initial structure, characterized by the control and power of autonomy.

Power and Control/Autonomy

Autonomy includes early initiatives to influence the group and much ambivalence regarding both potential freedom and existing limits. Just as the child might follow the early learned words of "Mom" and/or "Dad" with the ubiquitous "No," members seek and want freedom from "authority." They both want and deny approval from the practitioner and each other. They seek the power to maintain more control over how they and others know their public selves while also wanting more freedom to let aspects of their real, more private selves be known. Thus, the autonomy stage often involves two phases. First is the negative autonomy of control and power over others. Second is the positive autonomy of personal power, which emanates more from the real self and the responsible use of this power with others.

Once the initial trust concerns are fairly resolved through the decision of most members to become involved with each other in the group (or at least to try to get along together), power and control concerns emerge. The autonomy theme dominates. Commitment to the group increases fears of vulnerability and the search for security and autonomy through the control that is inherent in structural positions, statuses, and roles. The group shifts from a preoccupation with acceptance, approval, involvement, and definitions of accepted behavior to a preoccupation with dominance, control, and power.

The conflict that is characteristic of this stage is between members, or between members and the perceived leaders (e.g., the practitioner). Each member is involved in establishing a preferred amount of autonomy, initiative, and power. Gradually a status and control hierarchy, a social pecking order, is established. The movement is from "I'm O.K., I belong here" to "I'm O.K., I rank here." The group begins to be stylized through the evolving structure. Communication patterns become established and forces are at work to freeze these patterns. Members tend to find their security in the mutually formed positions, statuses, roles, and norms. Early high-status members, who often embody dominant norms in their behavior, tend to direct their comments to other high-status members; low-status members participate through those with higher status. The trust at this point is not so much in the members and the self as in people with common needs, purposes, and goals. It is more of a trust in a common predictable structure. Mutual aid is submerged in the dynamics of seeking power and control over others through positions, statuses, and roles in the group structure.

This phase can be quite destructive for some members. Those whose place as low person on the totem pole reinforces already low self-esteem may drop out and be hurt before the group has an opportunity to resolve the hierarchical conflicts of this stage. Subgroups tend to come to the fore as important islands of safety wherein members can coalesce with others to guard their flanks. The scapegoats and isolates who cannot coalesce into subgroups may be particularly vulnerable and powerless to rejection or attack by the power clique. This increases their fears, loneliness, and isolation in human relations.

The struggle for control is part of the process of every group. It is always present to some degree — sometimes hidden, sometimes smoldering, and sometimes in full operation. It may manifest itself in battles of will for power and control or in collusion to avoid autonomy conflicts by suppressing the expressions of individual will, creating a subtle pseudo-closeness. The dynamic at this point appears designed more to control the group together than to care about the group and its members — including what each may invest in and receive from the experience.

Many groups, ineffectively facilitated, may never move past this stage. In these, the practitioner, too, has sought power and has entrenched this structure. Such a practitioner creates dependence on his or her directiveness — for example, through overuse of structured exercises (Anderson, 1980b). This stage usually does not dissolve without the group confronting an impasse, a phase of giving up the old with increased, temporarily immobilizing fears of the new. The social worker's skills are needed more in this stage and in the impasse than at any other time to help members confront the obstacles to the evolution of mutual aid in group process. It is in challenging the structural obstacles to further development at this stage that the practitioner can most empower group process toward reciprocal growth for members and the group.

Often, the process of resolving the authority issue is the first piece of work for which members really need each other in the shared power of mutual aid (Berman-Rossi, 1992; Glassman and Kates, 1990). It is in dealing with the practitioner's difference, and his or her perceived place in this structure, that the group may begin to find its own inherent power. This power can develop more equitably distributed resources for meeting more of the needs of all members. For instance, the group can discover that the practitioner functions as a specialized member with certain technical skills; then, his or her contribution can be evaluated for its value to group goal achievement, rather than accepted or rejected because of the structurally based authority behind it. This frees members to discover the unique contributions all can make to the goals of the group and the meeting of their individual needs — the basis for closeness in the group.

Intimacy/Closeness

Closeness or intimacy follows when autonomous members choose to commit themselves more to each other and the group. There is an underlying awareness that members want to be together and, at least to this degree, care about each other and the group's purpose and work. There is the comfortable climate of the "campfire group" and the consensus that this group promises more authenticity when it is ready to stretch the comfort zone. It feels good.

This third potential stage evolves closeness and cohesiveness. Following the previous phase of covert and/or overt conflict, the group gradually develops into a cohesive unit. All members come into the group at this stage with some degree of equal importance to each other and to the group as a whole. There is an increase in morale and a deeper commitment to the group's human relations agenda in the service of needs and goals. Mutual trust grows in members as people and resources rather than in structural power and control. Spontaneous self-disclosures increase, particularly the sharing of feelings of closeness and here-and-now responses to the interaction. The group becomes a group in the deepest sense of the concept as absent members for the first time are really missed and are of concern to others. The "We-It" caring about the group now temporarily submerges the "I."

While a mutual aid system in the group is developing for intermember closeness and intimacy, there is some holding back of conflict-producing feelings. Compared to the previous stage, group interaction seems to be sweetness and light. The group basks in its glow of newly discovered unity. Eventually, however, the glow will pale and the group embrace will seem superficial and ritualistic unless authentic differences in the group are permitted to emerge. When the fear of authentic feelings is resolved in the interests of mutual aid, the group has reached the maturity of interdependence—a state that lasts for the remainder of the group's life, with possible periodic and brief phase recurrences to each of the earlier stage dynamics.

Differentiation/Interdependence

The differentiation, or interdependence, stage is marked by several dynamic balances of members' and the group's needs. Autonomous and interdependent concerns of members are fused. Cohesion remains strong and is the anchor for dovetailing the here-and-now process and content concerns (the "I-We-It"). The processes in a mature group involve "valid communication" (Bennis and Shepherd, 1956) in which the group as a whole and the individual members are expressively aware of what they are doing together. Members responsibly and spontaneously sense what self and others need to achieve their common tasks. They are given what they need in proportion to their needs. This consciousness of mutual aid taps the now-recognized resources for individual, interpersonal, and group work through open feedback channels. Members' needs and the group's goals are realized more fully, spontaneously, and creatively. Member differences are accepted, reached for, and used as resources in achieving the instrumental goals of the group. This interdependence occurs until the group terminates; members transfer their increased identity, energy, and skills from the group to other social systems; or new members are taken in and create some recrudescence to the themes of earlier stages.

Separation/Termination

The last, or termination, stage can come at any time in the group's development. If the group separates following the interdependence stage, members emerge with a strong sense of competency in relation to the situations they face in life outside of the group. With this sense of competency, wishes for meeting needs in human relations outweigh fears. Hopes are increased for more matching of members' needs with resources to meet these needs in their life situations. These outcomes in the group are tinged with some regression to behavior that is more reflective of the earlier stages in the group. This behavior is based on some inevitable, increased insecurities and is often a last attempt to deny separation through insinuation that members still need each other and the practitioner.

If the group terminates during the earlier stages, the reverse is likely: feelings of inadequacy, fears stronger than wishes, increased mistrust in self and others, and less hope and faith about need-meeting potentialities. The feelings about separation are denied expression even more strongly. Increases in absences and dropouts are likely to occur.

CONCLUSION

This model of group development aids the understanding of group dynamics and events at any point in the group process. It illuminates the current potentials for reciprocal growth in both members and the group-as-a-whole. Group empowerment entails facilitating members' interactions in such a way that the social system they are creating is moving from the trust and autonomy stages toward closeness and interdependence. The major task of the practitioner becomes one of helping members to challenge the obstacles to this developmental group process and to facilitate the members' movement together toward interdependent mutual aid. This aim is the basis of social work practice through group process.

part II

The Process Model

chapter 6

Overview of Social Work Practice through Group Process

HEADLINE: GROUP COPING SKILLS BOOST
SURVIVAL OF MELANOMA

> *In October 1993, several newspapers reported a study: melanoma patients who attended a brief support group after diagnosis had about one-third the death rate of equally ill patients who did not participate in groups. This was a finding of a five-year study conducted by UCLA Medical School.*
>
> *It was the second major study to find that improved coping skills learned through group process can help people survive after a cancer diagnosis. The earlier one involved women with breast cancer.*
>
> *Studied were 68 adults treated for Stage 1 (not widely spread) melanoma. Half attended weekly therapist-led groups. Among the findings:*
>
> - *After five years, 9 percent of group members died of melanoma versus 29 percent not in the groups.*
> - *Among those who did not attend groups, the first death came four months after treatment; for group alumni, it came four and a half years later.*
> - *Group members had better immune functions six months after their groups ended. This improved their survival rate.*

INTRODUCTION

What awesome power in groups! Here we see the power of life and death. How can we tap this power in our practice? The power comes from the practitioner who has learned to facilitate rather than to obstruct group process. Indeed, a generic helping process can instruct social work through group process with a wide variety of groups established for various purposes. The group process approach suggests a basic stance toward the group and particular sequential functions and skills in the pregroup phase, the stages, and the postgroup phase. These inform the helping process presented in Part II in this text. They are summarized in an overview in this chapter.

BASIC STANCE AND FUNCTIONS

Stance

No better word describes the social worker's basic stance in the group than *enabler*. The enabler makes able, capacitates, benefits, empowers. The practitioner empowers members through enabling the group process and each individual's potential. In enabling there is an element of facilitating, which implies assisting in progress by easing and accelerating. However, facilitation does not mean expediting the process by pushing members through the stages. Facilitation involves enabling members to use the power of their own choices and actions to progress — from *empowering*. The social worker's basic stance and actions need to make the group able to accomplish its developmental process and its shared content goals.

The social worker enables through respect and positive regard for each individual member and for the group-as-a-whole. He or she uses knowledge and skills that facilitate members' awareness of their needs and evolving goals and the obstacles in their group process. The model requires that the practitioner develop the expertise of process: how the content relates to this process (the "I-We-It" triangle in an ecosystems circle as it exists at any time for the group), what can be done to develop members' awareness of this process, and what can encourage their empowering choices as a result of this awareness.

The social worker is not expected to be an expert in the particular content areas that serve as the common theme for the group — the life of the adolescent truant, the abusing parent, the prison inmate. In fact, the practitioner in this model believes strongly that the experts in the particular life situations of members are the members themselves. She or he expects to learn about these situations as members teach each other about them — not to teach members how to live in these situations. The practitioner, however, can illuminate aspects of the life process that underlie these situations as they are reflected in individual and group development themes. He or she can also underscore the strengths they bring to these and lend a vision of growth.

The social worker, therefore, enables members to help each other through developing the group process. The tasks of this enabling are related to, but different from, the tasks of the members in the group. The helping process in fact is a *parallel process* (Schwartz and Zalba, 1971); this view implies that the tasks of the practitioner and those of members are not only different but must be clearly distinguished from each other. When one takes over the tasks of the other — as when the practitioner states the goals for the group — the typical result is confusion. The members have the task of establishing and committing themselves to common goals in the group. The social worker's task is to confront members with what they are doing to determine goals and how they are working or not working together to accomplish *their* goals. The principle of parallel process clarifies the different yet interdependent tasks of the worker and the group. Any obliteration of the differences between these two sets of processes, this division of labor, renders the work dysfunctional and the encounter itself manipulative, sentimental, and frustrating. It restricts empowerment. The work — and it *is* work — will not get done.

Functions

Several models identify the generic tasks of the leader in a variety of groups. (See Appendix D for comparative models.) The tasks cluster into four basic functions through which practitioners enable the group's work. The concept of function implies a combination of the *why* and the *what* in relation to tasks. That is, functions are marked by both their intent (why used) and their result (what is expected). The four functions are:

1. *Catalyzing:* This is the active catalyst task and roles of stimulating interaction and emotional expression through such skills as reaching for feelings, challenging, confronting, suggesting, and using program activities such as structured experience and modeling.
2. *Providing:* This is the provider task and roles of relationship- and climate-setting through such skills as support, affection, encouragement, protection, warmth, acceptance, genuineness, and concern.
3. *Processing:* This is the processor task and roles of expanding awareness of the meaning of the process through such skills as explaining, clarifying, interpreting, and providing a cognitive framework for change, or translating feelings and experiences into ideas.
4. *Directing:* This is the director task and roles through such skills as setting limits, rules, norms, and procedural goals; managing time; pacing; stopping; interceding; and suggesting procedures.

THE HELPING PROCESS

Preaffiliation/Trust

The task and skills for enabling group process relate to the four functions of catalyzing, providing, processing, and directing. In the first stage, the members' primary task is to develop trust. The practitioner's parallel task is to enable a climate for this trust. The task requires some directing, catalyzing, and processing and a great deal of providing. Providing comes first from attending, observing, and actively listening. It is experienced through the use of empathy, warmth, and respect. (All skills mentioned in this section are elaborated in the remaining chapters in Part II of the text.

See Appendix G for operational definitions and an instrument for measuring these skills.) In addition, providing comes from granting permission for members to both approach and avoid — through the conscious use of reinforcements and through satisfying members' needs, whether the needs be information, tension release, friendliness, security, or whatever. Activities are noncompetitive, experiences are nonfrustrating, and limits are nonrigid. The practitioner needs to be fair and consistent, to validate all members, and to provide the hope that members can achieve their group and individual goals — simply by expecting and encouraging their work toward their goals. This indicates that although members may be ambivalent, at best, the practitioner cares about the group.

Catalyzing involves sharpening and clarifying each member's communication, especially the "I-We-It" elements. The practitioner asks members to direct statements toward intended recipients in order to facilitate intermember dialogue and connections and to point out what they have in common. The practitioner also clarifies expectations, as these are hinted at implicitly in comments, and elicits, accepts, and supports members' goals. In gently inviting trust, the practitioner does not challenge the group for initiative and cooperation so early but supports each member's entry into the group by inviting participation and feeling expression and by personally responding to each member.

Directing involves contracting. The contract begins with a clear statement of purpose, the practitioner's stake in the process, general roles and procedures, and expectations of members' responsibilities. The practitioner also reaches for feedback regarding the contract, members' ideas about short-range and longer-term goals, and the specific agenda for future work. The contract, then, is the verbal and nonverbal agreement among the group members and between the members and the practitioner about the purpose of the experience, the nature of the content and tasks, and how they will work together to achieve these purposes (Kravitz and Rose, 1974). It is comparable to what in other skill models has been called "norming" and "task focusing" (Gill and Barry, 1982).

Processing in this first stage entails calling attention to members' initial wishes and fears, difficulties in exposing themselves and feeling free, and elements of trust in what is being discussed. These skills are not used in a confrontational manner or in an "I-know-something-you-don't" manner. These will increase tension, lead to denial, or quite often be completely ignored in interaction while stored away in resentment and resistance. The skills are best used in terms of the naturalness and universality of these issues for beginning groups. At the same time, the practitioner must not give the impression that this group is like all other groups and therefore is predictable — because it can never be. The processing includes some indication (and often is best put out as such) of the practitioner's experience of these issues within the self, as he or she is excited and also a little anxious about this group experience and its unique as well as universal elements. The practitioner also processes the feelings and unstated needs and goals behind communications by restating what he or she may have heard and observed about them, reaching for them, and checking them out. It is particularly important to introduce there-and-then content as it relates to here-and-now trust themes in beginning *this* group. Finally, the practitioner asks members to process what they are experiencing as commonness and difference and how they have proceeded to establish norms for their work together. Such processing itself is vital, as it helps to establish awareness of norms in relation to goals. Here-and-now awareness is among the most powerful mediums for what members will learn, especially in therapeutic groups. In other groups it teaches them how to stay alert to, confront, and deal with process obstacles for the potential achievement of their goals. They have more power to trust themselves.

EXAMPLE

The first meeting of an "empowerment group" (see Lee, 1995) in a homeless shelter for women and children demonstrates the directing via contracting and the providing functions. The group is co-facilated by two social workers: an African-American and a Caucasian woman. The eight shelter residents include four African Americans, one who identifies herself as biracial (African-American and Irish-American parents), a Mexican American, and two Caucasians (neither of whom identify with any particular ethnicity). Thus, this empowerment group meeting also reflects some of the multicultural aspects of practice noted in Chapter 4.

Beverly, the African-American co-facilitator, begins the group: "Welcome; Ellen (the other facilitator) and I have met with each of you individually and you have all agreed to join this empowerment group. To begin, we believe you likely want to know each other at least a little better. So why don't each of you tell each other a little about yourselves and why you're here at the shelter?"

They share their individual stories with several periodic echoes of "me, too" by members and with some restatement and reflection by Beverly and Ellen [providing through active listening and empathy]. Afterwards, Beverly says, "Everyone here has had a very rough time before coming to the shelter and feels to some degree that you've lost control over parts of your lives [empathizing]. That's very much related to the purpose of this group. The shelter, Ellen, and I all believe this group is an opportunity for you to talk about what you've experienced, especially in finding housing, and to help each other deal with the obstacles to getting what you believe you need. That's why we call this an empowerment group. Some of the walls you now face and want to break through might be personal, such as some of the trouble several of you expressed about your drug and alcohol use. Some of the walls may be like the ones you have described about your relationships with the people in your lives right now. Some may be more related to the way the systems you depend on and are supposed to help you actually treat you, including this shelter" [directing through contracting: stating purpose and practitioner's stake, pointing out common ground, suggesting possibilities for work]. Ellen adds, "What are your reactions to what Beverly just said? Did any of that especially strike you as useful?" [reaching for feedback]. Michelle immediately responds, "Oh, yeah. Especially the part about drugs. That's me!!" Janine quickly echoes, "Me, too. I just left _____ (a substance abuse treatment program) and have nowhere to go." Beverly provides more by reinforcing how brave it was for Michelle and Janine to share their stuggles and assures the group that we can work on such issues together here. This leads to a general discussion among members about how they have been disempowered ("oppressed," made a "slave" by, is a "fool," dug their own graves, etc.) by their own or others' substance abuse.

At the end of this discussion Maria, the Mexican-American member (age 18), tells how her stepfather's drinking and abuse drove her out of her mother's house. She concludes, "My biggest wall now, though, is federal housing. They lost my Section 8 application. I'm starting all over again." Several other members share her frustration but suggest that she does not have to start all over — that if she talks to the supervisor there is a good chance they will find it. Ellen, then, indicates, "The systems you need aren't always there for you. This really can hurt more than help [providing through empathy]. Working together to regain some power with them is also an important thing we can do in this group, just as you just did with Maria" [directing through contracting; emphasizing interpersonal and political empowerment].

Cassandra picks up on this and with strong emotion says, "Yeah, especially if you're black and a woman." Beverly responds, "You bet. There are definitely times when how you're treated comes from the ills in our society, like racism and sexism" [reinforcing critical consciousness]. The women of color in the group nod in agreement. Kathy, one of the Caucasian members, looks puzzled and says, "I don't know about that. I get treated like a nobody, too. I just think they believe we are a problem for them and that it's only our fault we need their help." The group suddenly grows silent. Ellen interrupts the rising tension by commenting, "Kathy, I heard your own experience of oppression in what you've said [active listening], but I wonder if you were also saying you did not understand that being poor, black, and a woman can be three walls together in our society" [clarification; demonstrating a willingness to talk about racial issues in the group]. "No," Kathy clarifies, "I don't mean that I don't understand that there is prejudice against blacks. I just mean we all got our crosses to bear." "Or battles to fight," snaps Janine. "Yeah, and battles to fight," continues Kathy; "but it's hard to fight back, especially when I'm so down." Beverly, then, seeks elaboration [while reflecting more empathy in providing]: "You feel depressed, and that makes it hard for you to fight for the things you want, Kathy. What are the things now that seem to be forcing you down? Tell us more." At this, Kathy and others continue the first meeting, describing their past and recent experiences with oppression. Some recount how they feel depressed; a few feel more anger.

The first meeting ends with a checking-out. Each member and the practitioners reflect in a sentence or less how they believe the group worked in this first meeting.

Power and Control/Autonomy

In the second stage, the members' primary task is to develop autonomy. The practitioner's parallel task is to enable a structure for the group in which members can assume responsibility for the work and discover the potential for interdependent mutual aid. This task requires a great deal of providing and processing, and some catalyzing and directing. Providing here entails responding to feelings and content and being concrete. Support is given to members who are not a central part of the group by helping them to state their experience of their position and to articulate the reasons for their choices (to be quiet, eccentric, critical, etc.). Check-ins and check-outs are used. This support also includes follow-up of dropouts and absentees.

Processing is probably more important at this stage than at any other, because the evolving group structure — patterned positions, statuses, roles, and norms — can become entrenched as obstacles to people-to-people (rather than role-to-role) relationships. To a large degree the members will be unaware of this structure; therefore, the practitioner must reach for processing from the group and add his or her own processing regarding the power and control (or "negative" autonomy) themes inherent in the current structure. This structure is processed in relation to the group's needs that it meets and obstructs, to the contract, and to how it helps or hurts particular members in meeting needs and achieving goals. It especially relates the structure and process that evolved here-and-now to there-and-then content (e.g., power struggles with authority figures and others) and vice versa. The practitioner processes the autonomy and closeness issues underlying the conflicts that tend to emerge at this stage and the norms that have evolved for handling them. This is especially so when the norms are defensively protective of conflict or influence conflict resolution in terms of win-lose positions. Similarly, the practitioner helps the group to process *how* it makes its innumerable decisions — both consciously and unconsciously.

The practitioner as catalyst reaches for the expression of feelings, especially ones in reaction to the structure. This includes clarifying the members' beliefs behind the feelings and the members' current perceptions of the reality of the group as it relates to feelings and beliefs. There is also a reaching for both the consensual view of reality (i.e., how all or most members view particular events) and the differences in these perceptions. To catalyze intermember interaction, the practitioner calls for the group to assume its responsibility for the process, deflects dependency on self, redirects interactions toward self to the members, and reaches for group responses to individual members. The practitioner also encourages the expression of feelings, feedback, and evaluation of how they are working together toward goals. And the practitioner shares his or her own feelings, observations, and interpretations.

Most significant in catalyzing is reaching for the anger toward the practitioner that is implicit in group interaction. Some disenchantment and anger toward the leader who is empowering is a common feature of small face-to-face groups in the autonomy stage, but this is by no means a constant process across groups or in form or degree.

One's behavior may potentiate or mitigate both the experience and the expression of rebellion. Invoking greater negative responses are those practitioners who are ambiguous or deliberately enigmatic, who are authoritative yet offer no structure or guidelines for members, and who overtly or covertly make unfulfillable promises early in the group. Suppressing the expression of hostility are those who present themselves as anxious, uncertain, or frail; those who collude with members to avoid all confrontations and settle for comfort as an end in itself; those who appear to need to be liked above all else; and those who remain so aloof and ambiguous that they give members nothing to attack.

The suppression of vitalizing ambivalent feelings toward the practitioner as authority inhibits group development. It can lead to a counterproductive taboo that opposes the desired norms of interpersonal honesty, feeling expression, and freedom. This will influence the "illusion of work" in relation to both content and process themes. It can rob members of the experience of nonlethal aggression and anger. It can create off-target displacement of resentment toward the social worker onto the members through such processes as scapegoating and encouraging and then destroying leadership attempts by other members. It is essential that the group feels free to confront the practitioner, who must not only permit but — in the function of catalyst — encourage such confrontation. In discovering the practitioner not as a role player but as a person who carries out certain functions of possible benefit to the group, the members have taken a giant leap. They move toward realizing that within the role-to-role interaction that has come with structure there is a subterranean gold mine of people-to-people events in the here-and-now of group process.

As director in this second stage, the practitioner facilitates member autonomy and interdependence by clearly and consistently demonstrating that he or she does not intend to coerce or suppress members, or to reinforce coercion and suppression among members. The social worker actively indicates the importance of all members and avoids manipulating or exploiting them. Directing involves limiting and guiding members, but not controlling them. The limits and guidelines occur in encouraging work, suggesting ways in which it may be accomplished, and protecting others from harm while maintaining the underlying freedom for the group to respect individual wills and to develop its collective will for interdependence or mutual aid. Despite conflicts among members and with the practitioner for power and control over the group resources, the practitioner needs to influence a group structure that promotes equal opportunity and freedom for all members. This, in microcosm, reflects the practitioner's faith in democratic processes as the basis of true mutual aid.

In sum, in this stage the practitioner must not sanction the autocratic members even though their high level of participation helps to keep the group going. He or she gives status and recognition to those who are denied them in the group; supports helpful "I-We-It" contributions and ignores others; teaches members, through modeling and feedback, to perform in ways that benefit the entire group; and consistently seeks and provides well-timed feedback about the power and control elements of group structure. Members then have the opportunity to discover obstacles to their personal power (their conflicts and exploitations), to compare their actions with their contract and needs, and to develop empathy for the needs and hurts of others. Again, the practitioner actively solicits the less conscious hostilities bestowed on him or her as the "leader" and, together with members, attempts to distinguish (1) those reactions that are due to him or her as an imperfect person, from (2) those that are projected onto his or her role and its symbol for members. Then, members may gain more recognition of their personal power to connect with other members.

> ### *EXAMPLE*
>
> This meeting is the third in a counseling group of separating and divorced women. Up to this point, the women have shared many common concerns: emotional and other intimidations from their husbands, financial stresses, their children's painful reactions. Several—Jane, Marlene, Carol, and LaSalle—still have their husbands in the house. In this meeting (which is about one-third through), these woman did all the talking. Jane talked about her own and her children's anger, fear, and confusion as her husband came and went at will, often spending several days at his girlfriend's. LaSalle has just finished describing her husband's unwillingness to move out even though he says their marriage is over. She shares feelings of being trapped and wishes he'd move out. Carol, Jane, and Marlene respond. Mary, the practitioner, notices that Margaret, Rosie, and Dawn, the members living without husbands, have sat in silence.
>
> Mary reflects, "It appears to me that those of you still to some degree living with husbands have been talking to each other. The rest have said little or nothing so far. Are any of you aware of this? If so, what seems to be happening here?" [processing]. Marlene says she hasn't noticed. Jane indicates that she saw this "split" but finds it hard to talk to those who have "done it." Mary asks, "Is this what's been happening—that we have two subgroups, and those with husbands are given the power in this group now?" [processing]. "Is this what you want together?" [directing].
>
> LaSalle then says, "I would like to hear from everyone, rather than keep going like this. I wonder how you, Rosie, were able to go through with your divorce." At this point, Rosie and the others begin to identify how they experienced similar issues and feelings and how their concern about themselves and their children empowered them to take action. This is especially helpful to Jane, who shares her ambivalence but also her increased desire to take her children with her to a shelter. They remark toward the end of this meeting that it was good that Mary "butted in," that they had been forming two subgroups, and that they liked the group more when everybody participated.

Intimacy/Closeness

In the third stage, when the members face the closeness theme, the practitioner's parallel task is to encourage members to take the personal risks of self-disclosure and feedback that meet intimacy needs. Here one serves primarily as a catalyst with higher use of providing and processing, and less use of directing. Catalyzing involves modeling here-and-now self-disclosure and feedback, encouraging intermember contact and self-explorations, reaching for feedback in interpersonal processes, reaching for the negatives underlying positive feelings, and reaching for growth needs. Providing requires personalizing meanings, problems, feelings, and goals and using genuineness and confrontation. It also requires providing opportunities for all members to come into the group with equal status as human beings. Processing entails detecting and challenging obstacles that obscure the common ground, relating there-and-then content to here-and-now process, clarifying positive and negative feelings and intimacy issues (especially in intermember conflicts), and confronting how particular norms can be changed to better meet needs and achieve goals. Directing necessitates clarification of the evolving purpose of members themselves and renegotiating the contract to maximize achieving this purpose.

All these functions facilitate the more authentic autonomy and interdependence in the closeness stage through explicit dealing with questions of direction and purpose. For instance, while the contract is directly renegotiated, the practitioner encourages more genuine commitment to an "I-We-It" balance as a means to achieve the chosen and stated goals of members. Often, this includes encouraging more commitment to the agenda of interpersonal relationship needs within the group, as well as to the content. Members are now expected to know more about what resources this group has to help them attain their goals. The attempt is made to help members interact as people-to-people rather than as role-to-role, revealing their wishes and fears for closeness, expressing their current goals, and asking for and accepting help. In short, they are held to their responsibility for themselves and others.

During the impasses that occur at the beginning of this stage, the practitioner needs to help members express (verbally and nonverbally) the fears experienced as they sense that the environmental supports of group structure are giving way to the autonomous self-supports of authentic and close human relations. The practitioner catalyzes this by expressing his or her own feelings; provides by accepting and personalizing these fears; processes by linking them to behavioral consequences through such questions as "What are we experiencing?" "What will be the consequences for us of continuing to do what we are doing now?" "How are we avoiding moving on?" and "How can we best proceed from here?"; and directs by invoking the contract and suggesting procedures for resolving the impasse. One trusts more that the shared, supportive power of closeness can be combined with challenges for risking change and growth.

EXAMPLE

This meeting in a male support group occurs during the intimacy/closeness stage. It demonstrates the exchanges of self-disclosure and feedback and the catalyzing function of the practitioner while the group directly deals with multicultural issues. Stan, the practitioner, is an African American. The members include three other African-American males (John, Maurice, and Lawrence), three Caucasians (Red, Sam, and Trent), and two Hispanics (Eddie, a Mexican American, and Mario, a Columbian American).

When Stan enters the group the members nod, and John looks at him and says, "We've been talking about the shit that goes down at work where we don't sit with the white guys, or the Hispanics." Maurice adds, "It's the dumb way the world works. It will always be that way." Lawrence agrees, "You bet. Like in here, we talk about making more informal contact with other men and then we hang with our homeboys, just like outside." Sam comments, "I saw you, Eddie, yesterday. Remember? You said 'hello' and then went back to talking Spanish with the guy you were with. I thought you didn't want me around." Eddie just looks puzzled at Sam. Lawrence chimes in, "My wife and I went with Red and his wife to a jazz club. We enjoyed it. We talked some about the social barriers that we experience at work and in here." John says, "Come on. We know we want it both ways like here — to bond with those like us and to integrate to get ahead." Stan now actively participates with "Wow! You all sure chose a theme for this meeting. John, can you say more about how what you believe makes you feel?" [catalyzing self-disclosure] "And I wonder how the rest of you are reacting to John and what he's said." [catalyzing feedback].

In the emerging discussion there is much talk about the ambivalence involved in bridging differences, especially when it is felt necessary to succeed in their jobs. They then talk more about the perceptions of efforts at bridging these differences in the group and some of their frustrations, including Eddie's, when they have felt misunderstood by certain other members.

Differentiation/Interdependence

In the fourth stage the members' primary task is to help each other through mutual aid. The practitioner's parallel task is to enable members to use the mutual aid system. All members now carry the functions earlier assumed by the practitioner. He or she (like all members) provides and processes and, less than other members, catalyzes and directs. Several models for these tasks in conjunction with group development suggest that the practitioner participate like any other member or become a full-fledged member without a separate function (Bonney, 1974; Klein, 1973; Levine, 1979). However, the fact that the practitioner has some expertise and special resources for helping members in this stage supports the continued use of parallel process. The practitioner, here, does tend to eliminate the use of catalyzing and directing; he or she trusts the group for these. In this sense, she or he is more an equal part of the membership circle. Nevertheless, the practitioner's special knowledge of the dominant issues and dynamics of this stage of group development, especially how members can use and learn from their differences, must be made available as resources for the group through providing and processing.

Through immediacy, genuineness, and self-disclosure, the practitioner provides an invitation for members to operationalize their individual and group goals and to develop special plans for achieving them. Much of the support is for the work that the group is doing. As this work gets done the practitioner illuminates the process, reminding the group of the reciprocal relation of the "I-We-It" both in the group and as connected to situations in their lives outside of the group.

Directing, providing, and processing involve offering program activities, experimental exercises, or techniques. These activities help the group and its members discover more concretely their specific needs and goals and their plans for meeting them. They may also promote action toward change or growth. These are offered and accepted freely as experiments to be used or not on the basis of their relevance to particular concerns of group members. They are not imposed on the basis of one's authority. They are suggested and explained in their functional relationship to the group's themes and needs. Their facilitation comes from their relevance and from the technical expertise of the practitioner. The power is in how members use them as a tool for their growth, not in who is presenting the tools.

EXAMPLE

This is a latter group process meeting with seven high school senior boys, all of whom were substance abusers (see Sheilds, 1985/1986). They are meeting on the grass during a picnic outing. The boys begin the conversation by joking and fooling about their marijuana use. Social Worker: "For the past two weeks in our group meetings we've talked about problems connected to getting high in school. Now I'm hearing some honest talk about the other side—the fun you see in getting high. Maybe you could tell me more about some of the good parts" [genuineness: almost a structured exercise]. The group is surprised by the question. The members look in a perplexed way at the social worker, then at each other. Andy: "What do you mean? The benefits?" Social Worker: "Yes, like what do you personally get out of it?" Dan: "You mean why?" Ron: "Well, music sounds better—I have more fun." Tim: "Yeah, you have a better time." (All agree.) Larry: (hesitantly) "I haven't smoked in two weeks." Richie: "Me either." (Members start joking and teasing each other about trying to "go straight.") Social Worker: (asks Richie and Larry) "How come you haven't smoked?" Larry: "I had no money." Richie: "I got drunk instead." Ron: "Oh, that doesn't count?" Richie: "No, it's different." (The group laughs.) Social Worker remains quiet [trusting mutual aid process]. Dan: "Oh, come off it, Rich, it's no different." Richie: "I think it is." Social Worker: "How is it different for you?" [reaches for difference]. Richie: "Well, I don't worry about it. (pause) Like sometimes I'm afraid if I smoke too much I'll become a burnout." Carl: "Sometimes, I don't even want to do it. But I do." Larry: "It's something to look forward to." Tim: "Like on a nice day like today—you get stoned outside—it's real nice." Carl: "I wouldn't." Tim: "Why not?" Carl: "It's too nice out. I can get high on this—on our being out and being together." Dan: "I would, just like to relax. I'm so tense after school." Social Worker: "What do you mean, tense?" [elaboration; reaching for self-disclosure]. Dan begins to talk about the pressure he feels in school. He shares with the group his worry that he won't graduate and how ashamed his parents will be. The others listen intently to these words and feelings, which are obviously very strong for Dan. The social worker asks, "Does anyone else feel discouraged and worried about graduation?" [reaches for common ground of mutual aid]. Then, others share their particular concerns, and a discussion ensues about the pressures of senior year and the weight of future decisions they have to face.

Separation/Termination

In the last stage, the members must separate from the group and transfer their learning to life situations outside of the group. The practitioner's parallel process is to enable this separation and transfer. To accomplish this task he or she will need to use high levels of all four functions: catalyzing, providing, processing, and directing. Catalyzing requires initiating the facing of termination by members and the inevitable ambivalences involved. Often the group avoids the difficult and unpleasant task of termination by ignoring or denying their concerns. The practitioner helps them keep this task in focus, by repeatedly calling the members' attention to the impending termination. If avoidance is extreme — manifested, for instance, by an increased absence rate — he or she confronts the group about their behavior.

Through providing his or her own feelings about termination, the practitioner supports the challenge of the reality of separation and the need to experience, own, and discuss it. In this discussion, one provides for facing ambivalences by reaching for the negatives behind positives and the positives behind negatives.

In processing, the practitioner responds to indirect cues for these ending feelings and their dynamics such as the absences, the difficulty in working, and the regressions. He or she also encourages an evaluation of the experience — the "processing" of the overall group experience. This processing links the ending to "globe" situations by encouraging the transfer of learning.

Directing entails making the limits of the group explicit by pointing out that the group will end and providing guidelines and, perhaps, exercises for this closing. Usually with a mature (interdependent) group, the best approach is a direct one. The members can be reminded that it is their group and that they must decide how to end it. It is important in this directing that the practitioner not bury the group too early; otherwise the group will likely have several ineffective and disillusioning "lame duck" meetings. Through directing, processing, providing, and catalyzing, one holds the issue of separation and termination before the group and yet helps it keep working until the very last minute.

EXAMPLE

The last meeting of a coed discharge planning group in the adolescent wing of a mental health facility reflects the ending themes and functions. The group consists of five females and four males.

The practitioner, Dale, had reminded the group that this tenth and last meeting was arriving over the last two meetings [providing and directing by pointing out the ending]. At this meeting Dale shares his satisfaction of being with them and in the group and his sadness that he will miss them [providing by owning own ending feelings]. All nine members express their feelings about ending. All but one, Judy, tends to share similar feelings: sadness, satisfaction, excitement, some fears of going it alone. Judy is especially disappointed, angry, and fearful because her plans to live with her older brother fell through because her brother's wife has decided not to take her. Her case manager is now looking for a group home placement. The members take some time to express their regrets at Judy's current reality and then make sure she has all their phone numbers, so that she can call any of them if she "needs a friend." Dale then asks each member to review their plans for discharge, along with what they now believe they most learned in this group [reaching for transfer of learning]. At the conclusion of this go-around, Dale requests: "Now, I find I learn more about how to work as best as I can by having members who have completed groups tell me honestly what they liked and what they think I could do differently in groups such as this" [directing evaluation]. Several members remark about Dale's sincerity, his caring about each of them and about the group. They especially like how he let it be their group, as this was not what they had expected and this was unlike the other groups in the hospital. Some suggest that he help more in the future around the skills for job interviewing. Dale thanks them for their honest and useful feedback. Then he suggests they find a way to say good-byes in the group. They decide that each member will write a thank-you note to every other member and then deliver it, saying goodbye in any way one prefers. This is how the group ends.

Within this helping process there is also a pregroup and postgroup phase that entails particular skills. The pregroup phase includes composing the group, conducting the intake interview, orienting members toward the group, and preparing oneself as the practitioner. The postgroup phase requires evaluation and follow-up procedures and skills.

SUMMARY

The social worker's functions flow from the basic enabling stance and the parallel tasks during the stages of group development. The most significant skills are those that implement these functions. Although all functions are used throughout to some degree, the primary functions are providing and directing in Preaffiliation/Trust; processing and providing in Power and Control/Autonomy; catalyzing and providing in Intimacy/Closeness; providing, processing, directing, and catalyzing through program activities and/or experimental exercises in Differentiation/Interdependence; and directing and processing in Separation/Termination.

Appendix E presents an instrument for self-assessing the functions in one's currently preferred leadership style. Appendix F provides a questionnaire for discovering leadership preferences in relation to the TACIT themes of these stages, and directions for the interpretation of this questionnaire. Appendix G includes an instrument for assessing the use of these skills in practice. Appendix H suggests a format for recording group practice consistent with the group process approach.

chapter 7

Preaffiliation Stage: Trust Themes

"Laurie was about three when one night she requested my aid in getting undressed. I was downstairs and she was upstairs and . . . well.

'You know how to undress yourself,' I reminded.

'Yes,' she explained, 'but sometimes people need people anyway, even if they do know how to do things by themselves.'

As I lowered the newspaper, a strong feeling came over me, a mixture of delight, embarrassment, and pride; delight in the realization that what I just heard crystallized many stray thoughts on interpersonal behavior, anger because Laurie stated so effortlessly what I had been struggling with for months, and pride because, after all, she is my daughter."

William Schutz (1958, p. 123)

INTRODUCTION

That people need other people as well as self-determination is the basis for our trust in group process. We do well to remind ourselves of these universal needs — especially in early meetings when members reflect their own mistrusts of themselves, others, and us in an ambivalent seeking to discover initial security and trust.

Members begin groups needing to know where they might go — the purpose of the group — and how they might get there — especially how they might be protected against harm yet experience hopes for growth and change. This is the trust issue. It marks the first stage of group development.

The preaffiliation trust themes begin before the group formally meets. In the pregroup phase, the "group" is a concept in the mind of the practitioner and a vague expectation for members. This phase affects what happens when the members actually meet face-to-face for the first time. Then, the trust theme predominates.

Therefore, the principles and skills for composing and convening the group come before the first meeting. This chapter presents this phase and then considers the early meetings. Part II, beginning in this chapter, uses two separate groups for detailed examples of the model in action. The first is a group of preadolescents in an elementary school. Examples are based on the recordings of one of the social work student practitioners. The second is a group of adolescents in a community setting. Critical incidents from this group are presented at the end of each chapter in Part II. This chapter concentrates on the helping process in the preaffiliation stage of group development. It considers member, group, and helping process in relation to the development of *initial* trust.

TRUST IN THE PREGROUP PHASE

There are three aspects of the pregroup phase (Hartford, 1971): the private, the public, and the convening. The private refers to the idea of the group as formed in the mind of the practitioner. The public is the announcement and explanation of the group to others. The convening includes the activities that go into setting up the first meeting. The common threads of this pregroup tapestry are the principles and skills for group composition, clarifying group purpose, and pregroup preparation.

Many recognize group composition as a vital element in successful groups (Bertcher and Maple, 1977; Melnick and Woods, 1976; Slavson, 1964; Yalom, 1995). There is, however, comparatively little tested knowledge about how to compose groups effectively. The work that has been done focuses primarily on the homogeneity (similarities) and heterogeneity (differences) of members. No consensus has evolved from this work. Some researchers suggest that homogeneity in relation to the task orientation of members is most important for predicting a cohesive group (Copeland, 1980; Yalom, 1995). Others suggest a principle of "complementary heterogeneity" wherein members are interpersonally compatible with at least some other members in relation to particular criteria (need for affection, control, inclusion; extraversion or introversion) (Rose, 1977; Schutz, 1958; Slavson, 1964). In general, the researchers agree that composition must support cohesiveness and provide for both the support of "sameness" and the challenge of "difference." In addition, they agree that too much difference is destructive of cohesiveness (Woods and Melnick, 1979). None draw a distinct line between what is an appropriate level of homogeneity and heterogeneity.

Irvin Yalom (1995) proposes that screening out is more useful than trying to compose the perfect group. Particularly important is consideration of the central tasks of the group and prospective members' current capacities to perform them. For instance, in an interpersonal therapy group members are required to engage in introspection, to share feelings, and to process their interpersonal behavior in the here-and-now of group interaction. Potential members who are especially disintegrated because of severe crisis or more chronically defended against examining aspects of their own behavior would not be up to tackling these tasks. Perhaps a different kind of group resource, if indeed any at all, would serve them and the group better. The intent in screening out, then, is to predict as well as possible and to eliminate the probability of any member being likely to deviate from the tasks and norms by which the group will function to achieve its central purpose. In short, we try to prevent this harmful deviance.

One model for group composition has been proposed by Harvey Bertcher and Frank Maple (1977). They suggest that the composition balance homogeneity in *descriptive* attributes and heterogeneity in *behavioral* attributes. Descriptive attributes include age, sex, educational level, and other such statuses as married, single, probationers, students, and so on. Behavioral attributes include such traits as talkativeness, introversion, dominance, clowning, and so on. In the domain of behavior, Bertcher and Maple propose that the range of rating on any one characteristic for all group members (e.g., conformity) not be too great. In other words, they support the rule of the golden mean in heterogeneity of behavioral attributes: too much or too little difference in important behavioral characteristics of members prior to joining the group can obstruct cohesion and productivity.

Initial trust in the group does depend on some sense of similarity for members. More so than particular descriptive and behavioral attributes, this trust evolves from a sense of similarity about goals. The initial question is not whether the other members will be exactly like me. Rather, it is whether the other members want the same thing from the group as I do—whether they share my goals. Members want to determine if their needs and goals (for both security and growth) could be as potentially important to other members as they are to one's self. They explore this question by assessing how the group does or does not work together and what the group is working on from the very first interaction.

Therefore, the skills for the pregroup phase require practitioners to communicate the purpose of the group to prospective members, to connect this purpose to our own stake and to each member's needs, and to "tune in" to the members' early fears and expectations about the group. An important principle for composition is that members share *common* life situations and themes that reflect some *common* needs and *common* goals and evidence capacities to perform the particular group's *common* tasks. Forming the group around a common stated theme that can be clearly and directly linked to members' felt needs to some degree and communicated to prospective members in a way that at some level they can understand aids this composition. Doing so supports initial trust and cohesiveness and challenges the group to work toward accomplishment of goals. One other important principle of group composition is "pairing" (Anderson, 1984) or "Noah's ark" (Reid, 1991). That is, one tries to ensure that for each individual in the group there is at least one other person who is compatible in some relevant characteristics.

In sum, the current weak state of verified knowledge about group composition does not justify a great deal of time and effort spent on composing the group. More useful is the tested knowledge that members' expectations translate into group goals and norms (Bond, 1983). One can clarify these expectations, influence those that are not definitive, and suggest specific ways in which the group might work together. Any plans for group composition should quickly advance from the private phase of our purpose and expectations to the public phase of involving prospective members and others in forming and convening the group.

Preparation

Preparation in the private phase expedites the public phase when it includes plans that can be communicated to the prospective members in individual contacts prior to the final group composition and initial group meeting. Suggested procedures are as follows:

1. What are the common needs (or "issues") that could be addressed by the group? (These would likely translate into group purpose.)
2. What are my general goals for the group? (These would certainly be renegotiated with members once the group begins to meet.)
3. What are the relevant themes for this group?
4. Based on these preliminary goals and themes, what are some of the critical attributes needed by group members, both descriptive (age, sex, education, statuses, etc.) and behavioral (abilities and experience)?
5. What are my plans regarding:
   A. *Support:* What do I have to do to create optimum conditions within my setting, or agency, for this group? With whom do I have to clear this idea?
   B. *Size:* How large do I want the group to be? How can I ensure a pool of prospective members to get sufficient numbers?
   C. *Environment:* Where will we meet? What needs to be done to make the meeting place conducive to the group's work?
   D. *Time:* When will we start? How long will the group experience last? How often will we meet? At what time of day?
   E. *Choice:* What will be the degree and nature of choices about joining the group? Will this be an open group (one that takes on new members after the group gets started) or a closed group (one that does not bring in new members once the group begins and supports group development more)?
6. How will I obtain information about the critical attributes for each potential member? How much and what kind of information will I need from referral sources, my own group or individual interviews with potential members, holding an orientation group session, and/or using members' self-reports on particular questionnaires or instruments? (See Appendix I.)
7. How will I compare and select potential members by using descriptive and balanced behavioral attributes and/or by determining common needs, expectations, and goals as related to the possible themes?
8. How will I notify potential members that they have, or have not, been selected?

As these procedures are planned and implemented, we have begun to prepare members for the group. An overall stated theme for the group can help clarify the common ground and imply group purpose. Members can begin to relate their needs and expectations to the purpose and the theme. Throughout this process of engaging members in the group, we must "tune in" to what potential members are experiencing in their wishes and fears for joining such a group. While preparing members, we need to prepare ourselves.

"Tuning in" is our skill for preparatory empathy (Schwartz, 1976). We anticipate the potential feelings and concerns of prospective group members. This attempt to guess accurately what might be going on for them while they are considering joining the group prepares us for reaching for indirect communications and for responding to them directly (Shulman, 1992). When we alert ourselves to what might be the wishes and fears of prospective members, we can help them express and clarify these concerns in our contacts related to forming the group. For instance, we tune in to the mistrusts and fears of parents who abuse their children as potential members of a counseling group with the theme of "Being More Effective Parents." When these parents ask us what will happen with the information they share in the group, we (if "tuned in") can respond directly to their fears of official retaliation by noting them and by clarifying the principle of confidentiality as it relates to the group. Basically, tuning in requires answering the following questions: What would I be experiencing in feelings and concerns if I were this person in this situation considering joining a group around this theme? How much of this might fit what they are currently experiencing? How might they "hint" at these, and how might I respond more directly to these indirect cues?

Example

Now let us look at these principles and skills of the pregroup phase in one of the groups mentioned throughout the chapters in Part II: group counseling using a group process model in a project with fifth-graders in the school. The practitioners are students in a BSW course on social work with groups that I taught.

The pregroup (private) phase began when I decided that the best way to learn to work with groups effectively was to actually work with one. At the same time, a teacher in an elementary school in my community consulted me regarding problems in her fifth-grade classroom. The school represented the microcosm of a mixed-race and lower socioeconomic part of the community. Several of the children in her classroom were resistant to learning activities and being especially disruptive. They prevented the learning of others. As we discussed this behavior in relation to their developmental needs, we grew excited about the possibility of a group service program for all the youngsters in both fifth-grade classes in this school. I clarified these needs as I understood them and developed a preliminary program for providing counseling groups to meet the needs through the students in my class. In conjunction with both fifth-grade teachers, the elementary guidance counselor assigned to the building, and the principal of the school, I drafted a proposal that won approval from the Director of Pupil Personnel Services and the Superintendent of Schools. Following are excerpts from this proposal:

The social worker's function in the public schools is one of mediating between the need of the child to use the school and the need of the school to serve the child. One of the barriers to establishing this common ground between the child and the school is the child's stage of psychosocial development in relation to the classroom environmental demands. Quite often the child's normal developmental tasks do not match with the school system's task demands. Enabling students to accomplish some primary developmental tasks can free them to use skills more effective for classroom learning.

The groups are established to help members accomplish peer-related developmental tasks. The specific objectives are related to the primary developmental tasks of preadolescents (age 9–13).

The point of departure of many programs with this age-group is the developmental theory of Erik Erikson (1950). Erikson views the most important psychosocial developmental task of preadolescence as industry, if accomplished, and the development of inferiority if social supports for industry skills are not forthcoming. The base for industry is the resolution of the earlier development of basic trust, autonomy, and initiative versus mistrust, shame and doubt, and guilt. These earlier tasks are primarily accomplished in relationship with adults in which the child experiences an orderly, predictable relationship, a sense of self-control without a loss of self-esteem, and a sense of direction for the child's own behavior.

The peer group is the major medium for learning industry without restricting feelings of inferiority. Socially, this stage is most decisive. The child needs to learn that industry requires cooperation with others, or mutual aid, and feeling a special sense of worth for what one produces with others. This interdependent work is based on mutual trust, autonomy (self-control), and initiative.

The intricate relationship of work to self-esteem at this stage of development often leads the child to look toward school as a chore rather than a delight. The excitement stemming from new learning and friendships needs concerted attention. Otherwise, many children begin marking time in school. Additionally, peer group norms take on primary significance. If the definition of success in the peer group counters the classroom norms, children may work hard (industry) on those tasks which defeat accomplishment of school work.

Some form of systematic program devoted to helping the child understand self and others can serve as a deterrent to the crushing of the child's interest in school at this stage of development. A TACIT theme-centered group program takes this important, perhaps most important, requirement for successful social functioning out of the realm of chance and into the mainstream of the school experience.

The purpose of group work with these students is the development of interpersonal and group membership skills which could enhance self-esteem. In this sense the group experience is developmental and structured in such a way that members can accomplish peer-related preadolescent developmental tasks. The intent is to have direct bearing on interpersonal and learning satisfactions in the existing classroom group and to provide for the learning of important preventative skills to ensure better use of the group-based learning experiences in the classroom and outside. Specific objectives are: (1) developing members' ability to relate to peers without giving in to antisocial peer group pressure; (2) developing the ability to cooperate with others toward accomplishment of group projects; (3) developing the ability to find a satisfactory place of belonging in reference to peer activities; and (4) developing a sense of self as worthwhile and competent.

The chosen theme, based on the common developmental tasks and the above objectives, is "Getting Along with Others in Groups." Relevant subthemes are "Letting Others Know Me," "Getting to Know Others," "Resolving Interpersonal Conflicts," and "Completing Group Projects Successfully." These subthemes in this order relate to both overall theme relevance and the sequential TACIT process "themes" associated with the stages of group development. Same-sex groups are composed from two fifth-grade classrooms in one school, as based on developmental needs and to increase homogeneity. Members from each classroom are mixed in composing the individual groups to ensure maximal heterogeneity within the commonality of developmental task. Each group meets for ten meetings weekly with two advanced BSW student coworkers.

The seven treatment groups are composed of five to six members. The counselor pairs are matched for complementary knowledge and experience in working with preadolescents and in using program activities. All groups meet in the school building for one hour per week for ten consecutive weeks on Tuesday mornings.

All group members are pre- and post-tested through two instruments. A Behavior Checklist is designed in conjunction with the teachers to rate behavior change both in the classroom and in the group. This checklist is marked by the teacher for each youngster, based on classroom observation, both before the first group meeting and at the conclusion of the group meetings. The same checklist is marked by the student group workers at the end of the third, sixth, and ninth meetings. This checklist serves also to indicate behavioral attributes used for composing the groups.

The second instrument is a sociometric instrument which requires group members to rank each other on three criteria: (1) ability to cooperate in the group; (2) confidence in self; and (3) caring about the group. These are administered at the end of the third and last meeting to measure increased accuracy in interpersonal perception (empathy) and to note particular self-concept changes during the experience.

The next step in this project involved helping the student social workers tune in to the prospective members in order to orient them to the groups. Classroom time was taken for them to review their knowledge of preadolescents. Then, they were asked to return in fantasy (or "visualization") to a day in their lives when they were fifth-graders. Discussion of the visualization experience sensitized the student social workers to such themes as the importance of their esteem as seen through the eyes of their peers, their need for close friendships, and their wishes and fears for closer relationships with adults—especially with parents and teachers. Next, they rehearsed explaining the groups to the fifth-graders in their own classroom, anticipating feelings and concerns, and encouraging the youngsters to join the group and get their parents' permission slips signed to permit their participation.

The actual orientation session with the fifth-graders closely approximated this "tuning in" experience. The preadolescents were excited about the groups, wondered about some of the activities they would experience as related to the theme, and had questions about how the groups would be composed. The social work students responded to these indirect cues by directly noting the children's fears (1) that they might be placed in groups with some kids whom they thought could not understand them, (2) that they might not think they could get along with certain kids in the group, and (3) that they might be required to do some things they would not really want to do. The social work students responded to these fears by giving some assurance that the youngsters would be in groups with at least some other kids who seemed similar to them, that the group together would plan the activities, and that no one would be required to participate in any activity if he or she did not really want to. The Parents' Permission Slips were given out and returned unanimously the next day. Then, a second orientation meeting was held wherein members discovered who would be in their particular group and who would be their student-counselors. The groups were ready to begin.

TRUST IN THE EARLY MEETINGS

Individual Process

When the group actually begins, the trust theme is reflected in members' orientation to each other ("I-We") and the content ("I-It"). On some level of awareness, each person coming into the group has three sets of questions for which he or she tentatively explores answers. The first set includes questions about *me* (the "I"):

> "How should I present myself here?"
> "What do I want and what do I have to do to get it?"
> "Can I be more who I am and belong to this group?"
> "What's safe to disclose and express about myself here?"
> "Will I be so different and not understood that I will feel left out, alienated, alone?"

Another set of questions relates to others (the "We"):

"Is there anyone else here like me?"

"Will I get understanding and support from anyone here?"

"How are they going to feel about me and what are they going to think about me?"

"What do they want from me and this group?"

"Do we share common goals and can we work together toward these goals?"

"Could I care more about their needs and they care about mine?"

The third set of questions relates to the practitioner and the process (the "It"):

"What are we going to be doing here?"

"What are the rules or expectations here?"

"What am I going to be required to expose about myself, or to discover about myself that I don't want to know or want others to know about me?"

"How will I be treated — judged? rejected? bullied? — or accepted and cared for?"

"How will this practitioner and this experience increase my competence?"

"What is the leader's stake in this process?"

"What kind of person is he or she?"

"Will he or she use power to protect me from getting hurt or hurting others?"

Group Process

The members explore answers to their questions about self, others, and us from the time they first sit face-to-face in the group. They seek some assurance of a climate for initial trust on which to choose to involve (not yet commit) themselves in the group. They approach and avoid participation in a cautious seeking of potential goals. They size up each other and us through an arm's-length exploration process. They search for a place and a viable role for themselves in the group. This enables them to feel secure, to experience an initial sense of belonging, and to feel important to the group. It provides security, protects members from early exposure, and yet gives them influence over the evolving group goals and norms.

Initial trust comes from each member's perception of group structure. As if they had entered a dark room for the first time and could not find the light switch, their fears are intensified until they feel their way around the structure of the room as related to expectations of where the furniture may be placed and where they may find some light. In the group they search for a structure that is familiar in terms of positions, statuses, roles, norms, and aspects of approval, respect, and domination.

This puzzled, testing, hesitant search is especially dependent. Members expect us to provide answers to their fearful and unstated questions and to direct them to a position and role for initial trust. They look to the practitioner as the leader to validate themselves. There is the underlying hope that "If this leader, this significant other, sees me as belonging and O.K., then I am O.K. in this group." Much of the early communication is directed toward us as leader. We are carefully, constantly, and subtly studied for expectations and rewards. Members manifest behavior that has gained approval from authorities in the past. They defend against perceived power and how its use might affect them. Therefore, they often do not connect with what other members have expressed and do not synchronize interaction.

As members are encouraged to interact with each other around the purpose or theme rather than with us (to connect the "I," the "We," and the "It"), they discover similarities and differences. As they follow general ground rules, they build group norms for meeting trust needs through security and consensus and a vague sense that their goals are shared—are "group goals." This climate, as it increases trust, builds a base for cohesiveness. The opportunity increases for risk of more authentic participation and the disclosure of differences. A structure evolves through which members can feel safe and can begin to trust that others might understand and care about them. The group, as a group, begins.

Helping Process

During the preaffiliation stage, our primary task is to enable a context in which members get answers to the trust questions they are silently asking. We need to carry out fully the providing function and moderately assume directing. We use less the catalyzing and processing functions. The skills for translating these functions into activities involve the following: attending, observing, contracting, active listening or empathy, clarifying, and elaborating.

Skills

Attending. We attend physically, contextually, and personally (Carkhuff, 1989). Attending physically means getting one's body ready to tune in to the members and to communicate interest. We need to face members as squarely as possible, to lean toward them, and to maintain face-to-face eye contact with all members if possible. This is just as important when we greet and communicate with individual members before the group begins as it is once we sit with the group in a circle. Attending contextually refers to arranging the group meeting environment to communicate our interest and support for group members. Chairs should be placed in a circle, which can facilitate the members' communication of interest and attentiveness to each other. Also, if possible, the chairs should be the same height to communicate equality and partnership rather than authority and power. Finally, attending personally may involve meeting the immediate physical needs of group members as well as using posture (squaring, eyeing, and leaning) that indicates warmth, respect, interest, and attentiveness. Attending to physical needs may include concern about each member's hunger and comfort as well as needs for solitude or activity. Depending on the times of group meetings and the "tuning in" preparation, we may attend to physical needs by offering snacks and drinks at the group meeting.

Observing. Observing includes noting the members' nonverbal communication, which can give messages about their energy level and feelings. The messages in groups come from body postures, facial expressions, appearances, spacing in relation to the group and other members, and seating patterns. These clues may be our most basic evidence to understand where other members are throughout the group experience. They especially help us to know members in the very first meetings when there may be incongruencies between what members communicate verbally and nonverbally. High energy and interest are often communicated by strong attending postures on the part of group members (squaring, eyeing, and leaning forward). However, there may be cultural differences in this posturing. Often, in the early meetings, members react to other members through posture and facial expressions more readily than through words. Reaching for the direct expression of these indirect cues can enable members to begin to relate to each other and invite more contact from individuals in the group. ("Jack, you were very interested and frowning as you were listening to Jill talk. I sensed some strong reactions in you to what she was saying. If I'm on target, could you share those with Jill and us?")

Contracting. Contracting involves three basic skills (Schwartz, 1976): clarifying purpose, clarifying roles and responsibilities, and reaching for members' feedback (their perception of their individual and collective expectations, goals, and stakes in the process). In the group process model, the purpose of the group should be stated simply, directly, and without jargon. It should openly reflect the stake of the setting and ourselves in the group's purpose and the possible stake of the members in the group process. In counseling the fifth-graders in groups, the student social workers could not clarify the purpose adequately through such jargon as: "We are here for you to experience the stages of group development so that you can move through trust, autonomy, closeness, and interdependence in order to increase your self-actualization and achieve more in your school classroom." The fifth-graders would likely be afraid that they would be given a vocabulary test and caught in not understanding! Or they would likely ask, "What in the world do you mean?" Rather, the student social workers began the contracting by clarifying purpose somewhat as follows:

My name is Trudy Sell and this is Joy Seavers. We are social work student-counselors. Your teachers asked us to help you learn to get along with each other better in groups. That is the theme for our group: "Getting Along Better in Groups." We believe we can help you talk about things and do things together in this group for you to learn to get more for yourselves and give more to others in other groups, such as your classroom. We know you are wondering what this group will be like and would like to answer any questions you have about what we have said.

Such a simple statement of purpose and theme calls forth a direct discussion of the members' feelings and concerns regarding trust. They do not have to use subtle messages and interaction to discover why we are there. We also need to anticipate their questions about how we might help. This concern, stated directly or indirectly, requires some attention to clarifying roles and responsibilities in contracting (Kravitz and Rose, 1974). We can introduce the ideas of the need to balance "I-We-It" interaction and some general ground rules, especially the "Be Your Leader" rule. We might indicate that each member's responsibility is to associate as much as possible to the group's purpose or theme, to select appropriate subthemes for each session, to get to know what the purpose means to each and every member, and to take responsibility for helping each other accomplish individual and possible group goals. The contract establishes the concept of parallel processes in the group process; that is, it specifies (1) our task as enabler as related to the purpose of the group within the specific setting and our stake in group process, and (2) the separate tasks of the members to use their personal power to relate as individuals ("I's") to each other ("We") around the purpose or theme ("It"). As Schwartz (1971) has noted:

> The convergence of these two sets of tasks — those of the clients and those of the agency — creates the terms of the *contract* that is made between the . . . group and the agency. This contract, openly reflecting both stakes, provides the frame of reference for the work that follows, and for understanding when the work is in process, when it is being evaded, and when it is finished. (p. 8)

Contracting is negotiating. Members and the practitioner are involved in this clarification of purpose, themes, and tasks. Therefore, reaching for member feedback is essential. Members are asked for their reactions and their suggestions on how to proceed. The negotiation itself contributes to initial trust by indicating our concern about the individuals in this particular group and our wishes to be accountable to them.

The contract permits group members, at least in theory, to hold us accountable for our actions. Even though members may feel powerless (and frequently may be) to confront us about upholding the terms of the contract, its use shows respect and encourages shared responsibility and collaboration in the work together. Contracts, in this sense, can help reduce group members' dependency upon us. They are not expected to enter into relationships with each other and us simply on the blind trust that their interests will be capably served.

Reaching for feedback in negotiating the contract is especially important in groups of involuntary members. These are groups in which members may be coerced to join — as in prisons, for parolees, with abusing parents, with those who are truant or "act out" in the schools, and so on. The "tuning in" anticipates member resistance, anger, and high levels of mistrust in beginning these groups. The members' discovery of our stake in their interest and their opportunity to influence the contract are vital dynamics to lessen this mistrust and to communicate respect for the choices they do have — their own level of investment and participation in the group.

The initial contract is then lived. We do not provide a wide range of activities to spark interaction. We help members get started on discussing the purpose and/or theme, and we use skills of active listening, empathy, clarifying, and elaborating to help members ("I's") focus interaction with each other ("We") around the initial work ("It"). We provide by balancing the "I-We-It" through the functions of catalyzing and processing member-to-member connections and with directing only when members need to be reminded of the terms of their contract.

One procedure for living the contract and carrying out these functions moderately to help the group get started is the "triple silence" (Cohn, 1972). In the triple silence members are asked to get into contact with (1) the overall group theme ("It"); (2) their own individual here-and-now feelings about being in the group ("I"); and (3) the other members in the group ("We"). For example, the student social workers asked the fifth-graders to shut their eyes and to become aware of their feelings about themselves in groups in which they have been members — perhaps their classroom, perhaps on the playground, perhaps with their families, and so on. (This invites a connection between the "I" and the "It.") Then they were told to open their eyes, to look around at the others in the group, and to become physically and emotionally aware of their reactions. (This can link the "I" and the "We.") Finally, the "I-We-It" connection was encouraged by the following directions: "Close your eyes again and please remain silent. In your imagination, picture a member of this group whom you might like to be more like in groups. Now, in your imagination, tell him or her why you would like to be more like him or her, and imagine his or her response."

Then we can introduce, or reintroduce, some of the ground rules deemed important and invite participation and interaction. One way of extending this invitation is to communicate as follows:

Now let's talk about whatever you want to — the theme, my suggestions to you, your thoughts, experiences, or feelings — whatever you want to talk about. Please be your own leader and try to get what you want from the group and to give what you want to give. I will do the same as my own leader and try to understand and help others understand what you are saying, what you want, and what you are experiencing here. Please interrupt when you are bored, distracted, angry, or experiencing anything that prevents your participation.

Often, an important element of contracting is establishing some general ground rules for suggested ways of proceeding to interact on behalf of group goals. This skill has been called "norming" in other models (Gill and Barry, 1982), as the ground rules present potential norms for members to use in pursuing their interactional concerns. With the exception of the "Be Your Own Leader" rule, which is usually best stated in the introductory procedures, these guidelines are often introduced when they are most appropriate. For example, the "Speak One at a Time" rule would probably not be mentioned at the beginning of the group but would be introduced only when several members are speaking at once, or when two or more members are making side comments to each other that are secondary to the main group interaction. These rules are presented as procedures or possible group norms to be kept in mind while pursuing interactional concerns. If followed as much as possible, they can facilitate the process. Seven potential rules are as follows:

1. *Be your own leader.* You are responsible for choosing what you want to talk about, share, and do in the group. Take initiative. Try not to merely react to others and to wait to be contacted by others. Reach out, and contact others. Try to be yourself, to share yourself, and respond to others genuinely. This includes choosing your own goal(s) for the meetings.

2. *Speak to individuals.* As a general rule, speak to individual members rather than to the group as a whole. This helps to establish and develop relations with individual members. You can be more direct, concrete, and specific in your interactions and get closer to each other.

3. *Speak as "I."* As much as possible use the pronoun "I" rather than such general pronouns as "we," "you," and "they," or such abstract and depersonalizing substitutes as "one" or "people" when speaking to the group. Strangely enough, the pronouns you use can make a difference in getting to know and getting closer to others.

4. *"Own" our interaction.* Part of taking initiative is "owning" the interactions of others. In the group, when two members speak to each other, it is not just a private interaction. All members "own" the interaction and need to contribute their own thoughts and feelings. This is particularly so when conflicts occur. Your tendency will probably be not to own the interactions of others because you do not want to "interrupt." Being tactless is one thing; spontaneous involvement and feedback, motivated by concern, is another.

5. *Deal with the here-and-now.* Try to establish some here-and-now immediacy. When you talk about things that are happening or have happened in the past outside the group (the there-and-then), try to relate what you are saying to the members in this group and how you see them affecting you. This does not mean that you should never deal with the there-and-then; but try to do so in order to further the task of establishing, developing, and learning from relationships within the group.

6. *Disturbances come first.* None of you can be fully involved in our group process as long as you are acutely bothered by something, experiencing emotional interference, or wanting to withdraw. There will be times when each of us will experience blocks to our involvement. At these times it is important that we try to share these disturbances with the group or reach for this sharing if we sense it in others.

7. *Speak one at a time.* Interaction can best proceed when we avoid whispered side conversations, do not all talk at once, and prevent the confusion of trying to listen to more than one speaker at a time. If we use the practical guideline of speaking one at a time, we can avoid much of this confusion and concentrate our energies on those individuals who are talking.

The ground rules are designed to enhance the learning of the autonomy ("be your own leader"; "disturbances come first"; "speak as I") and interdependence ("own interaction"; "speak to individuals"; "deal with here-and-now") that together constitute the assumption of responsibility within the group. The "speak one at a time" ground rule is the most practical; it is designed to avoid the confusion of several members speaking all at once and to teach members how to listen to each other within the group. Thus, ground rules are a tool to teach members how they can create, together, a therapeutic culture in the group.

Other techniques can help the group to focus on the theme of the meeting and to begin to experiment with using the ground rules. For example, in relation to "be your own leader," we might wonder aloud if a silent member is getting from and giving to the group as much as he or she would like. We might even encourage the silent member to take a few moments, while the group waits, to develop in fantasy his or her own "wishes" about what he or she would like to see happen within the remainder of the meeting—either in relation to himself or herself, to others, or to the theme. We might then, once the silent member has had the fantasy, encourage the member to try to make it occur in reality. The ultimate choice of whether or not the silent member verbally participates belongs to him or her (autonomy). The member may, as a result of our encouragement, begin to participate more fully (interdependence).

The practitioner, through the "disturbance" rule, encourages each member to let the group know when she or he is too distracted or preoccupied to partake fully in the here-and-now of group interaction. However, this kind of self-monitoring, which is difficult at best, may be especially burdensome at moments when a member is upset. Therefore, it is especially important for us to be aware of the signs of disturbance in any member and to encourage the member to express concerns to the group. It may often be sufficient for a member to simply talk about the feeling, especially if he or she then receives some understanding and/or support. At other times, especially later in the group process, structured experiments might be more appropriate. For example, the member who feels overwhelmed by a fear of rejection in the group might be encouraged to go around to each member and begin his or her statement with "I want you to like me for my _____"—which the member then completes differently in each instance. In using this rule, the practitioner attempts to limit the expression of each disturbance to the here-and-now context as much as possible. Its purpose is not to resolve severe personal disturbances but to help the member experience and "own" the distress to a point at which the member can return his or her attention to the group's work.

Another useful technique for operationalizing the "disturbances come first" rule is the "shuttling" procedure. When members or the entire group seem to be avoiding or resisting the work at hand, they are asked to shuttle between here-and-now contact of the group experience and there-and-then withdrawal in fantasy. For example, we may ask all members to go in fantasy to a place where they feel better than they do in the here-and-now and to get in touch with that experience. Then they are asked to return silently to the here-and-now of the group and to get in touch with their feelings about being "here" versus being "there." Next, they are instructed to return again to the more comfortable place, shuttle again back to the here-and-now, and discover what is "there" that is missing "here" for them. A third shuttle to there-and-then and here-and-now can be suggested, along with instructions that they try to bring more of what they experience in the then-and-there to the here-and-now. In other words, they are encouraged to try to "be their own leaders" and attempt to make the group more a resource for meeting the contact and/or withdrawal needs discovered in the fantasy shuttling.

One way of encouraging group members to discover that they are often others' best resources when they "own our interactions" is to "stop-action" and ask each member to share what he or she thinks is going on between two members, or between the practitioner and a member, in a particular interaction. Another technique for introducing this ground rule is to ask the members involved in the interaction to choose two or three other members who are not actively involved and check out what they were experiencing during the particular interactional episode. The goal is the opportunity for more active and responsible interaction from all members.

The "speak one at a time" ground rule is, in a sense, the most practical of the seven. It constitutes an attempt on our part to prevent the confusion of several members speaking simultaneously. All those wishing to speak could be encouraged to decide among themselves who will talk; or we could ask each of them to say quickly what he or she wants to say, like the snapshot technique mentioned earlier.

This rule is also invoked when there is only one member speaking as part of the formal group interaction and when subgroups have whispered separate conversations to this main speaker. We can encourage such subgroup members to make their statements, one at a time, to the group at large, since they reflect responses to the group process, or disturbance, and as such are an invaluable part of the group process. In other words, the content of these whispers is not seen as irrelevant to the group interaction. This request is never given as admonishment for the purpose of embarrassment. It is always asked in the spirit of concern for the members' interaction in relation to self-leadership, "speak as I," "disturbances come first," and owning the interaction rules.

Many of these procedures for contracting were used in the fifth-grade groups. The "triple silence" and introductory procedures got members started in living their terms of the contract. Then the social work students used more fully the active listening, empathy, clarifying, and elaborating skills.

Active Listening and Empathy.   Active listening involves responding to members with what one hears. Because the practitioner using a group process model wants members to respond actively and with empathy to each other, we do not use the skill of active listening after every member's comment (as it is often used in individual work). Rather, we use active listening under two special conditions: (1) when a member has risked communication in the group and no other members respond; (2) when responses by other members to a particular communication do not fit with the understanding we got from the message.

Active listening requires responses at three levels — often in sequence (Carkhuff, 1989). All three levels attempt to communicate understanding. Together they constitute the skill of empathy. Empathy involves suspending personal judgments. Through empathy, we try to see the world through the member's eyes and to understand what he or she is experiencing. Research has identified the empathy skill as a central one in successful helping (Carkhuff, 1969; Shulman, 1992; Truax and Carkhuff, 1967). Empathy is expressed through active listening at the levels of content, feelings, and the relation of feelings to content.

In responding to content, we share the degree of empathetic understanding of a message by paraphrasing in our own words the words heard from a particular member. Basically, we respond with something like "You're saying . . ." or "In other words, . . ." If this content is accurately reflected to the member, she or he should experience that we hear what the member has said. At that level the member feels attended to, listened to, and understood. It helps validate the other.

Responding to feelings requires reaching for the emotional part of the message, sharing "hearing" of the nonverbal or paraverbal feelings expressed in the way the message was delivered, and sharing how we understand the other would be feeling in the situation. These feelings include those that are directly expressed in the words and those that are picked up from indirect expressions or from the empathetic "guessing" about what they are. In essence, we listen to the music that accompanies the words. The members feel particularly understood when we (or other group members) can reflect their feelings at a level that is deeper than their own current awareness (Anderson, 1978; Carkhuff, 1969). This further validates.

The third, or deepest, level of active listening and empathy involves responses that connect feelings and content. These responses deepen the meaning and understanding for the members who communicated and for the understanding of other members. Feelings are always expressed in reference to content. They exist in certain contexts. When feelings are complemented with content in our responses, the person can feel uniquely understood. Feelings tend to be universal in group experiences (Anderson, 1980a). The individualized aspect of feelings is the specific content for the person who is experiencing them. We all experience love, pain, anger, joy, and fear. But we do not love or fear the same realities. Responding to feelings and content means putting the members' feelings into words and relating these feelings to the content of the message: "*You feel* unsure of this group *because* you don't believe others here can understand you." "*You feel* excited about what Jill said *because* you also have experienced the fears she is expressing." And so on. This especially validates.

Clarifying.   Clarifying skills entail helping members communicate accurately to increase the potential of their being understood and helping them direct this communication to the intended recipient. Active listening in itself is clarifying. As we feed back the message about content, feelings, and the relation of content to feelings, members are able to assess how their intended messages are being received — at least by us — and can alter communication to express the messages more accurately. This process clarifies.

Clarifying skills can also contribute enormously to the group's building of initial trust around common goals, themes, and other similarities. We can especially listen to what members are expressing indirectly about their expectations, wants, and/or goals for themselves and the group. This listening permits clarification of their commonness with others in the group and their relation to the group's stated purpose, theme, and contract.

Clarifying also involves using the ground rules to help members speak for themselves, speak to individuals, speak as I, and place disturbances first. In addition, clarifying requires questioning. We need to ask: "What is the statement behind your question?" "What are you saying about what you hope happens for you or others in this group?" "What is going on for you right now?" "Are you directing that message to anyone in particular in this group? (If so, who?)." The last question is especially important for clarifying early in the group. It encourages members to make contact with each other as a prerequisite for developing trust and initiating the group process.

Finally, a special use of clarifying in the early group process involves reaching inside silences. Silences are always meaningful. They are an important form of communication. When we ask for the meaning of a silence we do not understand, or when we share our own understanding of the meaning of a particular silence and check its accuracy, we clarify both for ourselves and for other members what the silence means.

Elaborating.   Elaborating skills are closely related to clarifying. The difference is that they are designed to move members farther in expressing understood concerns rather than to further the practitioner's and members' understanding per se. The elaborating skills include moving from the general to the specific, containment, focused listening, and questioning. In moving from the general to the specific we reach for the feelings behind content, seek the relation of a member's there-and-then concern to here-and-now group process, and try to obtain details of specific content and feelings. We try to get members to paint the pictures in their heads in such a way that we can see and feel them. Containment means actively not acting. That is, we choose to hold back responses to permit a member to elaborate on communications without premature interruption or closure and to permit openings for other members to respond. Focused listening involves "honing in" to the important aspects of messages to encourage elaboration. Particularly focused upon are the here-and-now components of a communication—the content, feelings, and goals related to the person's experience in this group at this time. Questioning in the elaboration process involves requesting more information on particular aspects of vaguely stated content, feelings, and/or goals.

DYNAMIC BALANCING

Dynamic balancing refers to our activity in ensuring that the group process does not remain overly focused on any one part of the "I-We-It" triangle. These skills help to dynamically balance the group. The skill lies in detecting those decisive points at which the group is becoming stuck and is therefore most ready for a shift of some kind—for instance, from "I" to "We."

Certain techniques are helpful in making these transitions. For instance, "checking in," "checking out," and the snapshot go-around techniques can be used to help the group know where each of its members is at any one time. In the latter device, we create a "stop-action" situation by snapping our fingers or doing some other "ritual" and saying: "Please try to pinpoint just where you were at the moment I snapped my fingers (stopped the action). Now go around, each in turn starting from my left, and give a brief statement of what your inner experience was at that point." It is important that we handle this activity in a disciplined way; each member is to be as brief as possible, and each person should proceed in order without spontaneous interaction. In other words, even though one member's experience may have involved negative comments about another (or us), the others (or we) are not given a chance to reply until a formal "go-around" has taken place. This is a relatively easy way to introduce a "We" focus and is designed to promote a greater sense of group cohesion. Dyadic interactions can be intensified by having two members in conflict line up facing each other at opposite ends of the room, walk toward each other in the center, and nonverbally respond to each other; or be asked to role-play each other and continue their dialogue; or be asked to express *both* their resentments and appreciations; or be asked to repeat *in their own words* what they heard the other saying, to the satisfaction of the other that this message was the intended one before making one's own response to the other. In these situations the "We" focus will be intensified, although now its scope will be reduced to two people instead of the entire group. If the group's theme relates to interpersonal relations, these techniques will simultaneously strengthen the "It" point of the triangle.

Gerald Gorey et al. (1992) recommend "checking in" and "checking out" as significant techniques for assisting groups and practitioners to stay attuned to where members are relevant to the "I," the "We," and the "It." Both are structured activities that require hearing from each member, without response, their reactions to a question(s) or assigned topic(s) at the beginning (checking in) and ending (checking out) of each meeting. A check-in for the first meeting might involve asking each member (in any order, but in such a way that the group hears from everyone) to share his or her response to the question: "What do you most hope to get from this group and what are you willing to do to get what you want?" A check-out for the initial meeting might be: "What do you believe was the most helpful part of this meeting?" Or: "In a sentence or two, or in a word or a sound, please state how you feel right now." We might need to remind members to abide by the rule that the check-in and check-out activities be structured simply, so as to hear from each member as briefly as possible and not to stimulate immediate interaction. This ensures room for all to keep in touch with each other.

A particularly useful technique for helping the group focus on the "We" dynamics of the evolving group structure is the following: The practitioner moves to the center of the group and says, "I stand for the group at this moment. I want each of you to place yourself nonverbally in the room in relation to me-as-the-group where you are presently experiencing your position in this group. Move around freely until you find a spot that best reflects this current experience of your place in the group. We will stop when everyone seems to have settled on a place." At the conclusion of this exercise the members are asked to hold their places and, through a "go-around" technique, to state how their physical place reflects their current experience of their position in the group.

In relation to the "It," we strive to keep the content theme in clear, not perpetual, focus throughout the group process. We give themes optimum, not maximum, attention. A continual theme focus produces oversaturation and fatigue. Just as the natural rhythm of the perceiver is such that one cannot keep a stimulus "figure" for too long without it becoming "ground" (Passons, 1972), group members can better attend to their themes if we occasionally allow them to recede into the background. Spontaneous interactions unrelated to the themes; statements of disturbance, humor, and laughter; brief "snapshots" in which each member states whatever he or she was experiencing at a particular moment regardless of whether or not it is theme-relevant—all have a place in the group. Our task is to return the group to its themes—sometimes subtly, sometimes obviously—but only when this is not done by the spontaneous behavior of the members themselves.

Expertise in the thematic area on our part is useful, but it is not absolutely necessary. For example, rarely in groups where the theme centers on members' common problems or life situations do we have as great an understanding of the content theme as do the members themselves. The focus is primarily upon members' give-and-take at their own level around their common goal—the theme. We need to come to meetings with some plans for the potential work, but the best principle is to "overplan and underuse" (Tropp, 1972). It is preferred that the group's own proposals approach the relevant themes, including those normally agreed upon and those that arise spontaneously. The "It," as all of the group process, is theirs. Our plans are basically on thinking through the possibilities of common meanings of particular themes for the group and how these might be explored. This planning can enhance the understanding of leads that come from the group and the offering of procedural suggestions if the group does not have any of its own. Decisions about focus and procedures are based on open agreement between us and the group and are related to the purpose and the time structure. Thus, meetings are not aimless and never-ending. We help ensure that time is not wasted. In a very real sense, our preparation and involvement suggest that we see that every moment is precious in the group.

PRINCIPLES IN THE FIRST MEETING

These introductory procedures and skills can be summarized in certain principles that provide structure for first meetings in group process practice:

1. We need to introduce members to each other.
2. We need to make a brief, simple opening statement of the purpose and potential themes. This statement tries to clarify the agency's or setting's stake in providing the group, as well as potential subthemes (issues and concerns) that members might feel as urgent.
3. We need to obtain feedback from the group members on their sense of fit between their ideas of their needs and our own and the agency's or setting's view (the contract).

4. We need to clarify our function, tasks, and roles.

5. We need to deal directly with any specific disturbances or obstacles to the group getting started (e.g., their stereotypes about groups, other members, or us as an authority figure; or in the case of an involuntary group, their anger).

6. We need to encourage intermember interaction rather than discussion only between us and individual group members.

7. We need to develop a supportive culture in the group in which members feel safe and begin to have their needs for trust met.

Example

The following example demonstrates the use of the understanding of these principles, procedures, and skills. It follows the earlier information on the counseling group project with fifth-grade preadolescents in school.

The social work student counselors with this group are Trudy (the recorder) and Joy.[1] The members are six boys who meet with the counselors in one of the two empty classrooms. They are Chris, Darren, Jeff, Mike, Randy, and Ricky. The overriding theme is "Getting Along Better with Others in Groups."

In the following recordings we see the wishes/fears of the preaffiliation stage in action. One student counselor, Joy, is ill and misses the first meeting. All members are present. Trudy begins by sharing her observations and feelings. (These are placed in parentheses throughout.)

MEETING 1

(I can point to the exact place at which our group process began. Its beginning was at the moment we walked down the hall into the classroom. Immediately, Darren and Chris argued over who was to lead the group [to the mystery of where we were actually going to go]. Randy followed Darren, and Chris wanted to lead also. Mike walked beside me, smiling, and Ricky followed close behind. Jeff took special caution to be in the back of the group as we walked toward the room. As I am looking back on that beginning experience, I am surprised to see that the individual participation patterns in this first meeting very much reflected what I have just illustrated.)

The group is fairly aggressive as a whole. Their fears, anxiousness, and confusions were masqueraded in their behavior. Except for Jeff, no one displayed initial phases of silence or uneasiness. They didn't wait for me to begin the experience. Darren immediately sat down at the teacher's desk. Chris stretched himself out across two desks and everyone talked at once, except Jeff. I suggested that we move into a circle. Everyone plopped down on the floor, responding. Darren moved the teacher's chair into the circle. I asked him to sit

---

[1]Ms. Trudy Sell. The other worker was Ms. Joy Seavers.

down with the group and he refused. Different members tried to get him to join us, but without success. Chris jumped to his feet, moved behind the chair, and dumped Darren to the floor. I hadn't even introduced myself yet. I picked up the teacher's chair, put it into place, and walked back to the group. Everyone was sitting in the circle. The episode was over, Chris had helped me, and Darren seemed content with where he was now sitting. I decided to leave it as it was.

I introduced myself and the members began to ask me many questions about my classes, my car, etc. I spoke of my brothers and they picked up right away on telling the group of their brothers and sisters. Darren spoke fast and very loudly when telling the others about his older brother's sex class. I happened to glance at Jeff and he started to talk about his sisters. I sensed that he felt he had to because everyone else did. He seemed uninterested in what he was saying. When Jeff finally began to feel more comfortable, Chris interrupted him; then Darren interrupted Chris, saying he was "tired of this stuff." I said that we would talk about something else when Jeff was finished speaking. I pointed out the fact that everyone else got to talk without interruptions. I moved back to Jeff, but anything that he wanted to say was gone. He was quiet again.

I was surprised at the way the group actually "helped" me move from one issue to the next. As I was just ready to discuss the theme, Chris asked, "What are we going to do here anyway?" Darren answered, mimicking someone's interpretation of the theme: "We're here to get along with everyone else." I ignored the sarcasm in his voice and asked the group what it meant to them. Everyone except Jeff and Ricky offered a meaning for the theme. They were all speaking at once. Ricky and Jeff eventually started also. I decided to hold on to the confusion for a few moments in order to see if it bothered anyone else. They became louder and louder until I finally yelled, "Wait a minute." Mike backed me up, yelling, "Talk one at a time." We then established our first ground rule, just as Mike had put it. Everyone agreed and if it happened again, it was an accident. They remembered the rule and became aware of when it was violated. I then used the "triple silence." Afterwards the discussion led to their suggestion that they play a game.

The group then decided to play a game with a nerf football, which was already in the room. As we played, I could see Jeff becoming more uncomfortable. Ricky loved the game and was a very good sport. Darren fought hard for attention and wanted everyone to throw the ball to him. He and Randy got into a shoving match over a dropped ball. I had to break it up, and said, "Is this any way to get along with others?" Darren said, "Yes," and Randy was silent. I handled the situation through the reactions that I saw. They both seemed very embarrassed and stood beside each other with no hostile feelings being evident. I decided that it was momentary anger — it was felt, expressed, and over. I didn't want to just end the game with that episode, so I made up another one with the nerf ball. Unplanned, but successful, this game proved to be a security activity and helped to rid Randy and Darren of their embarrassment.

One person stood in the middle, threw the ball in the air, and called some-one's name; that person then ran to catch it. The game was very noncompeti-tive, and it really seemed to unite the group (partially because it was an outlet for uneasiness caused by the fight, and also because it gave them the opportu-nity to relate to others, feeling secure when someone chose them to get the ball). It worked fine because there was absolutely no favoritism. The choosing was very well balanced, and I noticed the members working to "include" Jeff. He responded. He started clapping, laughing, and really getting into the game.

At the end of the meeting we talked about the next meeting. At their re-quest, I agreed to bring a snack. Chris was curious about Joy and wondered if she would be like me. I told him that she wouldn't, because we are two differ-ent people. We had a brief discussion of how people are different. I tried to make them realize that Joy would not be just like me, but that we were alike in certain ways. I explained that she was looking forward to being with us but that she couldn't because she didn't feel well. (I had explained this before, but they asked again.) I said that Joy was part of our group even though they didn't meet her in the first meeting.

MEETING 2

The continuance of trust themes and the beginning of autonomy themes took place in the second meeting.

I introduced Joy to the group and they readily introduced themselves to her. Joy had brought a blanket for us to sit on. Everyone except Chris and Darren seemed to like the idea. Chris and Darren sat on desks, refusing to sit down with the group. We asked them to tell Joy about our first meeting since she hadn't been here. Everyone started telling her about the games we played and how much fun they were. Darren was very quick to tell her how he fell over a few desks. He assumed the same role as in the previous meeting. Joy asked them what else they did, and I was disappointed because it was almost as if they couldn't remember anything but the games. I had to direct them to re-membering our discussion of the theme, of our ground rule of "speak as I," and the general purpose of the group. I even reminded them of the snack.

We introduced the subtheme of "Cooperating in Groups." Next was a con-versation about physical fighting, which really brought certain attitudes of members to the surface. I asked Darren if most of his punching around and hitting was for real or just for fun. He said that most of it was for fun, but that he likes to fight for real. Darren said he likes fights because he likes to see people bleed. I asked him why and he said he just likes it; no reason. I asked him if he likes people to hurt him and of course he said no. Then I said, "How do you feel when someone hurts you?" He said that he feels like hitting them back. I am sure that Darren knew exactly what I was trying to do, but he couldn't break through the barrier of the presence of his peer group watch-ing him and listening. I felt a definite need to have him start accepting re-sponsibility for himself, so I tried to share my feeling with him. I explained what it felt like inside when someone hurt me. He just looked around, saying nothing and feeling uncomfortable. He was afraid to get that close, so I didn't push it.

Another prevailing issue in this meeting was the struggle for power and control. This seemed to be reflected in the decision-making process. The group became tired of sitting around. "All talk and no action," as Randy put it. We proceeded to decide what we would do as an activity, but many conflicts arose. Chris and Darren wanted to go outside and play football. They wanted to do this, and that's what the group would do! Chris went over to get the football, and Darren jumped up, ready to go. Joy and I asked if everyone wanted to play football, but not everyone did. Chris was a little upset and Darren was angry. We told them we had to decide as a group. I was surprised that Chris suggested something else. He said that we would play records. I asked if anyone else wanted to do this and Jeff raised his hand, saying nothing. Everyone else said playing records would be fine, so Chris turned on the record player. Darren was upset, so we decided to play a few records, then go play football.

Chris stood at the front of the room with a make-believe microphone, singing with the music. Everyone ignored him, except me. I stood there and watched him. I told him that he had a good voice. (I felt that Chris needed recognition at times. There have been different instances when I have noted feelings of inadequacy from him. He is 13 years old, as opposed to the others who are 10 years old. One time the group told me about this, and he didn't like it because they explained his older age by telling me how many grades he had flunked. I noticed that he is more mature in certain ways, and I think that Joy and I should bring this maturity to the surface. Of all the members, he is the one whom I see as having a felt need for directly expressing how he feels. He seems to be close to understanding the reason for our project, and some individual focusing on him will help the group. For example, when Chris really wanted to play football but realized that not everyone else did, he was concerned about the confusion.) Everyone seemed to like the records and he was pleased. Even Darren temporarily forgot his anger at not being the decision maker and others sat around, watching and listening to the music. They didn't want to dance, but they said that they liked watching us. Jeff was moving to the music until he noticed that I saw him. He stopped, looking very embarrassed. Then he got up and started to walk around.

(Jeff is very afraid to become close to the group or anyone in it. It seems like he is holding so much back. He acts very nervous most of the time and I can feel his uneasiness. I've been trying to help him by deliberately directing small questions or just statements toward him. He never looks directly at me and usually his hands are moving as he does talk. He hasn't developed very much trust in the group. Only last week when we played the nerf ball game did I notice him responding to the group.)

We never did make the football game. More records were played than was planned, and we only had ten minutes remaining for our meeting. It didn't seem to bother anyone but Darren and Chris. Chris felt that we should still go out. Darren became furious and started blaming everything on Jeff. He was stomping on the floor and screaming about how it wasn't fair because we had decided to go out previously. It was difficult for me to understand what was going on because Jeff hadn't said anything. He had only raised his hand to show that he would like to play records. Darren kept saying that it was all that "stupid Jeff's" fault that we played records too long. I confronted Darren by asking him why he didn't interrupt the dancing if he wanted to go out so badly. He simply would not admit that it was fun playing records and he forgot about football because of this. He just blamed it on Jeff again. Jeff was very upset but didn't say anything to defend himself.

Ricky suggested that we decide on what we would do next week in the remaining minutes. Everyone agreed. Jeff was relieved that the conflict was over, and Darren stomped over to a desk to sit down with arms folded. We all decided to play football as soon as we got there next week. I asked Darren if he agreed and he just nodded his head. No one was really excited about the next meeting, though. It wasn't a good way for the meeting to end at all, but the time was up. Everyone said good-bye and we left. I glanced back into the room. Darren looked back at me and made sure I saw him pouting. He was still in the seat that he had gone to after the conflict.

In this meeting, group members were fearing a closeness that the group could provide them. The social work students had been trying to enhance autonomy through providing an atmosphere in which trust could be developed. Also, the members were given every chance to be involved in decision making. This very process of making decisions leads to the struggles for power and control.

SUMMARY

The preaffiliation stage involves a pregroup phase and the early meetings. The pregroup phase requires moving from the practitioner's private concept to the public announcement of the group and the plans for convening it. Group composition and pregroup preparation are two important elements of this planning. An overall theme might be chosen, potential members recruited and selected, and other plans for the first meeting finalized. Then the group begins.

The first meeting is significant for creating a climate of trust to meet members' needs. We need to carry out *fully* the providing function and *moderately* the functions of directing, catalyzing, and processing. These functions are carried out by the skills of attending, observing, active listening or empathy, contracting, clarifying, and elaborating. The first meeting follows principles designed to structure the group for members' trust, autonomy, and initial interaction. These include clarification of the purpose and of our parallel tasks and those of group members. Introductory procedures, proposed ground rules, and our responses manifest this stated contract and contribute to the establishment of initial trust.

An understanding of this stage and the concomitant principles and skills direct our activities in the first few meetings. These activities are demonstrated in a group with fifth-grade preadolescents in school. The group gets started, finds some initial trust in shared group goals and structure, and moves toward the process of the Power and Control/Autonomy stage.

CRITICAL INCIDENTS

Each chapter in Part II, beginning here, concludes with critical incidents from another group, this one involving adolescents. The critical incidents are presented for the purpose of reviewing and summarizing some of the skills discussed and to permit the reader to interact with the material by considering what you would do in response to these examples. A "critical incident" describes an event in the group that represents a significant point of choice for group members and the practitioner. Critical incidents have been used to demonstrate stages of group development (Cohen and Smith, 1976), to assess leadership styles (Wile, 1972), and to study comparative methodologies for group practice (Churchill, 1974; Corey, 1990b).

The critical incidents in Part II follow the format suggested by Arthur Cohen and Douglas Smith (1976), with some adaptation. Each incident includes the stated meeting subtheme, a statement of the group context of the incident, and the event preceding the choice point. At the choice point you are asked to give your preferred response as the practitioner and your rationale for this response. Finally, I present the response suggested by the group process model and a brief statement of its rationale.

The group consists of ten adolescents, five young men and five young women, all of whom were referred because of symptoms of school truancy. All had some history of substance abuse, and in a number of behavioral characteristics they all manifested much isolation and alienation from teachers, peers, and families. They decided to join the mutual aid group with the theme of "Helping Each Other Stay in School," for fifteen meetings after a joint referral from the local school system and the public agency for children and youth services. They were active clients in the latter as a result of their truancy, which was considered a "status offense" in their state's juvenile justice system.

The male members of the group are: Steve, a 16-year-old African American; Gomez, a 15-year-old Puerto Rican; Tom and Jerry, both 15 years old and Caucasian; and Mark, a 14-year-old African American. The female members of the group are: Cheryl and Chris, 15 years old and African American; Judy, a 16-year-old Caucasian; and Sandra and Jane, both 15 years old and Caucasian.

Critical Incident 1

Subtheme.   Getting Acquainted

Context of Incident.   This is the first meeting. The initial group climate is a mixture of awkwardness and anxiety. Members seem unsure of their direction and unfamiliar with one another. After the initial "triple silence," some particularly anxious members make a few statements to the group with little response. One group member, Steve, who appears somewhat more aggressive, has apparently decided to initiate some action. He begins to speak in a loud, demanding tone.

Choice Point

STEVE: "Hey, this is a waste of time! Let's get going. I think we should go around and each tell something about ourselves. You know, introduce ourselves and tell why we're here."

GOMEZ: "O.K. You start."

The group picks up on this idea and continues until everyone is finished. Now, it is your turn. Everyone is watching you closely and expectantly.

What would you do at this point? What is your rationale for this response?

Suggested Response.   The practitioner initiates work on the group theme via contracting skills. These skills involve introducing self, clarifying purpose and theme, clarifying roles and responsibilities, and reaching for feedback: "I am _____ and I am here to help you to learn to help each other to stay in school. Because I see this as a mutual aid group, one in which you help each other, I want to get to know you and help you get to know each other. I see my role as helping you to listen to, respond to, and help one another. In relation to the purpose of this group, I wonder how far this go-around has taken us in beginning to know each other. My guess is that it helped us break the ice and provide a way to fill in our time to relieve some of our fears. I think we may discover some more about each other toward the theme "Helping Each Other Stay in School," if each of you can share more of your individual goals for the group. That is, what do you want for yourself from being in this group? What do you think of what I have just said and of my suggestion?"

Rationale.   On the surface, this incident is a simple suggestion to put names and faces together in getting to know each other. It is an "ice breaker." At another level, the event reflects the group's reaction to the need for structure, their increased anxieties, and some feelings of dependency (their wanting to hear from you). They need, too, some encouragement to work and some trust that they can, with some initial guidance, do this work themselves. The response clarifies the group purpose and theme to provide some direction for the work, initiates a processing norm for the group (by referring to fears underlying interaction), and clarifies the practitioner's role directly and indirectly by providing some guidelines for proceeding and by reaching for feedback.

Critical Incident 2

Subtheme.   Developing Trust

Context of Incident.   This event occurred in the second meeting, during the early part of the group's life. The members were still in an exploratory, fearful, wandering phase. They tended to avoid dealing with strongly expressed needs of individual members. One member who was quite anxious made a request of the group. This request was ignored and the group started off in a new direction, discussing an altogether different topic.

Choice Point

JERRY: "Let's discuss things in the group that keep us from knowing each other. I'd like to see us start by telling what we dislike most about each other."

There follows a moment of awkward silence, then the group starts off on another topic as if Jerry's statement had not been made.

What would you do at this point? What is your rationale for this response?

Suggested Response.   The practitioner uses the active listening skill to respond to Jerry and contracting skills to suggest the "disturbance first" ground rule and to reach with empathy for the group's goals: "I need to interrupt. I am having trouble following this discussion because I am still with Jerry's comments. Therefore, before I can continue I need to hold myself to the 'disturbances come first' ground rule. I believe we left Jerry hanging. Jerry, I sensed your feelings of mistrust of where you stand with others in this group because you don't know them. My guess is that this is an issue for others, but we might be afraid to discuss this. I wonder if the group wants to continue without responding to Jerry. What were you experiencing when Jerry was talking and what do you want to do about this?"

Rationale.   The surface issue seems to be a legitimate request on the part of one member that was subsequently ignored by the others. The request was for personal and threatening information, however, thereby increasing mistrusts and fears. Other important underlying issues are the group's responsibility toward individual members and the norms governing topics for discussion. Finally, the theme of the group and the contract call for members' learning to deal with the needs of individual members as well as the process itself (by being aware of what it is doing and how it affects members), and to make more conscious decisions. Active listening responds to Jerry's feelings and content. Clarifying ground rules, goals, and norms for the group can help the group attend to the "I-We" interaction behind the "It."

Critical Incident 3

Subtheme.   Developing Trust

Context of Incident.   This incident also occurred in the second meeting. The discussion of the subtheme "Developing Trust" included several pessimistic statements by various group members regarding the lack of trust in the group, along with statements of their difficulty in trusting others. A generally gloomy prediction of the group's future came from Chris, who had been vacillating between being dependent and counterdependent thus far in the group meetings and who had made several attempts to lead the group.

Choice Point

CHRIS: "So what I guess I'm saying is I think this is impossible. I don't think I'm going to trust anyone in this group completely in fifteen weeks. It just . . . I don't know . . . can't be done."

Following her statement, other group members nod their heads pessimistically. There follows a long period of silence.

What would you do at this point? What is your rationale for this response?

Suggested Response.   The practitioner uses active listening skills to respond to Chris's feelings and content and reaches for wishes behind fears in Chris's ambivalence through elaborating: "You and others are discouraged about what we can accomplish in this group, and yet you do seem to want something to happen for you. What do you think may help you to trust other members more than you do now?"

Rationale.   The practitioner uses active listening to respond to both Chris and others. This is a group issue, yet the practitioner avoids intense processing or over-interpretations in this stage. The response is meant to establish a more supportive and free atmosphere, yet to create a climate for work. The noting of the naturalness of wish/fear ambivalences for Chris and the members invites her and others to express the wish side and to consider concrete solutions for resolving the surface and underlying issues of trust.

chapter 8

Power and Control Stage: Autonomy Themes

Johnny, an 8-year-old single child, shocked his parents when he returned home from school one day to find he could not watch his favorite cartoon show on TV until he cleaned his room. He raged against the house rules and defiantly announced, "I'm running away from home."

His mom and dad gathered their composure enough to respond, "Well, if you must, you must."

They watched from a distance as he went to his room and quickly packed his school bag with the odds and ends of his clothes that were strewn across his bedroom floor. They continued to watch as he walked with head held high and determined step through the front door and down the steps to leave home and enter the world on his own. They carefully observed through the window that he went half a block to the corner, where he met his neighborhood playmates and engaged immediately in their play.

Mom then went about preparing dinner. Dad set the table with the usual three places, then sat by the window, reading his paper and periodically glimpsing at Johnny's whereabouts.

In about two hours, the scene outside changed dramatically. All the other kids went home for dinner and Johnny was left alone. He sat on the curb by himself for what seemed like quite a while.

"What do we do now?" his parents asked each other. They decided to fill their own plates and his and to eat.

As they finished their meal, they saw Johnny get up and, as determined as when he had left, begin his return home. They were both sitting at the table when Johnny came in, threw his school bag in the corner, and sat down at his place to eat. No one said anything, and the comfortable silence turned into tension.

Just then, their pet collie walked through the dining room to check out possible scraps on the floor and wandered off to find her own food and water. Johnny broke the silence and quickly relieved the tension while quite skillfully maintaining his own sense of autonomy by remarking, "Oh, I see you still have the same dog."

INTRODUCTION

The power and control stage evolves as initial trust is established and most members have decided to involve themselves in the group. Then members seek autonomy in using the group's resources. This autonomy initially shifts members' preoccupation with acceptance, approval, and involvement to concern with dominance, power, and control. The group becomes a more potent instrument to help or to hurt. Unfortunately, too many groups do not resolve the power and control conflicts of this stage. They entrench themselves in this structure. They hurt powerless members and limit their potential of growth for powerful ones. Too often, the practitioner is an obstruction to the group's development beyond this stage toward more closeness and interdependence. At no point in the group's development are our functions and skills more vital to individual and group growth than during this stage.

In fact, many members entering our groups have little real hope that their wishes for more authentic closeness and mutual aid will be fulfilled. They expect the group to be similar to others in which they have found their satisfaction, if any at all, in positions and roles that confirmed some of their identity even though they might also have experienced the frustration of increased alienation and feelings of not being understood. Our family groups, classrooms, work groups, and even friendship groups may serve more as a battleground for conflicts over power and control than as empowering and mutual aid experiences. We expect competition for positions, statuses, and powerful roles. We doubt, even while we wish for, the possibility of cooperation toward mutual goals and having others be as concerned about our own needs as theirs. We learn to win or to lose, and we develop behavioral patterns in groups to increase our winning at the expense of others' losing. Social work groups, to make a difference, need to empower mutual aid. They need to enable members to regain faith in people and to risk moving beyond the competition for group resources to meet one's own needs at the expense of others. They need to provide an opportunity to expand the use of one's personal power to meet one's needs more functionally.

AUTONOMY CONFLICTS

Almost all the work done on the stages of group development views this stage in such terms as "frustration," "conflict," "counterdependency," "control," "fight," "negative autonomy," "competitiveness," "disillusionment," "anger," "rivalry," "storming," "power bid," "rebellion," "authority-orientation," "resistance," "structure," "aggression," and "dissatisfaction." These terms all imply an early crisis in the group. Much of this work signals the catastrophic side of crisis. It often is experienced as such by members and the group "leader." Some scholars (Bennis and Shepard, 1956; Glassman and Kates, 1990), for instance, note this stage as based upon an "authority crisis" wherein members wrestle with the leader for control of the group yet really want to be dependent on the leader for directing the group. These scholars propose that it is only when members can overthrow the leader in rebellion that they can resolve their ambivalence about authority and can use the leader's resources for resolving the "intimacy crisis" that evolves.

Crisis, however, involves both danger and *opportunity*. The autonomy crisis may be more pronounced in groups in which members sense a potential for more authentic interaction and whose members have decided to engage more to fulfill these wishes. At the same time, they develop a structure from their fears that these wishes might be fulfilled. We both want and fear closeness, self-disclosure, being understood, growth, and interdependent mutual aid. Even though the fears influence the structure, the conflicts, and the autonomy crises, the wishes remain and provide the opportunity—with help—for resolution. The crisis therefore reflects the seeds of closeness and interdependence. If there is fighting in this evolving structure, there is also the potential for caring in the group.

The most detailed models of stages of group development indicate that the resolution of power and control dynamics leads to group cohesiveness, harmony, affection, warmth, and the revision toward a more equitable and less hierarchical structure (Bennis and Shepard, 1956; Cohen and Smith, 1976; Garland, Jones, and Kolodny, 1973; Gibbard and Hartman, 1973; Hill, 1976; Lacoursiere, 1980; Sarri and Galinsky, 1974; Schutz, 1958; Tuckman, 1965). Models that focus on the leader's function and role in this development view this stage as an opportunity to resolve the negative autonomy of rebellion and to develop positive autonomy by members assuming responsibility—or using their personal power to act on behalf of their own and others' needs.

Members need to understand the evolving group structure and process and to choose to revise them more in line with wishes and less as defenses for fears. Movement is from "I won't" to "I want" and "I hope we want this, too." The suggested functions and skills of the practitioner range from processing group structure (Klein, 1972; Lacoursiere, 1980; Levine, 1979; Yalom, 1995) to modeling the empathy that can help members recognize the hurts of others, compare these with their contract and needs, and represent their wishes more than their fears in their choices in the group (Carkhuff, 1989; Corey, 1990a; Rogers, 1970). Principles and skills for the enabling functions of the power and control stage spring from the understanding of these wishes and fears of members and how these are reflected in group process and dynamics. The intent is to help the members discover that this can truly be *their* group within the reality of its purpose and sanction, when they are freed from their fears and take responsibility for the group's growth.

INDIVIDUAL PROCESS

The members in power and control have three sets of questions related to the "I," the "We," and the "It." The first set concerns the "I":

"Where do I stand and rank in this group?"

"Do I have enough power and control to get my needs met?"

"How can I get more status and power in this group?"

"Will I lose some of my position, status, and power if I am honest about my feelings?"

"Can I move beyond having to control for power to a deeper level of trust here?"

The second set involves the "We":

"Who's who in this group?"

"How do others get power in the group and how will they use it?"

"Can others care about me if I do not assume the position and roles they expect from me?"

"Who ranks ahead of or below me in this group?"

"Will the most powerful members continue to control this group for meeting their own needs at the expense of others?"

"How much of my personal power must I give over to the group as the price of the ticket to get 'in' now?"

The third set relates to the "It," especially the practitioner and the process of this particular group:

"What is the appropriate behavior (norms) of this group?"

"What is expected of us?"

"How does the practitioner give status to some members and deny it to others?"

"What would happen if we challenged the practitioner's power?"

"In our decisions, what does the practitioner really want and approve of without telling us?"

"Can the practitioner really care about me and this experience help me if I don't give away my personal power to go along to get along?"

These questions pepper interaction. The "It" is often disguised and is safe content that serves more as the battleground for forming "I-We" up-down relationships than as authentic focus on the group's purpose or theme. Individuals censor their responses through their perception of what the powerful others may want to hear. Others seek more powerful positions in which to control group resources. Or they take the roles of victim, scapegoat, or silent member—thereby demanding some attention by those who seem to be running the group. Members' individual "control dramas" are enacted. Some are not so entrenched in this structure, appear more committed to the group goals than to their own place in group structure, and tend to settle for more moderate status during the early power and control stage. These members have been called "independents" (Bennis and Shepard, 1956), as different from the "dependents" who seek direction from leaders and the "counterdependents" who express their dependency by aggressively fighting those with power and authority. Often the independents initiate movement from the negative autonomy of rebellion toward the positive autonomy of responsibility during this stage (when they assert the power of their own will for growth). Nevertheless, members' communications at this stage include many attempts to command a particular relationship with the group and us as well as to report information with relevance to the stated group purpose or theme.

The power differential especially relates to decision making. Members are particularly aware of how decisions are made. Although they find it difficult to reflect this awareness when asked, they are in constance vigilance for who most influences certain decisions (both formal and informal ones) and who benefits most from such decisions. The informal decisions are occurring all the time: Who selects topics, who initiates them; who changes them? The formal decisions occur when members are conscious as a group that they are making them. Effective groups, which can revise structure to move through this stage, consciously process their decision-making dynamics and make the informal decisions more formal ones.

GROUP PROCESS

As members move together from trust to autonomy, concerns of power and control dominate. The group develops a hierarchical structure of positions, statuses, roles, and norms for permitting certain members to control the allocation of group resources such as time, attention, status, and emotional contact. Members tend to compete for these resources. Conflicts evolve.

The conflict is between members or between the members and the practitioner as the perceived leader. The intent is often to win the power struggle. Each member negotiates a preferred amount of autonomy, initiative, and power. Gradually a status and control hierarchy, or a social pecking order, is established. The movement is from "I'm O.K. I belong here" to "I'm O.K. I *rank* here."

This structure stylizes the group. Communication patterns are established and forces are at work to freeze these patterns in mutually formed positions, statuses, roles, and norms. High-status members, who often embody dominant norms in their behavior, tend to interact more exclusively with other high-status members. Low-status members participate through those with higher status. Trust at this point is not so much in other members with common needs and goals who share a common theme. Rather, trust is in a common, predictable structure. Members trust *what they can control* more than *who they can contact.*

This stage hurts some members. Those low on the totem pole may be reinforced in their low self-esteem. They may drop out and be hurt before the group has a chance to resolve the hierarchical conflicts of this stage. Subgroups develop as important islands of safety where the members can ally with others to guard their flanks. Subgroups also serve as support for power in influencing group decisions. The scapegoats and isolates who cannot coalesce into subgroups are particularly vulnerable to power cliques. They may be rejected or attacked in a manner that increases their fears, loneliness, and isolation in human relations. If their hopes for acceptance and understanding were high, they may lose much of what might be little faith in themselves and others. The group experience could worsen rather than ameliorate their feelings of helplessness, powerlessness, inadequacy, and alienation.

Struggle for control is part of the process of all groups that take on significance for members. In the practice group, it is always present to some degree. Sometimes it smolders. Sometimes it is quiescent. Sometimes it rages fully. We contribute greatly to autonomy development by challenging these structural obstacles. For example, as the group deals with our place in this structure, it can discover its own authentic source of power in its potential for mutual aid and caring. It can develop its resources to meet the needs of *all* members.

The emergence of some ambivalence and some anger toward us is almost inevitable as the group confronts the authority theme of autonomy. Members project dependencies upon leaders as an omnipotent source of satisfying their needs. Simultaneously, their autonomy needs are seeking a climate that is free from domination and supportive of interdependence. We refuse to feed the hunger of the omnipotent mystique, hold out faith that members can assume responsibility to find their own direction, and expect only that they confront the obstacles to goal achievement as explicit in their purpose, contract, and tasks. This confrontation includes us as an obstacle as well. Then we can influence a group structure that promotes more equal opportunity and freedom for all members. For instance, if members can express their ambivalence and anger toward us, rather than off-target behavior directed toward the control of each other, they can get in touch with their own power to meet needs — both their own and others'.

When members discover that we function as a special member because of our technical expertise and skills, they can evaluate our contribution for its value to their goal achievement. They can accept or reject these activities on the basis of what helps, not on the early power and control basis of the authority symbol we represent. At this point the members are ready to discover the contributions they and all other members can make to the goals of the group and to its development. They can open up the structure for the equality, cohesiveness, and beginning interdependency of the intimacy stage.

HELPING PROCESS

The task of members and the group is to develop a structure that is supportive of needs and goals rather than a hierarchy for power and control. Our parallel task is to enable this functional, nonrigid structure. Therefore, we use the functions of providing and processing to a great extent and those of catalyzing and directing to a moderate extent. These functions relate directly to the findings of Morton Lieberman et al. (1973) about effective leaders. Their findings may be explained as follows: Those leaders who helped the group resolve autonomy themes were those with the highest changes and fewest casualties. These were leaders who used high levels of providing and processing and moderate levels of catalyzing and directing. These functions, carried out as such, prevent the destructive processes of this stage and enable members to confront obstacles to group development.

The providing skills personalize the feelings and content of this stage as it supports all members. The processing skills entail illuminating power and control dynamics, sharing feelings, relating here-and-now interaction ("I-We") to there-and-then themes ("It"), and reaching behind conflicts and decisions. The catalyzing skills include reaching for feelings and perceptions. The directing skills involve encouraging work and invoking the contract.

Skills

Personalizing.   Personalizing responses to feelings and content takes place on four levels (Carkhuff, 1989): (1) meaning, (2) problem, (3) feelings, and (4) goals. We personalize the meaning of the members' particular situation in the group to them by responses to their communication and behavior: "You feel left out because you did not get to participate much today"; "You feel afraid because you believe some members of this group will challenge what you have to say"; "You feel selfish because you believe you have been monopolizing the discussion." When we personalize the meaning of particular members' communications in relation to issues of power and control, members may at least feel understood by us and increase their awareness of how their status-seeking restricts the possibility of their growth needs being met. Here we do not respond to all communications. We personalize when other members do not respond or do not seem to understand the process (autonomy) message, and when we perceive dominant themes related to the current group structure in what a particular member expresses: "One thing you experience personally in relation to your current place in the group keeps coming up over and over . . ."

Personalizing the problem is a critical task in helping members and the group-as-a-whole to resolve power and control themes. It confronts the negative autonomy of dependency and control and calls forth the positive autonomy of responsibility.

Personalizing the problem is confrontative (Carkhuff, 1989). In responding to personalized meaning, we help members discover the impact of the group situation on the member. Personalizing the problem asks members to take responsibility for their situation in the group by becoming aware of how they contribute to the situation. This response entails feeding back how or what the member (or members) does or does not do that leads to the situation: "You feel left out because you can't take the opportunities you've had to participate in this group"; "You feel afraid because you haven't risked expressing yourself to see if other members of this group would agree with you or not"; "You feel upset because you weren't checking to see if other members felt left out by your talking"; "You (the group) are having trouble getting started and are looking at me as if I will direct, and you really haven't expressed this to check it out with me"; "On the one hand you have agreed to the subtheme for today, and on the other hand you have really not considered it. I wonder if we need to discuss a new subtheme or if there are other disturbances going on for you today." This personalizing of the problem provides opportunities for deeper awareness and understanding and for more responsible and need-meeting choice. It especially empowers through highlighting choice.

The next step involves personalizing feelings. This helps members to understand where they are in the evolving structure in relation to where they want to be. In this response, we help the members experience how they feel about themselves in terms of the particular issues and meanings of autonomy themes. It especially includes responding to disappointments and doubts: "You feel disappointed because you can't act immediately on your opportunities to participate, or check out others' reactions to you, or give others a chance to talk, and so on"; "You (the group) feel doubtful that you can make your own decisions because you have been depending on me too much."

Finally, we can personalize goals. This helps members (or the group) to understand where they want to be in relation to where they are. It is the flipside of personalizing the problem. It gets to the wishes that are so often indirectly expressed in feelings of disappointment, disgust, or doubt: "You feel disappointed because you can't act immediately on your opportunities to participate, or check out others' reactions to you, or give others a chance to talk, and so on, and *you want* to be able to"; "You (the group) are doubtful that you can make your own decisions because you have been depending on me to make them and *you now want* to make them on the basis of what you want rather than on your guess about what I want." If it is accurate, this personalizing of meaning, problem, feelings, and goals provides the basic support for members. They feel understood yet challenged to develop toward their fuller potential. These responses can reflect the caring that attends to others and intends what is best (most responsible) for them.

Illuminating.   Illuminating skills are related to personalizing but are intended to increase members' awareness and to attribute meaning to their group events. Irvin Yalom (1995) refers to this skill as "activation" and "process illumination" of the here-and-now. The focus is on the group examining itself, studying its own interactions, and integrating its experience into a conceptual understanding of what it is doing. Members look at their own process with our help. They illuminate what they are doing, how they are doing it, and why they are doing it in terms of what it means about aspects of their needs, their goals, and their relationships with each other. The illuminating skill for helping the group "process" itself may be the most significant of all for enabling members to resolve the power and control structure of this stage.

The illuminating skill requires that we focus the group on the here-and-now and establish the norm that the group discuss itself in the here-and-now: its positions, statuses, roles, norms, wishes and fears, needs, obstacles, goals. We then help to relate the effects of these on the group's ability to achieve the stated goals explicit in the theme and contract.

Illumination of process requires that we (1) recognize process, (2) bring group tensions to the surface, (3) attend to our own feelings, (4) provide activities that help group members assume a process orientation, and (5) facilitate members' acceptance of process illumination (Yalom, 1995). Recognition of process begins with a theoretical model of group process. If we understand TACIT process and dynamics, we are in a position to hypothesize the meaning of the data observed and experienced in the group. Particular data to observe are the nonverbal: Who sits where? Who looks at whom when speaking? Do some members look at us while addressing comments to other members? If so, they may be particularly dependent on our approval and conflicted about authority and therefore have difficulty in resolving power and control issues. Do members pull their chairs away from the center of the group while professing interest in the group? Does a particular member move from sitting close to us in one meeting to sitting across from us in the next, as a first flicker of expressing resentment toward us as "leader"? Who is absent, and how do these absences relate to group events? This nonverbal behavior frequently expresses elements of individual and group process of which members are not yet aware. We can use these observed nonverbal communications to illuminate process when they are shared or responded to by us or other members.

What is not communicated, or is omitted, may reflect process as much as what is done or said. For instance, the group that never confronts or questions us may be particularly conflicted about their autonomy in relation to our authority. Avoidance of such topics as power, money, status, sex, or death may also reflect process. Positions, statuses, and roles can come to the fore when they are shifting because one or two high-status members are absent.

Content itself can be a disguised and unacknowledged trial balloon of here-and-now process communication. (I remember how suspicion and mistrust of any leadership during Autonomy could be reached for behind discussions of President Nixon during the Watergate investigations.) Often, talk about people who could not be trusted, authorities who were unjust, and confidentialities that were violated is a reflection of the experience of these issues, or the fears of them, in the group.

We can bring group tensions to the surface by anticipating them and noting them in the group. The struggle for dominance in this stage creates much tension. As members jockey for position in the pecking order, members fear they will lose while others win. Even as the hierarchy is established and tends to be agreed upon, conflicts and tensions will flare up. The wishes and fears of individual members influence the wishes and fears of the group and create the tension manifested in such behavior as encouraging group leaders and then taking potshots at them, seeking evaluations from us yet resenting any interpretation that appears judgmental, and pushing for honesty yet disapproving of any expression of authentic anger. In all these situations, the behavior on one side — the wishes — increases the fears on the other side. Tension increases. Identifying this tension and helping members to stay with their feelings and become aware of what they are experiencing and doing can empower members to face the polarities of their wishes and fears. There is more opportunity for integration of these in the choices on how to proceed.

Our own feelings may be the most important clues to recognizing and understanding process. Our feelings can be a microscope for viewing slices of the group process. Our feeling of confusion may mirror the group's confused attempts to make us feel powerless and helpless. So, too, might be our feeling of being shut out. Often, during the conflicts of this stage we are put on the spot by the group in its dependency-seeking demand that we must direct the process to be helpful, or must disclose much more than any other member does. The feeling of being put on the spot can be used, if expressed, to illuminate the underlying process of expecting us to resolve the tensions of power and control conflicts rather than looking at how the group can resolve them itself.

Activities that help members assume a process orientation are those that help influence norms for the group's stopping, looking, and listening to where it is. They periodically tug members out of the here-and-now and invite them to consider conceptually the meaning of the transactions that have just occurred. We switch on a self-reflective beacon (Yalom, 1995). For example, we can interrupt the group at an appropriate interval and say: "We are about halfway through our meeting today and I wonder how everyone feels about our meeting thus far." We may share observations and reach for meaning: "I'm not sure what is going on in this meeting, but I am aware of some obvious communications. Bob has been very silent and staring at the floor; Joan moved her chair back several places while Jack and Jill were debating why we are having trouble getting started today. Joe has been glaring at me as if he is angry while this is going on. What ideas do you all have about what's going on here today?" Also, we may share observations, feelings, and our ideas about what these may mean in terms of group process: "I noticed so many of you looking at me while Jack and Jill were fighting and I felt put on the spot — as if I were to rescue you from the tension their fight created for you and the group. I believe these fights will be inevitable in the group, and you are now afraid to respond to them. Perhaps you are afraid to take sides in which you might win or lose — or to permit the group to develop a norm that supports honest confrontation. What do you think?"

Nonverbal activities are especially useful for helping members assume a process orientation. Members during this stage are often more able to show than to talk about the structural elements of group process. They can experience these together more strongly by acting them out. We can ask members to place themselves in relation to the center of the room and to other members in a manner that reflects their perception of their place in the group. Or ask them to form a single line that reflects their ranking of themselves and others in the group. Or ask them to use themselves physically to "sculpture" the group as they see it. Or suggest that subgroups who are involved in conflict have a "showdown" wherein they line up facing each other, silently walk toward each other, and express themselves to each other nonverbally. All these activities illuminate process when they are "processed" —that is, they are discussed verbally for the analysis of meaning of the data derived from the "experiment."

We need to facilitate members' acceptance of process-illuminating comments (Yalom, 1995). The principles of effective feedback, used by us and by members, help make the illumination palatable. This includes the avoidance of pejorative labels in interpretive remarks. Instead of saying "You are a manipulator," it is far more acceptable to the other (and far more true!) to say, "When you told me that you couldn't trust me because I haven't gotten angry yet, I felt manipulated. I believe you were trying to see if I would get angry because you wanted me to. Are you aware of this?" Especially in the conflicts of autonomy, members might hurl important feedback to one another and the group in such ways that the "truth" may be lost in the defensiveness of labels, exaggeration, or nontrusts. We need to help tone down the noise of these interactions to enable members to hear the tones that may resonate some accurate awareness: "Jack, you have shut out everything Jill has said about her anger at your monopolizing this meeting. Yet you have tried to corner her in her responsibility to initiate discussion, to be her own leader. You prevent yourself from getting anything different here. Will you try something? Ask yourself if there is *anything* in what Jill is saying that is true for you. What parts strike an inner chord of your awareness? Could you forget for a moment the things that are *untrue* and stay with those that are *true* for you?" Then later: "Jill, I'd like to ask you to do the same." Or, to the group, we may similarly say, "You really jumped on Joy for saying she felt most of you were acting phony in the group, that you were not honest and too polite. You accused her of being the one who was phony by not participating. Could you hold back your anger at Joy for a moment and consider if any of what she said may have hit home? Because you reacted so strongly, I suspect this is a very meaningful issue for more than just Joy in this group. Does this strike a chord with any of you?"

Through this feedback, through questions, through the activities that help members process, through attention to our own feelings, through surfacing tensions, and through recognizing process — we illuminate the here-and-now. The other side of illumination involves focusing members' attention and awareness to the here-and-now. This focus is the purpose of the next skill: relating here-and-now interaction to there-and-then themes.

Relating Here-Now and Then-There.   The skill of relating the here-and-now to the there-and-then, and vice versa, is the ability to connect the "I" and the "We" to the "It." Especially during this stage, when members are assuming roles in the group that are similar to those they tend to take outside, this skill is important. The problems that members experience in structure and the difficulty they have in admitting power and status needs are reflected in the content. This content often avoids here-and-now concerns in disguised attention to more abstract there-and-then themes. As we relate there-and-then themes to the here-and-now group process, members can increase their potential for learning. This skill does not suggest a rigid norm that requires all content to reflect the here-and-now. Research suggests that effective groups have open boundaries in their norms for appropriate content, which is in the control of group members rather than the practitioner (Bond, 1983). However, the connection of the "I" and the "We" of the group structure and process to the "It" of there-and-then content is inevitable in practice groups. Our task is to help members experience and become aware of these inevitable relationships.

First, we need to "think here-and-now" (Yalom, 1995). This permits us to shepherd the flock of group members into an ever-tightening circle by heading off errant, superfluous historical or outside material as strays and guide members back into the present circle. Whenever an issue is raised in the group, we can consider, "How can I relate this to the group's theme and its process? How can I make it come to life in the here-and-now?" These questions alert us to possibilities for helping members make contact by focusing from outside to inside, from the abstract to the specific, from the general to the personal.

The member who describes a hostile confrontation of a power and control conflict with a roommate or friends can be asked, "If you were angry like that with anyone in our group, who would it be?" or, "With whom in this group do you believe you might get into the same type of struggle?" If the member shares that one of her or his problems is that one stereotypes others, we can bring this to the here-and-now by asking the questions, "Can you describe the ways you've stereotyped some of us in the group?" and "Who do you feel has stereotyped you in this group?" If a member describes a there-and-then problem as being easily led, we can increase the here-and-now theme by asking who in the group could influence him or her the most and who the least. Those concerned about being humiliated can be asked who in the group they imagine might ridicule them. The here-and-now contact and learning can then be deepened by reaching for the responses of other members: "How do you feel about these stereotypes?" "Can you imagine yourself ridiculing him (or her)?" Toward this contact the simple techniques of asking members to speak as I, to look at one another, and to speak directly to the intended recipient of a message can be enormously useful.

We can anticipate resistance to this here-and-now interaction. Often these skills both steer members into more intense, real, and fearful here-and-now interaction and simultaneously interrupt the content flow in the group. Members may resent the interruptions. We must attend to these resentments as they, too, are part of the here-and-now. The group's flow and our concern for work in here-and-now needs to be expressed: "Jack, I had two reactions as you were talking. First, I was delighted that you feel comfortable enough now in the group to participate. Second, I felt that it is hard for the group to respond to what you're saying because it's so very general and far removed from you personally. I'm interested in what's been going on inside you in this group over the last several weeks. Although you've been silent, I sensed that you were very much aware of what we've been doing. Can you share some of these feelings and observations with us?"

Resistance also calls for responses that focus on positive interaction and on the safety and distance of "Ifs" to lessen the perceived threat of here-and-now content (Yalom, 1995). Such questions as "Who do you feel closest to in the group?" or "Who in the group is most like you (or most understands you)?" accentuate the positive connections. Use of the subjunctive "if" mood in such questions as "If you were angry at someone in this group for dominating you, who might this be?" and "If you could participate more like another person in this group, who might you wish to participate like?" provides some safety and more self-governed distance in here-and-now interaction during this stage.

If members resist risking personal disclosures (and during this stage they often do), they can be encouraged, at least, to risk disclosures about their disclosures (what Yalom, 1995, calls "metadisclosures"). For example, a member who has been silent and who has shared some general there-and-then content might be asked, "What was it like for you to talk in this group just now?" Others can be asked, "What's been the hardest thing for you to share so far?" or "When we ask you questions about yourself, how do you feel? How do we know when we might be pushing you too much or when you really want us to push you?" or "How do you rate the risk you just took as you are experiencing it inside — low, medium, high, or very high?"

Silences are particularly rich sources of data for here-and-now awareness of the group's process. These riches can be tapped by noting: "Much seems to be going on for us in this silence. There is valuable information for us here if we could only excavate it. I wonder if each of us could tell the group some of the thoughts we had during the silence that we thought of sharing but did not say." Often, this skill is best preceded by our own sharing: "I've been feeling antsy during this silence, wanting to break it, not wanting to waste time, but also feeling irritated because I seem to be the one always doing this work for the group. I wonder what you were experiencing during this silence."

The group can be encouraged to evaluate its own process in relation to individual members' needs and goals in the here-and-now. Such comments as (1) asking the group to imagine that the remaining thirty minutes of the group have passed and that they are on their way home, and (2) asking them to share their disappointments about the meeting today, can encourage this processing. Members can be asked to stop-action and reflect upon what has been the most productive (and/or least productive) part of the meeting so far. Often, when we can shift the group's attention and awareness from the there-and-then to the here-and-now, we perform an important service for the group. If the group succeeds in focusing upon itself, the result will likely be a more cohesive, interactional atmosphere that maximizes group development and therapeutic outcomes.

Implicit in this skill is the assumption that we know the most propitious direction for the group at a specific moment. The interpretation does not have to be perfectly precise and accurate, however; the timing does not have to be impeccable. Even incorrect or poorly timed comments relating the there-and-then to the here-and-now can focus on the current drama of group structure and process and illuminate the meaning of group events for members. The broad principles that provide helpful direction to us are those derived from an understanding of TACIT. In Autonomy, these suggest that the group's awareness of its own structure as implicit in all group events is a prerequisite for preventing the structural obstacles that prevent members' needs from being met in the group and in their lives outside. This very processing and attention to the subterranean data of the here-and-now activates the basic difference between this experience and others in groups. It increases the potential for the development of closeness and interdependence in group process.

Reaching behind Conflicts and Decisions.   A special use of the processing function is the skill of reaching behind conflicts and decisions. Most important is our helping the group to understand some of the inevitable impersonal elements of conflicts and how decisions are made. Members entrenched in these structural dynamics manifest more selfish power-and-status-seeking behavior, which is not considerate of others. Therefore, some members are hurt and resentful while others carry on business as usual without empathetic awareness of having hurt others in their interaction. Some hurts and resentments can be deflected, and powerful members can develop more sensitivity to their impact on others by understanding the impersonal and stereotypic dynamics of conflicts and decisions. They can begin to understand that real people with real feelings were experiencing these group events personally.

Reaching behind conflicts and decisions requires that we tune in to the personal reactions to impersonal interactions. For instance, we can illuminate these issues in our own experience: "Jack, you made several assumptions about what I am thinking and feeling in this group without bothering to check these out with me, to get to know me. I am uncomfortable about your stereotype of me as manipulating this group because I have not told you how to resolve this conflict. You don't really know me. I was sitting here feeling that Jill must be hurt by your anger at her as the manipulator you described—as I have felt with your anger at me. I would like to know more about how you see me in this group other than your label as manipulator. I will let Jill speak for herself, but she may also want more specific feedback from you."

We also need to draw feedback from the group on what each member is experiencing, especially during moments of conflict and decisions. These include such questions as: "I sense a tension in the group as a result of the conflict we just experienced. What is going on for you who are feeling tense?" or "We just made a decision to change the topic and move away from the anger that Jack expressed toward Jill without really being aware that we made such a decision. How did we make it and what do you feel about this?" We particularly can reach behind the conflicts and decisions by eliciting the hurts that members may be expressing nonverbally: "Jane, you looked as if you were going to cry while we were discussing our subtheme for next week. Are you willing to share with us what is going on for you? I would really like to know."

Finally, a useful technique in reaching behind conflicts in a way that increases intermember awareness and empathy is the "listening game." In this activity we ask combatants if they are willing to try something while they are interacting with each other. If they are, we suggest that they continue their interaction with one additional "rule." They must state in their own words what they heard the other (or others) say, and the other (or others) must agree that they were heard accurately before the restater makes his or her own comments. This "game" often defuses the structural elements of conflict—the struggles for power or dominance, or the win/lose—and brings the conflict to the real and often more resolvable level of person-to-person (rather than position-to-position or role-to-role) encounter. As this encounter continues, the group can be asked to suggest potential solutions to the conflict with only one "rule" for the suggestion. It must be a solution in which no one loses and both combatants win.

Similarly, we can enable the group to make more effective decisions by reaching behind the way decisions are made in a manner that "counts" certain members "in" and powerful and other members "out" and powerless. This requires us to adopt a style of decision making that supports the norms of shared power and influence among members so that every member "counts." When members discover that they all "count" and that their needs (rather than who has the power) constitute the major issue in decision making, they have taken a giant step toward resolving the power and control dynamics of group development.

When we help members to explore their "I count; you don't count" decision making, we introduce them to a model for "decision-by-consensus." The research shows this norm as most helpful (Hall and Watson, 1970). In consensus, the norms support decisions made on the basis of "I count; you count." In short, the group is encouraged to move beyond win/lose decisions to "no-lose decisions." We can show the difference by reaching behind decisions to see whether they were based on assessed needs of all members or on preconceived solutions by a few. As alternatives are proposed, evaluated, and ranked, we can ask which solution from among those generated meets the needs of all members, or how those selected can be modified to meet all members' needs. Again, we build a base for reaching behind decisions toward establishing consensus, equality, and mutual aid norms from our own influence on decision making: "You've decided to work on the subtheme of Resolving Conflicts today and now we're off the topic. I think it would be helpful to stop for a moment and discuss where we are as a group and how we would like to commit the rest of our time. What do you think about this?" We can also reach behind the consensual decisions for the positive experience and feelings: "The experience we just had is an example of decision by consensus. What did you observe about this process and how do you feel about it?"

Two of the greatest gauges of movement through this stage toward the more equal opportunity structure of the next are the group's ability (1) to resolve conflicts in a no-lose manner, and (2) to make decisions on an "I count; you count" basis. Reaching behind conflicts and decisions illuminates the obstacles to this process and empowers members to challenge these on behalf of their needs for more close, authentic, and interdependent encounters.

Reaching for Feelings and Perceptions.   Many of the aforementioned processing skills do catalyze members toward emotional contact in the here-and-now. However, the more moderate use of the catalyzing function during this stage includes some specific skills. One involves reaching for feelings and perceptions. This includes checking for underlying ambivalence, supporting communication in taboo areas, reaching for individual communication in the group, and reaching for the group response to the individual (Shulman, 1992). All these skills catalyze intermember contact and awareness.

One of the dangers in group practice is that a member or members may choose to go along with us or the group through artificial consensus or submission. Meanwhile, they may feel very ambivalent about a particular issue, decision, or seemingly agreed-upon procedure. In this situation it is vital for us to catalyze honesty by checking for underlying ambivalence: "You all seem to be agreeing with this decision, but I wonder if some of you don't feel quite so excited and positive about it. Do any of you really differ with this?" Similarly, members who express negative feelings about a particular event most often are resisting facing some of their positive feelings. Although members often fear conflict in this stage, they also sense excitement about the possibility of spontaneity and honesty in the group and may resist facing this side of the experience. We may say: "You have expressed your anger and concerns about this conflict we have experienced, but I wonder if you also may see some positives in this. Who is aware of some possible feelings you have on the other side of this conflict?" In general, it is a useful principle throughout the group process to reach for opposites in feelings and perceptions. When members evaluate the group or a particular segment with nothing but positives, it pays to reach for the negatives. Likewise, negative evaluations can follow with reaching for the positives.

Members who are involved in conflict are making some connection to each other. Although they may seem to be attacking each other, the fact remains that in the underlying process they have taken on significance to each other. Therefore, they become a source for learning more about the self, perhaps even taking back disowned parts of one's self projected onto the other(s) toward further integration. For instance, members who attack those who have assumed leadership positions and roles can be helped to get in touch with their own power and leadership needs. This task requires us to reach for the appreciations that accompany resentments: "Jack, you have told Jill what you resent about her influence on this group. Can you now tell her what you appreciate about her participation?" Realistic choices for the individual members, for interaction between and among members and for the group-as-a-whole, evolve from experiencing, being aware of, and "owning" ambivalences.

Support for members in taboo areas means reaching for feelings in relation to themes that are constrained because usual social norms define these issues as unacceptable (Shulman, 1992). One of our most powerful taboos, and one that restricts awareness and entrenches structure during Autonomy, relates to feelings toward authority. Parents, teachers, employers, and other authority figures tend to discourage feedback on the nature of our relationship to them. We learn very early in childhood that honest expression of our resentment toward those in authority is fraught with danger. People in authority have the power to hurt us, to shame us to feel "bad," and to restrict our autonomy in meeting our needs. At worst, we tend to please them by withholding our feelings about them. At best, we may hint at our feelings and reactions. Often, the expression of positive feelings toward authority is just as difficult. Because we fear that if we express the appreciations we may slip into sharing resentments, we hold on to all these feelings. Our peer group also tends to teach us that expressing positive feelings and reactions to those in authority is "butt kissing" and demeaning. The socialized taboo creates a formidable obstacle in the working relationship between us and the group when the authority theme is in the forefront of members' attention during this stage.

We need to catalyze a culture in which the norms resocialize members to confront the authority theme. We do so by reaching for their feelings — again, both positive and negative — behind the indirect cues reflecting authority issues. When catalyzing the authority feelings and perceptions, we must be comfortable with our own imperfections. This security can help members begin to see us as a person, rather than as a symbol — a significant step in members beginning to see themselves and others as imperfect, yet O.K., people rather than as symbols and stereotypes of positions, roles, and statuses. Surely when we reach for authority-oriented feelings and perceptions or for feedback on our own meaning to members in the here-and-now, we will be readily reminded of our imperfections. We will have made mistakes and members will have stored these mistakes vividly in their memories. Even most skilled practitioners will discover that they missed some members' communications or lost track of their function, or made a judgmental statement that implied lack of empathy for some of the real struggles members were experiencing. When given half a chance, members might readily share these reactions and feelings toward our mistakes and our inevitable imperfections. This expression of negatives in relation to the taboo of authority and the experience of understanding by us can provide a significant "corrective emotional experience" for members; free the group to frankly confront other taboo areas in their process (such as "sibling rivalry" for our attention); and, for those of us who especially need to be liked, the sharing of positive feelings toward us as both an "authority" and a person.

We deal with the authority theme and support members in taboo areas by reaching for their feelings and perceptions. When members talk about the there-and-then themes of a strict parent, a crooked cop, a teacher they don't respect, and so on, we can activate the here-and-now by asking: "I wonder if some of that message was directed toward me as an authority figure for you in this group. How do you see me in this way, and what feelings does this stimulate in you toward me?" Members who are habitually late or who disagree with all our responses can be confronted with the potential meaning of this behavior in relation to the authority theme: "I get the impression from your lateness (or from how much you disagree with me no matter what I say) that you have some particular feelings about your relationship to me in this group. How do you perceive me, and what are your feelings toward me?" The group as a whole often reflects its ambivalences about authority by asking for direction from us and then furiously resisting any suggestions we make. Here, we can catalyze a culture with norms that permit confronting authority through opening this issue up for the group by stating our own feelings as a person within our function and encouraging the members to share theirs. For instance, we can say: "I really feel in a bind. On the one hand, you are looking to me to direct the group at this point, to be the leader; on the other hand, when I have offered suggestions on how to proceed, you have seemed to resent this direction. I think I can be most helpful to you now, and you to me, if we can take time to talk about what's going on for you in relation to your perceptions and feelings about me and my role in the group."

In checking for underlying ambivalences and supporting communication in taboo areas, it is important for us to reach for individual communication in the group and for group responses to the individual. We should concentrate efforts in the early phase of each meeting on helping individual members to present their concerns to the group. A useful technique for this is "checking in" (Corey et al., 1992). Each session during this stage tends to begin as a slow form of feeling out the group. Members endeavor to determine who is attempting to capture the group's attention for their own issues and how these may represent the theme of the group's concern. Often, individual members' concerns reflect the group's major process (if not content) theme for the meeting. We need to consider: "What are we working on this session? How does this member's concern relate to the group's concern now? What are the themes in this interaction?"

We start here, where the group and individual members are. We do not rush in with an agenda simply because group members' communications seem unclear. Likewise, we do not assume that simply because the group had agreed to deal with a specific subtheme at the end of the previous meeting, this subtheme will be the topic for the current session. Even if members begin by addressing the subtheme, we should monitor the discussion in the early part of the meeting to sense whether the interaction confirms the selected subtheme or suggests that members are going through the motions for a group session.

Members are always working on something. Even though the content and interaction may not seem directed toward the group's purpose and stated theme, it is always purposeful. Even disturbances to the work reflect some present orientation to the group process. Often, members especially mirror this current process. Hence, there is the ground rule that "disturbances come first." When we tune in to early discussion with the questions of, "How does this connect to a theme and our work?" and "What is troubling this particular member?" we have increased the opportunity for helping the individual member relate a concern to the group. The group can attend to its own here-and-now concerns when we catalyze the expression of the individual by reaching for this communication to the group: "Joan, you want something from us today. I wonder what this is and how you see this group helping you with this."

The other side of this skill involves reaching for the group's response to the individual (Shulman, 1992). We then catalyze empathetic response from other members: "Do you understand what John is saying—what his concern is, and what he wants from us? Will you respond to this?" The need for this reacting is greatest when strong emotions are expressed. Often, however, during Autonomy, strong emotions tend to scare members into nonresponse. When this occurs, we may feel upset and angry. We may be shocked, discouraged, and surprised that group members appear not to be listening, that their eyes glaze over as if they are lost in their own thoughts, or that they quickly change the subject or rebuff the member who has bared such intense feeling. We must move from this natural reaction to an understanding of the situation, especially in its TACIT dimension. The group's response most likely is a signal—not that members are disinterested in the theme of the communication, but that the theme is having a powerful impact on them. Part of this impact is the intensifying of their fears of authentic interaction, closeness, and responsibility toward others at the same time as they wish for this relationship. We can best reach for the group's response by noting the avoidance of response, the naturalness of the fears, and redirecting attention to the individual's communication. For instance, we can say: "John just took a big risk with us by baring some of his pain with us. I believe we left him hanging by shifting the topic suddenly and diverting our attention to his needs. I sense that what he said had a powerful impact on you but you weren't sure how to respond to him or were afraid to stay with him. I wonder if we can take a few moments and stop and, in silence, become aware of what reactions his pain stimulated in us. Then perhaps we can return to John and share our responses with him. Is that O.K. with you, John?" (Shulman, 1992, p. 412). This response helps to challenge the obstacles to mutual aid that are inherent in this stage and reaches for the group's empathy in relation to the individual's current theme.

Encouraging Work. The directing function largely entails encouraging work and invoking the contract. This section examines the first of these skills — our ability to encourage work from the group. We do this by holding the group to focus, challenging the illusion for work, reaching for work when obstacles threaten, and focusing the group on problem-solving mutual aid (Schwartz, 1971; Shulman, 1992). William Schwartz (1971) described this skill in these terms:

> The worker also represents what might be called the demand for work, in which role he tries to enforce not only the substantive aspects of the contract — what we are here for — but the conditions of work as well. This demand is, in fact, the only one the worker makes — not for certain perceived results, or approved attitudes, or learned behaviors, but for the work itself. That is, he is continually challenging the client to address himself resolutely and with energy to what he came to do. (p. 11)

We particularly encourage work when we monitor when the group is working and when it is not and what the group is working on. Resistances to work are expected and, if experienced, can be the basis of choices for the group about what they are willing and able to work on. Particularly useful is holding the group to focus.

As the group deals with a specific subtheme, associations and other related concerns and issues may result in a form of rambling. The group, especially in this stage, finds great difficulty in concentrating on one theme at a time. We need to return the group to forgotten issues or themes when members do not do this themselves. The intent is to consider these themes with maximum, not optimum, attention. Often, the movement from one concern to another is an evasion of work. The group does not stay with one theme for fear the concern is very real for the group and members may have to deal with their associated feelings. When we address this rambling and hold the group to focus by reminding it of its purpose and evolving themes for the meeting, the group gets the message that we, at least, mean to discuss the tougher feelings and concerns.

One of the greatest threats to the effective group is the ability of the group to create an illusion for work. Groups can fall into a pattern of high participation around talk that is shallow, abstract, general, there-and-then, and safe. This becomes an illusion when we permit the interaction to substitute for the less comfortable struggle and growth that mark any TACIT development.

Schwartz (1971) commented on this illusion as follows:

> Not only must the worker be able to help people talk but he must help them talk to each other; the talk must be purposeful, related to the contract that holds them together; it must have feeling in it, for without affect there is no investment; and it must be about real things, not a charade, or a false consensus, or a game designed to produce the illusion for work without raising anything in the process. (p. 12)

The skill of challenging the illusion to work involves detecting the pattern for illusion over a period of time and confronting the group with the reality of evasion.

Challenging the illusion of work is one way of reaching for work when obstacles threaten. It requires the support of underlying empathy for the difficulty in moving on, mixed with the challenge of the reality of the group's purpose, theme, and contract. We note: "I know it is hard to confront how we really feel about each other today, especially after the tension of last week's conflict, but I wonder if you really want to spend the whole hour talking about yesterday's elections." A useful principle for reaching for work even when obstacles threaten is the movement from the general to the specific. Work is often avoided when members fear or resist the risks inherent in group process by expressing their concerns in general, abstract terms. We can encourage individual members to be more specific and concrete in elaborating these general themes, or the general concerns of one member can be made more specific for the group by asking other members whether they feel the same way.

The connecting of individual needs and issues, expressed as specifically as possible, with group concerns seeks the common ground that supports work. We focus the group on more problem-solving mutual aid when we recognize the common concerns among members, or help the group discover them, in a way that can translate into a common theme to which members can commit their efforts. The group is more ready to confront resistances and to work when they do feel the support of "being in the same boat" and when there is some potential for empathetic understanding from members toward increased mutual aid. We can focus on this potential by reaching for it when it appears to exist in the group. We can relate this mutual aid to encouraging work when confronting resistances in the power and control stage: "I sense that most of you are having trouble working on our theme today. Do any of you have any ideas about how we can help each other get past this resistance and get on to our work?" In other words, we promote mutual aid in the group's problem solving when we make the problem of individual members and the group-as-a-whole the group's problem — including the problems of the obstacles and resistances to work.

Invoking the Contract.   The second major skill of the moderately used directing function during this stage involves invoking the contract. We can use the contract terms as the model for exploring the group interaction, including our own role, and for encouraging members to make choices about their group structure and process. We invoke the contract when we ask: "Is this what we agreed to do together?" "Are we working on our stated group goals?" "Can we try to use the ground rules that we agreed on in our contract?" These questions and others remind members of the purpose of the group, the ways they have decided to proceed, and how they may be swerving off the course they have set for themselves.

If there is much digression from the terms of the contract, we may need to raise the question of its relevance and renegotiate its terms with members. However, this renegotiation is often premature: Group issues in power and control and resistance to work toward authentic themes may make any contract terms difficult to follow. In the stage that comes next, this renegotiation is more appropriate. It may be better to help members consider what it takes to uphold their initial contract than to attempt to renegotiate it so quickly. Often, the group decisions for interaction, when they are compared against the contract, can motivate the members to give more attention to the wishes for closeness and to the hurts and frustrations of others. Then they can recommit themselves to the work required. We, too, can consistently invoke the contract with ourself. The best guidelines for what we choose to do in the group are those that are consistent with what was agreed upon by members in the initial contract. When this contract is important to us as reflected in our living it, it becomes more real and meaningful for members.

PRINCIPLES FOR THE POWER AND CONTROL STAGE

The power and control stage can last for several weeks or several months of group meetings, depending on the nature of the members, the group, and the practitioner. Members who are particularly mistrustful of authority and involved in power and control may spend much of their process stuck in autonomy themes. These include teenage gang members, prisoners, and probationers, among others. Open-ended groups also may create longstanding autonomy themes.

I once consulted with a practitioner who had an open-ended group of fathers whose sons were involved in therapy for "emotional disturbances." This group had had forty meetings over a full year, with three fathers present from the beginning and three to four others joining and leaving the group after it had begun. It was not until the forty-second meeting—when a new member who entered the group initiated discussion about the group's structure and the members' rivalry for the practitioner's attention and then cried in desperation of his own needs for help—that this group resolved enough of the autonomy themes to begin interaction reflecting the intimacy stage.

Too many groups, because of the lack of the practitioner's knowledge and skills, never get through this stage. They begin and end with the practitioner's strong structure and direction of the process; they provide the illusion of work so that members' status needs are met in sibling rivalry for the leader's attention and approval. The most effective groups tend to resolve autonomy issues and conflicts early in their process.

The following principles integrate the skills we can use to enable this early resolution as much as possible:

1. We need to begin each meeting where the members are and be especially attuned to what individuals are working on and how this work relates to the current group process themes.
2. We need to monitor the evolving group structure and its reflection in group process events.
3. We need to activate a here-and-now focus in the group and to illuminate the here-and-now process through the systems of feedback in the group.
4. We need to help the group confront the authority theme with empathy for its taboo, with its reality for the group's process, and with support for members' abilities to take responsibility for themselves.
5. We need to increase the group's awareness of its norms for the expression of feelings, problem solving, conflict resolution, and decision making.
6. We need to discover subthemes to relate there-and-then to here-and-now concerns and to hold members to focus and work.
7. We need to encourage the group to evaluate its work in relation to its contract and to the needs and goals of members.
8. We need to ensure that the autonomy crisis is not relieved in illusion by our structuring the group and directing the interactions.
9. We need especially to trust the process; that is, we need to understand that the way around the power and control stage is *through* it and that members, when aware of their process and free to do so, will choose what is best for the group and themselves — a structure based on all members' needs; one that promotes equal opportunity, spontaneity, closeness, and empathy.

Example

These principles are reflected in the practitioner's use of self in the following example. The example demonstrates the autonomy crisis and its beginning resolution.

The example continues the counseling with fifth-grade preadolescents in groups that was begun in the last chapter. In this record, we find the power and control/autonomy issues emerging directly in the third meeting. They are resolved during this meeting and the next three. The four meetings are recorded below; the student social worker's observations, thoughts, and feelings are given in parentheses.

PREADOLESCENTS

Meeting 3

We played kickball instead of football at the beginning of the meeting. The changed decision was made quickly and smoothly. Joy wasn't feeling well, so she didn't take sides. She rolled the ball for both teams. The teams weren't really chosen, they just fell together. Everyone got along much better in this game than in the previous ones. There wasn't any fighting. It turned out to be a lot of fun, and the losing team (which I was on) didn't even mind the loss. Before we went out, Joy and I set the time limit of twenty-five minutes. They were upset when the time was up, but they were curious about what they needed the pencils for. (Their teacher had them bring pencils for the evaluation instruments.)

(I noticed that the members have now realized that we are a group because they show me in various ways that they are involved with one another. The "I-It" concern has fairly been resolved, and the fears of closeness that were very evident in Meeting 2 have brought the need for structure to most members. I saw this in today's meeting through members attempting to "fit" somewhere. The need for trust in different members is not as important now. Some initial trusts have mostly been established. The trust they are searching for now is in the group somewhere.)

The project of writing feelings about the group (the sociometric instrument) on a piece of paper proved to be very successful in providing Joy and me with insights of individuals that weren't previously expressed. But more important, this evaluation project gave individual members the opportunity to think about their position in the group. I was surprised that no one objected to this. They seemed to enjoy it after they got started, and they didn't even bother each other.

I really noticed the "peer court" being in session in this meeting. The members are very much aware of each other because of their need for position. A major process theme is the need for various members to gain power and dominate. Darren, wanting to lead the group, was the person who organized the decision of playing kickball instead of football. He asked for a show of hands in making the decision. "Unanimous," he stated. Ricky, who previously sat back, tried to influence the group to concentrate on the theme. He is emerging as a person who really wants the group to get along.

Through this exercise I used the skill of "illuminating group structure," especially interpretations of their roles. It seemed to initiate some thought about their place in the group; something that can't be accomplished fully when playing kickball or football.

Because of the need to understand their own roles and position in the group, I had them perform the exercise in which the members place themselves somewhere in the room, according to the closeness that they feel. Chris wanted to know if he could leave the room. We said "no," but he felt that far away to place himself at the edge of the room. He did so. Randy sat under a desk at the other end of the room. Jeff walked over to the window, gazing outside. Darren, Ricky, and Mike sat close to Joy and me.

This was such a good way to end the meeting. The way they placed themselves was very representative of what I have been perceiving. We asked why they positioned themselves in those ways. The three boys in the middle said they liked the group and felt good about it. Randy didn't know why he was under the desk, and Chris said that he felt far away. Jeff said that he just wanted to look out the window and feel the air come through the register. We asked them to think about the exercises that we did.

We had a few minutes to plan the next meeting. They wanted physical exercise but were not as intent on it as last week. I see some better understanding of purpose. Ricky suggested that we talk about the group again, after we played a game. Everyone seemed to agree.

(I think an important consideration in the next meeting would be to concentrate on resolution of hierarchical conflicts. It would be particularly harmful to certain group members if their lower self-esteem in relation to low status in the group was simply ignored.)

(I can now see some more of the group process coming into play, and this has really helped my own feelings about the group. I feel that I've been providing members with various things that meet their needs. Some of them need an atmosphere with security, some need friendship, and all of them have the need to release tension in various ways.)

Meeting 4

As we walked into the room today, everyone except Jeff and Ricky was in a single pile on the floor, wrestling. We stood there watching them for quite some time. They were just having fun with each other and I wanted to hold on to the togetherness for a while. Jeff and Ricky were also enjoying watching them. I could tell that neither of them felt excluded.

Darren noticed us watching them and began to get the group together. He told everyone to "knock it off" because Joy and I were "waiting." Gradually the boys got off the pile and moved toward the spot where we usually form our circle.

The cold, bitter weather today seemed to rule out decisions of going outside to play a game. There was a bit of reluctance to accept the fact, as various members opened the window, telling Joy and me how "warm" the air was. But as the cold air swept through the room, the window was closed and any decision for an outside game seemed to filter out.

We immediately introduced the idea of the exercise that we had planned with the blindfolds. Chris seemed a bit uneasy with this and brought up the idea of football. Everyone else was curious about this exercise, deciding that they wanted to do it. We checked further, giving a choice, and Chris said that it would be alright.

Joy and I put the blindfolds on everyone and a lot of them started wandering around, exploring the room. I got up and led them back to the circle. We explained that everyone had to be quiet as we passed particular objects around. Each person was supposed to explore the object, then pass it to his right. After one object went around the circle, we asked each person to take turns saying what they felt. No one was to say the name of the object while describing it. They each took a lot of time touching the soap, tea bag, and Band-Aid. Everyone followed the rules of the game. They were giggling and really getting into the game. I noticed them moving closer to each other. The fact that each boy was in the same situation, not being able to see, only relying on touch, seemed to provide something common for the group.

When the blindfolds came off, Ricky went to get his glasses and Chris and Jeff started playing with the balls. The fact that Jeff got up to interact with Chris was significant in indicating Jeff's conception of himself in relation to the group. He seemed very sure of himself as he threw the ball to Chris to catch. (It was distracting to the group, but in my thoughts, Jeff's new sense of "belonging" outweighed the need for them to join the group.) After a few minutes passed, we asked them to come back to the group. They both responded, Chris bringing the ball with him.

(I have developed an effective form of confrontation with Chris that is nonverbal. Somehow we have established a very good eye contact, and many times I only have to look at him to get a response. The ball in the group circle bothered me. I'm not quite sure how it happened; I didn't say a word when Chris looked at me. He felt my distaste with the object, looked at the ball, then at me again, and threw it to the side. He returned my smile.)

Joy and I then explained that there was something important that we wanted to talk to them about. With that, different members began running around the room. Mike and Darren stood on their hands. Jeff turned somersaults. Joy raised her voice, saying, "This is exactly what we want to talk to you about." Darren came in immediately, telling everyone to get "organized."

(Darren has emerged as a leader for the group. In previous meetings, he struggled for this position through displaying aggressiveness and overt behavior. Through those techniques, he did not achieve that position. Different members were bothered by his actions and resented them at times. I feel that I helped Darren deal with his need by using the skills of "stepping down strong signals." I never reinforced those actions and never showed any approval of them. I also knew that complete disapproval would not help him either. The need to lead is definitely present. I felt that in helping him realize this need, I could also see whether the need would result in destructive domination of the group. It has not. Darren has found his position, is very comfortable with it, and does not use it to overly dominate. What is equally important is the fact that most of the members are also comfortable with his position. Darren's strong signals are for the most part fully understood by Darren, and because of this, they are received without distortion by other members.)

The group followed Darren to the circle and Joy began to tell them that we become frustrated when everyone runs about, ignoring our needs to get together and discuss the progression of the group. The group members became silent as we both used the skill of "sharing our feelings." At the end of this self-disclosure, I asked if everyone understood what we were saying. Darren began, truly empathizing with our feelings. Randy quietly said, "He's taking up for them." Not everyone heard him, so I asked him to tell the group what he said. He didn't want to, but with some urging from me, he finally did, laughing. I asked Darren if that was true and he said "no," that his statement came from what he was thinking. Addressing Randy (who always sits near me), I asked him why he felt that way. He said he didn't want to be in the group and the only reason he was is because he didn't want to be left alone in the room when everyone else went to their groups.

(I didn't see Randy's statements as totally real. He projects too much enjoyment of the group, many times, for me to see such significance in his words. Instead I feel that Randy is experiencing ambivalence and possible hostility toward me. He really needs my approval and undivided attention. I have been catching little "flirting" facial expressions, in his search for my approval of him. When I don't acknowledge them, he seems to get upset. He is showing some hostility toward me because I show no favoritism. I feel that some jealousy came out as he saw that Darren is beginning to feel what I have been stressing all along. I am showing him that I do not intend to display the favoritism he wants. During further meetings, I plan to leave myself "open" for any hostility that Randy may feel. Suppressing this expression would only suppress his individual growth. I want to show Randy that I refuse to allow dependency upon me. I will make him aware of his exploitations so that he has the opportunity to develop autonomy and interdependence.)

(I believe that trust and autonomy are overlapping at this point. The members have decided to become involved with each other. But at the same time, "fears of intimacy" are still present. As we talked about the group [the first real discussion we've had], different members would quietly offer expression of how they feel. They weren't comfortable with those feelings to the point of fully and loudly verbalizing them. When we asked them to repeat what they had said, they would not. There is still resistance to self-disclosure on the part of certain members, especially Randy and Jeff. During today's meeting, though, I saw Jeff opening up a lot more. He is beginning to be less afraid of the more dominating members, realizing that he has a position in the group also.)

The members now realize that at the end of the group session we should plan for the next meeting. I was happy that they needed no direction with this at the end of the meeting. They are beginning to see the purpose of our meetings more clearly. Their focus on next week did not lean toward an outside activity. Instead, they were thinking of something that we could all do together inside. Chris became bored, put a record on the record player, and started dancing. I incorporated his own interest into something that would be good for not only him, but for the group. I said, "That sounds good, Chris. We can all listen to the music as we plan the next meeting." He came back to help us with the planning.

We all decided to have a party next week in keeping with our "Getting Closer" subtheme. Everyone decided what he could bring. I got a piece of paper and wrote down everyone's name and what he would bring. They all moved very close together as we planned the party. Chris said that he had a dollar saved and would spend that on the party. He said he really wanted to do that.

As the meeting ended, everyone was excited about next week. Joy and I left and Jeff followed, telling us to have a nice week.

(Because the opportunity to be one unit will exist next week as we have the party, I want to focus on that. I want to reinforce the emerging feeling that "I am important; I am a part of the whole.")

Meeting 5

When we arrived at the room, I noted the excitement about the party. Everyone had special concern in showing Joy and me that they had not forgotten to bring the food. Joy and I had forgotten the blanket, though, but it didn't bother anyone. As a group, we pushed desks together to make a long table. Everyone helped to organize the food, each boy walking around, giving everyone a portion of what he had brought. I sat down beside Jeff, who shies away from me a lot. He had brought cookies. They happened to be my favorite kind, so I told him. He seemed happy about that and he told me to let him know when I wanted more.

(Jeff is gradually reaching out, if only in small ways. I think it's very important at this point to direct him toward self-expression. The need is definitely there. Either he doesn't recognize this need, or he is having trouble understanding it. I have been using the skill of "reaching for feelings" with Jeff. He is struggling to accomplish his task, even though he may not understand what that task is. While the group is talking about something and Jeff is not responding, I have been directing questions to him. [For example, Darren was talking about preparing the drinks he had brought. We discussed how it felt to do things for the group. Jeff offered nothing, so I asked him what he thought about that.] In the initial moments of this confrontation [and many other instances of this], Jeff seems thrown off-balance and even confused by a very simple question. At times, I find it hard to believe that he really is that confused. So at the same time that I "reach for" feelings, I "wait for" them. Jeff becomes uncomfortable with the silence, knowing that I will not go away, and usually responds in some way. It's only in the past two meetings that I have been using these skills with Jeff. In prior meetings I think that I became equally uncomfortable with the silence, then left the situation. This wasn't helping Jeff. He desperately needs someone to identify with, and although it left him "off the hook," so to speak, I also helped him suppress expression.)

In the discussion that followed the distribution of food, I saw attempts to move into a whole unit as never before. But along with this movement came more frequent intermember criticisms. These criticisms were not really harsh and judging, but more "joking" with underlying attempts to justify individual positions. There was a subtle battle between Randy and Mike over athletic abilities. Mike is smaller but seemingly more knowledgeable about the sport of football. Randy explained his advantage in terms of strength and experience on the midget football team. I want to note that it was not an argument, but more of a "jockeying for position" as suggested in the TACIT approach. Up until this point, each boy seemed to hold an almost equal position in the group with respect to other group members. However, I believe that the need has emerged in each of them to find a somewhat "higher" position.

Ricky also became involved in this jockeying for position, but in a much different way. It is not in his nature to compete in this sense. He is not as conscious of his peers and their recognition. His needs seem to live more with self-recognition. In this meeting, it seems as though he felt the need to become a stronger member, and he acted upon this need. The boys were into a discussion about girls, and Ricky (who seems uninterested in the subject himself) didn't let this hold him back from participating. Instead, his involvement in the conversation was focused on different members, showing that he cared about their "girlfriends." This caring and being interested in other members is very real and the other boys realize this. As a result, Ricky constantly gains position — not by artificial means of a type of "proving" method that others employ, but by being himself.

(As all this overt jockeying finally emerged, Darren was overwhelmed. The position that he had found very comfortable was being challenged and he didn't know what to do. Most of the previous clues that Darren had put forth were verbal. But his reaction to others taking over, in a sense, led me to adopt the skill of "interpreting clues of nonverbal language." From Darren's previous behavior, I would have expected him to react to the situation in a much different manner. But as I learn more about the functioning of members within groups, I find that nothing should be based upon mere expectations. So many things happen that initiate deviations from a pattern of behavior. What's more, threatening or uneasy situations can change that behavior altogether.)

(Darren wasn't quiet, but he certainly wasn't as physically and verbally aggressive as he usually is. It was surprising, but I thought that maybe it was just a bad day or that he was becoming comfortable enough with his position that he could just sit back now. But after a while I realized that the lack of communication was a type of communication in itself. I began to understand that his silence indicated (1) that his leader position was being threatened, and also (2) that he was reaching out. After he grasped what was happening [a real withdrawal from the group], he communicated the need to be noticed, reached, and recognized [an artificial form of withdrawal that he probably felt would be manipulative]. Through this experience, I realized that all along I had been using the skill of "identifying patterns of behavior" without really identifying this skill. From the time the group began, I developed an understanding of repetitious forms of behavior. Because I understood Darren's verbal system of communication, it was easy for me to interpret his nonverbal signs and signals).

When the party was over, we decided to go outside to perform the breaking-in exercise. Darren showed deliberate defiance of what everyone else was doing — the simple matter of wearing a coat outside. With arms folded, Darren refused to get his coat. Seeking power and status, he implied that he was tough enough to go without one. I knew that if I let him go through with this, he would have achieved the powerful feeling that he wanted. It would have blocked his recognition of what he was actually feeling, because he would have regained his position in his own mind, not in the group's. I told him that we would not go out until he got his coat. Perceiving his facial expressions, I sensed his feeling that everyone wanted his position of power and leadership, even me. So I portrayed feelings of caring, not authority. I told him that I would feel terrible if he caught a cold and got sick. He looked at me for a few moments, then went to get his coat. We all went outside to do the "breaking-in" exercise. It turned out to be a game of strength and cunning. The underlying question of who was strong enough and smart enough to get in the circle was present. Just as everyone completed his turn, the time was up and we didn't have time to talk about it. Joy told them to think about the exercise until next week.

Meeting 6

(The excitement of the boys as we begin the sessions seems to be increasing with each meeting. This seems to reinforce me. I see the excitement and view it as a very positive channel in which I can work. I am seeing my own role much more clearly with each meeting, which is another thing that determines my effects on the group. I really believe that I am growing and learning through this experience, just as they are. I am providing them with help and direction; they are giving me feedback that serves as a basis for my continued help and direction.)

The boys were so excited that we had some trouble getting started. The boys were playfully pushing each other all over the room. They were running around, laughing, and having a good time with each other. All except Chris. He was standing high on a bookshelf, alone, at a corner of the room. He didn't seem very interested in what the other members of the group were doing. (At that moment I realized that I had possibly been ignoring Chris, unintentionally. There is something that has been holding Chris back, and I've known this. But just recognizing it is not enough. It is very difficult to get Chris involved in the group, and maybe I've been subconsciously hoping that the group would take the responsibility of doing this. When I saw Chris alone like that, I really felt terrible. Not only would emergence of his feelings and attitudes help him, but he would also be a positive contribution to the whole group. I had noticed this in the very beginning but failed to act on it. As a result, Chris is not getting very much from the group. And even though the members like him, they are not getting as much as they could from him. As I realized this today, I found that it is my fault, and I learned something very important about group work. It seems as though it is very easy to pick up on what certain members do and say. Some of them are simply easier to understand; even some members with negative feelings give adequate feedback upon which the worker can proceed. But then you have a member in your group who is much more difficult. You feel for that person and care very much, but he is very hard to understand. You want to take that person somewhere for the whole hour and concentrate on what is wrong. But that is not group work.)

(All along, I have been working very hard to prevent dependency on me. Now I realize that I have become dependent on group members to help me. It wasn't the most wonderful thing to realize, but I'm glad that I have. Throughout the rest of the meeting, I worked with Chris as I should have before. It was difficult for both of us, but we both accomplished a lot.)

I walked over to where Chris was as Joy waited for the others to get settled. I asked him why he was up there. He said he was up there waiting for everyone to go outside. I asked him to come down with the group. He jumped off the shelves and joined them. I told the boys that we had a lot of plans today and wanted to get a lot done. Chris looked disgusted when we told him our plans to do the same exercise again. No one else seemed very pleased either, but no other suggestions were made. I explained that there was a purpose behind the exercise and asked them to restate the theme. I wanted them to understand how the exercise related to the purpose of the group and asked them to think about how it felt when they couldn't get into the group. They seemed a little curious and started to decide who would go get the coats. (Some of the boys' coats are on the second floor because that is where their classroom is.) We have established a rule that only one boy gets everyone's coats. Randy and Mike were having a little battle over who was going to go. They were both begging with me to be the one to get the coats. I asked them to decide between themselves. They couldn't decide and the others were getting impatient, so I put my keys behind my back and told them to choose a hand. They were both satisfied with their choice; Mike won, and Randy took it well.

It was cold, so the exercise was a fast one and we all ran into the school together. Everyone helped to push the desks back so we could make room for our circle. We began with the go-around technique, asking each boy to take his turn expressing how he felt first being outside of the group, then becoming a part of it. Ricky and Mike said they felt mad when no one would let them in. Ricky said he was mad because he liked to be in the group more than being outside. Darren said he felt bad because he was cold and it was warmer in the group. Then he thought some more and added that he liked to be a part of the group. Chris had trouble as he usually does when asked about his feelings. He didn't have too much to say. Jeff is really coming out of his shell a lot more now. It takes a while for him to express himself. Sometimes that expression becomes suppressed because others get impatient and start moving around, uncomfortable with his silence. When this happened today, Joy and I reminded them of the ground rule "speak as I," and immediately went back to Jeff. It was really wonderful how Jeff responded to this. Instead of forgetting or losing grasp of what he was saying before, he looked at us and continued. (He is developing much more self-confidence in the group and is very happy about this. I believe he is finally understanding that he is an equal member. I was so glad to see this, because as I mentioned earlier, I have been trying to help him by showing that I won't let go when he has something to say. He understands this now and is also dealing with those silent moments when he collects his thoughts.)

(Randy has really overcome the need for my attention, and because of this he is relating to the other members in a much more positive way. For a while, I thought that some hostility was developing toward me. But now he accepts my role; he seems to accept everyone else's role and, most important, his own. I treated Randy in such a way that he understood the importance of equality in the group. He saw that even though I didn't give all my attention to him, I didn't give it all to anyone else either.)

After we finished talking about the exercise, I immediately proposed the idea of a fantasy. (I have learned that there needs to be some structure in the meetings, especially when dealing with this age group. They can, for the most part, deal with silence; but if Joy and I would sit there with no specific purpose in mind, they would detect this, I'm sure. It has happened before and I've learned through those experiences. In fact, this meeting was a very good one because we adopted the subtheme and planned to work on it. We didn't have to fight, so to speak, to direct them away from physical activities. The structure that we had was not an authoritative device. We suggested procedures and they had every opportunity not to accept them.)

I told them that no one could talk during the exercise and asked them to close their eyes and think about the group at this moment. I told them to remember what it was like before we had our group. I gave them many things to think about, such as what they would be doing at that time on Tuesday morning, how they felt about other members before we were together as a group, and so on. Then I asked them to remember the first meeting and what they were feeling then, and also how their feelings might have changed with each meeting. In ending, I brought them back to the group as it was, asking them to think awhile about what they have learned about themselves and others in the group.

What followed proved to be a very meaningful experience for all of us. The boys understood the fantasy much more than I had imagined they would. Everyone seemed very content to listen to others' explanations of what they thought about the fantasy. Ricky said that Joy and I were showing how nice it is to care about people. Everyone agreed, as Chris put his head on the floor. I asked Chris if he was learning anything and he just shook his head. I said, "What are you learning, Chris?" and he said that he learned to know everyone better. (When Chris is asked a question about his feelings, he becomes very uncomfortable. He usually bites his lip and looks around a lot. He is also relieved when his turn is over as we go on around the circle. He hasn't been verbally contributing anything in the sense of commenting on subjects that we discuss, unless it is his turn or he is asked.)

Everyone was talking about what they were learning about the group, paying attention to the "speak as I" ground rule, but Chris was just lying on the floor with his head down again. I took advantage of a moment of silence and reached for Chris, saying, "Aren't you interested in what we are discussing, Chris?" He said, "Yeah, I am." I asked him why he hardly ever looked at people when they were talking, and he shrugged his shoulders. For a long time I used the skill of "getting with the other's feelings." I was truly empathetic with Chris, I could feel his uneasiness, and this time I was going to work at bringing those feelings to the surface by helping him understand them. I said that I could understand why he wouldn't want to talk or comment if he didn't like what we were discussing or if he didn't like the group experience. He said no, that wasn't true. He didn't know what was wrong. As I tried to get at Chris's feelings, I used the skill of "making the problem the group's." I said, "Now I could be wrong: Does anyone else think that Chris is quiet a lot?" Everyone responded to this by acknowledging Chris's behavior. I suggested that maybe we could all help him understand why he didn't feel like getting into the group. I explained that he was part of the group and if one part of the group is troubled, it will affect the whole group. I stated my skill to them: "We are going to make this one problem, the group's problem, so that we can all help Chris." Everyone responded in a very positive way, truly concerned about Chris.

Now Chris was looking up at the clock and moving around uncomfortably. I moved down into the same position that Chris was in. Everyone followed; we were all lying on our stomachs, very close together. The group was ready to tackle the problem. Chris sensed everyone's sincerity, and everyone was silent as he felt that concern. I asked him if this was his usual behavior, wanting to know if he acted like this in school. Everyone answered "no" for him, and he smiled. Apparently, his behavior in school was completely the opposite. But he slowly implied that the school situation doesn't call for a projection of feelings. Then I realized that his withdrawal from the group had come about mostly in the last meetings when we were engaging in activities other than physical sports. He is comfortable in those situations, has confidence in himself, and knows that others accept him. His fears of intimacy seem to stem mainly from his need for someone to reach out and help him express the closeness and good feelings that he evidently has toward group members. I also believe that another factor affecting his behavior is his age. (He is 13; the others are 10.) In many ways the other members look up to him, his physical abilities, and his age. Because of the great influence of peers, someone with this image must find it very difficult to admit feeling hurt, disillusioned, or frustrated.

Someone asked him what he does outside of school, and he started explaining how he stands in front of Kentucky Fried Chicken and waits for them to close every night. The people who work there give him free chicken that they haven't sold.

At first it was very painful for Chris to know that he was, in a sense, in the "limelight" of the group experience. But as he talked, he became more comfortable and feelings came out about how much he appreciated what the restaurant staff did for him.

He had desperately needed the reassurance from the group that he belonged, and I could feel his happiness that everyone was listening and caring. He went on to say that a new boy was coming into their class, and we all talked about how it would feel to be a newcomer. (We related this to being outside of a group and then being accepted.)

Something very wonderful had happened to Chris, and he began talking with group members about everything that was brought up. There was little direction needed in the following discussions, because they were all very happy that we had helped someone in the group. No one mentioned going outside at all. It was almost as if I were sitting there watching them gradually move into a cohesive unit. It was a unique experience for me. I had such good feelings at that moment, that I knew if I didn't share them with the group, I would be holding in a very needed expression. I told them that I felt very good about the group and that they made me feel very happy. I explained that I thought they were grasping the purpose of the experience.

Many members started talking, including Chris. Darren also had something to offer at that moment, and he apparently felt that he had been interrupted. He started to yell very angrily about how it wasn't fair, defending himself with our ground rule. He said that we had made a rule to talk one at a time and it wasn't fair because he was being interrupted. He kept repeating this; Joy and I permitted him to express his anger. I didn't say anything until he finished, arms folded intentionally, and everyone agreed. Darren has a habit of violating the ground rule himself, but then he remembers it and lets the person go on. I reminded him of this, not by way of throwing the situation on him but in order to bring to his attention that sometimes interruptions are accidents. He agreed with this, stating that he does it unintentionally. But all of a sudden, the entire blame went to Chris. Darren said it was his fault; he was the guilty person who didn't want Darren to talk, and he began to call Chris all sorts of names. (Both lived in the "projects," as did the majority of group members. Darren's family was among a few Caucasian families who lived there.)

This was a very intense moment, and everyone was quiet. We had just done something meaningful for Chris (Darren was very helpful in that), and now someone was overtly attacking him. I was pleased at how Chris handled the whole situation. The confidence he had obtained just minutes before seemed to be very real. He was most expressive in telling Darren that he hadn't meant to interrupt, asking him to go ahead and proceed with what he wanted to say. Darren refused, telling us to look at Chris and his big white teeth. He certainly was trying everything. The concern that he had shown for Chris was seen as a threat to Darren. He hasn't felt comfortable with the quality that everyone else is feeling. His role as leader could be very helpful to the group if he would only understand that "leading" doesn't mean running the show. I really want to help him with this, and I tried very hard to explain the equality of each member, how everyone was just as important, and so on.

Just then, all the kids from the other groups started to come into the room. Every member in the group yelled at them to go away for a few minutes. They were very involved with the problem and very united. Chris walked over and stood beside Darren. The time factor bothered me and I wanted so much to be able to resolve the conflict. But I knew that I had to leave the problem with Darren and Chris. We decided that we could talk about the conflict next week. Darren said that he wanted that.

SUMMARY

This stage brings on a crisis of power and control in the group. Members seek positions, statuses, and roles for themselves to influence the allocation of group resources and norms that protect their fears of losing security. The group tends to stylize, and some members get their needs met at the expense of others. Frequently, work is avoided or evaded and members are constricted in their inability to confront the taboo of the authority theme.

We need to function highly as provider and processor and only moderately as catalyst and director to help the group through this stage. The skills for assuming these functions effectively include responding to feelings and content in a personalizing manner, illuminating process, activating the here-and-now, sharing our own feelings, reaching behind conflicts and decisions, reaching for feelings and perceptions, encouraging work, and invoking the contract. These skills can enable members to be aware of their conflicts and needs and the hurts and putdowns of others, and to compare these processes with their contract and goals. Members can risk moving from the security of trust in structure and toward the trust in each other as people. This discovery recommits members to each other and to the group's purpose, empowers more personally and interpersonally, and initiates the intimacy stage.

CRITICAL INCIDENTS

Critical Incident 4

Subtheme.   Being Responsible for Ourselves

Context of Incident.   This event occurred during the early part of the third meeting. The social worker had begun the meeting by stating the subtheme "Being Responsible for Ourselves" and asked members to take a few moments to think about this theme. When discussion was encouraged, a long, uneasy silence ensued. Then one member who appeared especially tense during the silence turned to the practitioner.

Choice Point

CHERYL: "I'm getting frustrated. I thought you were supposed to start us off and tell us what to do — otherwise, I don't know what to say. We're getting nowhere this way."

The group turns to observe the practitioner's reaction.
What would you do at this point? What is your rationale for this response?

Suggested Response.   The practitioner might use four skills here: (1) personalizing the content, feelings, and goals of Cheryl; (2) gently encouraging work; (3) relating the there-and-then to the here-and-now; and (4) illuminating the current authority crisis in the group process: "I certainly sense your frustration and anger at me, Cheryl. I guess you've had these feelings toward me before in the group and you'll probably have them again. You're mad at me, Cheryl, because apparently I haven't lived up to your expectations. You are used to leaders in groups—especially adults—telling you what to do, and you expect that from me. However, I see us working differently in this group. The subtheme for this meeting is Being Responsible for Ourselves, which I think requires you to be your own leader in this group. This may be difficult for you, as I'm sure it is for others. One of the major issues I see present in our group at this time is authority. My refusal to tell you all exactly what to do where seems to have a great effect on what is happening in our group. Maybe some other members would like to comment on this."

Rationale. This response legitimizes the genuine expression of feelings of Cheryl and these feelings in other members of the group. It brings to the surface the underlying issues of leadership, authority, and expected roles. It also invites further expression of these feelings and exploration of these issues. This processing is essential for members' increased awareness of the evolving structure and the opportunity to work more autonomously and responsibly in the group.

Critical Incident 5

Subtheme. Being Responsible for Ourselves

Context of Incident. This critical incident emerged soon after the previous one in the third meeting. The group was attempting to make a decision on its own as to what to discuss for the remainder of the meeting. During the tentative discussion, several members looked closely at the social worker, apparently attempting to see if he approved of the suggested topics. Some of the more aggressive members began to seek concrete rules to follow.

Choice Point

STEVE (TURNING TO SOCIAL WORKER): "How should we decide what to talk about—by majority vote, or should we have everyone agree?"

CHRIS: "Yeah, and after we make our decision, I'd like to know if you agree with it or go along with it!"

The group now sits silently waiting for your response, apparently in agreement with these two members.

What would you do at this point? What is your rationale for this response?

Suggested Response. The skill used here is reaching behind decisions: "You are asking me how to make decisions in this group. And yet (with a sense of humor in voice), you have decided that I can decide this, that my ideas count more than others' about this. I wonder if you want to count all members' ideas and how you will know you have counted them. You know this is the first decision we have talked about as a decision, but we have been making them all along."

Rationale.   On the surface, this incident is a straightforward request for information; yet substantive issues deserve recognition. Members are revealing underlying orientations toward leadership and authority, evidencing some dependent and counter-dependent behavior in relation to making decisions. The event also reflects some members assuming more power and control over the group and checking this position against the control of the practitioner. The response, therefore, must reinforce that the group belongs to the members, that they need to determine how to make decisions. However, the practitioner asks only that they consider who they are counting in their decisions and that they be conscious of how these decisions are made.

Critical Incident 6

Subtheme.   Being Responsible with Others

Context of Incident.   This happened during the early part of the fourth meeting. Two members have been building up, but suppressing, their anger at each other as they have resented each other's attempts to gain leadership in the group. They now exchange these hostilities as the group experiences a tense silence, seemingly immobilized by the confrontation.

Choice Point

CHRIS: "When Steve said that, I got mad as hell. You really piss me off, Steve!"

STEVE: "Well, I couldn't care less what you think, Chris! Why don't you just shut up and keep your opinions to yourself!"

The two continued to exchange angry looks while the group fell into an uneasy silence.

What would you do at this point? What is your rationale for this response?

Suggested Response.   Two skills are most useful here: illumination of process, and reaching behind conflicts. "I believe we are more aware of the tension that has been building between you, Chris, and you, Steve, than our silence lets on. This conflict has been really brewing between you. There are strong feelings and we are stuck, perhaps afraid, as to whether we wish to respond to them. We have feelings about Chris and Steve, and what went on between them. I believe we can stay with them and share our feelings and ideas if Chris and Steve would talk to each other, to respond aloud and tell each other what they think about what they have said to each other."

Rationale.   This response relates to the surface issue of hostile feelings between two group members, but it also challenges the group's immobilization in the face of interpersonal conflict. The conflict is made the group's, yet some direction is given to promoting a fuller, more authentic interchange between Chris and Steve. Finally, the illumination suggests that members can provide insight into the nature of the conflict and, in turn, develop more insight into the current obstacles to power and control in the group.

chapter 9

Intimacy Stage: Closeness Themes

Muzafer Sherif (1936) did classic studies on how group norms were created by members in their interaction and were internalized in behavior outside of the group. He ingeniously used the perceptual phenomenon known as "autokinetic effect." This means that a fixed point of light, when viewed in total darkness, appears to move spontaneously. Sherif used the autokinetic effect and asked participants—first individually, then with the same individuals in a fairly cohesive group, and again individually—to judge the amount of movement. Once the group decided how much the light moved, this norm persisted in the individual members' second evaluation of the perceived movement. Sherif's conclusion, supported by other significant research (Newcomb, 1961; Festinger, 1954), is that cohesive groups significantly define a social reality against which members test and change their personal realities. Such consensual validation in cohesive groups is a powerful force for change.

Solomon Asch (1956), in turn, did classic studies on how the power of the group related to conformity. Asch, who was an unusually independent person, was born in Poland in 1907, arrived in the United States at age 13, and completed his Ph.D. degree from Columbia University at age 25. It has been said that it took the least conformant of social psychologists (Asch himself) to defend conformity to group consensus and pressure as an underlying basis of trust in social life. At the same time, his studies point out that conformity can obstruct individual autonomy and learning from difference.

Asch asked participants in groups of 3 to 15 members to choose which of several lines came closest in length to a line they had just seen. There was obviously only one right answer. Many participants agreed to the group's consensual answer, which they privately saw as wrong. In other words, they would go along to get along, agreeing with an erroneous group judgment even when they knew it to be false. Obviously, cohesion does not equal synergy.

INTRODUCTION

The intimacy stage increases the power of the cohesive group to change members' constructs of reality. It represents a movement toward synergy — the combination of the strengths of individual members and the group-as-a-whole to use resources on behalf of each other's needs. Yet it is still not the evolution of mutual aid. In such interdependence, both consensus and autonomy flower.

The intimacy stage evolves from the resolution of the overt and covert conflicts over power and control and the revision of early group structure. Members move from tentative involvement in the group and the establishment of structural fences to protect them from the catastrophic expectations of the exposure that they fear. The wishes for closeness — for knowing others and being known authentically, for understanding and being understood — begin to motivate behavior in the group. The "I" attaches its identity to the "We," and members initiate discussion of the "It" in terms of these here-and-now "I-We" processes.

Cohesion becomes the glue for spontaneous interaction and support and the impetus for the challenge of work in the group's real agenda of interpersonal relationships and socioemotional needs. As Irvin Yalom (1995) has noted in his research and theory of group cohesiveness, it is the sine qua non for members' learning. Cohesiveness in the group process is analogous to relationship in individual helping. It is the heat that melts the iron. However, although the iron is hot, somebody must shape the horseshoe. The group develops a cohesion that ultimately moves from (1) the comfort of being part of the whole, to (2) support for risking honest and open self-disclosure and feedback. It seeks the differences that are so vital to interdependence and mutual aid — to growth.

In this evolving closeness many members may discover for the first time the potential to care about others and to be cared for. The newness of this experience for members — the very experience that makes the group such a powerful medium for change and growth — does produce some awkward and tentative trials of self-disclosure and feedback. In fact, this stage frequently begins with an impasse. The impasse is a period in which the group is stuck and somewhat immobilized. It has given up the old security of hierarchical structure without trusting the new support of authentic concern and interaction. Often, for one brief and dramatic moment, or for a total meeting or two, the group seems to regress to the preaffiliation stage and early trust themes. In one sense, they have. They start over. This beginning is marked, however, by an underlying warmth and respect that is so obvious to all members that the group structure is "buried" with little effort and the group is "reborn" in its transformation to cohesive trust. The doubts for closeness are quickly relieved. The buds of confidence find sunshine in the group's capacity to stay with each member, understand, and help. This confidence flowers in full bloom. The group basks in its glow. The basis of relationships moves from control to contact; from the power of positions, statuses, and roles to the power of care and concern.

INDIVIDUAL PROCESS

Each member's questions about the "I," the "We," and the "It" in this stage relate to disclosure, closeness, and cohesiveness. In relation to the "I," each member experiences such questions as:

"What can I do to allow these others to know me?"

"How can I communicate what I am experiencing and who I think I am — both the good and bad?"

"How can I overcome my fears of being known to achieve my wishes for being known?"

"How can I contribute to the needs of others that I am discovering?"

In relation to the "We," each member asks such questions as:

"How can I get to know others better?"

"How can I contribute to developing the trust that they need in order to be more honest with me?"

"What will others do to keep this warmth alive?"

In relation to "It" (the practitioner and/or content of the experience), each member wonders:

"When we get honest will he/she be able to protect me and others from getting hurt?"

"Will she/he push us toward more disclosure than we are ready for?"

"Will our discussion lead to so much difference among members that we lose this togetherness?"

"How will we handle the deep problems and feelings that are likely to be shared with us?"

"Can we draw a line between what we handle responsibly and what is too much for us to deal with without anyone being too hurt?"

Members manifest these questions in their risks of self-disclosure and feedback and in their attempts to protect and rescue members whom they perceive may be hurt by exposing more than the group can understand. They assert similarities before differences and are wary of conflicts that threaten cohesiveness. Yet they open up the structure and communication for needs to be shared. From their underlying caring, they discover that conflicts are inherent in the inevitable differences and that these differences are basic to authentic interdependence and mutual aid. They begin to accept both their own autonomy (difference) and interdependency (union with others), not as opposites but as connected poles in the process of growth and development.

GROUP PROCESS

In this stage of the formative group, the theme of intimacy comes to the fore-front. The members' attraction for the group, significance attached to it, and strong feelings of bond in its "We-ness" constitute cohesiveness. As during auton-omy, covert (and often overt) conflicts are resolved in the interest of relating as people rather than as roles; through this, the group gradually evolves into a cohe-sive unit. All members come into, or are directly offered the opportunity to come into, the group. They all share some degree of equal importance to each other and to the group as a whole. Morale increases. So does commitment to the group's purpose, goals, and tasks. This commitment includes a deeper invest-ment in the agenda of dealing with the group's human relations in the service of needs and goals.

A different level of trust is established. Whereas initial trust was based on shared goals and a predictable structure, trust now entails a feeling that other mem-bers can care for each other. Mutual trust grows in people and resources rather than in structural power and control. This trust is an impetus for spontaneous self-disclosures. Members especially disclose their feelings of closeness and their here-and-now responses to the interaction (i.e., their feedback). The group becomes a group in the deepest sense of the concept when absent or silently withdrawn mem-bers are really missed for the first time. The group begins to say to itself and to members who have not been previously central to the process, "We're O.K. We have something special to offer to each other."

Even though a mutual aid system is developing for meeting closeness needs, the group does tend to suppress feelings that may produce conflict. Compared to the previous stage, there is a calm after the storm. Interaction seems to be all sweet-ness and light at first, as the group basks in the glow of its newly discovered unity. Eventually, however, the group's embrace will seem superficial and ritualistic unless authentic differences are permitted to emerge.

The content tends to dovetail with the process. The themes reflect here-and-now feelings and concerns. The "I-We-It" seems more balanced, as what is discussed relates more to what is being experienced at the moment in the group. The topics especially relate to intimacy needs and relationships outside of the group.

Some initial conflicts may arise in these discussions. Often, however, these con-flicts reflect problems with intimacy, not with power. For instance, jealousies that underlie the surface conflicts are those related to closeness, not to status. The group responds to these conflicts and supports initial risks but tends to smooth them over quickly in the interest of cohesiveness.

The group begins to allocate statuses in this stage on the basis of who embod-ies the norms of honesty and openness in self-disclosure and feedback. The "good member" is perceived as one who helps the group by taking risks in expressing here-and-now feelings. All members are respected as belonging, however, and the difficulties in risking tend to be appreciated as well. The recommitment to stated group purpose and themes and the discovery of how members may help each other toward more mutual aid lead them to renegotiate the contract. The group now knows what it can accomplish. It can autonomously incorporate its own model for effective participation and group functioning into its contract. This contract, as renegotiated, often serves as the springboard for the group's entry into Differentiation/Interdependence.

HELPING PROCESS

The group's task is to use cohesiveness to develop authentic closeness and mutual aid. Our parallel task is to enable the self-disclosure and feedback that contributes to closeness and intermember help. We function as a catalyst and provider with moderate use of directing and processing. The catalyzing skills include modeling self-disclosure and feedback, encouraging intermember contact, and reaching for empathic feedback. The providing skills are the personalizing ones presented in Chapter 8, as well as those of genuineness and confrontation. Directing entails following the leads of members and using the skills of clarifying purpose and renegotiating the contract. For processing, we need to detect and challenge the obstacles to work, especially during the early impasses of this stage, and to illuminate the process by relating there-and-then concerns to here-and-now process when members themselves do not make these connections.

Skills

Modeling Self-Disclosure and Feedback. The members seek ways of being known and getting to know others and of building the trust for free-flowing interaction. The procedures for meeting these needs in group process are self-disclosure and feedback. When we model these skills, we are providing useful tools for members. A helpful model for understanding the procedures of self-disclosure and feedback and their contribution to group process is the Johari Window (Luft, 1970). In fact, the Johari Window can be presented to the group to catalyze members' finding ways to interact on behalf of their needs and goals. This "window" is depicted in Figure 9.1.

The "window" is divided into four "panes" representing the dimensions of "known or unknown to self" and "known or unknown to others." Any single person in the group, or any single group event, can be characterized by these four quadrants. What is known both to the self and to others (Open Area of Quadrant 1) increases trust. However, members often have had impact on others without knowing how others have experienced them. In other words, the impact as experienced by others is "known to others" but "unknown to self" (Blind Area of Quadrant 2). Then, too, members have aspects of themselves or experiences in the group that have not been shared. This content is "known to self" but "unknown to others" (the Hidden Area of Quadrant 3). Finally, there are forces at work in the here-and-now that may be largely unconscious; that is, they are "unknown to both self and others" and likely will remain as such (the Unknown Area of Quadrant 4).

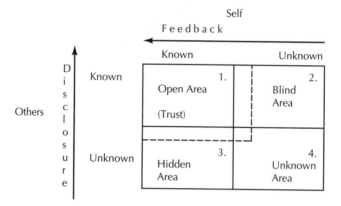

FIGURE 9.1 Johari window

In any interpersonal systems that promote growth, trust is basic. This process is particularly true of our practice groups. The increase of trust demands the enlargement of the Open Area of Quadrant 1 and the shrinking of the Blind and Hidden Areas of Quadrants 2 and 3. This alteration of the panes of the Johari Window, the central trust process in the group, requires disclosure and feedback. Self-disclosure extends the Open Area by shrinking the Hidden Area (depicted by the arrow extending alongside Quadrant 3 to Quadrant 1). Feedback enlarges the Open Area by diminishing the Blind Area (depicted by the arrow extending from Quadrant 2 to Quadrant 1). The surest way of opening up trust and empathy in the group is for members to exchange self-disclosure (reducing the Hidden Area) and feedback (reducing the Blind Area). As members give ("disclose") and receive feedback, they increase the opportunity for trust and for open, free-flowing communication.

We model these procedures for establishing trust by disclosing our own feelings and by providing feedback to members and the group through sharing observations, perceptions, and interpretations. To serve as a model, our feedback needs to reflect the principles for effective feedback in groups and other interpersonal systems. The principles are as follows:

1. *Feedback must stem from a concern for the other and a desire to improve your relationship with him, her, or the group.* We are most open with those we care about (Carkhuff, 1969). From this concern, feedback aims to create a shared understanding of the particular relationship. Moreover, if we give feedback, we should be ready to receive it in return.
2. *Feedback should be descriptive rather than evaluative, whenever possible.* Feedback should be more the message of "This is how your (specific) behavior affects me" rather than "You are a manipulator." In this sense, effective feedback focuses on the nature of observed and perceived behavior rather than on the inferred nature of the person. We share observations rather than inferences. As much as possible, we need to suspend our judgments to permit

unclouded observations. In addition, we can best give feedback in terms of "more or less" rather than in terms of "either-or." Then we can describe behavior in terms of quantity and patterns rather than in terms of quality or judgments. Judgments come out in terms of good or bad, right or wrong, nice or not nice. Descriptions and observations reflect a continuum of measurement of the meaning of behavior: high participation/low participation; often directs comments to practitioner rather than group/seldom directs comments directly to practitioner; and so on. An example of effective descriptive feedback is: "This is the third time in this meeting that I noticed you changing the subject when someone was talking about something potentially powerful for them. You seem to be trying to avoid this pain or to protect others and the group from experiencing it. I'm not sure this is helpful to the group at this time. I wonder what is going on for you inside about our dealing with painful topics and about what I am saying to you now."

3. *Feedback should be specific rather than general.* The focus on description rather than evaluation and on behavior rather than the person, as in the above example, helps to keep feedback specific. So does the focus on the here-and-now rather than the there-and-then." The message above was put into such terms as: "This is the third time in this meeting . . ."; not in terms of "Do you always avoid painful topics with others?" The potential for feedback to improve the relationship and to be meaningful to the receiver increases when it is tied to place and time, especially the here-and-now.

4. *Feedback should be well timed.* The focus on actual time and place helps feedback to be timed more appropriately. Timing is especially appropriate when feedback is given as close in time as possible to the actual occurrence that is described. Timing is particularly destructive when observations and feelings (especially resentful ones) are accumulated over a period of time and then are dumped all at once: not, "I have been concerned from the beginning of this group about your . . ." but, "Just now while Jill and I were talking, you . . ."

5. *Feedback should be directed toward behavior that the receiver can do something about.* This principle reflects the aim of feedback to be helpful to the receiver and the relationship, not destructive. Included in this principle is the choice of the amount of information given. How much information we give needs to be based on what the person (or group) receiving it can use rather than on the amount we might like to give. For instance, we do not give feedback on the group's size being a deterrent to its interaction, when the group has already been formed and the current size cannot be modified. Nor do we share an informed dissertation about the theory of group size in relation to interactional problems. Instead, we can note that several members have commented in this meeting about the group being experienced as too large for them and therefore serving as an obstacle to their participation. We can then ask the group how it might deal with this perceived obstacle to break down some of this barrier for members.

6. *Feedback should be checked out.* In the group there are two useful ways of checking out feedback to ensure accuracy and communication. The first involves asking receivers to paraphrase what they heard in the feedback. The second involves asking other members whether the feedback makes sense to them (i.e., fits their impressions and opinions of their perceived and described behavior). Feedback that is most useful in the group is that which is more consensual, or shared by others.

There are two ways in which effective feedback is shared: by describing one's own feelings ("I feel hurt by what you just said"; "I like what I saw you doing just now"), and by describing one's own perception of the other's behavior ("You cut in before I finished my sentence"). When feelings are shared, it is important that they be recognized and expressed as temporary and capable of change, not as permanent attitudes. Compare: "At this point I'm irritated with you" with "I dislike you and I always will." When we take the risk to share feelings in such a way that others may get angry or hurt and put these in the temporary terms that more accurately reflect the meaning, members can discover the value of feedback designed to increase mutual trust. They may be more ready to move beyond their fears of their own feelings as destructive to themselves and others and to risk acceptance of their central place in the close, authentic, and interdependent relationships that we all so desperately need. The group is on its way to becoming "real." It is ready to invite this realness from all its members.

Encouraging Intermember Contact.   We can catalyze intermember contact by encouraging the use of ground rules, directing messages to the intended recipient, and amplifying the expression of the feeling component in intermember communication. Ground rules that especially aid members to make contact with each other are "speak as I," "speak to individuals," and "own our interaction." The skills and techniques for establishing and reinforcing these ground rules are most useful. The group in Closeness has rediscovered purpose and increases its motivation for tapping mutual aid resources. It is frequently very ready to intensify the use of norms that can be explicated through these ground rules.

When we direct messages to the intended recipient, we listen to the "I-You" aspect of "We," "They," or "the Group" communication. We encourage members to consider to whom their messages are specifically directed and to try to use more direct communication to meet their needs. The person who notes that "We have been getting very close to each other in the group" is encouraged to express this experience more directly: "To whom do you feel very close in the group? Can you tell them this and what it means to you?" and "To whom do you feel less close in the group right now but would like to be closer to? Can you tell them directly, face to face, what you are feeling and what you want?"

Amplifying the feeling component of interaction between and among members includes reaching for more concreteness in the general feelings expressed, helping members get in touch with the feeling component of their reactions to others, and suggesting activities that increase the nonverbal expression of feelings toward other members. To amplify general feelings, we can ask directly what these may be: "You told John you thought he didn't like you. How does this perception of your relationship with him make you feel about yourself and him? Can you tell him this?" We can help members get in touch with these feelings more by asking them to take the time to tune in to what they are experiencing: "John and Mary, are you willing to try something right now to help you get more in touch with your feelings about each other? Close your eyes and imagine the two of you at each end of a football field, walking toward each other in the middle. As you walk toward each other in your imagination, focus on the other and then become aware of what you are feeling. . . . As you get closer and can see each other better, do these feelings change? . . . What feelings do you have when you get toe to toe and nose to nose with each other in the middle of the field? . . . Now open your eyes, look at each other, and share whatever you wish about what you experienced in this fantasy."

Finally, a frequent dynamic of this stage, when members are feeling closeness toward each other, involves (1) the spontaneous impulse to make physical contact with each other — to touch — but (2) the repression of this impulse because of the social taboo that relates touch to sexual intimacy. With our encouragement, members can find some freedom from the restriction of this taboo for communicating nonsexual intimacy and feelings. The norms for touch and physical contact can be reformed: "John, you felt like giving Mary a hug. Why don't you?" "Jill, I want to hug you right now. Can I?" In the previous fantasy activity with John and Mary, we might intensify the emotional contact by having them stand at opposite sides of the room, walk toward each other in silence, and allow things to happen *nonverbally* when they meet in the middle. All these skills can enable members of the group to make the emotional contact with each other that grows out of and increases initial closeness — and that members very much need at this stage.

Reaching for Empathic Feedback.   When members in the group express intense here-and-now feelings, these churn in the guts of other members (Anderson, 1980a). The chords that are struck are the basis for spontaneous empathic responses. However, members frequently are thrown by the intensity of what these feelings stir up in themselves. Especially during the early part of this stage, they may fear the intensity and honesty of their own reactions and be embarrassed about expressing their responses. We can catalyze this most empathic emotional connection by reaching for these responses.

The skill at this time is really rather easy. Members are more ready than not to share their own feelings as stimulated by those expressed, and they are drawn toward those who have expressed such intense feelings. They wait for permission. We grant this permission and extend an invitation by noting: "We have reacted greatly to Jack's pain/joy/grief/fear (or whatever). I can sense we have been drawn to him. I think it would be helpful for him and for us if we share some of our reactions with him." Most often this comment, or a similar one that invites response, stimulates a great deal of empathic feedback and self-disclosure in relation to the theme of the feelings expressed. In these moments the members often experience their humanity and its connection with all humans most fully, especially in relation to those in the group. They trust the salve of this humanity to heal their wounds. They learn the power of bearing pain for growth when one does not have to suffer alone.

Genuineness.   Chief among the providing skills during Closeness are the personalizing ones that were discussed in Chapter 8. These include personalizing meanings, problems, feelings, and goals. Another skill that enables the group by providing support during Closeness is genuineness. Genuineness is authenticity—the ability to be honest with others. Our words, in short, are closely related to our feelings. Robert Carkhuff (1969) writes about the relationship of the skill of genuineness to such elements as warmth and respect in these words: "In addition to constituting a necessary dimension of the experiential base and indeed the goal of helping, one of the potentially critical dimensions of genuineness is the respect it communicates—we are most genuine with whom we care most" (p. 181). He also conveys the relationship of genuineness to self-disclosure: "Although a helper may be genuine and not self-disclosing or self-disclosing and not genuine, frequently, and particularly at the extremes, the two are related" (p. 187). Our genuineness invites more closeness in the group. If other members recognize our sincerity, they will risk greater genuineness themselves. The bond of genuine closeness increases the odds for the group's dealing with the real needs and concerns of members, not just those deemed safe or socially acceptable. We are genuine when our verbal and nonverbal communication is congruent, when it reflects our here-and-now experience, when it includes both positive and negative feelings, and when it risks challenging our relationship with the group or with particular members.

Genuineness is "selective authenticity" (Cohn, 1972). What is "selective" about it is our focus on the group's purpose and/or theme and how "It" relates to ourselves as an "I" in the "I-We-It" interaction. In other words, we share those parts of our own life and here-and-now experiences that *relate to the purpose and/or theme.* This keeps our genuineness related to the parallel task and does not pull us into entering the group as a member for the purpose of meeting our own needs. To be genuine and yet to accomplish the parallel task of enabling group members to meet each other's needs, we may use the ground rule of "disturbances come first." When we find ourself disturbed by a there-and-then situation, especially during this stage when it does not spark the power and control conflicts, we can share the disturbance with the group. Confrontation of the disturbance in the here-and-now usually serves us, as it does members, to move beyond it toward more effective functioning in the group. This selective authenticity does tend to promote more equality and closeness in the group. Again, as members experience us as a person with a function rather than a symbol of power authority, they are more ready to experience themselves and others in the same way. In brief, genuineness begets genuineness.

Confrontation.   The skill of confrontation is a special case of feedback. Confrontation is feedback addressed to discrepancies in words and deeds. Through confrontation, we provide the group and/or specific members with a difference to consider in the process of self-awareness and self-evaluation. In effective confrontation, we must feel our own sense of caring and the basic understanding of the other (or at least the desire to understand). Confrontation springs from this empathy. Then we feed back discrepancies and the specific directions in which they lead (Carkhuff,

1969). These elements of confrontation are reflected in the following example of a practitioner's response to a group member. The group member has said, "I really can't make friends here. I think most of the members are out for themselves. They don't care about me." The practitioner confronts: "You say you want to make friends, to get closer to others in this group, yet you seem to be excusing yourself when you find it difficult to reach out to the others here. As long as you make excuses and write them off as not caring, you will feel this emptiness."

This confrontation is best, of course, when the member has actually felt some empathic understanding from us. Although confrontation in itself can be most empathic, the understanding part of the message could increase the use of confrontation in providing an opportunity for self-awareness and self-evaluation. For instance, one could follow the above confrontation with: "You're probably hurt by what I've said, but I believe you really want something different for yourself; and facing this difference between what you are saying and doing here might be helpful. What do you think? Is there any truth that hits home to you in what I've said?" If confrontation of discrepancies increases the other's awareness of specific contradictions, the other can choose to bring behavior more in line with words or wants. The member, or the group, can act in ways that contribute more effectively to meeting needs.

Clarifying Purpose.   We clarify purpose by asking the group to weigh its current interactions against its desires. In short, we note and ask, "This is what we have been doing. Is this what we want to be doing here?" Much of this clarification relates to the leads of the group during Intimacy/Closeness. These leads hint at members' wishes to use the group differently. As the members express their readiness to redefine and recommit themselves to the group's purpose, we make this message explicit and nudge the group to work on stating what they want. For instance, the group that expresses low energy in the beginning of the meeting through difficulty in getting started and through several members' expressing their difficulty in feeling "with" the group today can be asked to shuttle in fantasy between a place outside of the group (there-and-then) that seems to meet their needs and then to the group (here-and-now). This shuttling is encouraged until members discover what is "there and then" that is lacking for them "here and now." Next, they are asked what they want from the here-and-now and how they can make it a more viable place and time to meet their needs.

In clarifying the purpose, we need to be alert to what the group is working on. The major group themes can be brought to the surface through self-disclosure and feedback or through reaching for feedback in the group. Members are asked, "What are we working on?" and "What do you want to work on?" These questions help produce a relevant agenda and energize the group toward activity that is consistent with achieving its clarified purpose or overriding theme.

Renegotiating the Contract.   During the intimacy stage, when members are involved in knowing what the group resources for their needs really are, members not only are more willing and able to clarify purpose but also are ready to renegotiate a more meaningful contract. The contracting skills discussed in Chapter 7 are vital now for this renegotiating. These include clarification of purpose, of roles and responsibility, and of useful ground rules in a simple statement of the purpose, major themes, and relevant subthemes. They also entail the reaching for feedback and making decisions of the contract that are truly consensual reflections of the group's cohesiveness and collective will. The contract at this stage no longer provides a structure for the group to discover its own needs. Conversely, the contract now serves group autonomy. The group can account for its own needs and autonomously develop a structure that promotes the matching of these needs to group resources. Thus, the renegotiated contract operationalizes the group's sense of mutual aid.

Illuminating Process. The skill of illuminating process, which was introduced and presented in Chapter 8, is used in a special sense here. The members themselves tend to carry the processing function during this stage. They often demand staying in the here-and-now and, with little encouragement, self-reflect on their process. Frequently, we can help the group examine whether it has over-restricted the norms of content. Most themes benefit from relating the here-and-now to the there-and-then. Members during Closeness often choose more open content boundaries for addressing this relationship.

When we relate the here-and-now to there-and-then and vice versa, we illuminate the connection of these processes. We might ask the member who shares fears of closeness with friends outside the group to explain whom he or she fears getting close to most (and least) in the group. We might encourage a member who has spontaneously hugged another inside the group to reflect on how she or he might use this behavior in relationships outside the group. We might invite the group, while it basks in the warmth of its cohesiveness, to consider what made a difference in this group so that members discover more of a conceptual framework to initiate and influence closeness in their natural groups in social living. The greatest value of the group experience for members lies in this very ability to relate learnings inside the group to situations outside the group. The group itself will not last forever, but the process and learning it sets off in members may.

Detecting and Challenging Obstacles to Work. A special skill related to closeness themes involves detecting and challenging the obstacles to work (Schwartz, 1971; Shulman, 1992). This skill was discussed in Chapter 8 in relation to the autonomy theme of authority. In Intimacy, we can especially use this skill during the early impasse that marks the transition to this stage and later in relation to the closeness theme.

The major obstacles to work during the impasse are the members' catastrophic expectations and fears as they give up the old belief system of trust in structure and have yet to develop the new one of trust in people. When the environmental supports of group structure and power and control begin to give way to the self-supports of authentic interaction, the members fear a loss of self and are stuck. They seem unsure of where to go or how to get there. We help the group by naming this obstacle ("We seem stuck. I believe we have reached an impasse.") and calling for the experience of both the fears and the wishes ("I wonder what we're afraid of?" and "What is it that you would like to see happening here now, would like to do next, if you weren't afraid?"). Sometimes the group can literally "bury" itself, or have a funeral in which they symbolically reflect an old group culture leaving and a new one being born. In fact, I have found that merely suggesting such an activity in the group is enough for the group to move through its impasse by experiencing it and moving on to a new level of work — even though the group did not pick up on the suggestion and go through with the exercise!

The closeness theme can create an obstacle to work when members hold on so desperately to the warmth and intimacy they are experiencing that they fear the disclosure of authentic differences. So, too, can this theme led to the expectation that we will become a friend and not provide the difference of our parallel task and specific function that at times require specifically encouraging work. In these events, we must detect and challenge the obstacles. We name them or give feedback about our observations; we ask members: "Is this what we want? Is this going to help us achieve your goals?" We can self-disclose: "You have been acting like I wasn't here when I asked you if you were working on what you want to work on. I felt a little silly, like I am out of place. Yet I believe it is important for me to help you by raising the question or I wouldn't have asked. Your reaction leaves me feeling even more that it is important for you to consider if we are going to use the good feelings we have about each other to float along where we are now or to grow together. I really need to ask: Is this what you want? Is this what you're here for?" If we trust the process, we know that members will want to work toward more interdependence and will need little more than periodic nudges to confront the obstacles to this process.

PRINCIPLES FOR THE INTIMACY STAGE

The following principles incorporate these skills as guidelines for the practitioner:

1. We need to provide the difference to hold members to experiencing the impasse that often portends the transition from autonomy to closeness themes.
2. We need to initiate and help members develop the processes of self-disclosure and feedback.
3. We need to help members learn to give and receive empathic feedback through use of the principles for effective feedback.
4. We need to help members to reclarify the group's purpose and major themes, and to renegotiate a contract in which members are more genuinely committed to group goals, selected subthemes, each other, and useful ground rules for achieving their goals. The current "I-We-It" is weighed and evaluated against the wanted "I-We-It," and the group chooses procedures to close the gap between the real and the ideal.

5. We need to help the group get its underlying human relations agenda on the table by encouraging intermember contact, reaching for feelings and empathic feedback, and comparing its contract and needs against the needs and hurts of members.
6. We need to help the group to transfer here-and-now themes to members' there-and-then situations and to activate there-and-then themes in here-and-now process.
7. We need to more freely use our own "selective authenticity" to risk genuineness, self-disclosure, and feedback (as much as is expected of any other member) within the boundary of our function and parallel tasks.
8. We need to reach for the common ground, or similarities in experienced differences, and reach for differences in experienced similarities. Also, we reach for the positive in the negatives and the negatives in the positive.

Example

In the continuing scenario of the group of fifth-graders in school, we find the intimacy stage flowering in Meetings 7 and 8. Facilitation of more authentic autonomy and interdependence in this stage requires more explicit dealing with questions of direction and purpose. The contract can be directly renegotiated. The goals are more feasible to sustain effort and to reinforce emerging hopes for success. More commitment is encouraged for dealing with interpersonal relations as well as the group's purpose and themes. Members are invited toward interdependent mutual aid; interacting with each other as person-to-person rather than as role-to-role; revealing their wishes and fears and asking for and accepting help; and taking responsibility for themselves and others.

Meeting 7

The conflict involving Darren and Chris last week was not yet resolved. As the members sat down in the circle, I could sense that they had not forgotten. This verified my feelings that "We" concerns were beginning to emerge. I opened the meeting by saying, "We have a discussion to finish, if you all remember." Darren, looking unusually embarrassed, said, "I remember." But before focusing completely on Darren, I asked the group to verbally remember what had happened at the close of Meeting 6. (I wanted to include the group when taking up the issue again. After all, I had used the skill of "making the problem the group's," and I felt that it was very important to follow through with this. I thought that my suggestions of the importance of unity would reinforce the individual feelings of "We-ness" that were gradually coming to the surface. Another objective in including the group was to permit Darren to understand group concerns, since he had felt threatened in the last meeting.)

(I have no indication whatsoever that the expressed anger and anxiety have anything to do with any other members or even the group situation itself. Instead, they seem to be stemming from conflicts within Darren himself — unfulfillment of personal needs. As I think about the group in between meetings, I have different views of his behavior. I was completely disillusioned and confused with him at the onset of the group experience. Then he moved into the experience, displaying behavior that actually defined the direction in which the group would move for a while. I have a very strong feeling that he sensed this almost as much as I did.)

(In last week's recording, I expressed the attitude that Darren must learn to differentiate between being a strong but equal member of the group and being one who runs the show. I had to admit to myself since then my perceptions and anger with him at that point. Later on, I realized that Darren's behavior had disrupted and imposed a closing conflict on the meaningful meeting that we had all achieved. But conflicts are meaningful too. Perhaps that is one of the most difficult things for the practitioner with groups to understand. I know now that Darren's anger in no way stopped or stunted our togetherness. It gave us yet another device by which to become united. But that was only secondary. The primary consideration was Darren's feelings. He doesn't want to run the show. Instead, he wants to be reassured, just like every other member, that he is an important part of the group. Especially now, as togetherness is being experienced more and more, each member has the need to contribute to that growing feeling of unity.)

His anger with himself because of feeling threatened was imposed on Chris during the last meeting. From what I observed today, he had begun to understand this. He was embarrassed by last week's behavior and told the group that he still thought it wasn't fair that he had been interrupted. However, this time the blame was shifted toward the situation. No mention was made of Chris being the cause of his anxiety.

I helped Darren deal with his feelings through "redirecting the signal to intended recipient." The attack he was making was on the situation and himself. I helped him realize this by "reaching for feelings" of how he felt during the situation, then pointing out that what he had just expressed was not anger toward Chris but toward the fact that he had been interrupted. (I didn't think it would be wise to come right out and say that I thought he felt threatened.) Instead, I again stressed the equality of group members, and the fact that he was right in saying that the situation was unfair for him (an equal part of the group). This was very successful. He said he now understood that it was an accident, and throughout the rest of the meeting he assumed the more helping role that he had had before.

Darren's insight seemed so genuine that I felt no reservations when pursuing the issue further. Joy also sensed Darren's ability to deal rationally with the conflict, and together we "reached for feelings" from other group members. We asked them what their reactions were at the time when Darren was expressing his anger. This worked out very well. While Darren spoke, they listened intently. Prior to Darren's disclosure, we included the other members in restating what had happened. Now we followed through with this, by indicating that their feelings about the situation were also important.

(The members are now sharing their feelings with increasingly authentic and real expressions.) Ricky immediately offered his feelings, saying, "I was mad at Darren because we helped Chris and then he made him feel bad." He said that the situation also made him feel bad, along with being mad. There were other expressions of feeling bad about what had happened. Randy said that he was upset because Darren kept saying things over and over again, not getting anything accomplished. Darren listened to these comments and reacted beautifully. He didn't see them as an attack and showed no need to defend himself. We concluded that the whole situation was not exactly pleasant for anyone. Through this experience the entire group had a hand in the problem. Darren was helped to understand his own actions, and the group moved yet another step closer together.

Chris seemed more involved than before because of last week's conflict. He was more comfortable when we talked about "group feelings." He still becomes uneasy at certain moments, but his behavior exhibits more real feelings of belonging.

Jeff was quiet for a while in this meeting, and the group jumped at the chance to deal with that also. They pointed out the fact that he was quiet a lot in school. Ricky said that when he went to visit Jeff at home, he wasn't quiet. He also told us that if Jeff went to visit him, he was afraid to go into Ricky's house. Jeff agreed with this and laughed. Then he told us that sometimes he just didn't have anything to say. Even Jeff is feeling much more that he belongs in the group. Though expression is not frequent, it is put forth with less confusion. His explanations of his behavior are moving away from the "I don't know" toward real attempts to bring his feelings into words.

We discussed ideas of things that we could do as a group. Someone suggested singing songs. Everyone agreed, and Chris got the music books. Everyone had a good time singing together, clapping, and laughing at our mistakes. We planned a football game with Don and Audrey's group, but before we went out we pushed the chairs and desks back together. Everyone waited together in the hallway and we had a pep talk. The game was competitive, but they handled it well. We lost, and they handled that even better. Chris said, "We'll get them next time," and everyone ran into the school.

Meeting 8

We formed our circle; everyone very enthusiastic. (I'd like to note the procedure that we have developed in forming the circle. It was Darren's idea, a few meetings ago. Upon his words, "Let's go!" we all hold hands, forming a circle. We remain holding hands, until we all are seated on the floor in our circle. It is beautiful. The feeling of "We-ness" that shines through as we do this is amazing. If someone outside of the group were to enter the room as we join hands to form our circle, it might seem insignificant. But working with the group all these weeks, nothing is small. Everything is so important. As we formed our circle today I took a few moments to reflect upon our meetings, starting from the first. We have come a long way.)

Everyone had a turn at sitting in the middle of the group. Then we used the go-around technique, each member saying one thing that he liked about the person who was sitting in the middle. This exercise worked out so well that it practically lasted throughout the whole meeting. It seems as though the members could go on and on about each other's good qualities. In fact, some of the boys got impatient if the person before them was taking too long. They couldn't wait to have their turn.

I was so happy with Jeff's participation. Ricky was first to go into the circle and Jeff listened intently, watching Ricky being in the center. I was surprised because as we finished with Ricky, Jeff took a deep breath and said he would like to be next. As he first entered the circle, he was a bit uneasy but very proud that he had volunteered. I was proud of him too. It took a lot of courage. In fact, as I remember then, he hesitated to participate. Jeff just glowed with pleasure as his fellow members verbally expressed to him that he was "O.K.," that he "belonged." It was wonderful to see the other members reinforce Jeff's conception of himself. It is definitely not just Joy and me who help the less confident members. It is a group effort now, and as a result, the confidence level of those members has increased significantly. Jeff has obviously been the most withdrawn member. It had been evident to every boy in the beginning; they almost ignored his silence because they were uncomfortable with it. But the comments they gave to him today brought out such a positive reaction. They turned his shy silence into something meaningful for the whole group. Darren said, "I like Jeff because he never interrupts anyone." Mike said that he liked Jeff because in the last couple of meetings he had "joined" the group.

The boys did a very responsible job with the exercise. Not only did they understand what we were doing, being very serious about it, but they also gave examples, as they explained why they liked a person. I had to hold myself back from running to Jeff and giving him a big hug as he left the group. Smiling, he said, "Thank you." He really meant it.

(I am learning a lot about holding myself back when need be. I care so much about the members; but many times, directly displaying those feelings could be very wrong. Jeff gained independence while he was in the circle. If I had acted upon my feelings [giving Jeff a hug, as I explained], I would have taken away from that newly found freedom of autonomy that is now emerging. I realized that indirectly we had all embraced him.)

No one mentioned an outdoor activity. Everyone was having a great time being together. The comments about members were taken very seriously. But we also laughed and had a good time discussing past experiences. "We" statements were frequent throughout the entire meeting.

(We are now a cohesive unit. My role in this meeting mainly involved sitting back and understanding how we got here. To be truthful, I could never have imagined this success during our first meeting. We have grown together. I have learned so much through each one of the boys, and I feel that they have learned from me. My main goal for the group has gradually been met. And I certainly didn't do it by myself. Our theme of learning to get along with others is in full focus now. Today, I sat back and watched the shared responsibility and shared leadership. I observed and participated in the closeness that we all enjoyed.)

(I also tried to prepare myself for the termination of this experience. I believe that much of my reflection on past meetings today had a lot to do with the realization of the few meetings that we have left. My direction was vital in the beginning. They have responded positively to this and have reached a point where they can direct themselves. However, they will need as much help leaving the group as they did coming in. My goal now is to direct them toward applying what they have learned here to experiences outside of the group. What they have learned today should provide a basis for deeper evaluation. I would like this to be the focus for next week.)

SUMMARY

During the intimacy stage members build and use a culture of mutual trust, closeness, and cohesiveness. They confront the impasse in the transition of the security of structure in Power and Control/Autonomy to the yet-discovered security of real trust in others. They develop more processes for exchanging self-disclosure and feedback. The purpose of the group becomes clearer for members. They recommit themselves to the goals and tasks explicit in this purpose. They renegotiate and live the contract more fully.

We enable the evolution of this culture through high use of the catalyzing and providing functions and moderate use of the directing and processing functions. Catalyzing requires modeling self-disclosure and feedback, encouraging intermember contact, and reaching for empathic feedback. Providing involves personalizing, genuineness, and confrontation. Directing entails clarifying purpose and renegotiating the contract. Processing comes from relating here-and-now themes to there-and-then themes. These skills enable the group to risk more authentic interaction. Such interaction inevitably confronts the differences in members that surface when they trust the process enough to be themselves. The experience of these differences and their use in the members' process within and outside the group mark the beginning of deeper mutual aid — of differentiation and interdependence.

CRITICAL INCIDENTS

Critical Incident 7

Subtheme.   Responding to Others

Context of Incident.   This incident occurred in the sixth meeting. The group had been discussing such values as trust, intimacy, sharing, and group norms for the disclosure of personal problems. During this discussion, one member of the group remained quiet and seemed fearful of joining in group discussions. Finally, two other members noticed this situation and commented.

Choice Point

TOM: "Mark, I notice you haven't said anything or contributed in any way to our discussion."

JUDY: "Yeah, I noticed that, too. Why haven't you said anything?"

MARK (WITH EMOTION IN HIS VOICE): "I'll tell you why! I don't feel I can trust you guys not to laugh at me or make fun of me if I make a mistake or say something personal and foolish."

This statement appears to have immobilized the other group members, and they all focus their attention on Mark.

What would you do at this point? What is your rationale for this response?

Suggested Response. The practitioner uses self-disclosure and some confrontative feedback and encourages intermember contact: "I'm really excited to hear you say what you did, Mark, because I experience a very honest statement and one that I respect. I believe your sharing these feelings is a big risk for you. I feel that while you say you've been afraid of the risk to speak up, your statement to the group represents a greater risk than in remaining silent and not disclosing yourself. I wonder what impact Mark's statements make on the rest of us, and I bet Mark does, too."

Rationale. The surface issue is Mark's reluctance to share in the group discussion and risk personal disclosure. At a deeper level the issue involves trust, the level of disclosures, and mutual concern for other members. The practitioner needs to enable the establishment of norms that permit freedom to deal with personal issues at many levels and that therefore can support this group process as it strengthens a climate of trust and closeness. The practitioner responds to Mark's concerns as well as attempts to establish the responsibilities of group members for each other. In doing this, the practitioner also models some self-disclosure and feedback.

Critical Incident 8

Subtheme. Responding to Others

Context of Incident. In this meeting after the members responded supportively to Mark, especially to affirm the risk he took and their appreciation of it, a brief silence ensued. During the silence, another member who had remained silent through most of the discussion suddenly began to cry.

Choice Point

SANDRA (CRYING): "I wouldn't want anyone to open up inside, not anyone! It's horrible and it can make you miserable. I've tried it and I know! It's too big a risk to take!" [*Sandra continues to cry.*]

The other members appear shocked and taken aback by this incident, some silently looking at Sandra and a few at you.

What would you do at this point? What is your rationale for this response?

Suggested Response. The preferred response initially is silence, or the active containment of a response. This containing by the practitioner can encourage the group to make contact with Sandra's pain and fears. If the group seems immobilized, the practitioner can model self-disclosure and feedback: "Sandra, I know you're hurting right now, and I respect your saying you aren't willing to risk disclosing your insides. Yet I appreciate what you've shared. I feel much closer to you now than when you were silent. I don't know what the others feel, and I hope they might tell you, but you've had an impact on me. When you risk disclosing your insides as you just did, I am drawn to you, wanting to get even closer to you."

Rationale. The surface issue is to decide whether to respond personally to Sandra's distress. Underlying issues center around the group's concerns about trust, closeness, and fears of closeness and risk. The trust issues for the group are: "How can I trust myself—and others?" "How far can I go in revealing myself?" "How far do I want other members to go?" "What are the responsibilities of members to those who choose to reveal personal data?" "Will I be hurt or will I hurt others when we open up?" The practitioner needs to respond to Sandra with genuine care and concern, share the impact she had made on him, and reach for the empathic responses and contact of other members (if the group is not ready to initiate these responses).

Critical Incident 9

Subtheme. Helping Others in the Group

Context of Incident. This occurred toward the end of the seventh meeting. The group had made a few tentative thrusts at dealing with emotional issues. Several members revealed personal concerns to the group, accompanied by appropriate emotional expression. Following these disclosures the group responded supportively and then tended toward quietness and a tranquility, with members reaffirming the importance of personal disclosures. Some inertia has evolved in relation to the emotional intensity, leading to a group collusion to avoid painful issues in the future. It appears that the group considers their responses to be a final, token gesture to the emotional aspects of the group's work. They want to close the group on this more calm and supportive atmosphere; they fear opening up more painful conflict. Several members actively take this stance.

Choice Point

JANE: "I really feel close to Sandra after our talk; I think I know, now, how she really feels."

GOMEZ: "I think we're all closer than we've ever been. It seems we really trust each other."

CHRIS: "I feel the same way. This group really seems together."

STEVE: "You know what we ought to do? We should all get together and go somewhere and have a party."

Other members continue the discussion along the same lines, none of them actually picking up on the idea of the party.

What would you do at this point? What is your rationale for this response?

Suggested Response. The practitioner here clarifies purpose, begins to renegotiate the contract, illuminates process, and detects and challenges the obstacles to work: "I think it would be helpful if we stopped and looked at what might be happening here. We are feeling closer to each other, but I sense a closure in what you are saying. It's like we have gotten here through some pain and it feels better now, so we don't want to open any more wounds. I think we now know what potential we have to help each other—to achieve our purpose in this group. I wonder if you really want our group process to end like this—that you don't want to go any deeper in honest disclosure and confrontation? And I wonder what we may be afraid of now?"

Rationale. The practitioner attempts to illuminate both surface and underlying issues in terms of positive and negative aspects of the process—to support the disclosure and cohesiveness, while at the same time gently encouraging work by subtly discouraging a premature closure of authentic emotional expression and contact. This requires enabling the group to clarify purpose and goals and to decide how to work in the direction of achieving them. The practitioner both supports prior work and challenges the group to contemplate future growth. In reacting to emerging conflict and tensions by holding onto early closeness, by circling round and round the work it has done to reach this sense of well-being by restating its history, the group risks inertia rather than looking to its future.

chapter 10

Differentiation Stage: Interdependence Themes

There is a Hasidic story about the Rabbi who had a conversation with the Lord about Heaven and Hell: "I will show you Hell," said the Lord and led the Rabbi into a room. In the middle of the room was a very big, round table. The people sitting at it were famished and desperate, evidencing all the worst potentials of human nature. In the middle of the table there was a large pot of stew, enough and more for everyone. The smell of the stew was delicious and made the Rabbi's mouth water. The people around the table were holding spoons with very long handles. Each one found that it was just possible to reach the pot to take a spoonful of stew; but because the handle of the spoon was longer than their arm, they could not get the food back into their mouths. The Rabbi saw that their suffering was terrible. "This is Hell," said the Lord.

"Now I will show you Heaven," said the Lord and they went into another room exactly the same as the first. There was the same, big round table, and the same pot of stew. The people, as before, were equipped with the same long-handled spoons—but they were well nourished and plump, laughing and talking; evidencing all the best potentials of human nature.

At first the Rabbi did not understand. "It is simple, but it requires a certain skill," said the Lord. "You see, they have learned to feed each other."

INTRODUCTION

In the differentiation stage, the group moves from the mutual trust of Closeness to the mutual aid of Interdependence. The evolution of trust, autonomy, and closeness permits the emergence of difference. When these differences become resources for both individual learning and group growth, the interdependent mutual aid system in the group is established.

"Mutual aid" is a phrase coined by Petr Kropotkin (1908). His seminal study of animal and human evolution suggests that the species that have survived and progressively developed have not been the dominant, destructive, or competitive ones. The "fittest" have been those most able to cooperate with one another through interdependent mutual aid. This mutual aid marks both the healthy person and the healthy group.

Ruth Benedict (Maslow and Honigmann, 1970), an anthropologist, discovered a similar interdependence in her study of healthy cultures. She termed this mutual aid "synergy." In cultures with synergy, members' own selfish and vital need-meeting is interdependently connected with that of others. Most acts toward self-actualization contribute simultaneously to both the good of the self and the good of the group. In synergy, or mutual aid, there is no inherent conflict between individual and group needs and goals. Members build a healthy system on which they depend for their own growth and development. The mutual aid relationship is readily assumed by members during this most mature stage.

Dominique Moyse Steinberg (1993) has recently elaborated on the place of differentiation in mutual aid:

> mutual aid may simply be defined as the process of group members helping one another think things through — not by the gift of advice, but by sharing of life experiences, opinions, feelings, and attitudes. . . . [It] embraces many types of possible interchanges, including those which are confrontational in nature. This is not to say that expressions of sympathy do not reflect mutual aid. They may or may not. Sometimes it is more helpful . . . to be challenged . . . and there are many moments in which the expression of difference is far more helpful than murmurs of compassion. (pp. 27 – 28)

INDIVIDUAL PROCESS

The three sets of questions that members have regarding the "I," "We," and "It" of group process during Differentiation/Interdependence are not experienced as separately as in the earlier stages. These elements of group process fuse for members. In fact, the work of the group is marked by this fusion. The "questions" at this stage also tend to be statements. Individual members now experience their own needs as these dovetail with the group resources. Their autonomy and differences as well as their interdependence and sense of group needs come out in statements about "I" such as:

"I want to grow."

"I'm O.K."

"I am different from yet similar to you."

In relation to "We," the statements involve:

"We can grow together."

"We're O.K."

"We are different yet similar."

"We do know and have known what we've been doing together."

"We know what we can do to maximize the growth of all members of this group."

Toward the "It," or the practitioner and the helping process, each member believes:

"It — this group — can and will help us as well help each other."

"It — this group — knows its resources, including the practitioner, and will tap them as needed to achieve our purpose, themes, and goals."

"It — this group — will stay on target and will meet individual members' needs in proportion to what these needs are."

"It — this group — will help each and every member to discover his or her special and unique self and to use this self as the basis for authentic and close relationships with others."

The overriding question, which members seldom ask but consistently work on, is: "What can we do before we end and while we have these resources to meet the needs of all members, starting with those whose needs seem strongest and most pressing for their individual growth?" In brief, each member assesses and acts to contribute as fully as possible to achieving the purpose of the group.

GROUP PROCESS

This stage is marked by several dynamic balances of members' and the group's needs. Members fuse autonomous and interdependent concerns. Cohesion strengthens and balances work for the "I," the "We," and the "It." This balance anchors the connection of here-and-now process to content — both in the here-and-now and as related to and transferred in learning to the there-and-then. The interaction, although consistent with purpose and attending to these dynamic balances, is fluid, spontaneous, and creative.

Members of this mature work group are now facing reality. Through "valid communication" (Bennis and Shephard, 1956), members reflect a consensual reality in which individuals and the group as a whole are expressively aware of what they are doing together. Members responsibly and spontaneously sense what self and others need to achieve their common tasks and purpose. Foremost, members are creatively given what they need in proportion to their needs. This consciousness of mutual aid taps the group resources. Differential work occurs at the "I," the "We," and the "It" levels as pertinent to the needs that emerge.

The group's awareness of these needs springs from open feedback channels. The Open Area of the Johari Window presented in Chapter 9 has enlarged to the point at which members know what self-disclosure and feedback are most immediately pertinent to the needs of individual members and of the group. Members' differences are sought, accepted, and used to achieve the group's goals. This process includes a respect for the practitioner's professional difference in expertise and experience and the contribution of this difference, valued no more than any other member's, to the group's growth and learning.

HELPING PROCESS

The group's task now is to tap its resources for mutual aid. Our parallel task is to enable the group to use its mutual aid resources. Toward this end, it is best for us to stay out of the way of the group's process and to serve as a consultant to the group when it perceives this need and calls upon us. We, as a member, function in providing and processing (much as any other member). As consultant, we may be called upon to function in directing and catalyzing. The skills for providing and processing are those presented in previous chapters — personalizing, self-disclosure, feedback, genuineness, and illuminating processes. The new skills for directing and catalyzing involve offering experimental activities, exercises, or techniques that may serve as tools for members to resolve the specific themes that emerge.

Skills

Offering Experimental Activities.   This skill for serving as a consultant to the group is quite complex. It may require us to have the creativity borne of study and experience to set up (1) experiments based on the group's needs for learning, and (2) a compendium of activities and techniques that can be used differentially in response to specific needs.

The "experiment" is a cornerstone of experiential learning (Zinker, 1977). It entails structuring a situation in the group in which the member can try (and "try out") new behavior and study the consequences for self and others within the safety of the group as a lab. The results, if successful, can then be risked in behavior outside of the group. Experiments help members to enact wishes in ways never tried before.

Joseph Zinker (1977; 1980) describes the use of experiments in this stage of group development. He notes about this stage (Zinker, 1980): "The group takes on more clarity, thematic pointedness and elegance in resolution. The leader tracks the themes of the ongoing action effectively and suggests original ways of resolving group dilemmas [through experiments]. The leader reveals himself or herself as a group member with a special task rather than as an insulated role-bound genius" (pp. 69–70). As Zinker reflects, these experiments cannot be preplanned totally. They must evolve in response to the emergent themes in the here-and-now group process. They may be a part of our repertoire because they have been developed before in similar situations or were used as a structured exercise. Often, they are created on the spot by us and/or by members.

If we listen for expressed wishes, we can play these through in terms of how they may be enacted in the group. For instance, the member who discloses that he or she wants to be freer in expressing nonverbal affection can be asked to try an experiment wherein he or she goes to each member of the group and expresses experienced affection nonverbally and differently to each. Metaphors in the individual member's or group's themes can be enacted in experiment. A member who expresses a desire for a fresh start can be "reborn" through the group's acting out, together, the metaphor of giving birth.

In enacting group wishes and metaphors, the members are especially creative, spontaneous, and involved during this stage. In fact, this creativity is often the best source of our experiments. When asked by the group what we can do to help a member resolve a particular theme, we can ask the group what might be done to create an experiment wherein the member can try to resolve the theme in action in the here-and-now in a way that he or she wishes. Also, the member himself or herself might be able to design this experiment. When the particular member or the group seems stuck, then perhaps we can draw on our own knowledge and experience to construct a relevant experiment. The key principle is to translate wishes into a way of being enacted and to structure a laboratory experiment in the group in which the member or members can try this enactment — to see if it fits, if it meets wishes or needs. Most often, the group is ready to help the member to process the experience itself. They share its impact on them through feedback and seek the meaning through self-disclosure. They generate the data needed to assess the results, positive and negative, of the experiment. If this processing is not initiated by the group itself, it is imperative that we seek it.

Using Structured Exercises. Structured exercises are also experiments and should always be presented as such. However, they are experiments that have been used by others and are available in catalogues or compendiums assembled by experienced group leaders. There are some general principles (Anderson, 1980b) for the use of structured exercises.

A structured exercise is a practitioner's intervention in group process that involves a set of orders, instructions, or prescriptions for the behavior of group members (Lieberman, Yalom, and Miles, 1973, p. 409). These prescriptions specify certain members' behavior alternatives at a particular moment in the group. For example, if we say, "Pick out the member of this group you feel most different from and we'll go around for each of you to tell that person how you feel, why you think you feel that way, and what you appreciate about his or her difference," we are using a structured exercise. Each group member can choose whether or not to carry out the directive. However, if the member chooses to participate, the behavior alternatives are limited by the interactions. The exercise calls for trying out specific new behavior as focused on an identified theme.

On the other hand, if we say, "How different do you feel from other members of this group?" we are not using a structured exercise. In this example we specify the content of the interaction, but members can choose how to approach this content—the process of this interaction. A particular member may discuss his or her perspective of one other member. Or he or she may address feelings about us or the group as a whole. Or the member may describe feelings about several members. This question, therefore, does not constitute a structured exercise. It does not instruct the group in both the content and process of its interaction and consequently limits its choices for participation for the duration of the exercise.

A structured exercise may take only a few minutes—"Tell Jack why you feel closest to him in the group"—or it may consume most of the group meeting (Pfeiffer and Jones, 1979). It may be primarily verbal or nonverbal ("Stand up, Jack and Jill, face and walk toward each other, and without talking, let happen whatever happens"). Finally, the exercise may involve a number of different participant combinations:

1. The group as a whole: "Sculpturing"—arranging members into a group statue that represents their image of the group.
2. One member vis-à-vis the group: "Breaking in"—one member attempts to break into the group physically while the others form a tight circle with arms interlocked and attempt to keep him or her out so that the member has to use his or her own power to get in.
3. The entire group as individual members: "Go-around"—each member in a "go-around" is to give, in order, his or her opinion of what the group could do in the next ten minutes to begin to meet its most pressing need.
4. Pairs: "Mirroring"—the group is broken into twos, and each pair is to "mirror" (or imitate) nonverbally the behavior of each other in order.
5. One particular pair: "Arm wrestling"—two members who are afraid of their own power are asked to arm wrestle each other.
6. Each of the members independent of the group: "Fantasy trip"—the members are asked to imagine individually taking a trip through the woods and visiting a wise person in a mountain retreat to whom they ask a very important question for which they need a very wise answer.
7. One particular member: "Empty chair"—a member is requested to have a dialogue that gives voice to two conflicting forces of his or her current internal life and to move to the empty chair when it represents the other side of the conflict, such as the fear of confrontation that opposes one's desire to assert oneself more.

We can develop a mental file of these structured exercises from the various catalogues that have been published (e.g., Johnson and Johnson, 1987). Yet there is a danger that those of us who are familiar with a compendium of structured exercises will draw upon them too often, especially early in the group when members are struggling for structure and the interaction wanes. Research suggests that these exercises can become a serious obstacle to group development and rob members of the opportunity to develop authentic autonomy and interdependence (Anderson, 1980a). In brief, these exercises are most useful only when the members do not need them for structure but seek a structured intervention for meeting a particular need of the group or its members. Then they are truly perceived and used as "experiments" (such as during Closeness, and particularly during Interdependence).

I offer five principles for the use of structured exercises at any point in the group's development. These principles are derived (1) from the theory and research on these exercises, and (2) from my own experience with them.

1. *Don't use structured exercises to enliven the group or its members emotionally.* Too often, structured exercises seem to be used as emotional space fillers or as something interesting to do when the group seems at loose ends. This is a mistake. Members of the group are alive; and if they seem to need to be energized by us, if meetings seem listless, if we believe we must constantly spark more lively activity, the problem most likely lies within the group process and will only be compounded by accelerating devices. This developmental obstacle can best be explored rather than circumvented. We and the group need to consider together the obstructions to members' involvement through attention to such areas as the current norms operating in the group; the relationship of these norms to the group's goals and to each member's primary tasks; and the members' perceptions and feelings toward us, each other, and the experience. This principle does not suggest that we refrain from asking members to stand up and stretch, for instance, when they seem physically fatigued and therefore stuck in devoting energy to the task at hand. However, it instructs us to control any impulse to use a structured exercise to enliven interaction solely for the sake of energizing or "sparking" emotional expressivity.

2. *Don't use structured exercises to accelerate "breakthrough."* Similar to the Principle 1, this one is concerned about the proclivity in practice for accelerating interaction in the group. Indeed, structured exercises are effective for accelerating groups to bypass the early, "slower" stages of development and plunging members into "instant intimacy" through the expression of positive and negative feelings. But they do not accelerate the individual and group growth process through these "breakovers." It is the "breakthrough" that can significantly aid this growth. We can best help the group and its members to get *through* anxiety, *through* the impasses or difficulty stages, rather than *over* them. The struggle with timidity, with mistrust, with resistance, with authority, with developing mutual aid relationships, and the development of competencies to move beyond them in real relationship with others constitute the very stuff of growth in group process, not an impediment to it. It is these skills that are transferred to the world outside of the immediate group experience on behalf of one's further development.

3. *Use structured exercises to increase awareness of group process.* This principle evolves from Principle 2, in that structured exercises used to control rather than to illuminate group process create more obstructions than they prevent. Exercises to increase closeness by bypassing the "trust"

and "autonomy" stages of group development rob members of the opportunity to (1) develop skills to confront structural barriers to interpersonal closeness and mutual aid, and (2) experience the power of their own choice to work through these obstacles within and outside of the group. On the other hand, there are structured exercises that can be introduced to, or created by, the group for the purpose of increasing the group's awareness of what is occurring in its structure and process so that it can choose to alter its focus and participation in line with individual and group goals. Such structured exercises are not designed to bypass these obstacles to group development; they are designed to confront them directly. Some are activities such as suggesting that members compile a list of what they think the current norms are in the group — the do's and don'ts about how to become a "good group member" if someone new to the group wanted this information; asking members to place themselves physically in the room in a place they believe represents their position in the group at that point in time in the group process; having a "go-around" in which members share their reactions regarding what the most (or least) meaningful part of the group experience (or meeting) was for them thus far. Always, these exercises are best introduced as "experiments" and as optional for the group or any members to try; what members do with the "data" they collect from this "experiment" is their own choice.

4. *Use structured exercises to increase autonomy and interdependence.* The activities suggested in Principle 3 and the way they are introduced and used are designed to increase, not decrease, a member's autonomy and interdependence. We best suggest a *means* to discover more about important aspects of the group's structure and process, not a preconceived *end* of how this information is used. It is the group's responsibility, and each member's, to choose what will be done with what they know. In the further interest of helping the group and its members to increase their awareness of what they do, we can provide or solicit more information on what they have done with their awareness — including, perhaps, denial of why it is so. But here, too, *they* must choose to act on their awareness. The autonomy and interdependence in achieving goals for the group experience is theirs, as it must be; the degree to which they experience this through our behavior is the degree to which they are empowered to use it on their own behalf, both within and outside the group.

5. *Help the group and its members to evaluate realistically the structured exercises that are used.* Because the research consistently demonstrates that structured exercises feed the omnipotent mystique of the practitioner and result in the erroneous evaluation of a powerfully effective group for members in their own eyes, it is most important that members get help to put the experiences that are used into a proper, more realistic perspective. Group members can be aided in their awareness that the structured exercises that are perceived as especially meaningful to an individual member's growth or to the group as a whole were tools to their awareness

on which they chose to act. There is nothing magical about the exercises or the person who suggested them. They served, for the most part, as a way of concentrating awareness on what is. This awareness is an important step, but only a step, in the process of growth. What probably made the difference in the actual growth experienced was in fact the *responsibility* that members of the group took to act upon this awareness. And in the final analysis, only they could do this for themselves. They used their own power.

PRINCIPLES FOR THE DIFFERENTIATION STAGE

There are few principles for guiding our work with the group during Differentiation/Interdependence. These are:

1. We need to trust the group.
2. We need to maintain a consultant role to the group, keeping interventions few and far between.
3. When called upon, we need to make experiments, exercises, and techniques available to the group at the appropriate level of the group process — the "I," the "We," and the "It."

Example

Meetings 8 and 9 of the ten meetings demonstrate the interdependence of this stage and the social worker's use of functions in the preadolescent groups in school. Meeting 8 was described in Chapter 9 and should be reviewed with Meeting 9, which follows.

Meeting 9

(Along with this stage has come decreased defensiveness among members. Because of this, they seem to have discovered a freedom to experiment with each other. I noticed the rediscovery of fellow members. Questions directed toward members reflect curiosity about why others feel and react as they do. This was all very evident in today's exercise.)

The boys were very responsive when we told them about the "secret" exercise. As I handed them pieces of paper, they stressed the importance of being alone to write their secrets, as much as Joy and I did. In comparing their participation in exercises from beginning meetings until now, there is a remarkable difference. In the beginning, there was much ambiguity over such exercises because of fears and unclear understanding of our purpose. Although the exercises that we do now are of the same type, the boys' responses are much different. The declining reluctance to participate in these awareness activities showed me increasingly clear conceptions of the theme in relation to our existence as a group. This has resulted in enthusiasm and enjoyment of the exercises. Before, the boys almost demanded knowing the purpose before involving themselves. Now they know that the purpose of the exercise can only be realized to the fullest extent through participation and post-discussion. They trust our direction and their own.

Everyone took this exercise as a very serious matter. Even Randy, who has a tendency to joke around about everything, sat in his corner, very involved in his secret.

There were questions about the exercise from those who did not clearly understand. In emphasizing our progress, I will again reflect back on earlier meetings. If we would be doing an exercise early in the experience, questions weren't asked, even though they were present. The boys would rather write anything than reveal that they were confused. Now, trust has developed, permitting them to expose the true confusion or misunderstanding that they experience from time to time.

(The secrets are placed in one pile anonymously. Each member selects one — preferably not his own — reads it, and comments on how he might feel if this secret were his.)

Each person read the secret that he had chosen, freely commenting on how he felt about it. There was quite a variety of secrets. But every secret, no matter how different from the one before, showed much concentration on inner feelings.

There were two secrets in particular that dealt with feelings about the group. Chris read the first one, which said that the group had provided that person with very good feelings about himself and others. We talked about this for a while, relating it to the members. It was the first secret, and the true owner of it had come forth. Mike quietly said, "I'd like to tell you all that it is my secret." Darren felt that this type of thing should not be a secret. He said that it is something important to the group and should be voiced instead of kept quiet. Darren's contribution wasn't hostile or joking at Mike's secret. Instead, he was displaying the real type of disclosure that he had learned in the group. He knows that our experience permits freedom of opinion. Equally important, Mike understood what Darren was saying. As I "reached for Mike's feelings," I discovered why he chose this as a secret. His thoughts during this meeting were concentrated on the unity that had emerged. It was all a secret to him simply because he felt that he had never *voluntarily* said how meaningful the group was to him. His positive feelings had always been voiced because we used the go-around technique. Now, he did want everyone to know how he felt. I noted his good feeling about getting it out. This also showed me that Mike clearly understood the purpose of our group. To me, there is a clear difference between expressions of feelings that come out because of norms that have developed and expressions of feelings that are truly experienced and real.

Ricky's secret, which was directed toward the group experience, was read by me. Darren jumped in again, saying that for some reason he didn't feel this should be a secret. This gave me a good opportunity to discuss means by which our group situation could be beneficial in the area of self-actualization. I initiated a discussion of reasons why individual feelings can be helpful to the group. I asked the boys why they thought our group had become so close. There were different responses, all pertaining to the fact that we had all engaged in some form of self-disclosure (e.g., "It happened because we say what we think"). We discussed the fact that this type of interaction enabled us to learn more about each other. It was meaningful because the discussion focused on the connectedness on which interdependence is based. I tried to emphasize the individual autonomy; we all had the choice of accepting or rejecting those relationships.

(Darren's theme-centered feelings had been expressed, and they were worked through and understood by group members. What is most important is the fact that the closeness theme did not become so illuminated that the members could not understand that "I" is separate from "We." They have realized that being a group is rewarding and wonderful. But at the same time, there has been spontaneous actualization that "I" am at the core of my experience. For the most part, members have shown me realization of their individuality, even at the peak moments of our togetherness.)

SUMMARY

When interdependence evolves, the group develops a synergistic mutual aid system. It quickly resolves any remnants of the prior stages, in order, and monitors itself for the members' most pressing needs. These needs are met in proportion to what they are. The creative, spontaneous, and purposeful interaction ensures a balance of the "I-We-It" on behalf of the group's and each member's growth.

As practitioners, we stay out of the way of this process. We serve as a consultant only when the group members somehow request our expertise. Then we can help the group and/or members to enact wishes through experiments, exercises, or techniques. These are offered and used as trials or experiments and are designed to increase awareness of wishes and behavioral alternatives within and outside of the group. Basically, however, we, no less than the group members, need to trust the group process and its growing capacity for mutual aid. This aid empowers the group and us to carry out mutual need-meeting interaction and activities until termination.

CRITICAL INCIDENTS

Critical Incident 10

Subtheme.   Developing Mutual Aid

Context of Incident.   During the eighth meeting, the group followed the needs that seemed most pressing for individual members. These needs became most immediate for the group as a whole. Interactions were sharpened. When the group finished one such interaction, they sensed a few loose threads but some completion.

They had just finished talking about why a particular group member — Jane — did not risk a response to a member who reached for her feedback, and what they could have done to help her and to help the group.

Choice Point

JUDY: "I guess we can move on."

GOMEZ: "Yeah, but I feel like she's still on a hot seat, kind of . . ."

STEVE: "I feel that too. But I don't know what else to do. I feel like we're hanging."

CHERYL: "I feel like she's hanging."

JERRY: "I feel like we all are, and we can't move from here!"

What would you do at this point? What is your rationale for this response?

Suggested Response.   The practitioner uses a structured exercise to extend members' individual awareness as well as offer them a "break" in the interaction: "I'd like to suggest something. At this point I suggest we just take a couple of minutes, stand up, and turn around with our backs toward the group, and think what you could personally do when we come back to get us unstuck. Otherwise we might just sit here and be stuck. Would you be willing to try that?"

Rationale.   The surface issue and real issue are the same: When has an issue been worked? How can we move on without avoiding issues or imposing group needs on individuals? With the help of a break in the action through a structured exercise, the members can resolve this issue themselves.

Critical Incident 11

Subtheme.   Using Mutual Aid

Context of Incident.   This critical incident occurred during the tenth meeting. The group had talked primarily about personal feelings over the last several meetings. During the middle of a personal disclosure by one group member, another group member inserted a nonconnected question about planning a party.

Choice Point

TOM: "I've been really preoccupied lately with death. I've been afraid of dying all my life, and I feel really alone since my dad died last year. In here, I've been afraid that I'm going to lose some of you and this feeling makes me think a lot about my own death."

STEVE: "I wonder if we could discuss the party we're supposed to have so we can start planning for refreshments and entertainment."

JANE: "How can you talk of something like that after what he just said!"

MARK: "Hey, man, didn't you hear what he just said? How can you completely ignore his feelings? Don't you give a damn about him?"

JERRY: "Did what Tom said about death scare you, Steve?"

What would you do at this point? What is your rationale for this response?

Suggested Response.   Trust the group. Do nothing.

Rationale.   The group members have demonstrated that they wish to confront this issue themselves. They have indicated that they can respond to this with responsibility for others and accountability for what they and others do to each other. They can tap this mutual aid and develop it further through use of the group's own potency.

Critical Incident 12

Subtheme.   Using Mutual Aid

Context of Incident.   This event occurred during the tenth meeting, close to the termination of the life of the group. Up to this point all members had been working toward helping each other within and outside of the group, especially sharing very deep, meaningful feelings and information about themselves. Now, a dramatic shift is evident. The members begin the meeting talking about lighthearted, irrelevant, or amusing things, as if deliberately to avoid further involvement on a personal level. This has continued for almost five minutes into the meeting. Finally, one member who has expressed considerable sensitivity and empathy over the last several meetings begins to speak.

Choice Point

GOMEZ: "You know something? I wonder why we're talking about all these things. It's almost like we're all withdrawing from the group even though we have three meetings left after this."

The group remains silent, considering its past behavior.

What would you do at this point? What is your rationale for this response?

Suggested Response.   Trust the group. Do nothing. (If the group cannot increase awareness of its own process on its own, and wants to, the practitioner could use the "shuttling fantasy" structured exercise.)

Rationale.   Both surface and underlying issues have been recognized and dealt with by a group member. In doing this, Gomez is fulfilling the processing function of a group leader — instilling in others the responsibility for distributive leadership and shared power. This is a sign of interdependence in the group. This taps mutual aid.

chapter 11

Separation Stage: Termination Themes

Mark Twain, the first great American humorist, and his good friend, the writer William Dean Howells, were leaving church one Sunday when it started to rain heavily. Howells looked up at the clouds and said, "Do you think it will stop?" Twain replied, "It always has."

A more recent American humorist, Woody Allen, has said, "I'm not afraid to die. I just don't want to be there when it happens."

INTRODUCTION

Indeed, all things come to an end. The termination of the group process takes on particular significance for members and the practitioner. The special concerns and issues depend upon when the group ends — and it always will.

Termination does not necessarily follow Differentiation and Interdependence. The group can end at any point in its development. When groups end during earlier stages, the termination is marked by decreased confidence and hopes, and by high fears in interpersonal relationships. The members regret and project the blame for expectations unfulfilled. They mistrust.

The group that terminates after achieving Interdependence, or at least Closeness, may experience increased ambivalence about separation; but members basically sense the power of their own autonomy and responsibility to meet their needs more effectively in interpersonal relationships. They increase their basic trust.

Whenever separation occurs, it is a stage in which members need our difference for them to use it to its fullest advantage. Our task can be very difficult because we, too, are experiencing the end. We may share the members' regrets and/or their desire to hold on to the illusion that the group will not really terminate. Many models of stages of group development, especially those developed outside of social work, assume the termination stage without separate coverage of it. Bruce Tuckman (1965), for instance, added "adjourning" to his stages of "forming," "storming," "norming," and "performing" only after revisiting research of these stages in a later review (Tuckman and Jensen, 1977). (For a review, see Keyton, 1993.)

In general, the termination themes in the group reflect the stages of death as first conceptualized by Elisabeth Kübler-Ross (1969). They often begin in denial, avoidance, and some shock; move through anger, regression, and flight; to a period of bargaining (when members communicate that they still need the group). From the bargaining evolves the first step in facing the reality of the impending ending, as in dying, through depression and grief or sadness; and then the acceptance that leads to review, evaluation, and transfer to the new state of being, or what Kübler-Ross (1969) calls "decathexis." The members, if helped through this process, are ready to face the new beginnings of life without the group. The group experiences the reframing that Kübler-Ross gave death when she labeled it the "final stage of growth."

INDIVIDUAL PROCESS

Each member often experiences the process of stages of ending mentioned above. The group's ending is experienced symbolically as a death for each individual member. If the group terminates after achieving Interdependence, each member also experiences a set of questions toward the "I," the "We," and the "It." About "I," each member asks:

> "Can I transfer what I have learned here to life outside of the group?"
> "Can I use my personal power as I did in this group?"
> "Did I do everything I could to get the most from this experience?"
> "Will I be able to do more in the future if I were to be in such a group?"
> "Do I still need the group?"

In relation to "We," each member asks:

> "What will become of the others when the group ends?"
> "Will I find others elsewhere who are as strong and understanding?"
> "Will we continue to meet after the group ends?"
> "Do they still need the group?"

Toward "It," members wonder:

> "Will the practitioner ever work with another group like ours?"
> "Does this really have to end?"

"What was it that we did that we can take into our other groups?"

"Will we always remember this experience together?"

As members manifest the behavior that seeks to answer these silent questions, the separation stage evolves. It may last for one or several meetings and is often stimulated by our reminding members of their already-sensed inevitable ending. The group process takes on a special character for the remainder of this stage in the group.

GROUP PROCESS

Although termination can come at any time in the life cycle of the group, its date is often set when the group begins. If the group separates after the latter stages of intimacy and differentiation, members often emerge with a strong sense of competence in relation to their lives outside of the group—even with renewed ambivalences. The wishes for autonomous and interdependent human relations that satisfy needs far outweigh the fears. Feelings of alienation decrease, and trust and hopes for mutual aid relationships increase. Members feel willing and able to captain their own ships to the shores of interpersonal growth.

These outcomes are colored by regression to behavior that is more characteristic of early stages. Members may seem detached and to be losing their affiliation with the group. This behavior, based on some insecurity, is less a rejection of the group than an insinuation that members still need each other, us, and the group. The group moves from denial, then anger, to the bargaining for extension or continuance of time together. When bargaining fails, the group faces its underlying grief and sadness, its depression through inactivity, and then its painful acceptance and final closure through involvement in its ending work and movement away from the group and toward life situations outside.

If termination occurs during the earlier stages, the reverse is likely. Members experience feelings of inadequacy, fears stronger than wishes, increased mistrust and alienation, and less faith in their potential for self-actualization. The feelings about separation are denied awareness and expression even more strongly, preventing an effective ending process. Absences and dropouts are likely to increase. Unstated regrets and resentments predominate.

Because the group often avoids the unpleasant work of termination, we must help it keep this task in focus. The end of the group can be a real loss for us as well as for members. All gradually come to the realization that the group can never really be reconvened. Even if they continue relationships with certain members, the group as an entity is gone forever. It will be missed. For all, it may have been a place of pain, conflict, and fear but also a place of love, joy, and great meaning. Some of life's most poignant and fulfilling moments can occur in the microcosm of a developed group. We, therefore, like all other members of the group, must go through the ending process. Our acceptance in the face of ambivalence is vital for enabling members to terminate effectively.

HELPING PROCESS

The task of members is to terminate effectively. Our parallel task is to enable separation and the transfer of learning from the group. This usually requires that we carry all four functions of group leadership at a high level: catalyzing, providing, processing, and directing. The catalyzing and processing skills require initiating termination, focusing, and reaching for feelings and evaluation. The providing skills demand sharing one's own feelings. Directing involves holding out the ending and facilitating closing. In addition, there are our skills for the postgroup phase. These skills include evaluation and follow-up.

Skills

Initiating Termination.   We initiate termination by pointing out the ending. Because of the difficulty members have in facing feelings about ending through denial, we must provide time for these feelings to be sorted out. This time comes from our pointing out endings, or reminding the group of its impending ending (Shulman, 1992). Through this reminder, we initiate termination. Such catalyzing is followed by helping members to focus on their ending feelings.

Focusing.   Focusing involves acknowledging the behavior and feelings that reflect the ending. We reflect the denial and sadness that come from members starting to arrive late for meetings, having difficulty getting started, creating lulls in the interaction, and so on. As we focus the group's and specific members' attention on these behaviors and reflect their feelings, we are able to reach for the ending feelings more directly and specifically to catalyze their expression.

Reaching for Feelings and Evaluation.   We reach for members' feelings about ending by encouraging members to share them and to stay with them. Indirect cues of anger and grief are responded to directly. As always, it is most important that we reach for the ambivalences in these feelings. When the positives are expressed (e.g., the sense of accomplishment), we reach for the negative (the sense of loss). When negatives are expressed (the anger), we reach for the positives (the caring).

Similarly, we reach for evaluation. Members are asked for their feedback about the group, themselves, and us. Again, we reach behind the positives for the negatives (e.g., what we did that they did not appreciate as well as what they appreciated) and behind the negatives for the positives (e.g., what the group did accomplish, as well as what was left unfinished). We must help the group avoid the "farewell party syndrome" (Shulman, 1992) wherein no negatives are faced. Especially important in this evaluation is helping members to credit themselves. As with a graduation ceremony, the members' fears of "going it alone" may detract from their confidence that they are taking something new in themselves with them. We need to help members credit themselves for what they have accomplished as individuals and as a group—to graduate with "honors" due them.

Sharing Our Own Feelings.   A particular skill that provides the group with the support for working through the ending involves sharing our own feelings. Often, we must first risk our own feelings of ending in order for members to feel free to risk themselves. Both may feel vulnerable, but it is part of our function and a measure of our professional skill to take the first, hard step. In this expression, we best model the importance of tuning into and sharing the positives and the negatives. The reality of ambivalences, even though one side of the feeling may outweigh the other in intensity, is as ubiquitous for us as for the members during Termination.

Holding Out the Ending.   We assume the directing function by unyieldingly holding out the ending and encouraging work through it. We need to avoid being seduced into the denial phase by joining the group's taboo against mentioning it, or by permitting members to decide to extend the group meetings or to party their way through the ending. This requires that we stay tuned to our own feelings so that they do not blind us to the meaning of the group's process at this time.

We hold out the ending not only in the process but also in the substantive content of the group — the "It" as well as the "I" and "We." Here we direct the group to identify major learnings and direct members to identify areas for future work. We also help members to connect this difficulty in ending to other endings in their relationships outside of the group, and to discuss how they can transfer their learnings in the group to their life situations outside.

Closing.   Closing involves providing a way for members to say their final goodbyes to each other in the group. It is the structure for leaving. An exercise or ritual is suggested (if the group has not developed one of its own) for this purpose. I prefer to use a "symbolic closing exercise" that requires the group to go outside (if possible) together nonverbally and to follow me to an open space where we can form a circle. As we look at each other in the circle for almost the last time, I am the only one who talks. I then ask members to turn their backs to the group and walk out far enough so that they can't see other members out of the corner of their eyes. When they reach this spot, they are to become aware of their separateness from the group and to take several minutes to tune in to the meaning of this. After these few minutes, during which most members feel their sadness *and* their strength, I instruct them to walk back to the center slowly and to literally bump up against each other in a solid circle of bodies. After a minute of experiencing the strength of this solidness, I ask them to form a circle again with our arms around each other. When face-to-face and arm-in-arm, I suggest that this is our very last opportunity in the group itself to say what we want to say so that we won't regret not having said it in the group. When everyone who wants to has had his or her say, I instruct the group once more to spread out as they were and to take a brief moment when they are out of peripheral vision to become aware in silence of what they as individuals are taking from the group. With this accomplished, the exercise, the meeting, and the group, as such, end.

Evaluation.   Our special skill for evaluation involves the assessment of specific outcomes of the group. This skill requires a knowledge of evaluation research methodology and its use in group practice. The methodology is discussed in Chapter 14.

Whenever possible, we need to operationalize group outcomes such that instruments may be used for more precise measurement of the results. A variety of instruments with demonstrated validity and reliability are available for measuring process and outcome variables in groups. When these are used in pre- and posttests, we gain additional data for evaluating the group's success and/or lack of success in accomplishing particular goals. Although this procedure lacks controls and therefore limits the validity of the findings, nevertheless the data tend to be more reliable than the testimonies of group members. These instruments and measurements can also reflect particular needs in follow-up.

Follow-Up.   Follow-up skills enable us to check on graduated group members to provide further support for changes, to encourage more transfer of learning, or to get additional group or other service if needed. This follow-up can range from a self-addressed and stamped postcard asking members to check how they are doing in particular areas, to a questionnaire, telephone call, or personal interview. It is usually best to wait for this follow-up until three to six months after the group ends. Research indicates that change is maintained or not after this period, as much as after any longer period (Lieberman, Yalom, and Miles, 1973). Many of us carry out some informal follow-up of group members, whether or not they initiate the procedure. Usually, this involves members who were high changers and doing well in their own life situations; or, conversely, those who were negative changers or casualties who are in further, or perhaps even deeper, trouble. The skill is designed to formalize the procedures for follow-up. The concerned practitioner does not forget about his or her responsibility to (not for!) members after the group terminates.

PRINCIPLES FOR THE SEPARATION STAGE

During Termination, our functions and skills suggest some overall principles:

1. We need to initiate the ending process by reminding the group of its impending ending in time for it to work through members' feelings.
2. We need to be particularly aware of our own feelings during termination and to share these with the group.
3. We need to reach for both the positives and the negatives of members' feelings and evaluations during separation.
4. We need to hold the group (and ourselves) to the ending time and its work on ending.
5. We need to credit members and the group for what was accomplished.
6. We need to help the group relate the here-and-now ending process to members' there-and-then content — the "I-We" to the "It" as a there-and-then theme. This enables members to transfer their learning.

7. We need to seek or provide a procedure for closing the group.
8. We need to consider methods for formal evaluation and follow-up.

Example

The following example reflects the last meeting in the group we have been considering throughout Part II. Meeting 10 of the preadolescent group reflects the themes and dynamics of termination.

> ### Meeting 10
>
> I got to the meeting ten minutes late. The boys were all very happy to see me, and one of them was worried that I had been in a car accident. Darren ran to greet me, telling me how he was afraid that I wasn't going to be there to say good-bye. He has been very conscious of this ending during the past few meetings. He has truly understood this experience and has benefited from it. Darren and I have become very close, which is ironic when viewing our first meeting. I would have expected him to be a definite barrier to the group's progress. Instead, he became one of the most important contributors to the group's growth. I have learned so much about being the counselor within a group through him. Many times I could have very easily denied him the opportunity to be aggressive, bold, and very physically active. For a while his actions did bother me and the other group members; and there were ways that I could have stopped it, but I didn't. The important point is that my allowing him to "act out" was an experiment. Of course, I wanted him to understand his actions, but I have never worked with a group before. I didn't know what would result from my behavior. But I did learn from this that I had reacted to Darren in the way that provided him with the best means to understand his own behavior. It helped me tremendously with other members. I gradually learned more about my own goals in helping others. Darren's behavior is right for Darren. It is natural and need not be changed, but more fully understood by him. I really believe that I have helped this understanding to take place through our experience. Throughout the entire meeting Darren stayed close to me, repeatedly saying that he would really miss me. At one point, he whispered to me that I had helped him to want to be nice to other people. He had also been doing a lot of reflecting back to earlier stages of our experience. He even asked me if I remembered how he "used" to act. He felt that I liked him more now than I did in the beginning. I explained that it may seem that way because of the process of getting to know each other. He agreed that people can show each other their feelings much more after a bond of trust has been developed. He truly understood, giving me he example of how he used to act with Jeff. He used to "pick on" Jeff, more because of not knowing how to react to their differences than because of actually disliking him. He explained to me that because he and Jeff were in the same group, he got to "know him a lot better, and like him more."

I sat down to join the party. It took only a few moments for me to see the chaotic state that was present. For the most part, all members' fears have been resolved through our experience. These resolutions freed us all of barriers that could have prohibited us from real interaction. But today another type of fear was present. It was evident that there were fears of ending our group. This took many different forms. Some of the members simply chose to ignore that our experience was over. Others repeatedly expressed feelings about the separation. But there was one thing common to all group members: regression to behavior that was characteristic of earlier meetings.

For the first time in many, many meetings, Chris again retrieved the ball that had been his outlet for uncomfortable feelings. He continuously bounced it all around, as he had done before. Randy joked about the ending of our group, just as he had at the beginning. Ricky was as serious as ever about our group, expressing his sadness over the ending.

Every member, no matter what behavior they retreated to, was very aware of our task of termination. They all knew that our group would soon be an experience of the past. I tried to help them deal with this, while using the go-around technique, asking them to say a few words that expressed their feelings at this point. It seemed as though everyone wanted to be first to explain his feelings. But once a few members had their turns, it became even more evident that we were going to leave each other in this situation. The go-around technique didn't really work. As in an earlier meeting, I would have had to push too hard for its completion. Darren put his head down on the desk and wouldn't look at the rest of the group. I explained that throughout our lives we become involved with many groups, none of them exactly the same. I said that it's not easy to say good-bye to people whom we have grown to know and love in certain degrees. But I asked them to think back to how we gradually got to know each other. I "shared my feelings," telling them that I felt sadness in saying good-bye, but that every one of them had brought me learning and happiness that I'll never forget. I told them that the experience has been something that we can take with us— what we have learned here can be applied to other groups. (I must admit that I was happy to have the role of giving direction in this meeting. If I had not been so aware of the need for this, I could have easily behaved like the boys. The group has given me more than I could ever explain, and I felt very confused about the termination myself. This was evident as I think about my personal preplanning for this meeting. This time it wasn't as extensive. I feel this is partly because of me as a member [I probably wanted to ignore the termination more than I really was aware of] and partly because of my role as a leader [I really had no idea of what to plan or expect today from the members]. But as I saw the strong need for my direction, I thought of nothing else. I assumed the leader role, wanting to provide as much for them now as I ever did.)

As in Trudy and Joy's group, the BSW students were able to use the TACIT process model to help group members achieve both group and individual developmental tasks. They were able to use themselves and theme-relevant program activities to influence the group process toward mutual aid. This movement occurred to a degree in all treatment groups and in all cases culminated in the group project of a party in which members took pride in the accomplishment of group goals. The contract formulation and renegotiation as related to the group's purpose and work also stood as a gauge in all treatment groups for successful efforts at both using the group process methodology and achieving the developmental objectives.

DATA ANALYSIS: EVALUATION OF EFFECTS

Outcome data included the ratings on the Behavior Checklist. These measured sensitivity, prosocial behavior, physical aggression, collaborative behavior, and feeling expression. The data were analyzed via the t-test for all pre- and posttest scores. The total scores on the Behavior Checklist rated by teachers are shown in Table 11.1. The student social workers' ratings of behavior in the group with this checklist could not be used in analysis, as inter-rater reliability was only .59. However, teacher ratings showed an increase in desirable behavior in the classroom for all but 6 of the 40 members. The highest increase occurred in the members of the group

TABLE 11.1 Behavior checklist scores

		Boys					**Girls**			
Group	*Member*	*Pre*	*Post*	*Difference*	*Group*	*Member*	*Pre*	*Post*	*Difference*
1	1	22	23	+1	5	23	23	28	+5
(Total	2	13	22	+9	(Total	24	21	25	+4
increase	3	18	23	+5	increase	25	17	26	+9
= +21)	4	27	23	−4	= +29)	26	21	31	+10
	5	14	24	+10		27	9	14	+5
2	6	13	17	+4		28	28	24	−4
(Total	7	28	30	+2	6	29	23	32	+9
increase	8	17	22	+5	(Total	30	14	16	+2
= +23)	9	16	30	+14	increase	31	28	30	+2
	10	15	16	+1	= +13)	32	12	12	0
	11	15	12	−3		33	30	30	0
3	12	9	12	+3		34	16	16	0
(Total	13	21	25	+4	7	35	19	22	+3
increase	14	26	28	+2	(Total	36	26	28	+2
= +20)	15	13	19	+6	increase	37	26	28	+2
	16	24	29	+5	= +24)	38	10	22	+12
4	17	9	22	+13		39	30	32	+2
(Total	18	12	26	+14		40	14	17	+3
increase	19	8	23	+14					
= +55)	20	20	27	+7	Totals	40	367	433	+66
	21	26	30	+4	X		18.95	23.63	
	22	26	29	+3	s.d.		18.08	22.55	
					s^2		326.92	505.58	

$t = 1.440$
$p < .07$

used in the above case study (Group 4). The total increase and its statistical significance were as true for the behavior of boys as of girls.

Table 11.2 presents the subscales of the Behavior Checklist. Two subscale changes are statistically significant. Greatest change occurred in the decreased use of physical aggression (p < .03). However, increases were consistent in the other four subscales: decreased action against group norms, or attention-seeking deviant behavior (p < .07), and increased sensitivity to other (p < .06), expression of feelings (p < .05), and collaborative behavior (p < .07). All subscale changes approach significance. One of the major behavioral outcomes appears to be the movement from physically aggressive behavior (used to express feelings) toward more frequent verbalization of feelings. This change is reflected in the statistically significant findings of these two subscales of the Behavior Checklist.

The Group Survey is a sociometric rating scale that provided two additional evaluation scores: an empathy score and a self-concept score. In this instrument the members were asked to rank each group member, including him- or herself, on three criteria: ability to cooperate, confidence in self, and caring about the group. On the basis of deviancy or accuracy with the pooled group ranking, an individual member empathy score was derived. Empathy is therefore operationalized as an ability to perceive (rank) the self and others as consensually perceived (ranked). The self-concept score was derived from the total of each member's own rank on the three subscales. Used in pre- and posttests, this scale allowed measurement of empathy development and self-concept change during the experience — two of the major objectives of the program.

Table 11.3 summarizes the data on empathy development for members. All members increased in their ability to perceive themselves as others perceived them and to perceive others as others perceived themselves within their group. This development of empathy was statistically significant (t = 2.632; p < .01).

Self-reported self-concept scores increased similarly to the empathy scores. All

TABLE 11.2 Behavior checklist subscale score

Subscale	Pre	Post	Difference	t	p
Sensitivity to others' needs	Sum = 156 Mean = 3.9 s.d. = 1.234	Sum = 183 Mean = 4.6 s.d. = 2.438	+27	1.620	<.06
Action against group norms	Sum = 168 Mean = 4.2 s.d. = 2.150	Sum = 196 Mean = 4.9 s.d. = 2.210	+28	1.434	<.07
Use of physical aggression	Sum = 185 Mean = 4.6 s.d. = 2.441	Sum = 222 Mean = 5.6 s.d. = 2.338	+37	2.041	<.03
Collaborative behavior	Sum = 145 Mean = 3.6 s.d. = 1.319	Sum = 167 Mean = 4.2 s.d. = 2.158	+22	1.422	<.07
Free expression of feelings	Sum = 150 Mean = 3.7 s.d. = 1.234	Sum = 175 Mean = 4.4 s.d. = 2.338	+25	1.670	<.05

TABLE 11.3 Empathy scores

	Boys					Girls			
Group	*Member*	*Pre*	*Post*	*Difference*	*Group*	*Member*	*Pre*	*Post*	*Difference*
1	1	11	23	+11	5	23	11	26	+15
(Total	2	7	22	+15	(Total	24	10	25	+15
increase	3	9	23	+13	increase	25	9	20	+11
= +59)	4	14	20	+6	= +74)	26	11	25	+14
	5	8	24	+16		27	5	20	+15
2	6	7	19	+12		28	14	18	+4
(Total	7	14	30	+16	6	29	12	30	+18
increase	8	9	22	+13	(Total	30	8	20	+12
= +81)	9	8	27	+19	increase	31	15	27	+12
	10	8	20	+12	= +58)	32	6	13	+7
	11	8	17	+9		33	19	20	+1
3	12	5	22	+17		34	8	16	+8
(Total	13	12	25	+13	7	35	10	22	+12
increase	14	14	28	+14	(Total	36	13	24	+11
= +72)	15	8	20	+12	increase	37	13	26	+13
	16	13	29	+16	= +75)	38	5	22	+17
4	17	5	25	+20		39	20	30	+10
(Total	18	7	28	+21		40	7	19	+12
increase	19	5	24	+20	Totals	40	392	935	+66
= +110)	20	11	27	+16	X		9.8	23.37	
	21	13	30	+17	s.d.		4.51	4.41	
	22	13	29	+16	s^2		20.34	19.45	

$t = 2.632$
$p < .01$

but seven members increased their self-concept (esteem) via their self-ratings. Table 11.4 reports these data. This change in self-esteem, operationalized as perception of self as increased cooperativeness, confidence, and caring about the group, was the most statistically significant finding ($t = 4.710$; $p < .001$). As predicted, members seem to have developed more sense of self-worth as a result of the group accomplishments. Unlike empathy, however, this change did not correlate significantly with rated behavioral changes ($r = .21$; NS).

In sum, the findings indicate an increase in acceptable classroom behavior and a decrease in unacceptable behavior. This change is most significant in the ability to express feelings in more acceptable ways while decreasing unacceptable ways such as physical aggression. Members also increased their ability to empathize with (accurately perceive) other members and their self-esteem in relation to self-report ratings.

Interpretation of Findings

These findings must be viewed cautiously, as there were no controls to increase confidence in the group process experience as the cause of these outcomes. There is no doubt that changes did occur. The majority of the changes relate to the theoretical hypotheses of both the developmental tasks of preadolescents and the group

TABLE 11.4 Self-esteem scores

	Boys					Girls			
Group	Member	Pre	Post	Difference	Group	Member	Pre	Post	Difference
1	1	8	12	+4	5	23	13	15	+2
(Total	2	11	14	+3	(Total	24	11	16	+5
increase	3	6	11	+5	increase	25	8	14	+6
= +22)	4	5	11	+6	= +19)	26	9	12	+3
	5	9	13	+4		27	13	15	+2
2	6	10	12	+2		28	16	17	+1
(Total	7	18	18	0	6	29	3	11	+7
increase	8	17	17	0	(Total	30	16	16	0
= +2)	9	14	16	+2	increase	31	9	11	+2
	10	17	17	0	= +29)	32	3	12	+9
	11	15	13	−2		33	9	15	+6
3	12	18	17	−1		34	16	16	0
(Total	13	13	17	+4	7	35	12	13	+1
increase	14	17	18	+1	(Total	36	18	17	−1
= +10)	15	15	16	+1	increase	37	15	17	+2
	16	8	12	+4	= +15)	38	14	16	+2
4	17	12	18	+6		39	9	15	+6
(Total	18	10	17	+7		40	12	16	+4
increase	19	7	16	+9					
= +39)	20	8	16	+8	Totals	471	601		
	21	12	18	+6	X	11.77	15.03		
	22	15	18	+3	s.d.	4.135	1.430		
					s^2	17.10	2.05		

$t = 4.710$
$p < .001$

process model. Certainly, a plausible explanation is the direct influence of the experience, capably facilitated by the social work students, on these outcomes. The permanence of these changes, as much as the other possibly strong influences on them, depend on the classroom experiences of the youngsters involved. There seemed to be a great deal of reciprocal reinforcement between the attitudes and behavior of the counseling group and those of the classroom. The "I-We-It" triangle in the group appears to have reciprocated with the ecosystem of the school and classroom.

Conclusion

Both the "efforts" and the "effects" evaluations generally support the efficacy of this group process model with preadolescents in school. Group members were able to increase their empathic perception of each other and their sense of self-esteem during the experience. Their classroom behavior increased in interpersonal sensitivity, ability to collaborate, and ability to express feelings appropriately. Their classroom behavior decreased in physical expression of aggression and in attention-seeking deviance from classroom norms. These behavioral changes are the sine qua non of appropriate classroom learning norms, which are vital to the achievement of the school's objective for the child. Again, there were no control groups or other controls in this evaluation. The pre- and posttest design is suggestive but limited.

However, social work practice through group process, as used in this project, does seem especially applicable to operationalizing the social worker's function of mediating between the need of the child to use the school and the need of the school to serve the child. The results of this project attest to the fruitful possibilities of this approach, the developmental needs and strengths of the preadolescents involved, the actual skills of the student social workers, and the desire of the school to serve the child.

SUMMARY

Termination, whenever it occurs, is marked by ambivalence for practitioners, members, and the group-as-a-whole. Termination early in group development causes the negative to be experienced more intensely than the positive. If termination occurs later in group development, the positive outweighs the negative and the members can experience the ending process effectively. They can move beyond the group by working through the separation.

We enable this process by catalyzing, processing, providing, and directing. We come to terms with our own feelings and use this difference to help members (1) understand what they have accomplished, and (2) package their experience in such a manner that they can unwrap it and discover the gift of their own abilities to make what happened for them in the group more real for them in their separate social worlds. The end, then, is a real beginning for them. This beginning, when successfully evolved from mutual aid in the group process, includes an increased sense of one's personal, interpersonal, and/or political power.

CRITICAL INCIDENTS

Critical Incident 13

Subtheme.   Focusing Learning

Context of Incident.   This incident occurred in the thirteenth meeting. During the meeting, members discussed how their learning in the group had helped them outside. Most comments were positive, yet not very intense. One member has been looking very hurt and pained.

Choice Point

JERRY (IN A STRAINED VOICE): "I've had trouble using what I've learned here in school. They don't seem to care about me. When I get honest with people there, as I am in here, they come down harder on me. I really wonder what to do about this!"

A few members attempt to offer some help, mostly reassurance, but with little success. Finally, the group falls silent.

What would you do at this point? What is your rationale for this response?

Suggested Response.   The practitioner focuses on the ending and reaches for feelings and evaluation: "I believe we have difficulty owning the negative feelings and evaluations we have now that we are close to ending. Jerry has started to express this negative in his experience. It is almost as if we will feel less good about our experience together if we accept that some aspects of this group experience haven't worked. This stance prevents our really helping Jerry. Perhaps we can talk about some of our less positive feelings and evaluations about our group and its ending, and then come back to Jerry and his specific situation. Is that O.K. with you, Jerry?"

Rationale.   Group members can help Jerry, but they are blocked because of how his comments stir up their avoided feelings about ending. The surface issue of transfer of learning from the group is a real one for all members, clouded here by the underlying issue of the group experience and its ending.

Critical Incident 14

Subtheme.   Preparing for Termination While Still Working

Context of Incident.   This was the fourteenth meeting, and the incident involved one member's expressed anger during a discussion when several members disclosed what they assessed as unfinished business for themselves as the group was drawing to a close. The member's anger was intense and displaced.

Choice Point

CHRIS (IN A VERY ANGRY TONE): "You guys are kidding yourselves. If that much is unfinished for you, it's your own fault! You could have gotten more from this group if you would've tried harder!"

The group seems taken aback by Chris's outburst and lapses into silence.

What would you do at this point? What is your rationale for this response?

Suggested Response.   The practitioner shares his or her own feelings and reaches for the positives behind negatives and the negatives behind positives: "Chris, you're really angry because you don't want members to have any bad feelings about this group. I wonder if maybe that is because you're fighting your own feelings, which aren't so positive about the group and having to leave it. I ask because I was aware of something like that in me as Cheryl, Sandra, and Tom were talking about unfinished business for themselves. I felt good about their honesty and the awareness they took from the group. Yet I was aware of some anger and realized this was from my own frustration about not finding ways to help them with some more of this in the group. Then I realized that there is always unfinished business; that this is life. A part of me wants to hold on to this group. It has been such a good experience for me, and I will always remember it much more positively than negatively. Yet these negative comments have me thinking about working with future groups, and I appreciate this feedback for my learning. Perhaps we can all try to share both the positive and negative feelings we now have about ourselves and the group experience. I would especially appreciate both the positive and negative feedback each of you could give me about my function and role in this group."

Rationale.   Members will manifest individual styles centered on the same underlying issues regarding ending. Most will be more immediately aware of one side of their positive/negative ambivalences. Chris reacts to the negatives in others, displacing anger that may be related to her own frustrations, and the surface issue becomes the tension of her hostility censoring honesty in the group. Chris and the other members need encouragement to confront the ending authentically, both with positives and with negatives. The practitioner shares these, and the difficulty in being in touch with them in ending, in a manner that defuses the hostility and tension and legitimizes ambivalence in disclosure and feedback.

Critical Incident 15

Subtheme.   Saying Good-Byes

Context of Incident.   This event occurred during the fifteenth and final group session. Group members had generally finished saying their good-byes, and the atmosphere was one of resignation and sadness. In general, all immediate unfinished business had been completed and there was a reluctance to stay and yet a greater reluctance to break up the group and leave. The majority of the group members were quiet and contemplative, feeling a sense of intimacy and yet not really knowing how to express the sensation of "oneness" with the group.

Choice Point

The members sit in silence, feeling somewhat peaceful, yet sad and depressed. A few signs are expressed and the silence appears long.

What would you do at this point? What is your rationale for this response?

Suggested Response. The practitioner uses the skill of holding out the ending by directing the closure: "It's always hard to say good-bye, especially to people we've grown quite close to. I don't know of any way of really saying it that can escape the sadness yet the appreciation we feel. I'd like to suggest something at this point that may help us express our good-byes in a meaningful way. I want each of us to close our eyes for about one minute and get in touch with our feelings about ourselves and each other. At the end of a minute, I want us to get up slowly with our eyes still closed, move around the room, and simply do whatever we feel like doing — all without talking. Let's just see how we all end up, without planning or thinking, or talking, and then we'll all leave. O.K., let's close our eyes . . ."

Rationale. The issue, both surface and underlying, is one of needing direction for a significant and meaningful way to say good-bye and leave. The practitioner provides a closing exercise that deals directly with the group's expression of feelings and permits members to balance their autonomy and interdependence in the termination — as throughout the group process.

part III

Implications

chapter 12

Direct Practice Groups

"Once upon a time, some of the creatures who lived in the sea decided that they had to find a way of helping their young to survive the pollution, predators, and other dangers of their world. They decided to form a group to teach these survival skills to their young. In this group was a porpoise, a crab, an oyster, a sailfish, and a moray eel. An octopus was chosen as the group leader because he had eight arms and could control the group better.

"The octopus talked to many sea creature parents, and it was decided that the group would work on the following 'problems':

1. How to dislodge a hook from the mouth;
2. Breathing air on the surface;
3. How to camouflage oneself among the rocks;
4. Running from predators.

"The octopus decided that each creature should be proficient in each of these areas before he or she could 'graduate' from the group.

"The sailfish was excellent at spitting a hook out of her mouth as she jumped high out of the water. Unfortunately, she could not breathe air very well or camouflage herself among the rocks. Since she was having trouble in these areas, the group leader really pressured her and made her work on her deficiencies. This continued until the sailfish's bill was battered from digging into the rocks and she hyperventilated from getting too much air. As a result, the sailfish became only mediocre at spitting a hook out of her mouth.

"The oyster was excellent at camouflaging himself among the rocks, but he soon had to drop out of the group because he couldn't reach the surface to breathe air or spit a hook from his mouth. (He didn't have a mouth!)

"The crab was very good at camouflage, running from predators, and spit-ting the hook out of her mouth. The only problem was that she wanted to do it her own way. When spitting out the hook, she simply took it out of her mouth with her claw. Since the crab didn't jump out of the water to spit the hook in a 'correct and acceptable' manner, the group leader was very unhappy. He contin-ually watched and pressured the crab to make sure she was conforming to the norm of the group.

"The porpoise excelled at breathing air and running from predators. How-ever, she soon developed severe bruises on her stomach from trying to mimic the way the moray eel slid in and out of the rocks.

"The moray eel was a real loner in the group. He kept to himself and didn't come out of the rocks. He threatened to bite anyone who tried to put a hook in his mouth or make him go to the surface to breathe.

"After several months of constant pushing, prodding, and confrontation, the octopus decided that the group was a failure. They would never be able to learn, and they deserved everything that happened to them. Disgustedly, the octopus left for the solitude of his coral reef." (Merritt and Walley, 1977, pp. 3–4)*

INTRODUCTION

The octopus in the parable above exaggerates one extreme of contemporary prac-tice with groups. This is a parenting skills group of the structured genre directed by the many long arms of a leader with little respect for autonomy and interdepen-dence and, thus, for group process. What difference, even in current work with a structured parenting skills group, does social work bring to such practice? This chapter addresses the question. It focuses on the overview of groups used in con-temporary direct practice and on how the group process model informs this prac-tice in *social work* with groups. It continues to underscore the notions of empow-erment and mutual aid. Indeed, these aims and principles stand in stark contrast to the work of the octopus in the parable. Empowerment aims and mutual aid princi-ples distinguish the social worker's competence and difference in direct practice through group process.

THE SMALL GROUP IN DIRECT PRACTICE

Direct or clinical social work practice builds on and integrates the generalist per-spective discussed in Chapter 3. It entails a concentration on therapeutic work face-to-face with client systems in their own behalf (or what is identified as Quadrant A of Figure 3.1 presented in Chapter 3). It requires more breadth and depth of knowl-edge and skills. It involves more depth in differential and sophisticated application

---

*From *The Group Leaders Handbook*, by R.E. Merritt and D.D. Walley. Champaign, IL: Research Press, 1977. Reprinted with permission of Ray E. Merritt.

of these skills and knowledge in engagement, assessment, intervention, and evaluation in behalf of these client systems — individuals, families, small groups, and other interpersonal systems — as well as breadth to address the resource systems that are pertinent to attention to the person-in-environment.

Group approaches that are emphasized in such practice have specific therapeutic objectives (e.g., counseling, psychotherapy, skill training, emotional support, and coping). Models for this practice tend to be those that appear in the first two rows of Table 3.1 presented in Chapter 3. The generic models emphasize individual and interpersonal problem solving and include prevention or more remedial work. The specific models tend to fall on the outer columns of Table 3.1 with an emphasis on either prevention/enhancement or therapy/correction/remedial purposes.

OVERVIEW OF CONTEMPORARY DIRECT APPROACHES

There have been many reviews of approaches to contemporary social work practice (Brown, 1991; Lang, 1979; Middleman and Goldberg, 1987; Papell and Rothman, 1980; Reid, 1991). Generally, this work compares and contrasts (1) the "mainstream" approach of social work with groups with (2) group psychotherapy and structured group approaches. Attention to the therapeutic uses of groups is incorporated here, in terms of the group process model as well as counseling, "mutual aid" or support groups, and correctional groups. Each approach is compared (see Table 12.1) in relation to its major theoretical construct of the "I," the "We," and the "It" — or of the members, the group, and the major activities undertaken. Also compared are the conception of the practitioner's role and the major functions through which this role is operationalized in practice.

Group Psychotherapy

In most group psychotherapy approaches it is assumed that members ("I's") enter the group with special clinical needs. Each member experiences chronic emotional or mental disorders. Members can function, at least to a limited extent, to carry required group tasks (e.g., talking and listening to others, processing or interpreting, and developing awareness of their own behavior and how it affects others within and outside the group). However, their dysfunctions are chronic, being of fairly long duration. Thus, the approach expects therapeutic change in the group to take time. The prototype for group psychotherapy is the long-term (one to three years) outpatient adult group (Yalom, 1995).

In most models for this approach, it is assumed that each member can benefit from small group therapeutic norms. These norms support and challenge interpersonal learning (i.e., the exchange of feedback and self-disclosure) and interpersonal experiences that can be "emotionally corrective" (i.e., can change the patterns from past emotional consequences that have led to current emotional or mental disorders).

TABLE 12.1 An overview of work with groups in direct practice

Group Psychotherapy	Group Counseling	Mutual Aid/Support Groups	Structured Group Approach	Group Correctional Approaches	Social Work through Group Process
"I"	*"I"*	*"I"*	*"I"*	*"I"*	*"I"*
Group members experience more chronic emotional or mental disorders; need therapeutic norms and individual corrective emotional experiences within particular interpersonal relationships in the group	Experiencing current problems in living; need problem-solving norms that use cognitive, emotional, and behavioral data and the reality test and support of others in the group	Experiencing current or chronic crises in coping with debilitating situation; need mutual aid as shared understanding and support and different models for coping with similar situations	Experiencing need for interpersonal and problem-solving skills; need group learning norms to create a context to increase skills	Experiencing antisocial or personally destructive behaviors; need norm changes from antisocial to prosocial or from self-destructiveness to self-control and recovery	Experiences underlying developmental needs for both increased autonomy and interdependence; to some degree may be blocked in current life situations; need norms that promote the development of as much autonomy and mutual aid as possible while gaining power and control in less need-meeting life situations
"We"	*"We"*	*"We"*	*"We"*	*"We"*	*"We"*
Group development as recurrent themes and more phasic; group as microcosm of each member's interpersonal styles and situations; group norms established early and promote both here-and-now experience and awareness and "transferences"	Group development moves progressively through stages toward cohesiveness; group is laboratory for reality testing and problem solving; group norms for problem swapping and problem solving	Group development moves toward closeness and open sharing of concerns in current or chronic crisis situation; group as community of sameness where members look out for each other; group norms for understanding and support and emotional communication	Group development as structured around how individuals, subgroups, or groups as a whole are resources for learning curriculum; group as resource for understanding and practicing skills; group norms as safety to experiment with skill behaviors and transfer learning	Group development as increasing norms for encouraging and reinforcing behavioral and attitude change; group as socialization medium; group norms as strong counters to members' individual and shared antisocial or personally destructive norms	Group development as stages that evolve in a spiral-like fashion more naturally toward increased autonomy and interdependence in group process; group as a process for therapeutic growth and empowerment in relation to life situations; group norms evolve and are shaped to promote autonomy and mutual aid

"It"	"It"	"It"	"It"	"It"	"It"
(Task & Activities) Reflective and verbal activity foremost; focus on covert content; some increasing use of activities other than reflection; insight into one's own role in interpersonal consequences	Reflective and verbal activity foremost; focus on conscious and "preconscious" content; sharing specific problematic situations through self-disclosure and giving and receiving feedback related to problem solving	Verbal communication and community-like activities; focus on emotional concerns and understanding; supporting others through "being with" them; life-sustaining and life-promoting identification through support of group and models for coping derived from this identification	Structured experiences or discussions; focus on concepts and skills deemed crucial for members; involvement in learning activities and practicing learning within and outside of group	Discussion of past patterns and principles for changing these; focus on attitudes and behavior (e.g., substance abuse, violence) in relation to current and future consequences for self and others; some increasing use of reliving and reparenting activities as well as spiritual experiences	More spontaneous and creative as well as planned; focus on common goals in relation to individual goals and "ranges from pursuit, processing, and achievement of group goals to focus on interpretation of individual and/or interpersonal dynamics, maximizing mutual aid, development of group into an autonomous system, and when necessary, the practitioner member exchange" (Middleman and Goldberg, 1987, p. 718)—as dependent upon purpose and needs of group; range of topics and/or activities proposed by either members or practitioner to practitioner-designed structured experiences to achieve specific short-term goals

(continued)

TABLE 12.1 An overview of work with groups in direct practice *(continued)*

Group Psychotherapy	Group Counseling	Mutual Aid/ Support Groups	Structured Group Approach	Group Correctional Approaches	Social Work through Group Process
Practitioner's Role	*Practitioner's Role*	*Practitioner's Role*	*Practitioner's Role*	*Practitioner's Role*	*Practitioner's Role*
Prescribed expert; high directing and processing; controls and/or catalyzes interaction for therapeutic goal-achievement	Consultant on group process and specific problem situations; high providing and directing; controls focus and "shepherds" members to keep it	Convener and initiator; high providing and catalyzing; provides setting, climate, and some direction of members' connection around common needs	Trainer; high directing; controls processing experiences and curriculum content while members make connections to their own needs	Changer; high directing; establishes and controls group norms and holds to work for change	Enabler or empowerer; high levels of providing and processing and medium levels of directing and catalyzing

In general, the group (or "We") is significant in terms of how its recurrent themes resonate with individual members' clinical themes (Whitaker and Lieberman, 1965). Group psychotherapy approaches tend to conceive of the group-as-a-whole as a composite of the social microcosm that each member has attempted to carve out. It is a mosaic of the current levels of functioning and dysfunctioning in members' interpersonal styles and patterns. Prevailing concepts of dysfunctional themes include interpersonal issues such as power and intimacy (Bennis and Shepherd, 1956); "fight," "flight," and "pairing" (Bion, 1959); dependence, counterdependence, and independence (Yalom, 1995); and "inclusion," "control," and "affection" (Schutz, 1958). Priority is placed on the practitioner's establishing therapeutic norms very early in the group, especially through "ground rules." These demand here-and-now intermember interactions and interpretations. Interpretations of the interaction focus on members' transferences and how these serve functional or dysfunctional purposes in the group and in members' emotional and mental functioning in contexts outside of the group.

The approach primarily makes use of reflective and verbal activity as the tasks ("It") considered necessary to accomplish individual and group therapeutic goals. The focus is on gaining awareness and insight about one's communication and interpersonal patterns within and outside the group. Special content includes the covert, or less conscious, influences on these patterns in members' talk and behavior. There is a trend toward increased use of activities other than reflection wherein the practitioner suggests experiments in interpersonal communication and action designed to change patterns without reflective insight. However, these do not characterize much of group psychotherapy observed in practice or depicted in the literature. Considerable practitioner-to-member and member-to-member discussion is intended to increase a member's insight into his or her own autonomous role in his or her interpersonal consequences. This painful awareness is used as leverage for change in chronic dysfunctional patterns.

In group psychotherapy, the practitioner's role generally reflects a medical model of practice. Hence, practitioners are the prescribed experts, both on the members' disorders and appropriate treatment and on the therapeutic process in the group. Practitioners use high levels of the directing, processing, and catalyzing functions. They avoid using the providing function, with the expectation that such personal involvement would create dysfunctional transferences for members and countertransferences for the practitioners. They do tend to direct strongly. They especially attempt to control group interaction in a way that shepherds member and group discussions to in-group interpersonal styles and reactions as related to areas of diagnosed pathological function in contexts outside of the group (Yalom, 1995).

Group Counseling

Counseling groups differ from psychotherapy groups because they focus on identifiable problems that members are experiencing in their present situations. Members ("I's") are assumed to be experiencing very immediate problems in living. Whether these problems are chronic or situational, members need to find ways of coping with them as well as possible and as soon as possible. Practitioners consider shorter-term (4 to 16 weeks) and, most often, closed groups (keeping the members together for the duration of the group) as most responsive to the individual members' needs and goals. Practitioners assume that members need a group that shares individual problem-solving goals. Group norms would promote such problem solving, especially through the generation of cognitive, emotional, and behavioral data. The norms regulate the problems and solutions through their relevance to other members in the group and through support to initiate action to solve particular problems differently.

The group ("We") is important in three major respects: (1) its development through stages to cohesiveness supports the shared problem-solving work (Corey, 1990a); (2) it serves as a laboratory for consensual reality-testing during problem solving; and (3) it develops norms that affirm the strengths of identifying and working on problems through "problem swapping" in group discussion and supporting and challenging each member's actions toward more effective resolution of identified, immediate problems.

In the task and activity dimension ("It"), group counseling approaches also favor reflective and verbal activity. However, the focus is consistently on conscious and "preconscious" content; that is, what members are aware of — if only dimly — regarding their beliefs, feelings, and behavior patterns and the connections among them. Much activity reflects members' sharing of problematic situations through both self-disclosure and the giving and receiving of feedback related to this problem solving.

Practitioners tend to assume a consultant role in the group (Corey et al., 1992). They suggest ways to enhance the development of the group's process in behalf of therapeutic cohesiveness and to approach problem identification, assessment, and solution activities among members. Thus, they make high use of providing and directing functions (Carkhuff, 1989; Egan, 1975; Ivey, 1973). The intent is to establish a climate of safety and understanding. From this base of support, they challenge the group and individual members to keep focus and to mobilize resources in behalf of the problem situations they address (Jacobs, Harvill, and Masson, 1988).

Mutual Aid/Support Groups

"Mutual aid" or emotional "support" groups are offered to persons who are experiencing current acute crises (e.g., bereavement, acute illness, or criminal victimization) or more chronic stresses (e.g., diagnosis of debilitating illness, stresses from socially stigmatized ascriptions such as sexual preference or interracial marriages.) The groups come together around the common need for mutual aid, support, and other help in coping with situations that may not appear to be changeable (e.g., loss, imminent death, permanent "handicap," or socially ascribed status). Members need understanding and emotional support, as well as coping skills developed through their interaction with others who are coping with similar situations (Silverman, 1980).

The emphasis on emotional support influences conceptions of the group ("We") as developing toward closeness. This closeness promotes a sense of belonging and allays feelings of loneliness and alienation. At the same time, it provides a climate that is supportive of open sharing of feelings and concerns in members' chronic or current crisis or stress situations. It validates increased competence in coping. The primary group model is of a "community" of people in relatively similar situations who likely have much in common from which to share and to look out for each other. The group norms emphasize mutual understanding and support, and emotional bonding and communication among members (Wassermann and Danforth, 1986).

Tasks and activities ("It") entail verbal communication and discussion as well as other community-like activities (e.g., games, dances, lectures, fund-raisers, and excursions). Through any activity the emphasis is on emotional connections, concerns, and understanding. The reciprocal supporting of others by being with them during times of need can increase mutual identification among members through the support of the group, the members as models, and information on coping.

The practitioner's role is generally one of concern and initiation. There is fairly high use of the providing and catalyzing functions. Practitioners provide the setting and climate in which members can make emotional connections, and they offer some direction for how members may connect around their common needs. This often includes mediating between members and the people and information deemed functional to an understanding of their needs and coping alternatives.

Structured Group Approach

Perhaps no aspect of direct practice with groups has expanded as greatly in recent years as the structured group approach (Drum and Knott, 1977). Workshops for skill training are offered both to the general population and as an adjunct to treatment in a variety of therapeutic settings. Generally, though, individual members ("I's") in this approach are assumed to need interpersonal, communication, emotional management, and/or problem-solving skills. The group context is a resource for this skill learning, especially when (1) its norms mobilize members to use the planned program to increase their skills, and (2) it presents opportunities to experiment with and practice these skills.

Thus, the group ("We") is conceived of to a degree as a controlled laboratory whose development is consciously planned through a practitioner-initiated structure. Often this structure moves from individual experiences, through subgroup activities, to use of the group-as-a-whole for learning the specific curriculum. The group, when considered in the structure, is a resource for understanding and practicing particular skills. Group norms tend to be "ground rules" designed to cultivate experience with skill behaviors and to transfer learning connections to each member's individual needs and goals.

Program activity ("It") includes many structured experiences and discussion of them. The discussion generally is initiated and focused by the practitioner; it underscores concepts and skills deemed crucial for members. The major tasks relate to involvement in the planned learning activities and the practice of this learning as relevant within and outside the group.

Practitioners conceive of their role primarily as "trainers" or "workshop leaders." There is high use of the directing and processing functions. The approach is especially marked by directing through structured experiences and interpreting them in reference to (1) the skill models used, as well as (2) how members see the content fitting their needs and individual situations. For example, recent program material for directing these groups makes extensive use of audiotapes, videotapes, and participant manuals (Research Press, 1994).

Group Correctional Approaches

Correctional approaches involve people who evidence antisocial behavior (e.g., juvenile and adult offenders, batterers) or self-destructive behavior (e.g., alcoholics, overeaters). Individual members ("I's") are assumed to be needing corrective or recovery ("healing") experiences. Emphasis is on resocialization through developing a group culture that enforces norms that are prosocial as opposed to antisocial (Vorrath and Brendtro, 1985) and oriented toward self-control and recovery as opposed to self-destruction (Levine and Galoghy, 1985).

Group development in correctional groups highlights the norm regulation process. The intent is to form a "We" with increased norms that encourage and reinforce changed attitudes and behavior. In taking on significance and power for members, the group serves as a medium for socialization. A group with strong prosocial or prorecovery norms is necessary to counter the members' individual and shared antisocial or personally destructive norms in their lives outside of the group.

Primary activities involve discussion of past patterns and norms, their costs and benefits to members, and ways for changing now and in the future. The "It" focuses on attitudes and behaviors (e.g., substance abuse, violence) in relation to current and future consequences for self and others. More recently, these groups make use of reliving and reparenting activities as well as spiritual experiences (Bradshaw, 1990, 1992).

The practitioner is a changer. There is high use of directing to establish group norms and of catalyzing members' painful feelings as leverage for motivating change in attitudes and behaviors. The practitioner establishes and controls group norms via clear ground rules and keeps members and the group at work for change that is more responsible to self, others, and/or society (Vannicelli, 1992).

SOCIAL WORK THROUGH GROUP PROCESS

The group process model for social work with groups in direct practice considers individual members ("I's") as experiencing the normal developmental needs for autonomy and interdependence. To some degree, these needs may be stunted through obstacles in members' current life situations. In this regard the most pertinent therapeutic factors in the group are the norms that foster the development of as much autonomy and interdependent mutual aid as possible. Through these processes, members gain more personal power and control in their current life situations inside and outside of the group.

The group process, or "I-We," is the major agent of therapeutic change. It involves the group's development through stages in a spiral-like fashion, evolving toward increased autonomy and interdependence. This underlying evolution promotes both therapeutic growth and empowerment in relation to members' life situations and environmental contexts. Group norms may also evolve from negotiation of how best to achieve the group's purpose; they can be shaped to cultivate a group culture that is responsive to members' developmental needs for autonomy and interdependence.

The tasks ("It") involve spontaneous and creative as well as planned activities. They contribute to accomplishing group goals in a manner that enables individual and group autonomy and the synergistic sharing of power and resources. This taps the potential for interdependence and mutual aid. As Ruth Middleman and Gale Goldberg (1987) state, the focus on common goals ("We") in relation to individual goals ("I") generates tasks and activities ("It") that "range from pursuit, processing, and achievement of group goals to focus on interpretation of individual and/or interpersonal dynamics, maximizing mutual aid, development of groups into an autonomous system, and, when necessary, the practitioner-member exchange" (p. 718). These are dependent on the purpose and needs of the group. The range of topics and/or activities in mainstream group practice includes those proposed by members or the social work practitioner, as well as practitioner-designed structured experiences to achieve short-term goals determined in collaboration with the group and its members.

The practitioner's role vis-à-vis the group is enabling. In this empowering orientation, there is high use of providing and processing and moderate use of directing and catalyzing. These functions and their concomitant skills provide direction when tied to the stages of the group's development. They facilitate the group's process toward the evolution of more autonomy and interdependence.

When these therapeutic groups are used in social work, practitioners are encouraged to incorporate as much of the social-work-with-groups vision as possible. The group process model instructs such practice. The core of this model includes its concept of group process as the stages of group development, the value of both autonomy and interdependence in this process, and the differential use of functions and skills to enable development.

CONCLUSION

The variants of direct practice groups emphasize aspects of process as related to purpose and context. The group process approach presented in this book can expand the attention to process to ensure that empowerment is accomplished as much as possible in all practice with groups.

chapter 13

Task Groups

"A camel was a horse designed by committee."

INTRODUCTION

The delivery of human services encompasses working in task groups, which require group development on both interpersonal and task dimensions. The problem in understanding and facilitating this development is that the dimensions can evolve at different rates, whereas the full evolution of a task group requires their mutual progression.

TASK GROUP MODEL

TACIT is also an acronym for the sequential steps in group problem solving. These are Task Orientation, Accommodation, Communication, Integrative Problem Solving, and Task Completion. Members of task groups begin with *task orientation* activities. This orientation involves the initial determination of each member's position in the group as well as clarification of the nature of the task and what each member brings to it. Next, the exploration begins to focus more directly on *accommodation*. That is, members adapt to each other and the task, often by confronting and resolving (directly and/or indirectly) conflicts regarding positions, task expertise, interpersonal relationships, and group values and norms. Once this organization and structure for work has been established, more negotiation, data flow, or *communication* evolves. If the communication is open and flows freely regarding both the interpersonal and task dimensions of members' transactions, then members to some degree develop a contract with one another about the nature of their individual and interdependent tasks; in this way the potential for *integrative problem solving* evolves. Integrative problem solving connotes fuller incorporation of the resources of individual members and the group. It is based on decision making and action that reflect "synergy," or a performance on the team in *task completion* that surpasses the work of any member of the group working on one's own. Thus, the evaluation in task completion reflects an outcome of quality that is superior to the performance of less-developed groups or to the outcomes of individual problem solving.

The potential for synergy, the mark of an effective task group, requires simultaneous development in both TACIT interpersonal and TACIT task processes. Apparently, only in a group wherein interdependence in interpersonal relationships evolves can consistent, integrative problem solving occur. Problems in task group functioning can be tracked as deviations from this optimum level of development and assessed in relation to the team's current level of TACIT development in either the interpersonal or task dimensions. Figure 13.1 diagrams this general assessment model, wherein optimal development occurs diagonally toward the 4.4 interrelationship of interpersonal and task processes.

LEADERSHIP AND MEMBERSHIP SKILLS

A fairly extensive volume of model-building (Bales, 1950; Brill, 1976; Dyer, 1977; Fiedler, 1967; Hooyman, 1984; Kane, 1975; Maier, 1970; Sherwood and Hoylman, 1977) and of research (Bales, 1950; Hackman, 1968; Reitz, 1977) propose specific sets of interpersonal maintenance and task skills that are pertinent to leadership and membership effectiveness in task groups. The work to date, however, has not considered these skills in the context of stages of interpersonal and task development in groups (with the possible exceptions of Brill, 1976, and Hooyman, 1984).

FIGURE 13.1   Task group development

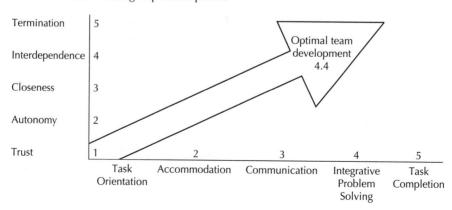

Research on leadership styles that focus on both personal and task dimensions in process-oriented groups (J. Anderson, 1984; Bolman, 1971, 1973; Hurst et al., 1978; Lieberman, Yalom, and Miles, 1973; O'Day, 1974) and in task-oriented groups (Hackman, 1968; Maier, 1967) has consistently identified a particular set of functions to distinguish among various leadership styles and their relationship to group outcomes. These are similar to directing, providing, processing, and catalyzing. For example, Maier (1967) refers to these equivalent functions in task groups as structuring, responding, process observing, and expression management.

The functions in task groups are defined here as follows:

Directing: At both the task and interpersonal dimensions, this function refers to leader behaviors that set and maintain limits (e.g., setting goals, assigning roles and tasks, prescribing norms, managing time, stopping, interceding, and suggesting procedures).

Providing: At both the task and interpersonal dimensions, this function refers to leader behaviors that set the climate (e.g., expressing affection, praising, communicating genuineness and empathy, and showing concern for each member and the group as a whole).

Processing: At both the task and interpersonal dimensions, this function refers to leader behaviors that expand members' and the group's awareness of process (e.g., explaining, clarifying, interpreting, giving feedback, and labeling processes).

Catalyzing: This function refers to leader behaviors at the interpersonal dimensions that stimulate interaction and emotional expression (e.g., reaching for feelings, sharing own feelings, challenging, and confronting). At the task dimension, this function includes behaviors with the intent of motivating for work (e.g., encouraging work, challenging obstacles to work, and sharing feelings).

To date, the research suggests that these functions cluster into a variety of task group leadership styles that are dependent on their degree of emphasis (or use) by particular leaders. Group outcomes relate to these leadership styles at two levels: the degree of task completion, and the degree of members' satisfaction with the group's functioning. Table 13.1 summarizes the major leadership styles and hypothesizes their relationship to outcomes, as based on current findings.

Enablers generally emphasize high use of the providing and processing functions and moderate use of catalyzing and directing. This style tends to promote both autonomy and interdependence as balanced with focus on the task. Responsiveness to group purpose and individual and group needs seems prerequisite for a high level of both task accomplishment and member satisfaction. *Social engineers* are similar to enablers with the exception of very little or no use of catalyzing. This style tends to accomplish a fairly moderate level of task completion and member satisfaction. The underuse of catalyzing can lead to unresolved interpersonal conflicts and more unchallenged resistance to the work, which often results in some members not per-

TABLE 13.1   Leadership styles and predicted outcomes

	Function					Outcome
	Providing	*Processing*	*Catalyzing*	*Directing*	*Task Completion*	*Degree of Satisfaction*
Enablers	H	H	M	M	H	H
Social Engineers	H	H	L	M	M	M
Energizers	H	L	H	H	L	H
Laissez-faires	L	H	L	L	L	M
Managers	L	L	H	H	L	L

H = High Emphasis; M = Medium Emphasis; L = Low Emphasis

forming to their potential (or actually "dropping out"). Next in effectiveness are *energizers*. They are highly directive, supportive, and stimulating (more "charismatic") and low in reflecting upon interpersonal and task processes. Their groups tend to accomplish tasks at a level of quality that is lower than that of enablers and social engineers. However, they often draw a high rating of member satisfaction. Their high level of activity as both task and maintenance leaders impresses members but can greatly restrict members' autonomous functioning. This impedes their fullest contribution to the task accomplishment. *Laissez-faires* are the opposite of energizers; they provide little except feedback designed to increase members' awareness of what they are doing (at task and interpersonal dimensions). Because members experience autonomy in their group, the satisfaction outcome is often medium. However, the quality of task completion is usually low, reflecting too little interdependence in the final product. The least effective team leaders appear to be *managers*. They tend to "boss" the group. They attempt to control the means and ends of the process by using high levels of the directing and catalyzing functions and low levels of providing and processing. The outcomes of the manager style are the lowest, both in terms of quality of the completed task and team member satisfaction.

As in other group practice, the group evolves best through enabling. The leader as enabler must use all four functions, with higher use of providing and processing and moderate use of directing and catalyzing. However, their use varies according to the stage of interpersonal or task process. That is, combinations of these functions and the skills that serve them for enabling development are differentially used in response to the interpersonal and task process needs of the group. Table 13.2 summarizes the functions and skills deemed most enabling for each stage of task group development.

In the best of task groups the functional aspect of leadership is shared among members, especially as the group evolves. Different members contribute to the process as well as to the products of teamwork through their natural strengths and skills that serve particular functions needed by the group. For instance, some members have stronger orientations and skills related to task processes than to interpersonal ones; others have the opposite strengths. These members contribute differen-

TABLE 13.2   Leadership functions and skills

T-Stage (TRUST and TASK ORIENTATION)

Interpersonal	*Task*

*Providing
  Encouraging
  Supporting/Attending
  Gatekeeping
	*Directing
	  Contracting
	  Initiating
	  Giving and receiving information
	    Standard-setting

**Catalyzing
  Reaching for participation
*Directing
  Contracting
	**Processing
	  Illuminating task-orientation process

A-Stage (AUTONOMY and ACCOMMODATION)

*Providing
  Harmonizing
  Individualizing
	*Processing
	  Task process
	  Observing and interpreting

*Processing
  Interpersonal process
  Observing and interpreting
	**Directing
	  Initiating agenda
	  Monitoring building work
	    Elaborating and clarifying tasks

**Directing
  Norming
	Giving and receiving options
	  Standard setting

**Catalyzing
  Compromising
  Consensus-building
	**Catalyzing
	  Reaching for ideas and opinions
	  Deciding by consensus

C-Stage (CLOSENESS AND COMMUNICATION)

*Catalyzing
  Sharing own feelings
  Reaching for feelings related
    to work
	*Processing
	  Elaborating and clarifying task

*Providing
  Harmonizing
  Individualizing
	**Directing
	  "Recontracting"
	  Promoting consensus
	    decision making

I-Stage (INTERDEPENDENCE and INTEGRATIVE PROBLEM SOLVING)

*Providing
  Encouraging and supporting
	*Catalyzing
	  Giving and receiving feedback

*Processing
  Challenging process obstacles
	**Directing
	  Coordinating

T-Stage (TERMINATION and TASK COMPLETION)

*Providing
  Crediting
	*Directing
	  Initiating task review

**Catalyzing
  Sharing own feelings
  Reaching for feelings
	**Processing
	  Summarizing and evaluating

*High use
**Moderate use

tially to the overall task by functioning naturally with skills that can enable the fullest development of the group's processes. In optimal team experiences, members' strengths in carrying these critical process functions are not only freely used but tend to be more broadly developed. All members increase in skills that address both the interpersonal and task process needs. This explains why there seems to be no better way of learning effective team leadership (one who can enable group development toward the higher levels of task completion as well as personal satisfaction on the part of members) than through the experience of membership in a more optimally functioning task group.

Thus, explication of the functions and skills of task group membership is similar to the leadership model presented in Table 13.2. When all members are using their strengths and skills to contribute to carrying functions that serve the team, leadership is experienced not as a position or as embodied in a single person designated "leader." Instead, leadership becomes an overriding function that is shared by all members and implemented through the diversity of strengths and skills of each.

As Table 13.2 notes, during the T-Stage the most important functions are *providing* in relation to interpersonal processes and *directing* in response to task process needs. Providing the opportunity for initial trust often involves: (1) encouraging members to get to know each other; (2) supporting members through attending (or paying attention to their individual interpersonal orientation and needs); and (3) gatekeeping through opening opportunities for them to interact and get to know each other personally, as well as through helping to make personal connections between and among members. Directing requires enabling the accomplishment of task orientation through contracting. This involves clarifying and negotiating the purpose and objectives of the team, its goals, the nature of the task, and an agreement on general expectations about how to proceed toward task accomplishment. This entails skills in initiating the contracting, in giving and receiving information that is useful for clarifying and negotiating such "contracts," and for beginning to clarify standards about the quality of the work and how it can best be accomplished.

At this stage, moderate to low use of catalyzing and processing is appropriate. Catalyzing here primarily serves to reach for participation through encouraging reactions and feedback; processing occurs through feedback that illuminates for all the current task-orientation needs of individual members and the team's beginning process.

During the A-Stage, the *providing* and *processing* functions need high use whereas directing and catalyzing are carried to a moderate degree. Interpersonal autonomy evolves from a more trusting climate and requires such providing skills as harmonizing and individualizing. The skills build a generally harmonious climate in the team yet demonstrate concern and respect for each individual's autonomy. They are most significant in promoting members' assertions of their strengths and individual contributions with an appropriate sense of responsibility to others and the team. They (1) hold in check the members' power and control impulses and fears and (2) channel them through a growing sense of responsibility to both self and group in interpersonal transactions within the "team." Processing skills contribute to interpersonal autonomy by sharing and eliciting reactions, observations, and interpretations regarding how members seem to be affecting each other and the team's functioning as *people* in the group. Task accommodation requires a similar processing, with special focus on where the team is and where it wants to be regarding its structure and performance toward achieving current objectives.

The A-Stage's moderate use of directing and catalyzing reflects additional leadership and membership skills. The directing and catalyzing to promote more interpersonal autonomy comes from the conscious establishment of norms to regulate and enable effective social interaction and from asserting compromise and consensus-building procedures to resolve interpersonal conflicts. For task accommodation, directing entails such skills as initiating agenda building, elaborating and clarifying the tasks, giving and receiving opinions, and the continual development of appropriate standards. Catalyzing especially involves reaching for ideas and opinions regarding the task and encouraging team decision making that addresses the differences of ideas and opinions through appropriate levels of consensus.

During the C-Stage, *catalyzing* and *processing* evolve as the most significant functions; directing and processing are more moderate in importance and use. For closeness or cohesiveness to evolve more fully in interpersonal processes and for the flow of communication that is necessary for work on the task, there needs to be interpersonal catalyzing through the sharing of feelings. This helps to put the interpersonal agenda more directly on the table. So does the reaching for feelings. Task processing here involves elaborating on and clarifying the work assignments in relation to autonomous needs, wants, and strengths and the interdependent purpose. With the recognition that by now the team has a wisdom of its own, borne of knowing its own resources, directing can promote even more consensual decision making and more specific "recontracting" in relation to task completion. Likewise, providing comes from the harmonizing and individualizing begun earlier.

During the I-Stage (wherein there is an evolution of a balance of autonomy and interdependence in both the interpersonal and task processes), *providing* and *catalyzing* are the predominant functions for all members of the team to carry. Processing and directing, also carried by all members, are best used in moderation. Providing through encouraging and supporting invokes the team's underlying interpersonal capacity to care. Catalyzing through the giving and receiving of feedback taps the team's ability to now use individual member differences more directly. These can become effective contributions toward, rather than obstacles to, task completion and the achievement of purpose. Processing still serves to challenge the obstacles to autonomy and interdependence when they arise. Directing coordinates individual members' efforts, now more consistently and creatively integrated with team problem-solving processes.

During the T-Stage of termination and task completion, *providing* and *directing* again require higher use. Feedback — especially the crediting of interpersonal process contributions — needs to be initiated through providing. Directing involves initiation of the review of task accomplishment and individual and team performance. This is true whether the group ends after substantial development or terminates its work together after evolution only slightly through the first T-Stage or at the beginning of the A-Stage. Similarly, the processing function — through such skills as summarizing and evaluation — is moderately needed. However, when the group is terminating after having achieved a more optimal level of development, catalyzing also takes on some significance. The breakup is experienced as a real loss — a special human process wherein one lived for a time with certain special people and worked close to one's fullest capacity. The resultant feelings of loss and the sense of increased competence also need to be lived through the ending by sharing and reaching for the feelings that give increased meaning to the experience.

CONCLUSION

This chapter presented a model based on TACIT themes and procedures for task groups. The model considers the functions and skills for leadership and membership that are most pertinent for the optimum development of task groups.

chapter 14

Practice Evaluation

"Seeing Is Believing"

INTRODUCTION

Social work authors have appealed for the practitioner to act as an evaluation researcher in social work, as well as for greater collaboration between researchers and practitioners (Bloom and Fischer, 1982). The gap between research and practice appears even stronger in social work practice with groups. Investigators of group process and outcomes often detach from the real groups we serve in social work. They frequently take refuge in isolated environments with greater controls over experimental variables. Social work practitioners, on the other hand, often try to understand groups without consulting the research. Or they dismiss the bulk of empirical work on groups as irrelevant, or related only tangentially to actual practice.

Recent developments both within and outside social work make it clear that practitioners and researchers can no longer afford to maintain such gaps. Some (Bloom and Fischer, 1982) argue that the very survival of social work as a profession requires more active integration of research and all areas of practice. From outside, the call for professional accountability means that legislators, insurance companies, and service consumers are increasing their demands for information on the efficacy, safety, and cost-effectiveness of social work services. From inside the profession, the Curriculum Policy Statement (CPS) of the Council on Social Work Education (CSWE, 1994) requires the integration of research and practice in the foundation competencies of students. Students must learn to use research to evaluate their own practice systematically.

Social work as a profession that works with group process is not the only area that experiences a gap between practice and research. One author (Parloff, 1980) has lamented "an anaclitic depression" between group psychotherapy and research. Another (Kiesler, 1981) finds the supposed relation of research to clinical psychology practice a myth—particularly in relation to the use of group psychotherapy. Others (Bednar and Kaul, 1979; MacKenzie and Dies, 1982) focus on the variety of professions involved in practice with therapeutic groups and judge all of them unaccountable in their integration of practice and research.

These authors suggest three avenues through which to build a bridge between practice and research in work with groups: (1) identifying the use of empirical process in all practice; (2) building instrumentation into social work practice with a group; and (3) using single-system designs for evaluating this practice.

PRACTICE AS HYPOTHESIS-TESTING

In basic attitudes, good practice and good research are most compatible. In group psychotherapy, one review submits that "the polarization of therapy-softness and research-rigorousness is artificial and does not represent a complete picture of what is required for high level clinical service" (Bednar and Kaul, 1979, p. 318). The authors suggest that effective clinical group practice and effective research require similar dispositions, attitudes, and intellectual skills. Formulating research hypotheses based on the theory and understanding of the empirical literature is not unlike planning interventions in groups based on the theory and understanding of group process. Another reviewer (Kiesler, 1981) suggests that all clinical practitioners and scientists employ identical processes in their work:

> Both start with empirical observations (systematically measured or not) from which generalities are abstracted and treatment or manipulative hypotheses are deducted, applied, and subsequently validated empirically (through systematic observations or not). Both . . . involve at their core a hypothesis-testing procedure. (pp. 213–214)

When working with groups, we first observe members' interactions within meetings and listen to their reports about transactions within their worlds outside of the group. Then, we generate conceptualizations of their behavior and its relation to group process from which we form hypotheses for intervention. When we use these interventions, we observe again to assess or evaluate their effectiveness. Thus, in practice we move from observation, to conceptualization, to intervention, to validation. This very practice is a scientific event, encapsulating the application (whether systematic or not) of the empirical process to the single case of the group. The difference in this hypothesis-testing between the practitioner and researcher lies in the use of scientific method in two areas: (1) whether the inductive-deductive logical process operates implicitly or explicitly; and (2) whether systematic or unsystematic observation occurs. To make one's efforts scientific, the practitioner needs only to explicate the conceptualizations of client change and to apply some form of empirical measurement so that the data base can be objective, replicable, and thus in the public domain (Dies and MacKenzie, 1983; Kiesler, 1981).

In other words, in social work practice with groups, the integration of practice with research requires more systematic use of the common empirical process through specific operationalizing and measurement of group process and outcome variables. A first step would be to build instrumentation into our actual practice with groups.

INSTRUMENTATION IN SOCIAL WORK WITH GROUPS

Instrumentation in group work has the potentially powerful appeal for combining research and practice with mutual benefits. For example, it can be most practical and serve as feedback on elements of the group process. This can help prevent the development of destructive processes that are highly correlated with psychological injury for members of groups (Lieberman, Yalom, and Miles, 1973). Robert Dies and K. Robert MacKenzie (1983) suggest that instrumentation used for evaluation research in groups can move practitioners from thinking only in terms of research with a "capital R (Random, Representative, and/or Robust samples, Rigorous methodological controls, Reined statistical operations, and Resplendent computer technology)" to considering its contribution for improving the quality of group treatment. Instrumentation, especially when combined with single-system research designs, permits the practitioner and members to both monitor and study the group more intensively and empirically. This action research can form the basis for decisions regarding intervention.

Instrumentation, therefore, is the use of systematic and repeated observations throughout the course of the practice group process. It permits one to study and monitor the possible connections between process and outcome variables in the group experience. Earlier work (Pfeiffer, Heslin, and Jones, 1976) and more recent work (MacKenzie and Dies, 1982) have assessed the benefits and disadvantages of instrumentation in work with groups and have provided useful batteries for initiating its integration with practice. Among the major advantages of this instrumentation are that it (1) encourages member involvement in the group process; (2) fosters open reaction to personal feedback; (3) clarifies members' goals and facilitates contracting for new behavior; (4) increases the objectivity of measuring member change; (5) provides for comparison of individual members (especially in treatment or therapy groups) with normative groups; (6) facilitates longitudinal (before, after, follow-up) assessment of change; (7) sensitizes members and practitioners to the multifaceted nature of change in group process; (8) gives members a sense that the practitioner is committed to effective work or treatment; (9) improves communication between members and practitioners; (10) allows practitioners to focus and direct the group more effectively; (11) aids the establishment of processing norms for the group; and (12) provides members some cognitive frameworks for understanding their group experience and transferring learning to their life situations outside the group.

Dies and MacKenzie (1983) especially note some of the disadvantages of instrumentation. These include member and practitioner resistance to giving and receiving information and feedback, misuse of the measures, interference with "treatment" precipitated by the measures, and the experience of intrusiveness on spontaneous group process. Dies and MacKenzie suggest that these pitfalls can be easily prevented by following some basic guidelines. Fully explaining their potential value to members can remove the mystique surrounding measures. Describing their contribution to understanding group process and outcomes can reassure members that every precaution will be taken to guarantee the responsible use of the findings.

Instrumentation, or the systematic use of empirical measures, can improve our immediate practice with groups. It also can narrow the gap between research and practice. As practitioners learn that data-collection procedures are not always time-consuming, inconvenient, and intrusive for work with groups and can actually contribute to efficacy in providing service, their personal resistance to research (especially "capital-R" research) may diminish. In fact, they may search for a source of appropriate and valid instruments. One resource is the CORE Battery, an outcome evaluation kit developed by the Research Committee of the American Group Psychotherapy Association (MacKenzie and Dies, 1982). This battery meets the major criteria for selecting and using suitable change-measures or outcome packages for instrumentation with groups. It includes multiple measures; elicits both objective and subjective viewpoints and evaluates subjective impressions as compared with behavioral observations; combines individualized and standardized measurements; assesses various areas of members' functioning (e.g., self-esteem, interpersonal satisfaction, and social role) draws on various sources of information, including practitioner, group member, and significant others; and represents instruments that strike a reasonable compromise between comprehensiveness and realistic time demands.

SINGLE-SYSTEM DESIGNS IN SOCIAL WORK WITH GROUPS

Outcomes

The use of such a package, or parts of it, and other outcome measures can lead to simple pre/post single-system design studies. For instance, one of the instruments in the CORE Battery is the Self-Report Symptom Inventory. This checklist is a standardized instrument with extensive norms and broad empirical support (Derogatis, 1977) that can be used to investigate outcomes in treatment or therapy groups. Members can readily complete it on their own time, and it can be easily scored. Because the test is brief and has obvious face validity, group members appear quite willing to take it (Dies and MacKenzie, 1983). If it is used in pretesting as an initial assessment it can be compared against later posttesting as an evaluation measure. Because it is standardized, it enables us to assess members against norms. We can measure individualized change goals by incorporating a self-anchored target goal or goal grid scale into the pre- and posttesting. These require members to identify specific and personal change goals that can be quantified and evaluated in terms of members' achievements in the group process (Coche, 1983). For therapeutic groups, one could use the goal-setting schedule presented in Appendix I of this text. Other social work outcome instruments can be found in Walter Hudson (1982) and in Joel Fischer and Kevin Corcoran (1989).

If practitioners were to use these measures in a simple pretest/posttest design with their groups, they would be taking important steps in practice evaluation research. Simultaneously, they would be clarifying the nature of group member outcomes. This could encourage group members to establish more concrete goals in the contract for and evaluation of change. Thus, the pretest contamination in small group "capital-R" research becomes a distinct advantage as part of the contract for therapeutic group work.

We can refine the simple pre/post design by using additional outcome measures — but only a few relevant ones. The selection depends on what is to be measured, the validity and reliability of available instruments, a repertoire of data-collection strategies, and alternative approaches to designing one's own instruments. These decisions require homework on the part of the practitioner in (1) conceptualizing and operationalizing group process and outcome variables, and (2) discovering appropriate instruments in the empirical literature.

We need to decide if we want to focus on particular symptoms, attitudes toward self, or specific areas of interpersonal or social functioning. Within time or resource limitations, we need to adopt different strategies with different groups. In one setting with one kind of group, our focus may be on remediating symptoms; in another, on functioning in certain social roles or targeting specific community action. Ideally, in much of social work practice with groups, the targets would include both personal *and* social change; and we would use multiple measures to assess outcomes in the same group.

Pre/post designs, even refined with appropriate and multiple outcome measures, have limitations. Although they may demonstrate the general efficacy of the group in practice and can aid contracting, they do not really link outcomes to process. This limitation is particularly serious for social work, as our models for work with groups (such as TACIT) reflect hypotheses that focus on group process.

A preliminary step to link outcomes with process involves administering change-measures in a time-series format throughout the group experience rather than in simple pre/post designs. The repeated assessment is often best based on the same easily administered instruments. They support replications, help keep members task-oriented, provide data for regular monitoring of group process and each member's progress, and permit changes in our interventions that are more appropriate to the group members' current needs (Dies and MacKenzie, 1983).

Process

In addition to repeated outcome measures in single-system design research, practitioners can use other process and leadership measures. When we add a few selected process and leadership measures, the goals of evaluating both process and outcome, using instrumentation to enable group process, and deriving an empirical base for future group practice might all be more effectively achieved. For instance, the practitioner can use a critical-incident format, a scale based on change mechanisms in groups, or a member journal (Corey et al., 1992). These all require a few minutes of each member's time after each meeting. One way to measure the evolution of therapeutic factors during each meeting is to administer the scale included in Appendix J of this text.

As practitioners find these instruments useful, they might want to build more systematic and readily scorable group process measures into their work with groups. Some are available that are high in face validity, easily scored, assess key dimensions of group process perceived as relevant by members, and provide useful data for influencing intervention. These include the Group Climate Questionnaire (GCQ) (Lieberman, Yalom, and Miles, 1973), the Group Norms Checklist (Bond, 1983), and the cohesiveness scale presented in Appendix K of this text. Dies and MacKenzie (1983) imply how these instruments can enhance group process and the achievement of individual members' outcomes, especially by providing data to members for discussion and decision making during the group process. Alternatively, members themselves could construct instruments and complete measurements for such evolving group themes as member/leader role expectations, group norms, self-disclosure, and interpersonal feedback. When we use empirical measures in this way to assess group process, they tend to be accepted as a vital component of the group by both practitioners and members.

This process instrumentation can be valuable in preventing casualties of the group experience. Research indicates that members are more aware than practitioners of those group members who are likely to have a detrimental group experience (Lieberman, Yalom, and Miles, 1973; Schopler and Galinsky, 1982). When these members are identified early through self-reports and other member-derived data, our capacity for preventing casualties increases. Thus, use of these measures might compensate for practitioner insensitivity.

Leadership

Group leadership measures can enhance the practice evaluation as well as the integration of practice and research in single-system designs. Social work practitioners can use a variety of instruments to gather data on how group members perceive them. Several researchers (Bolman, 1971; Lieberman, Yalom, and Miles, 1973; Lundgren, 1971; Hurst, et al., 1976) have developed measures that reflect leadership functions and styles. The Instrument to Measure Skills, presented in Appendix G, is useful in this regard.

By using these scales, practitioners can obtain feedback to monitor their leadership style. The instruments can be modified to focus on areas the practitioner deems most in need of self-monitoring and professional development. When such data are accumulated throughout the group process, rather than simply in a pre/post design, the practitioner can gain valuable insight into perceptions of leadership functions and skills throughout the stages of group development. Replication of these studies might tie process to outcomes with leadership functions and skills as an intervening variable. These findings could enhance the empirical base of group practice.

CONCLUSION

The call for accountability both within and outside of social work requires more practice evaluation research. This can help to close the gap between research and practice in social work with groups. The bridge might best be built on understanding the empirical process in all effective practice and adding systematic observation and measurement through instrumentation and single-system design. As we find more acceptance of the research base for practice, the potential increases for discovering other contributions that research can make to practice and practice to research. Such a coalition in social work with groups has been needed for a long time.

Afterword

This book has been about social work through group process. The process is a holistic reality, much more than the sum of its parts. At this level it cannot really be analyzed. What I have done is to attempt to sketch a map of the process, a model for understanding and negotiating its territory. As Edward Schumaker (1977) noted:

> One way of looking at the world as a whole is by means of a map, that is to say, some sort of plan or outline that shows where various things are to be found — not all things, of course, for that would make the map as big as the world, but the things that are most important for orientation: outstanding landmarks, as it were, which you cannot miss or which, if you did miss them, leave you in total perplexity. (p. 87)

In this book I offer a map of the territory that may help you to negotiate group process in your social work practice. You know from traveling that the map is not the territory; it is a model of group process, not the process itself. It is a two-dimensional representation of (at least) a three-dimensional reality. To the degree that it helps you negotiate group process without experiencing too much perplexity or without getting lost, it is useful.

If your objectives are to empower members to develop their autonomy as well as their interdependence, this map includes some valuable landmarks. I can think of no more pertinent aims for social work through group process. In life, we are alone and we are not alone. We are separate and we are united. We are autonomous and we are interdependent.

Through developing group process, we confront the paradox of this growth in the question attributed first to Rabbi Hillel over a thousand years ago:

If I am not for myself, who will be for me?
If only for myself, what am I?
If not now, when?

Diversity Awareness Inventory

1. *Accepting and Understanding Others:*

1	2	3	4	5
I am critical and caustic, disregarding feelings of others.	I am frequently indifferent to what others are saying.	I listen to what others say but am not aware of their real feelings.	I try to listen with openness and expectancy to others' feelings as well as to their ideas.	I am able to accept and understand some of the reasons for others feeling as they do.

2. *Being Accepted and Understood:*

1	2	3	4	5
I am afraid if I speak up my ideas would appear feeble or irrelevant.	At times I feel ignored or judged and am defensive.	I usually feel accepted but not free to say what I really think.	I feel free to express myself and believe others try to listen to me with openness and expectancy.	I feel free to express my real self and feel considerable understanding and acceptance from others.

3. Verbal Communicating:

1	2	3	4	5
With diverse groups I often interrupt others, interjecting irrelevant ideas.	I feel I usually talk too much when I am with people of diversity.	In diverse groups, I make an effort to curb my talking.	In diverse groups, I hold back my ideas until the appropriate time.	I feel a responsibility to allow others to express their ideas.

4. Participating and Interacting:

1	2	3	4	5
I usually feel like an observer.	I become slightly involved with others.	I enter into discussions primarily to convince others of my position.	I enter into discussions primarily to "work through" the concern with others.	I feel involved by trying to help others clarify their feelings just the same as I try to make clear my own convictions.

Value Orientation Inventory and Profile Sheet

NAME:_____ SEX:_____

DATE:_____ ETHNICITY:_____

This inventory concerns your preferences regarding conceptions of the world and human affairs. For each item, please rank order — 1,2, and 3 — your preference.

1. Which time orientation is the most important to you? (Please rank order all three)
   ___ Past
   ___ Present
   ___ Future
2. What kinds of activities do you value most? (Please rank order all three)
   ___ Doing (accomplishing tasks)
   ___ Being (enjoying the present)
   ___ Becoming (working toward future goals)
3. What kinds of human relationships do you prefer? (Please rank order all three)
   ___ Autonomy (where own needs are met)
   ___ Hierarchy (where the roles and statuses are clear)
   ___ Interdependence (where the relationship is paramount)
4. What do you believe is the basic relationship between people and nature? (Please rank order all three)
   ___ Mastery (people can triumph over nature)
   ___ Harmony (there is no clash between people and nature)
   ___ Subjugation (people must surrender to nature)

5. What do you believe is the basic nature of human beings? (Please rank order all three)

___   Neutral (not bad or good)

___   Evil (animalistic if not socialized)

___   Good (well-intentioned by nature)

VALUE ORIENTATION PROFILE

Please place your rankings in the following chart, as compared with the value orientations identified for middle-class North Americans.

Question	*Middle Class*	*Yours*
1. Time	(1) Future	
	(2) Present	
	(3) Past	
2. Activity	(1) Doing	
	(2) Becoming	
	(3) Being	
3. Human Relations	(1) Autonomy	
	(2) Interdependence	
	(3) Hierarchy	
4. Person-Nature Relationship	(1) Mastery	
	(2) Subjugation	
	(3) Harmony	
5. Basic Nature of Human Beings	(1) Neutral	
	(2) Evil	
	(3) Good	

Five-Stage Models of Group Development: Some Chronological Examples

Author and Date	*Types of Groups*	*Stage 1*
Bennis and Shepard, 1956	Training/Adults	Dependence
Stock and Thelen, 1958	Training/Adults	Individually centered/Exploration
Garland, Jones, and Kolodny, 1973	Social work/ Children	Preaffiliation
Tuckman, 1965; Tuckman and Jensen, 1977	Review/Several types	Forming
Yalom and Moos, 1967	Training and therapy/Adults	Orientation/Anxiety
Northen, 1969	Social work/Adults	Orientation/Inclusion/ Exploration/Testing
Klein, 1973	Social work/Adults	Orientation
Lacoursiere, 1980	Review/Several types	Orientation
Henry, 1981	Social work/Adults	Convening
MacKenzie and Livesley, 1983	Review/Several types	Engagement
Anderson, J., 1984	Social work/ Children and adults/ Review/Several types	Trust

Stage 2	*Stage 3*	*Stage 4*	*Stage 5*
Counter-dependence	Enchantment/ Disenchantment	Consensual validation	Termination
Frustrations/conflict among stereotypes	Attempted group harmony, feeling and work not integrated	Productivity and flexibility, integration of feeling and work	Good work with withdrawal of feelings
Power and control	Intimacy	Differentiation (reality-based relations)	Separation
Storming	Norming	Performing	Adjourning (added 1977)
Demands for structure	Resolution to go deeper, backing off	Meaningful interaction	"Disengagement and testimonials"
Dissatisfaction/ Power conflict	Mutuality	Work	Separation/ Termination/ Transition
Resistance	Negotiation	Intimacy	Termination
Dissatisfaction	Resolution	Production	Termination
Forming/Conflict	Maintenance	Work	Termination
Differentiation/ Individuation	Intimacy	Mutuality	Termination
Autonomy	Closeness	Interdependence	Termination

Group Leadership Functions:
Some Models for Comparison

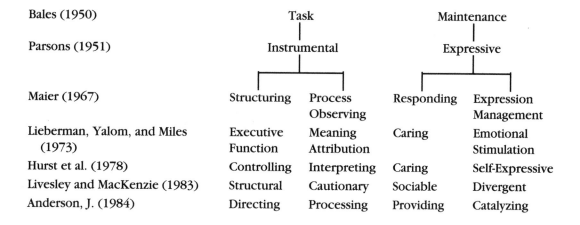

	Task		Maintenance	
Bales (1950)				
Parsons (1951)	Instrumental		Expressive	
Maier (1967)	Structuring	Process Observing	Responding	Expression Management
Lieberman, Yalom, and Miles (1973)	Executive Function	Meaning Attribution	Caring	Emotional Stimulation
Hurst et al. (1978)	Controlling	Interpreting	Caring	Self-Expressive
Livesley and MacKenzie (1983)	Structural	Cautionary	Sociable	Divergent
Anderson, J. (1984)	Directing	Processing	Providing	Catalyzing

Group Leadership Functions Scale and Interpretation Sheet

FUNCTIONS SCALE

Instructions: Respond to each of the items below with respect to your general preferences and tendencies as you now know them. Consider the entire 1 to 7 scale for each item.

As the practitioner with a therapeutic group, I would likely . . .

	Very Low			Moderate			Very High
1. reveal my own feelings about members	1 ___	2 ___	3 ___	4 ___	5 ___	6 ___	7 ___
2. show understanding of members	1 ___	2 ___	3 ___	4 ___	5 ___	6 ___	7 ___
3. clarify members' feelings	1 ___	2 ___	3 ___	4 ___	5 ___	6 ___	7 ___
4. suggest or set limits for the group	1 ___	2 ___	3 ___	4 ___	5 ___	6 ___	7 ___
5. offer my friendship to members	1 ___	2 ___	3 ___	4 ___	5 ___	6 ___	7 ___
6. challenge members' behaviors	1 ___	2 ___	3 ___	4 ___	5 ___	6 ___	7 ___
7. conceptualize group events for members	1 ___	2 ___	3 ___	4 ___	5 ___	6 ___	7 ___
8. directly elicit members' reactions	1 ___	2 ___	3 ___	4 ___	5 ___	6 ___	7 ___
9. manage my time and that of members	1 ___	2 ___	3 ___	4 ___	5 ___	6 ___	7 ___
10. confront members	1 ___	2 ___	3 ___	4 ___	5 ___	6 ___	7 ___
11. interpret members' communications	1 ___	2 ___	3 ___	4 ___	5 ___	6 ___	7 ___
12. praise members	1 ___	2 ___	3 ___	4 ___	5 ___	6 ___	7 ___
13. accept members	1 ___	2 ___	3 ___	4 ___	5 ___	6 ___	7 ___
14. spur reactions from members	1 ___	2 ___	3 ___	4 ___	5 ___	6 ___	7 ___
15. manage group activities	1 ___	2 ___	3 ___	4 ___	5 ___	6 ___	7 ___
16. explain situations to members	1 ___	2 ___	3 ___	4 ___	5 ___	6 ___	7 ___
17. participate actively	1 ___	2 ___	3 ___	4 ___	5 ___	6 ___	7 ___
18. question members	1 ___	2 ___	3 ___	4 ___	5 ___	6 ___	7 ___

	Very Low	Moderate	Very High
19. express warmth to members	1 ___ 2 ___ 3 ___	4 ___ 5 ___ 6 ___	7 ___
20. summarize members' statements	1 ___ 2 ___ 3 ___	4 ___ 5 ___ 6 ___	7 ___
21. suggest procedures for work	1 ___ 2 ___ 3 ___	4 ___ 5 ___ 6 ___	7 ___
22. be genuine with members	1 ___ 2 ___ 3 ___	4 ___ 5 ___ 6 ___	7 ___
23. take emotional risks with members	1 ___ 2 ___ 3 ___	4 ___ 5 ___ 6 ___	7 ___
24. translate behavior to ideas	1 ___ 2 ___ 3 ___	4 ___ 5 ___ 6 ___	7 ___
25. develop close relationships with members	1 ___ 2 ___ 3 ___	4 ___ 5 ___ 6 ___	7 ___
26. show how to make decisions	1 ___ 2 ___ 3 ___	4 ___ 5 ___ 6 ___	7 ___
27. help members understand their experiences	1 ___ 2 ___ 3 ___	4 ___ 5 ___ 6 ___	7 ___
28. use personality to inspire members	1 ___ 2 ___ 3 ___	4 ___ 5 ___ 6 ___	7 ___

Scoring and interpretation instructions are below. To understand functions and more of your own leadership style, please take the scale first.

INTERPRETATION SHEET

The Four Functions

1. Catalyzing

Release of emotions by demonstration; leader as center; challenging-confronting function; modeling; stimulating emotion

Items: 1, 6, 10, 14, 17, 23, 28

Group Tally

High > 41 ___

Your Score   Medium 15–41 ___

Low < 15 ___

2. Providing

Care-oriented; supportive; warm; understanding; specific, definable personal relationships

Items: 2, 5, 12, 13, 19, 22, 25

Group Tally

High > 41 ___

Your Score   Medium 15–41 ___

Low < 15 ___

3. Processing

Cognitizing behavior; naming function; translation of feelings and behavior into ideas for both group and individual members

Items: 3, 7, 11, 16, 20, 24, 28

Group Tally

High > 41 ____

Your Score   Medium 15 - 41 ____

Low < 15 ____

---

4. Directing

Conducting; providing meaning; limiting pacing; sequencing; expression of emotion through suggestion

Items: 4, 8, 9, 15, 18, 21, 26

Group Tally

High > 41 ____

Your Score   Medium 15 - 41 ____

Low < 15 ____

Group Leadership Styles and Functions Questionnaire

Directions: This questionnaire presents 15 situations that sometimes occur in counseling groups in social work. You are asked to indicate how you would respond if you were the practitioner in the group. Nine alternative responses are provided for each situation.

The group is a coeducational group of eight members, all adolescents between the ages of 15 and 17 and on probation for a series of offenses that include truancy, substance abuse, and petty theft. A common goal for the members (who have volunteered for the group) is learning to develop more prosocial and fulfilling friendships. The group meets for ten meetings around the general theme of "Choosing and Being Friends."

On a separate answer sheet, use three columns to record your preferences. For each situation:

a. List (in column 1) the numbers of *all* of the responses among the nine that you might consider making if you were the practitioner facing this particular situation.
b. Then, choose from among your selections the *one* response that you feel is most important to make, and write its number in column 2.
c. Record in column 3 the responses you might make that have not been included on the list.

SITUATION 1: STARTING THE GROUP

You are the practitioner in this group, which is meeting for the first time. All eight members, adolescents who volunteered for the group, are present as you enter the room and sit down. You introduce yourself and the members introduce themselves. Then everyone turns and looks at you expectantly. There is silence. What do you do?

1. Do nothing.
2. Describe how they seem to be expecting you to start things.
3. Reassure them that a certain amount of tension is typical in the beginning of a group.
4. Describe the silence as an expression of their anxieties about the group.
5. Ask what they think might be going on in the group.
6. Say how you are feeling (example: tense and expectant).
7. Ask how they feel in this first meeting (about being in the group or about each other).
8. Describe the purposes and procedures of the group.
9. Use a nonverbal or structured verbal procedure to "break the ice" (examples: milling around; a dyad discussion about each other's goals in the group).

SITUATION 2: CHAIRPERSON

Later in this first meeting, someone suggests the group appoint a member to serve as chair to conduct the meetings. This idea is received enthusiastically. They explain that this will permit the group to function in a more orderly fashion. Everyone appears to agree with the idea. What do you do?

1. Do nothing.
2. Reflect that the group appears upset about the lack of direct leadership thus far in this first meeting.
3. Say that you are willing to go along with whatever the group decides about this.
4. Say, "What happened that made us decide we need a chair for this group?"
5. Interpret their discussion as a way of dealing with the ambiguity of this group situation.
6. Say how you are feeling about the situation.
7. Ask how they feel about the way the group has been set up.
8. Reach for their feedback about the way the group has tried to use the discussed procedures to achieve its purpose in this first meeting.
9. Ask them to role-play how the group would be with a chair.

SITUATION 3: A FILIBUSTER

The group spends much of the second meeting talking about "crooked politicians and cops." No one appears displeased with the discussion, and it looks like it may continue for the remainder of the meeting. What do you do?

1. Do nothing.
2. Reflect that they seem to be satisfied about how the group is going today and ask, "Is this really how you want to use your time together?"
3. Encourage them to talk more about themselves.
4. Ask what they think might be going on in the group today.
5. Suggest that their interest in crooked politicians and cops may have something to do with their concern about authority in the group.
6. Say how you are feeling (examples: bored; in a bind because you want the discussion to be more personal and on-theme but don't want to force this).
7. Ask how they feel about what has been going on.
8. Suggest that the "contract" for the group requires them to talk about more immediate things.
9. Have them break into dyads and discuss their individual goals for the group and what each can do to achieve his/her goal during the remainder of this meeting.

SITUATION 4: THE ATTACK

After spending much of this second meeting talking about crooked politicians and cops and the fun of drinking, the group suddenly turns on you, accusing you of being uninvolved, distant, and uncaring. What do you do?

1. Do nothing.
2. Reflect that they are really mad at you for not providing more direction for them and that they want you to be more active for now in directing the group.
3. Talk in an approving way about the directness and honesty with which they are able to say how they feel.
4. Ask what they think might be going on in the group today.
5. Suggest that they are disappointed because you are not the inspiration and protective leader they had wanted you to be.
6. Say that you are feeling trapped and are irritated about this, that you wanted to change the direction of the meeting but did not want to direct the topics of discussion.
7. Ask how they feel when they are criticizing you.
8. Say that they are expecting you to be the chair of the group and you expect them to be their own chair, that it is up to them what happens in the group — not you.
9. Use a nonverbal procedure (example: find a spot in the room that expresses where each stands with you and with each other right now).

SITUATION 5: A GROUP SILENCE

The third meeting begins with a silence. Several minutes pass and still no one says anything. It is beginning to look like the silence may continue for some time. What do you do?

1. Do nothing.
2. Say, "You seem to be expecting me to initiate this meeting, and I prefer to wait for your concerns to be expressed. What do you think of this?"
3. Say, "Silences are often anxious but productive in groups. I wonder what you were thinking and feeling during this silence."
4. Say, "It seems no one wants to talk today."
5. Interpret the silence as a struggle to see who is going to lead this group by initiating discussions.
6. Say, "How are you feeling?" and ask if the silence includes fears left over from the leadership confrontation of the last meeting.
7. Ask how they feel when everyone is silent.
8. Ask how this silence and your breaking it fits in with the "contract" for the group.
9. Encourage them to remain silent and express themselves nonverbally to the person to their right.

SITUATION 6: A DISTRESSED MEMBER

Later in this third meeting, one of the female members describes how her boyfriend just broke up with her. She seems quite upset, skipping from one idea to another, and returning repetitively to the same few despairing thoughts. She has been looking directly at you from the beginning of her remarks, ignoring the rest of the group. When she finishes talking, she asks for your comments. What do you do?

1. Do nothing.
2. Say, "You are quite upset and seeking our help. Because your needs are so strong right now, I sense we both want to and are afraid to respond to you."
3. Express interest in her and concern about her difficulties.
4. Ask what they think might be going on in the group today, especially how they were experiencing their relationship to the distressed member and the group-as-a-whole.
5. Describe how the group has accepted the role of passive observer during this communication.
6. Share your own reaction.
7. Reach for reactions of other members.
8. Suggest that she ask the group rather than you.
9. Use a role-playing procedure to obtain a more here-and-now expression of what happens with her boyfriend.

SITUATION 7: THE MONOPOLIZER

For several meetings now the discussion has been monopolized by one of the female members. Her monologues and interruptions interfere with the development of meaningful interaction among members. She has had the floor for most of the first half of this fourth meeting. What do you do?

1. Do nothing.
2. Say, "From your frequent participation in discussion, you really seem to want to get some things out of this group for yourself. What are these, and how might the group help you get them?"
3. Suggest that the group seems to be letting one member carry the discussion load for it, and ask if this is what they want.
4. Ask how they would describe what has been going on in this meeting.
5. Describe what is going on as a two-party interaction wherein she monopolizes and others allow and perhaps even encourage her to do it.
6. Say how you are feeling (example: irritated with her for monopolizing and at the group for letting her).
7. Ask how they feel about one person doing all the talking.
8. Direct the group to consider the reasons it has established this pattern of one person doing most of the talking through the last several meetings.
9. Break into dyads and have members "mirror," verbally and nonverbally, each other's behavior thus far in the group.

SITUATION 8: THE QUIET MEMBER

One of the males has said very little throughout the meetings, although he seems to follow with interest everything that has been happening. It is now the middle of the fourth meeting, and some of the others are finally beginning to question him about his silence. He remains basically uncommunicative, however, and the group seems uncertain about how to pursue the matter. What do you do?

1. Do nothing.
2. Say, "The group seems to be wanting to get to know you better, but you seem to be getting tight about this discussion. Could you share some of what you are experiencing right now and what you wish the group would do with their concern for your silence?"
3. Say that each person is free to decide when he wants to talk, adding that you would like to hear from him when he does feel like talking.
4. Describe how the group seems uncertain about how to discuss this with him.
5. Ask the group why his silence now seems to be such a concern for them.
6. Say how you are feeling.
7. Ask how he feels about what the group is saying to him, and ask how they

feel about his reactions to their remarks.

8. Encourage him to talk about himself (example: ask if he is usually quiet in group situations).
9. Ask him to engage in a role reversal exercise with one of the members who has been questioning him about his silence.

SITUATION 9: TRUANCY PROBLEM

In the fifth meeting, one of the male members talks about his truancy problem. The others offer numerous suggestions. He listens to each of them one at a time and then explains why that particular suggestion will not work. What do you do?

1. Do nothing.
2. Reflect his fears about committing himself to work on his problems.
3. Show interest in him and express concern about his difficulties.
4. Describe how he and the group have decided to focus on his request for help through giving advice and that this procedure does not seem to be working.
5. Interpret that he is the focus around which all other members are projecting their own problems by giving advice that may have more to do with them than with him.
6. Ask members how they feel about him after his exchange.
7. Ask how he feels about the group response to his problem, and ask how they feel about his reaction to their suggestions.
8. Direct him to talk about his problem in behavioral terms.
9. Use a role-playing procedure to determine more the causes of his truancy.

SITUATION 10: A MEMBER CRIES

It is the middle of the sixth meeting. A female member, who has been unusually silent for the first half of this meeting, makes a brief attempt to fight back tears and then begins to cry. No one says anything about it. What do you do?

1. Do nothing.
2. Reflect that she really seems hurt and wants some attention to her needs from the group.
3. Express concern and encourage her to talk about her situation, what you want to hear about it.
4. Say that someone in the group is crying and the group seems uncertain about how to respond to her.
5. Describe her crying as a personal risk, reflecting her willingness to involve herself personally in the group.
6. Say how you are feeling (example: moved; drawn to her).

7. Ask about feelings (examples: encourage her to put words to her feelings; ask the members how they feel about her crying).
8. Ask each member in a go-around to tell her what her crying means to him/her right now.
9. Ask her to role-play the situation that her crying is about.

SITUATION 11: THE GRUMPY GROUP

Meeting seven is characterized by a general mood of irritability and negativism. A member can hardly start talking before another interrupts to say that he/she is bored. No one seems pleased about anything. The warm, involved mood at the end of the previous meeting seems completely forgotten. What do you do?

1. Do nothing.
2. Reflect that they feel in a fighting mood today.
3. Reach for the positive feelings that may be there.
4. Ask what they think might be going on in the group today.
5. Say that there seems to be an unspoken decision among members to disagree with everything, and ask if this is what they really want to do today.
6. Say how you are feeling.
7. Ask them to express what they most resent and most appreciate about the group thus far.
8. Suggest that they use their time more constructively.
9. Have them arm wrestle each other to get more in touch with their competitive feelings.

SITUATION 12: THE POLITE GROUP

The eighth meeting begins in a mood of superficial agreeableness. Everyone is being super polite. Rambling remarks, evasive comments, behavior that ordinarily would immediately be challenged — all are being tolerated. It is clear that the group is protecting itself against any possible expression of aggressive feeling. What do you do?

1. Do nothing.
2. Reflect that they seem to fear more fighting in the group, and ask how they want to deal with conflict together.
3. Suggest that the more superficial level of interaction seems to be a reaction against the anger of the last meeting.
4. Describe the group mood of politeness.
5. Say that there seems to be an unspoken agreement among the members to be polite and avoid anything that might rock the boat.
6. Say how you are feeling.

7. Ask how they feel about what has been going on.

8. Suggest that they get down to real feelings.

9. Use a nonverbal procedure to get at the underlying feeling.

SITUATION 13: A GROUP ATTACK

Throughout the meetings one of the male members had been insisting he has no problems. In the middle of the eighth meeting, the group attacks him for "hiding behind a mask." At the present moment the whole interaction seems to be gaining intensity—he responds to their accusations by increasing his denial; they respond to his denial by increasing their attack. You are not sure how he is being affected by it. What do you do?

1. Do nothing.

2. Reflect that he feels attacked by the group's pushing him and yet the group does seem to want something more from him.

3. Suggest that he stop for a minute and determine if there is *any* truth in what the group is saying.

4. Ask the group what they think is going on.

5. Describe the interaction as a standoff that is not meeting his or the group's needs.

6. Say how you are feeling.

7. Ask how he feels about what they are saying and how they feel about what he is saying.

8. Ask him and the group if they can design an experiment to give him more effective feedback.

9. Suggest that he and another member role-play each other's side in the argument.

SITUATION 14: THE FIGHT

In the ninth meeting, two male members get into a heated argument over a minor point. The real reason for the argument appears to be their rivalry for the attention of one of the female members. Finally, one of the males jumps up and threatens to hit the other. What do you do?

1. Do nothing.

2. Reflect on their feelings of rivalry and jealousy, and ask them how they think they can work this out between them without fighting.

3. Tell them you want neither to be hurt, and ask the group to help you deal with this conflict.

4. Ask what might be going on between these two.

5. Attribute the argument to competition between the two for the attention of the female member.

6. Say how you are feeling.
7. Ask other members to express their feelings about this situation.
8. Ask the members what they want to do about this situation.
9. Use a nonverbal procedure (example: arm wrestling).

SITUATION 15: ENDING

The tenth and last meeting begins like the third with a long group silence. What do you do?

1. Do nothing.
2. Reflect that the ending is difficult to begin.
3. Indicate that you want to help them end this experience in the best way possible for them.
4. Ask the group what seems to be going on in this silence.
5. Suggest that if they do not start they may feel they do not have to end this meeting and, therefore, the group.
6. Say how you are feeling.
7. Ask them to express their feelings about ending.
8. Ask if they have any specific ideas about how they would like to use this last meeting.
9. Suggest a closing exercise (example: saying goodbye, nonverbally, to each and every member).

INTERPRETATION OF GROUP LEADERSHIP STYLES QUESTIONNAIRE

To score and interpret the questionnaire, you need to know that in every one of the responses #2 through #8 represent particular functions. In all cases, all 15 situations, #2 and #3 represent Providing functions in use; #4 and #5 Processing functions; #6 and #7 Catalyzing functions; and #8 and #9 Directing functions. In all cases, #1 is do nothing and is not counted. Thus, you can examine how often you preferred and considered responses utilizing one of these four functions. In each, the functions were similarly represented. The following format was used:

Providing
2. Sharing perceptions and understanding
3. Reassuring or supporting

Processing
4. Offering own interpretation
5. Asking for members'/group's interpretation

Catalyzing
6. Expressing own feelings
7. Reaching for members' feelings

Directing
8. Contracting for work
9. Using a structured exercise or experience

There are no "right" answers to this questionnaire. Some elements of your preferred style might be reflected in the high, moderate, or low use of each of these four functions. In addition, how your current preferences relate to the TACIT model of this book might be considered. For that purpose, the following list indicates the TACIT themes incorporated into each situation and the number(s) of the responses most suggested by the TACIT model:

    1. TRUST, with some early AUTONOMY
       Preferred TACIT responses: #2 or #8
    2. AUTONOMY, with some remnants of TRUST
       Preferred TACIT response: #2
    3. AUTONOMY, with some remnants of TRUST
       Preferred TACIT responses: #4 or #5
    4. AUTONOMY
       Preferred TACIT response: #4
    5. AUTONOMY, with some early CLOSENESS
       Preferred TACIT responses: #2, #4, #6
    6. CLOSENESS, with some remnants of AUTONOMY
       Preferred TACIT responses: #6 or #7
    7. CLOSENESS, with some remnants of AUTONOMY
       Preferred TACIT responses: #2 or #4
    8. CLOSENESS, with some remnants of AUTONOMY
       Preferred TACIT responses: #2 or #6
    9. CLOSENESS, with some remnants of AUTONOMY
       Preferred TACIT response: #7
   10. CLOSENESS
       Preferred TACIT responses: #6 or #7
   11. CLOSENESS
       Preferred TACIT responses: #2 or #7
   12. CLOSENESS
       Preferred TACIT responses: #2 or #7
   13. CLOSENESS
       Preferred TACIT response: #7
   14. CLOSENESS, with more INTERDEPENDENCE
       Preferred TACIT responses: #1, #7, #8
   15. TERMINATION
       Preferred TACIT responses: #2, #8, #9

Instrument to Measure Skills

SCALE: 0 — Not Used; 1 — Poor; 2 — Ineffective; 3 — Minimally Effective; 4 — Good

Stage, Function, and Skill	Operational Definitions	Scale
PREAFFILIATION STAGE		
Providing		
1. Attending	a. Leans forward, faces other squarely, maintains eye contact	0 1 2 3 4
	b. Arranges setting to promote interaction	0 1 2 3 4
2. Observing	a. Actively notices and accurately reads nonverbal communication	0 1 2 3 4 0 1 2 3 4
3. Actively listening and empathy	a. Responds to content	0 1 2 3 4
	b. Responds to feelings	0 1 2 3 4
	c. Connects feelings and content	0 1 2 3 4
Directing		
4. Contracting	a. Clarifies purpose	0 1 2 3 4
	b. Clarifies roles and responsibilities	0 1 2 3 4
	c. Reaches for feedback	0 1 2 3 4
	d. Establishes them	0 1 2 3 4
	e. Introduces ground rules	0 1 2 3 4
Catalyzing/Processing		
5. Clarifying	a. Brings individual goals to surface	0 1 2 3 4
	b. Questions toward specificity	0 1 2 3 4
	c. Reaches inside silences	0 1 2 3 4
6. Elaborating	a. Moves from general to specific	0 1 2 3 4
	b. Contains responses	0 1 2 3 4
	c. Requests more information	0 1 2 3 4

SCALE: 0 — Not Used; 1 — Poor; 2 — Ineffective; 3 — Minimally Effective; 4 — Good

Stage, Function, and Skill	Operational Definitions	Scale
POWER AND CONTROL STAGE		
Processing		
7. Illuminating	a. Actively recognizes process	0 1 2 3 4
	b. Brings group tensions to surface	0 1 2 3 4
	c. Shares own feelings as linked with process	0 1 2 3 4
	d. Increases members' awareness of process	0 1 2 3 4
8. Relating here-now to there-then	a. Interprets the relation of content to group process in the here-and-now	0 1 2 3 4
9. Reaching behind conflicts and decisions	a. Checks for underlying ambivalences	0 1 2 3 4
	b. Shares own reactions	0 1 2 3 4
	c. Brings all sides of conflict to surface	0 1 2 3 4
	d. Reaches for empathy in members	0 1 2 3 4
	e. Reflects norms used in decision making	0 1 2 3 4
Providing		
10. Personalizing	a. Personalizes meaning	0 1 2 3 4
	b. Personalizes problems	0 1 2 3 4
	c. Personalizes feelings	0 1 2 3 4
	d. Personalizes goals	0 1 2 3 4
Catalyzing		
11. Reaching for feelings and perceptions	a. Checks for underlying ambivalences	0 1 2 3 4
	b. Supports communication in taboo areas	0 1 2 3 4
	c. Reaches for individual response	0 1 2 3 4
	d. Reaches for group response	0 1 2 3 4
Directing		
12. Encouraging work	a. Challenges illusion of work	0 1 2 3 4
	b. Reaches for work when obstacles threaten	0 1 2 3 4
	c. Focuses group on problem solving and mutual aid	0 1 2 3 4
13. Invoking the contract	a. Questions about what is happening in relation to contract	0 1 2 3 4
INTIMACY STAGE		
Catalyzing		
14. Encouraging intermember feedback	a. Encourages use of ground rules	0 1 2 3 4
	b. Directs messages to intended recipient	0 1 2 3 4
	c. Amplifies feeling messages	0 1 2 3 4
15. Reaching for empathic content	a. Invites intermember responses	0 1 2 3 4
16. Confrontation	a. Feeds back discrepancies between words and deeds	0 1 2 3 4
Providing		
17. Modeling self-disclosure and feedback	a. Discloses appropriately	0 1 2 3 4
	b. Uses feedback consistent with principles	0 1 2 3 4
18. Sharing own feelings	a. Shares own feelings and ideas in relation to theme and members	0 1 2 3 4

SCALE: 0 — Not Used; 1 — Poor; 2 — Ineffective; 3 — Minimally Effective; 4 — Good

Stage, Function, and Skill	Operational Definitions	Scale
Processing		
19. Clarifying purpose	a. Aids group in discovering what it wants	0 1 2 3 4
	b. Encourages group to weigh interactions against desires	0 1 2 3 4
20. Illuminating process	a. Brings there-then to here-now	0 1 2 3 4
21. Detecting and challenging obstacles to work	a. Names obstacles	0 1 2 3 4
	b. Reaches for ambivalences	0 1 2 3 4
	c. Elicits feedback about obstacles	0 1 2 3 4
Directing		
22. Renegotiating the contract	a. Reclarifies purpose	0 1 2 3 4
	b. Reclarifies roles and responsibilities	0 1 2 3 4
	c. Reclarifies theme, subthemes, and ground rules	0 1 2 3 4
DIFFERENTIATION STAGE		
Providing/Processing/ Catalyzing/Directing		
23. Offering experimental activities	a. Helps ground design experiments related to individual members' needs	0 1 2 3 4
	b. Uses structured exercises appropriately	0 1 2 3 4
SEPARATION STAGE		
Directing		
24. Initiating termination	a. Points out ending	0 1 2 3 4
25. Holding out ending	a. Continually presents the reality of ending	0 1 2 3 4
	b. Gently demands work on ending	0 1 2 3 4
26. Closing	a. Provides structure for final good-byes	0 1 2 3 4
Processing		
27. Focusing on ending	a. Acknowledges the behavior and feelings that reflect ending	0 1 2 3 4
28. Evaluating and following-up	a. Assesses specific outcomes	0 1 2 3 4
Providing		
29. Sharing own feelings	a. Expresses positive and negative feelings in ending	0 1 2 3 4
	b. Credits individual members and the group for efforts and effects in their own behalf	0 1 2 3 4
Catalyzing		
30. Reaching for feelings and evaluation	a. Encourages expressing and staying with feelings related to termination	0 1 2 3 4
	b. Reaches for both positive and negative feelings	0 1 2 3 4
	c. Reaches for both positive and negative feedback	0 1 2 3 4

Group Process Inventory

GROUP _____   OBSERVER(S) _____

DATE OF MEETING _____

Names of members present during meeting:

Names of members absent — possible reasons for absence:

Major theme(s) manifested during this meeting (check):

____ Trust ____ Autonomy ____ Closeness ____ Interdependence
____ Termination ____ Other (list)

For each theme, identify the underlying group process in terms of:

(a) Specific underlying shared needs/wishes reflected:

(b) Specific underlying shared fears reflected:

(c) How group dealt with wishes and fears (i.e., enabling or restrictive function of current group solution):

Relation of underlying theme to previous meetings (especially last meeting):

Group development stage:

Group and individual manifestations of this stage:

Group tasks necessary for group to evolve successfully through this stage:

Special current obstacles occurring in this meeting or likely occurring in group or for particular members:

Particular functions and skills most likely to enable group process at this point:

appendix I

Therapeutic Group
Goal-Setting Schedule

Group _____

Name _____ Date _____

INSTRUCTIONS: At the time of beginning a therapeutic group, many persons have goals for themselves in terms of changes they would like to make. Here are some statements of goals for group learning made by members of other groups.

What changes do you personally feel you want to make on each item below? For each item, check the column that most nearly represents the amount of change you feel you want to make on that item. If you are relatively satisfied with yourself in an area, you should mark the "remain the same" answer. Notice that you may choose to increase <u>or</u> decrease certain kinds of behaviors and feelings.

Please check the column for each item to indicate one of the following answers.

I want to decrease markedly

I want to decrease somewhat

Remain the same

I want to increase somewhat

I want to increase markedly

1. My comfort when a person challenges my opinions

2. The ease with which I can take part in other types of groups

3. My understanding of my faults and limitations

	I want to increase markedly	I want to increase somewhat	Remain the same	I want to decrease somewhat	I want to decrease markedly
4. The degree to which a group stimulates my mind					
5. My discouragement when my ideas are not accepted					
6. My interest in other people					
7. My self-consciousness					
8. My ability to admit I am wrong					
9. My tendency to take part in planning and carrying out activities					
10. My ability to talk with new acquaintances					
11. The number of congenial associations I have with people outside this group					
12. My tendency to oppose ideas different from my own					
13. My understanding of other people's points of view					
14. My self-control					
15. My ability to make decisions without help from others					
16. My activities with other people					
17. My ability to express myself					
18. My sense of humor					
19. My self-confidence and composure on meeting new people					
20. My ability to listen to people — their ideas and their feelings					

304

	I want to increase markedly	I want to increase somewhat	Remain the same	I want to decrease somewhat	I want to decrease markedly
21. My ability to attend to and identify my feelings — my subjective reactions					
22. My ability to accurately perceive people — to judge people correctly and efficiently					
23. My ability to understand myself — to know who I am at a given time					
24. My ability to express my own feelings					
25. My ability to be spontaneous and creative					
26. My ability to respond to other people's feelings					
27. My ability to relate to others — to have more complex, deeper interpersonal relations					
28. My ability to make personal decisions					
29. My ability to begin to engage in the directions I choose					
30. My ability to communicate more effectively with other people					
31. My ability to trust other people					
32. My ability to overcome fears and doubts					
33. My feelings of adequacy					
34. My ability to make lasting commitments					

In the spaces below, write the number of your three most important goals:

_____ _____ _____

Other goals not mentioned above: _____

_____

Therapeutic Factors Scale

Name _____   Group Meeting Date _____

DIRECTIONS: Using the following scale, please circle the number that reflects how much you perceived each of the eleven (11) therapeutic factors operating in this meeting:

0 — Not at all   1 — Minimally   2 — Moderately   3 — Much   4 — Very Much

0 1 2 3 4   1. *Instillation of Hope:* Expectations that this group can meet one's needs relevant to this experience.

0 1 2 3 4   2. *Universality:* Recognitions of similarities to others, that others share similar issues and underlying concerns.

0 1 2 3 4   3. *Imparting of Information:* Giving and getting ideas and data useful for members.

0 1 2 3 4   4. *Altruism:* Efforts at giving members what they appear to need in the group.

0 1 2 3 4   5. *Corrective Family Recapitulation:* Working through aspects of unfinished business from family of origin with particular members of the group.

0 1 2 3 4   6. *Socializing Techniques:* Development of specific social skills in more effective interactions among members.

0 1 2 3 4   7. *Imitative Behavior:* Members using each other as models for learning and growth.

0 1 2 3 4   8. *Interpersonal Learning:* Exchanges of self-disclosure and feedback that increase members' awareness and/or experimentation in interpersonal relationships.

0 1 2 3 4   9. *Cohesiveness:* Sense of common bond and significance of the group.

0 1 2 3 4   10. *Catharsis:* Expression and acceptance of members' negative and/or positive feelings.

0 1 2 3 4   11. *Existential Factors:* Recognition that members are responsible for their own choices and lives and their growth toward authentic self-actualization.

Feelings about the Group (Cohesiveness) Scale

Name _____   Group Meeting Date _____

Answer the following questions in terms of your feelings at the present time. Circle the best answer.

1. How well do you like this group?
   A. I like it very much
   B. I like it pretty well
   C. It's alright
   D. Don't like it too much
   E. Dislike it very much

2. Do you feel that work in this group will enable you to obtain most of your goals for this experience?
   A. Definitely
   B. Very likely
   C. Likely
   D. Uncertain
   E. Very unlikely

3. If you could replace members of your group with other "ideal" members, how many would you exchange?
   A. None
   B. One
   C. Two to three
   D. Three to four
   E. More than four

4. To what degree do you feel you are included by the group in the group's activities?

    A. All the time
    B. Much of the time
    C. Some of the time
    D. Little
    E. None

5. How do you feel about your participation and contribution to the group's work?

    A. Very satisfied
    B. Satisfied
    C. So-so
    D. Disappointed
    E. Very disappointed

6. How accepting do you feel the group members are to you?

    A. Very
    B. Mostly
    C. Somewhat
    D. Little
    E. Not at all

7. Compared to similar groups, how well would you imagine your group works together?

    A. Probably the best
    B. Much better than most
    C. Average
    D. Not quite as well
    E. Probably the worst

References

Abramowitz, S.L., and Abramowitz, C.V. (1974). Psychological-mindedness and benefit from insight-oriented group therapy. *Archives of General Psychiatry, 30,* 610–615.

Abrecht, L., and Brewer, R.M., eds. (1990). *Bridges of power: Women's multicultural alliances.* Philadelphia: New Society Publications.

Addams, J. (1902). *Democracy and social ethics.* New York: Macmillan.

Adler, P. (1975). The translational experience: An alternative view of culture shock. *Journal of Humanistic Psychology, 15,* 13–23.

Alissi, A.S., and Casper, M. (1985). Time as a factor in social group work. *Social Work with Groups, 8,* 3–16.

Anchor, K.N. (1979). High and low risk self-disclosure in group psychotherapy. *Small Group Behavior, 10,* 279–283.

Anderson, J. (1984). *Counseling through group process.* New York: Springer.

———. (1981). *Social work methods and processes.* Belmont, CA: Wadsworth.

Anderson, J.D. (1992). Family-centered practice in the 1990s: A multicultural perspective. *Journal of Multicultural Social Work, 1,* 17–30.

———. (1991). Group work with families: A multicultural perspective. In K.L. Chau (ed.)., *Ethnicity and biculturalism: Emerging perspectives of social group work.* New York: Haworth.

———. (1985). Working with groups: Little-known facts that challenge well-known myths. *Small Group Behavior, 16,* 267–283.

———. (1984). Responsibility group counseling. *Social Work with Groups, 7,* 37–53.

———. (1980a). The communication of feelings in today's groups: An evolutionary perspective. *Social Work with Groups, 3,* 51–59.

———. (1980b). Structured experiences in growth groups in social work. *Social Casework, 61,* 277–287.

———. (1979). Social work with groups in the generic base of social work practice. *Social Work with Groups, 2,* 281–293.

———. (1978). Growth groups and alienation: A comparative study. *Group and Organizational Studies, 3,* 85–107.

————. (1976). *Intensive small group experiences and alienation.* London: Universities International.

————. (1975). Human relations training and social group work. *Social Work, 20,* 195–199.

Anderson, J.D., and Paik, S.J. (1994). *The T-group in preparation for clinical practice with groups: An explorative study.* Norfolk, VA: School of Social Work, Norfolk State University.

Asch, S.E. (1956). Studies of independence and conformity: A minority of one against a unanimous majority. *Psychological Monographs, 70* (9, Whole No. 416).

Ashkenas, R., and Tandon, R. (1979). An eclectic approach to small group facilitation. *Small Group Behavior, 10,* 224–241.

Austin, M.J., Kopp, J., and Smith, P.L. (1986). *Delivering human services: A self-instructional approach* (2nd ed.). New York: Longman.

Bales, R.F. (1950). *Interaction process analysis: A method for the study of small groups.* Cambridge, MA: Addison-Wesley.

Balgopal, P.R., and Vassil, T.V. (1983). *Groups in social work: An ecological perspective.* New York: Macmillan.

Ball, S. (1994). A group model for gay and lesbian clients with chronic mental illness. *Social Work, 39,* 109–115.

Banet, A.G. (1976). Yin/yang: A perspective on theories of group development. In J.W. Pfeiffer and J.E. Jones (eds.)., *The 1976 handbook for group facilitators.* La Jolla, CA: University Associates.

Bassin, A. (1962). Verbal participation and improvement in group therapy. *International Journal of Group Psychotherapy, 12,* 369–373.

Bean, B.W., and Houston, B.K. (1978). Self-concept and self-disclosure in encounter groups. *Small Group Behavior, 9,* 549–554.

Bednar, R.L., and Kaul, T.J. (1979). Experiential group research: What never happened? *Journal of Applied Behavioral Science, 15,* 311–319.

Bednar, R.L., and Lawlis, G. (1971). Empirical research in group psychotherapy. In A. Bergin and S. Garfield (eds.) *Handbook of psychotherapy and behavioral changes: An empirical analysis.* New York: Wiley.

Bednar, R.I., Melnick, J., and Kaul, T.J. (1974). Risk, responsibility, and structure: A conceptual framework for initiating group counseling and psychotherapy. *Journal of Counseling Psychology, 4* (12), 31–39.

Bell, D. (1973). *The coming of a post-industrial society: A venture in social forecasting.* New York: Basic Books.

Bennis, W.G., and Shepard, H.A. (1956). A theory of group development. *Human Relations, 9,* 415–457.

Berman-Rossi, T. (1993). The tasks and skills of the social worker across stages of group development. *Social Work with Groups, 16,* 69–81.

————. (1992). Empowering groups through understanding stages of group development. *Social Work with Groups, 15,* 239–255.

Bernstein, S., ed. (1973). *Further explorations in group work.* Boston: Milford House.

Bertcher, H.J., and Maple, F.F. (1977). *Creating groups.* Beverly Hills, CA: Sage.

Bion, W.R. (1959). *Experiences in groups and other papers.* New York: Ballantine Books (1966).

Birnbaum, M., and Auerbach, C. (1994). Group work in graduate social work education: The price of neglect. *Journal of Social Work Education, 30,* 325–335.

Bloom, M., and Fischer, J. (1982). *Evaluating practice: Guidelines for the accountable practitioner.* Englewood Cliffs, NJ: Prentice-Hall.

Blumberg, A. (1971). *Sensitivity training: Process, problems and applications.* Syracuse, NY: Syracuse University Press.

Bolman, L. (1973). Some effects of trainers on their T-groups: A partial replication. *Journal of Applied Behavioral Science, 9,* 534-539.

———. (1971). Some effects of trainers on their T-groups. *Journal of Applied Behavioral Science, 7,* 309-325.

Bond, G.R. (1984). Positive and negative norm regulation and their relationship to therapy group size. *Group, 8,* 35-44.

———. (1983). Norm regulation in therapy groups. In R. Dies and K.R. MacKenzie (eds.), *Advances in group psychotherapy.* New York: International Universities Press.

Bonney, W.D. (1974). The maturation of groups. *Small Group Behavior, 5,* 445-461.

Bostwick, G.L. (1987). "Where's Mary?" A review of the group treatment dropout literature. *Social Work with Groups, 10,* 117-132.

Boyte, H.C., and Reissman, F., eds. (1986). *The new populism: The politics of empowerment.* Philadelphia: Temple University Press.

Bradford, L.P., ed. (1978). *Group development* (2nd ed.). La Jolla, CA: University Associates.

Bradshaw, J. (1992). *Creating love.* New York: Bantam.

———. (1990). *Homecoming.* New York: Bantam.

Breton, M. (1990). Learning from social group work traditions. *Social Work with Groups, 13,* 21-34.

Brill, N. (1976). *Teamwork: Working together in the human services.* Philadelphia: J.B. Lippincott.

Brody, C.M., ed. (1987). *Women's therapy groups: Paradigms of feminist treatment.* New York: Springer.

Brower, A.M. (1989). Group development as constructed social reality: A social-cognitive understanding of group formation. *Social Work with Groups, 12,* 23-42.

Brown, L.N. (1991). *Groups for growth and change.* New York: Longman.

Bugen, L.A. (1978). Expectation profiles. *Small Group Behavior, 9,* 115-123.

Carkhuff, R.R. (1989). *The art of helping* (vol. 6). Amherst, MA: Human Resource Development Press.

———. (1969). *Helping and human relations: A primer of lay and professional helpers* (vol. 2). New York: Holt, Rinehart and Winston.

Cartwright, D. (1968). The nature of group cohesiveness. In D. Cartwright and A. Zander (eds.), *Group dynamics: Research and theory.* New York: Harper and Row.

———. (1951). Achieving change in people: Some application of group dynamics theory. *Human Relations, 4,* 381-392.

Chau, K.L. (1992). Needs assessment for group work with people of color: A conceptual formulation. *Social Work with Groups, 15,* 53-66.

Chestang, L. (1982). Racial and personal identity in the black experience. In B. White (ed.). *Color in a white society.* Silver Spring, MD: National Association of Social Workers.

Chunn, J.C., II, Punston, P.J., and Ross-Sheriff, F, eds. (1983). *Mental health and people of color: Curriculum development and change.* Washington, DC: Howard University Press.

Churchill, S. (1974). A comparison of two models of social group work: The treatment and reciprocal model. In P. Glasser, R. Sarri, and R. Vinter (eds.), *Individual change through small groups.* New York: Free Press.

Cobbs, P.M. (1972). Ethnotherapy in groups. In L.N. Solomon and B. Berzon (eds.), *New perspectives on encounter groups.* San Francisco: Jossey-Bass.

Coche, E. (1983). Change measures and clinical practice in group psychotherapy. In R.R. Dies and K.R. MacKenzie (eds.), *Advances in group psychotherapy: Integrating research and practice.* New York: International Universities Press.

Cohen, A.M., and Smith, D.R. (1976). *The critical incident in growth groups: Theory and techniques.* La Jolla, CA: University Associates.

Cohn, R.C. (1972). Style and spirit of the theme-centered interactional method. In C.J. Sager and H.S. Kaplan (eds.), *Progress in group and family therapy.* New York: Brunner/Mazel.

Cooley, C. (1918). *Social process.* New York: Scribner's.

Copeland, H. (1980) The beginning group. *International Journal of Group Psychotherapy,* 30, 201–212.

Corey, G. (1990a). *Theory and practice of group counseling* (3rd ed.). Pacific Grove, CA: Brooks/Cole. (1st ed., 1979)

————. (1990b). *A manual for theory and practice of group counseling.* Pacific Grove, CA: Brooks/Cole.

Corey, G., et al. (1992). *Group techniques.* (2nd ed.). Pacific Grove, CA: Brooks/Cole.

Council on Social Work Education. (1994). *Handbook of accreditation standards and procedures.* Washington, DC: Council on Social Work Education.

Coyle, G.L. (1959). Group work in psychiatric settings: Its roots and branches. *Social Work,* 4, 89–96.

————. (1949). Definition of the function of the group worker. *The Group,* 11, 1–9.

————. (1947). Social group work in recreation. *Proceedings of the National Conference of Social Work, 1946.* New York: Columbia University Press.

————. (1946). On becoming professional. In *Toward professional standards.* New York: American Association of Group Workers.

————. (1935). What is this social group work? *Survey,* May, 3–14.

Cozby, P.C. (1973). Self-disclosure: A literature review. *Psychological Bulletin,* 79, 73–91.

Dana, R.H. (1993). *Multicultural assessment perspectives for professional psychology.* Boston: Allyn and Bacon.

Davis, L.E., and Proctor, E.K. (1989). *Race, gender and class: Guidelines for practice with individuals, families, and groups.* Englewood Cliffs, NJ: Prentice-Hall.

DeJulio, S., Bentley, J., and Cockayne, T. (1979). Pregroup norm setting: Effects on encounter group interaction. *Small Group Behavior,* 10, 368–388.

Derogatis, L.R. (1977). *The SSL-90-R: Administration, scoring and procedures manual.* Baltimore: Clinical Psychometric Research.

DeVos, G. (1968). National character. In D.L. Sills (ed.), *International encyclopedia of the social sciences* (vol. 11). New York: Macmillan.

Dewey, J. (1916). *Democracy and education.* Chicago: University of Chicago Press.

————. (1899). *Schools and society.* Chicago: University of Chicago Press.

Diamond, J.M., and Shapiro, J.L. (1973). Changes in locus of control as a function of encounter group experiences: A study and replication. *Journal of Abnormal Psychology,* 82, 514–518.

Dies, R.R., and MacKenzie, K.R., eds. (1983). *Advances in group psychotherapy: Integrating research and practice.* New York: International Universities Press.

Dorfman, R.A., ed. (1989). *Paradigms of clinical social work.* New York: Brunner/Mazel.

Drum, D.J., and Knott, J.E. (1977). *Structured groups for facilitating development: Acquiring life skills, resolving life themes, and making life transitions.* New York: Human Services Press.

Dyer, W. (1977). *Team building: Issues and alternatives.* Reading, MA: Addison-Wesley.

Egan, G. (1975). *The skilled helper: A model for systematic helping and interpersonal relating.* Monterey, CA: Brooks/Cole.

Ephross, P.H., and Vassil, T.V. (1988). *Groups that work: Structure and process.* New York: Columbia University Press.

Erikson, E. (1950). *Childhood and society.* New York: Norton.

Erlahaus, P. (1983). Culture and the attribution process. In W. Gudykunst (ed.), *Intercultural communication.* Beverly Hills, CA: Sage.

Estes, R.H., and Henry, S. (1979). The therapeutic contract in work with groups. *Social Service Review,* 50, 611–632.

Evans, C.R., and Dion, K.L. (1991). Group cohesion and performance: A meta-analysis. *Small Group Research,* 22, 175–186.

Evans, N.J., and Jarvis, P.A. (1980). Group cohesion: A review and reevaluation. *Small Group Behavior,* 11, 359–370.

Fatout, M.F. (1992). *Models for change in social group work.* New York: Aldine De Gruyter.

Feldman, R.A. (1986). Group work knowledge and research: A two-decade comparison. *Social Work with Groups,* 9, 7–14.

Festinger, L. (1954). A theory of social comparison process. *Human Relations,* 7, 117–140.

Fiedler, F. (1967). *A theory of leadership.* New York: Macmillan.

Fischer, J., and Corcoran, K. (1989). *Clinical measurements for social work practice.* New York: Macmillan.

Flexner, A. (1905). Is social work a profession? In *Proceedings of the National Conference of Charities and Corrections.* Chicago: Hillman.

Follett, M.P. (1918). *The new state.* New York: Longmans Green.

Freire, P. (1990). *The pedagogy of the oppressed.* New York: Continuum.

Galinsky, M.J., and Schopler, J.H. (1989). Developmental patterns in open-ended groups. *Social Work with Groups,* 12, 99–114.

Garland, J.A., Jones, H.E., and Kolodny, R.L. (1973). A model for stages of development in social work groups. In S. Bernstein (ed.), *Further explorations in group work.* Boston: Milford House.

Garvin, C. (1992). A task-centered group approach to work with the chronically mentally ill. *Social Work with Groups,* 15, 67–80.

———. (1987). *Contemporary group work* (2nd ed.). Englewood Cliffs, NJ: Prentice-Hall.

———. (1985). Task-centered groups. In A. Fortune (ed.), *Task-centered practice with families and groups.* New York: Springer.

Gemmill, G., and Schaible, L.Z. (1991). The psychodynamics of female/male role differentiation within small groups. *Small Group Research,* 22, 220–239.

Germain, C.B. (1981). The ecological approach to people-environment transactions. *Social Casework,* 62, 323–331.

Getzels, J.W., and Thelen, H.A. (1960). The classroom as a unique social system. In N.B. Henry (ed.), *The dynamics of instructional groups.* Chicago: University of Chicago Press.

Gibbard, G.S., and Hartman, J.J. (1973). The oedipal paradigm in group development. *Small Group Behavior,* 4, 305–324.

Gill, S.J., and Barry, R.A. (1982). Group-focused counseling: Classifying the essential skills. *Personnel and Guidance Journal,* 60, 302–305.

Gitterman, A., and Shulman, L., eds. (1988). *Mutual aid groups and the life cycle.* Itasca, IL: F.E. Peacock.

Glasser, P., Sarri, R., and Vinter, R., eds. (1974). *Individual change through small groups.* New York: Free Press.

Glassman, U., and Kates, L. (1990). *Group work: A humanistic approach.* Newbury Park, CA: Sage.

Goldberg, C,. and Goldberg, M.C. (1973). *The human circle: An existential approach to the new group therapies*. Chicago: Nelson-Hall.

Goldberg, T., and Lamont, A.E. (1992). The impact of a generic curriculum on the practice of graduates: Does group work persist? *Social Work with Groups*, 15, 145–156.

Goldstein, M.J., Bednar, R.L., and Yanell, B. (1979). Personal risk associated with self-disclosure, interpersonal feedback, and group confrontation in group psychotherapy. *Small Group Behavior*, 9, 579–587.

Grotjohn, M. (1972). Learning from dropout patients: A clinical view of patients who discontinued group psychotherapy. *International Journal of Group Psychotherapy*, 22, 306–319.

Gudykunst, W.B. (1991). *Bridging differences: Effective intergroup communication*. Beverly Hills, CA: Sage.

Gutierrez, L.M. (1990). Working with women of color: An empowerment approach. *Social Work*, 35, 149–153.

Gutierrez, L.M., and Ortega, R. (1991). Developing methods to empower Latinos: The importance of groups. *Social Work with Groups*, 14, 16–32.

Hackman, J.R. (1968). Effects of task characteristics on group products. *Journal of Experimental Social Psychology*, 39, 97–128.

Hall, E.T. (1976). *Beyond culture*. Garden City, NY: Doubleday.

Hall, J., and Watson, W.H. (1970). The effects of normative intervention on group decision-making performance. *Human Relations*, 23, 299–317.

Hartford, M.E. (1971). *Groups in social work*. New York: Columbia University Press.

Heap, K. (1977). *Group theory for social workers: An introduction*. New York: Pergamon.

Heider, F. (1958). *The psychology of interpersonal relations*. New York: Wiley.

Henry, S. (1992). *Group skills in social work* (2nd ed.). Pacific Grove, CA: Brooks/Cole. (1st ed., 1981)

Hewstone, M., and Brown, R., eds. (1986). *Contact and conflict in intergroup encounters*. Oxford, UK: Basil Blackwell.

Hill, W.F. (1976). Systematic group development theory. In A. Jacobs and W.W. Spradlin (eds.), *The group as an agent of change*. New York: Behavioral Publications.

———. (1975). Further considerations of therapeutic mechanisms in group therapy. *Small Group Behavior*, 6, 421–429.

Ho, M.K. (1987). *Family therapy with ethnic minorities*. Newbury Park, CA: Sage.

Homans, G. (1950). *The human group*. New York: Harcourt-Brace.

Hooyman, E. (1984). Teambuilding in the human services. In B. Compton and B. Galaway (eds.), *Social work process* (3rd ed.). Homewood, IL: Dorsey.

Horney, K. (1951). *Neurosis and human growth*. London: Routledge and Kegan Paul.

Hudson, W. (1982). *The clinical measurement package: A field manual*. Homewood, IL: Dorsey.

Hurst, A.G., Stein, K.B., Korchin, J.J., and Soskin, W.F. (1978). Leadership style determinants of cohesiveness in adolescent groups. *International Journal of Group Psychotherapy*, 28, 263–277.

Ivey, A.E. (1973). Demystifying the group process: Adapting microcounseling procedures to counseling in groups. *Educational Technology*, 13, 27–31.

Jacobs, A. (1974). The use of feedback in groups. In A. Jacobs and W.W. Spradline (eds.). *The group as an agent of change*. New York: Behavioral Publications.

Jacobs, E.E., Harvill, R.L., and Masson, R.L. (1988). *Group counseling: Strategies and skills*. Pacific Grove, CA: Brooks/Cole.

Johnson, P.W., and Johnson, F.P. (1987). *Joining together* (2nd ed.). Englewood Cliffs, NJ: Prentice-Hall.

Kane, R. (1975). The interprofessional team as a small group. *Social Work in Health Care*, 1, 19–32.

Kaplan, A. (1964). *The conduct of inquiry: Methodology for behavioral science.* San Francisco: Chandler.

Katz, R. (1989). Empowerment and synergy: Expanding the communities' healing resources. In J. Rappaport et al. (eds.), *Studies in empowerment.* New York: Haworth.

Kaul, T.J., and Bednar, R.L. (1986). Research on group and related therapies. In S. Garfield and A. Bergen (eds.), *Handbook of psychotherapy and behavior change* (3rd ed.). New York: John Wiley & Sons.

Kellerman, H. (1979). *Group psychotherapy and personality: Intersecting structures.* New York: Green and Stratton.

Keyton, J. (1993). Group termination: Completing the study of group development. *Small Group Research*, 24, 84–100.

Kieffer, C.H. (1984). Citizen empowerment: A developmental perspective. *Prevention in Human Services*, 3, 9–36.

Kiesler, D.J. (1981). Empirical clinical psychology: Myth or reality? *Journal of Consulting and Clinical Psychology*, 49, 212–215.

Klein, A.F. (1973). *Effective groupwork: An introduction to principle and method.* New York: Association Press.

———. (1970). *Social work through group process.* Albany: School of Social Welfare, State University of New York at Albany.

Kluckhohn, C. (1961). Value orientations. In F.R. Kluckhohn and F.L. Strodtbeck (eds.), *Variations in value orientations.* Homewood, IL: Dorsey.

Kluckhohn, F.R. (1954). Dominant and variant value orientations. In C. Kluckhohn and H.A. Murray (eds.), *Personality in nature, society, and culture.* New York: Knopf.

Knowles, M., and Knowles, H. (1972). *Introduction to group dynamics* (rev. ed.). New York: Association Press.

Kochman, T. (1981). *Black and white: Styles in conflict.* Chicago: University of Chicago Press.

Konopka, G. (1963). *Social group work: A helping process.* Englewood Cliffs, NJ: Prentice-Hall.

———. (1958). *Eduard C. Lindeman and social work philosophy.* Minneapolis: University of Minnesota Press.

———. (1956). The generic and specific in group work practice in the psychiatric setting. In *Groupwork in the psychiatric setting.* New York: Whiteside, Morrow.

———. (1954). *Group work in the institution: A modern challenge.* New York: Whiteside, Morrow.

———. (1951). Similarities and differences between group work and group therapy. In *Proceedings of the National Conference of Social Work, 1951.* New York: Columbia University Press.

Kravitz, D.F., and Rose, S.D. (1974). *Contracts in groups: A workbook.* Dubuque, IA: Kendall/Hunt.

Kropotkin, P. (1908). *Mutual aid: A factor of evolution.* London: William Heinemann.

Kübler-Ross, E. (1969). *On death and dying.* New York: Macmillan.

Kurland, R., and Salmon, R. (1992). Groupwork vs. casework in a group: Principles and implications for teaching and practice. *Social Work with Groups*, 15, 3–14.

Lacoursiere, R. (1980). *The lifecycle of groups: Group development stage theory.* New York: Human Services Press.

Lang, N. (1987). Social work practice in small social forms: Identifying collectivity. *Social Work with Groups*, 9, 7–31.

———. (1979). A comparative examination of therapeutic uses of groups in social work and adjacent human service professions. Part I. *Social Work with Groups*, 2, 101–115; Part II, 2, 197–221.

Leavitt, H.J. (1951). Some effects of certain communication patterns on group performance. *Journal of Abnormal and Social Psychology*, 46, 38–50.

Lee, F., and Bednar, R.L. (1971). Effects of group structure and risk-taking disposition on group behavior, attitudes, and atmosphere. *Journal of Counseling Psychology*, 24, 191–199.

Lee, J.A.B. (1994). *The empowerment approach to social work practice*. New York: Columbia University Press.

———. (1992). Jane Addams in Boston: Intersecting time and space. *Social Work with Groups*, 15 (7), 22.

———, ed. (1988). Special issue: Group work with the poor and oppressed. *Social Work with Groups*, 11, 5–11.

Lee, J.A.B., and Swenson, C.R. (1986). The concept of mutual aid. In A. Gifferman and L. Shulman (eds.), *Mutual aid groups and the life cycle*. Itasca, IL: F.E. Peacock.

Levin, E.M., and Kurtz, R.R. (1974). Participant perceptions following structured and non-structured human relations training. *Journal of Counseling Psychology*, 21, 514–532.

Levine, B. (1979). *Group psychotherapy: Practice and development*. Englewood Cliffs, NJ: Prentice-Hall.

Levine, B., and Galoghy, V. (1985). *Group therapy with alcoholics: Outpatient and inpatient approaches*. Beverly Hills, CA: Sage.

Levine, N. (1971). Emotional factors in group development. *Human Relations*, 24, 65–89.

Lewin, K. (1951). *Field theory and social science*. New York: Harper.

Lewis, H. (1982). *The intellectual base of social work practice*. New York: Haworth.

Lieberman, M.A., Yalom, I.D., and Miles, M.B. (1973). *Encounter groups: First facts*. New York: Basic Books.

Lindeman, E.C. (1939). Group work and democracy: A philosophical note. In J. Lieberman (ed.), *New trends in group work*. New York: Association Press.

Livesley, W.J., and MacKenzie, K.R. (1983). Social roles in psychotherapy groups. In R.R. Dies and K.R. MacKenzie (eds.), *Advances in group psychotherapy*. New York: International Universities Press.

Lofland, J. (1971). *Analyzing social settings*. Belmont, CA: Wadsworth.

Luft, J. (1970). *Group process: An introduction to group dynamics*. Palo Alto, CA: National Press Books.

Lukes, C., and Land, H. (1990). Biculturality and homosexuality. *Social Work*, 35, 155–161.

Lungren, D.C. (1977). Developmental trends in the emergency of interpersonal issues in T-groups. *Small Group Behavior*, 8, 179–200.

MacKenzie, K.R., and Dies, R.R. (1982). *The CORE battery: Clinical outcome results*. New York: American Psychotherapy Association.

MacKenzie, K.R., and Livesley, W.J. (1983). A developmental model for brief group therapy. In R.R. Dies and K.R. MacKenzie (eds.), *Advances in group psychotherapy*. New York: International Universities Press.

Maier, N.R.F. (1970). *Problem solving and creativity in individuals and groups*. Belmont, CA: Brooks/Cole.

———. (1967). Assets and liabilities in group problem solving: The need for integrative function. *Psychological Review*, 74, 239–249.

Manor, O. (1986). The preliminary interview in social groupwork: Finding the spiral steps. *Social Work with Groups*, 9, 21 – 40.

Martin, J.M., and Martin, E.R. (1985). *The helping tradition in the black family and community*. Silver Spring, MD: National Association of Social Workers.

Martin, L., and Jacobs, M. (1980). Structured feedback delivered in small groups. *Small Group Behavior*, 11, 88 – 107.

Maslow, A.H., and Honigmann. (1970). *Motivation and personality* (2nd ed.). New York: Harper and Row.

McGoldrick, M., Pearce, J.K., and Giordano, J., eds. (1982). *Ethnicity and family therapy*. New York: Guilford.

McIntosh, P. (1989). White privilege: Unpacking the invisible knapsack. *Peace and Freedom*, July/August, 10 – 12.

Melnick, J., and Rose, G.S. (1979). Expectancy and risk taking propensity: Predictors of group performance. *Small Group Behavior*, 10, 389 – 401.

Melnick, J., and Woods, M. (1976). Analysis of group composition research and theory for psychotherapeutic and growth-oriented groups. *Journal of Applied Behavioral Science*, 12, 493 – 512.

Mennecke, B.E., Hoffer, J.A., and Wynne, B.E. (1992). The implications of group development and history for group support system theory and practice. *Small Group Research*, 23, 524 – 572.

Merritt, R.E., and Walley, D.D. (1977). *The group leader's handbook*. Champaign, IL: Research Press.

Mezzano, J. (1967). A consideration for group counselors: Degree of counselees investment. *School Counselor*, 14, 167 – 169.

Middleman, R.R. (1978). Returning group process to group work. *Social Work with Groups*, 1, 27 – 38.

———. (1968). *The nonverbal method in working with groups*. New York: Association Press.

Middleman, R.R., and Goldberg, G. (1987). Social work practice with groups. In *Encyclopedia of social work*, (18th ed.). Silver Spring, MD: National Association of Social Workers.

Miley, K.K., O'Melia, M., and DuBois, B.L. (1995). *Generalist social work practice: An empowering approach*. Boston: Allyn and Bacon.

Miller, N.B. (1982). Social work services to urban Indians. In J.W. Green (ed.), *Cultural awareness in the human services*. Englewood Cliffs, NJ: Prentice-Hall.

Milne, A.A. (1954). *Winnie-the-Pooh*. New York: Dutton.

Minahan, A., ed. (1987). *Encyclopedia of social work* (vol. 18). Silver Spring, MD: National Association of Social Workers.

Moreno, J.L. (1934). *Who shall survive? A new approach to the problem of human interaction*. Washington, DC: Nervous and Mental Disease Publishing Co.

Morris, R.M., ed. (1971). *Encyclopedia of social work* (vol. 17). Silver Spring, MD: National Association of Social Workers.

Morrow, D.F. (1993). Social work with gay and lesbian adolescents. *Social Work*, 38, 655 – 660.

Naisbitt, R. (1984). *Megatrends*. New York: Warner.

Napier, R., and Gershenfeld, M. (1981). *Groups: Theory and experience* (2nd ed.). Boston: Hougton Mifflin.

Newcomb, T.M. (1961). *The acquaintance process*. New York: Holt.

Nixon, H. (1979). *The small group*. Englewood Cliffs, NJ: Prentice-Hall.

Northen, H. (1989). *The expanded definition of clinical social work—skills and knowledge*. Silver Spring, MD: National Association of Social Workers.

———. (1988). *Social work with groups* (2nd ed.). New York: Columbia University Press.

———. (1969). *Social work with groups*. New York: Columbia University Press.

O'Day, R. (1974). The T-group trainer: A study of conflict in the exercise of authority. In G.S. Gibbard, J.H. Hartman, and R.D. Mann (eds.), *Analysis of groups*. San Francisco: Jossey-Bass.

O'Hare, T., Williams, C.L., and Ezoviski, A. (1996). Fear of AIDS and homophobia: Implications for direct practice and advocacy. *Social Work*, 41, 51–58.

Ohlsen, M.M., and Pearson, R.D. (1965). A method for the classification of group interaction and its use to explore the role factors in group counseling. *Journal of Clinical Psychology*, 21, 436–441.

Otto, H. (1970). *Group methods to actualize potential.* Beverly Hills, CA: Holistic Press.

Papell, C.P., and Rothman, B. (1980). Relating the mainstream model of social work with groups to group psychotherapy and the structured group approach. *Social Work with Groups*, 3, 5–23.

———. (1966). Social group work models: Possession and heritage. *Journal of Education for Social Work*, 2, 66–77.

Parloff, M.B. (1980). Psychotherapy and research: An anaclitic depression. *Psychiatry*, 43, 279–293.

Parloff, M.B., and Dies, R.R. (1978). Group therapy outcome instrument: Guidelines for conducting research. *Small Group Behavior*, 9, 243–286.

Parsons, R.J. (1991). Empowerment: Purpose and practice principles in social work. *Social Work with Groups*, 14, 7–21.

Parsons, T. (1951). *The social system*. New York: Free Press.

Passons, W.R. (1972). Gestalt therapy interventions in group counseling. *Personnel and Guidance Journal*, 51, 183–189.

Pedersen, P. (1988). *A handbook for developing multicultural awareness*. Alexandria, VA: American Association for Counseling and Development.

Pernell, R. (1985). Empowerment and social work. In M. Parenes (ed.), *Innovations in social group work: Feedback from practice to theory*. New York: Haworth.

Pettigrew, T.F. (1979). The ultimate attribution error. *Personality and Social Psychology Bulletin*, 5, 461–476.

———. (1978). Three issues in ethnicity. In Y. Yinger and S. Cutler (eds.), *Major social issues*. New York: Free Press.

Pfeiffer, J.W., Heslin, R., and Jones, J.E. (1976). *Instrumentation in human relations training* (2nd ed.). La Jolla, CA: University Associates.

Pfeiffer, J.W., and Jones, J.E. (1979). *Reference guide to handbooks and annuals* (3rd ed.). La Jolla, CA: University Associates.

Phillips, H.U. (1957). *Essentials of social group work skill*. New York: Association Press.

———. (1954). What is group work skill? *The Group*, 5, 3–10.

Pillnick, S. (1971). Crime and delinquency: Guided group interaction. In *Encyclopedia of social work* (vol. 1). New York: National Association of Social Workers.

Pinderhuges, E. (1989). *Understanding race, ethnicity, and power: The key to efficacy in clinical practice*. New York: Free Press.

———. (1983). Empowerment for our clients and ourselves. *Social Casework*, 64, 331–338.

Polanyi, M. (1966). *The tacit dimension*. London: Routledge and Kegan Paul.

Priestley, P., et al. (1979). *Social skills and personal problem solving: A handbook of methods*. London: Tavistock.

Psathas, G., and Hardert, R. (1966). Trainer interventions and normative patterns in the T-group. *Journal of Applied Behavioral Science, 2,* 149 – 169.

Ramirez, M., III. (1991). *Psychotherapy and counseling with minorities: A cognitive approach to individual and cultural differences.* New York: Pergamon.

Rappaport, J. (1986). Collaborating for empowerment: Creating the language of mutual help. In H.C. Boyle and F. Reissman (eds.), *The new populism: The politics of empowerment.* Philadelphia: Temple University Press.

Reid, K.E. (1991). *Social work practice with groups: A clinical perspective.* Pacific Grove, CA: Brooks/Cole.

Reitz, H.J. (1977). *Behavior in organizations.* Homewood, IL: Richard D. Irwin.

Research Press. (1994). *Catalog: Books and video programs.* Champaign, IL: Research Press.

Reynolds, B. (1941). *Social work and social living.* New York: Citadel Press.

Richmond, M.E. (1917). *Social diagnosis.* New York: Sage.

Roberts, R.W., and Northen, H., eds. (1976). *Theories of social work with groups.* New York: Columbia University Press.

Robinson, K.R. (1991). Gay youth support groups: An opportunity for social work intervention. *Social Work, 36,* 458 – 459.

Rogers, C. (1970). *On encounter groups.* New York: Harper and Row.

Rose, S. (1990). Putting the group into cognitive behavior treatment. *Social Work with Groups, 13,* 71 – 84.

———. (1977). *Group therapy: A behavioral approach.* Englewood Cliffs, NJ: Prentice-Hall.

Rosenzweig, S., and Folman, R. (1974). Patient and therapist variables affecting premature termination in group psychotherapy. *Psychotherapy: Theory, Research, and Practice, 11,* 76 – 79.

Rotter, J. (1966). Generalized expectancies for internal versus external control of reinforcement. *Psychological Monographs, 80,* 1 – 28.

Ryan, W. (1972). *Blaming the victim.* New York: Random House.

Sampson, E.E. (1988). The debate on individualism: Indigenous psychologies of the individual and their role in personal and social functioning. *American Psychologist, 43,* 15 – 22.

———. (1985). The decentralization of identity: Toward a revised concept of personal and social order. *American Psychologist, 40,* 1203 – 1211.

Sarri, R.G., and Galinsky, M.J. (1974). A conceptual framework for group development. In P. Glasser, R. Sarri, and R. Vinter (eds.), *Individual change through small groups.* New York: Free Press.

Satterley, J.A. (1995). Needed: A fresh start for psychiatric inpatient groups. *Social Work with Groups, 17,* 71 – 81.

Schatz, M.S., Jenkins, L.E., and Sheafor, B.W. (1990). Milford revisited: A model of initial and advanced generalist social work practice. *Journal of Social Work Education, 26,* 217 – 231.

Scheidlinger, S. (1980). The psychology of leadership revisited: An overview. *The Group, 4,* 5 – 17.

———. (1966). The concept of empathy in group psychotherapy. *International Journal of group psychotherapy, 16,* 413 – 424.

Schmitt, D.M., and Weaver, DC (1979). *Leadership for community empowerment: A sourcebook.* Midland, MI: Pendell.

Schopler, J.H., and Galinsky, M.J. (1981). When groups go wrong. *Social Work, 26,* 224 – 229.

Schutz, W.C. (1973). *Elements of encounter.* Big Sur, CA: Joy Press.

———. (1958). The interpersonal underworld. *Harvard Business Review, 36,* 123 – 135.

Schwartz, W. (1985/86). The group work tradition and social work practice. *Social Work with Groups, 8,* 7 – 28.

————. (1977). Social group work: The interactionalist approach. In *Encyclopedia of social work* (vol. 2). New York: National Association of Social Workers.

————. (1976). Between client and system: The mediating function. In R.R. Roberts and H. Northen (eds.), *Theories of social work with groups*. New York: Columbia University Press.

————. (1971). Groups in social work practice. In W. Schwartz and S. Zolba (eds.), *The practice of group work*. New York: Columbia University Press.

————. (1961). The social worker in the group. In *The social welfare forum, 1961*. New York: Columbia University Press.

————. (1959). Group work and the social scene. In A.J. Kahn (ed.), *Issues in American social work*. New York: Columbia University Press.

Schwartz, W., and Zalba, S., eds. (1971). *The practice of group work*. New York: Columbia University Press.

Seeman, M. (1985). Alienation studies. In M.J. Coleman and N. Smelser, eds. *Annual Review of Sociology*. New York: Macmillan, pp. 91–128.

Seitz, M. (1985). A group's history: From mutual aid to helping others. *Social Work with Groups*, 8, 41–54.

Seligman, M.E.P. (1982). *Helplessness: On depression, development and death*. San Francisco: Freeman.

Shaefor, B.W., and Landon, P.S. (1987). Generalist perspective. In A. Minahan (ed.), *Encyclopedia of social work* (vol. 18). Silver Spring, MD: National Association of Social Workers.

Shaffer, J., and Galinsky, M.D. (1989). *Models of group therapy* (2nd ed.). Englewood Cliffs, NJ: Prentice-Hall. (1st ed., 1978)

Shapiro, J.L. (1978). *Methods of group psychotherapy: A tradition of innovation*. Itasca, IL: F.E. Peacock.

Shaw, M.E. (1984). *Group dynamics: The psychology of small group behavior* (3rd ed.). New York: McGraw-Hill.

————. (1981). *Group dynamics: The psychology of small group behavior* (2nd ed.). New York: McGraw-Hill.

Shean, G.D. (1985). Rehabilitation: Social skills groups. In R.K. Coyne (ed.), *The group workers' handbook: Varieties of group experience*. Springfield, IL: Charles C. Thomas.

Sherif, M. (1936). *The psychology of social norms*. New York: Harper.

Shernoff, M. (1995). Gay men: Direct practice. In R.L. Edwards (ed.), *Encyclopedia of social work*, (vol. 19). Washington, DC: National Association of Social Workers.

Sherwood, J.J., and Hoylman, F.M. (1977). *Utilizing human resources: Group approaches to problem solving and decision making*. Lafayette, IN: Purdue University Press.

Shields, S.A. (1985/86). Busted and branded: Group work with substance abusing adolescents in schools. *Social Work with Groups*, 81, 62–82.

Shulman, L. (1992). *The skills of helping: Individuals, families, and groups* (3rd ed.). Itasca, IL: F.E. Peacock.

Shumaker, E. (1977). *A guide for the perplexed*. London: Jonathan Cape.

Sibergeld, S., Thune, E.S., and Manderscheid, R.W. (1979). The group therapist roles: Assessment in adolescent coping courses. *Small Group Behavior*, 10, 176–199.

Silverman, P.R. (1980). *Mutual help groups: Organization and development*. Beverly Hills, CA: Sage.

Simmons, K., and Parsons, R. (1983). Developing internality and perceived competence: The empowerment of adolescent girls. *Adolescence*, 18, 917–922.

Slavson, S.R. (1964). *A textbook in analytic group psychotherapy*. New York: International Universities Press.

Snortum, J.R., and Myers, H.F. (1971). Intensity of T-group relations as function of interaction. *International Journal of group psychotherapy*, 21, 190–201.

Solomon, B. (1976). *Black empowerment: Social work in oppressed communities*. New York: Columbia University Press.

Solomon, L. (1977). Team development: A training approach. In W. Pfeiffer and J. Jones (eds.), *The 1977 annual handbook for group facilitators*. La Jolla, CA: University Associates.

Specht, H., and Courtney, M.E. (1993). *Unfaithful agents: How social work has abandoned its mission*. New York: Free Press.

Spiegel, J. (1982). An ecological model of ethnic families. In M. McGoldrick et al. (eds.), *Ethnicity and family therapy*. New York: Guilford.

Spradley, J.P. (1979). *The ethnographic interview*. New York: Holt, Rinehart and Winston.

Stava, L.J., and Bednar, R.L. (1979). Process and outcome in encounter groups: The effects of group composition. *Small Group Behavior*, 10, 200–213.

Steele, S. (1990). *The content of our character*. New York: St. Martin's.

Steinberg, D.M. (1993). Some findings from a study on the impact of group work education on social work practitioners' work with groups. *Social Work with Groups*, 16, 23–39.

Stewart, J., and Thomas, M. (1990). Dialogic listening. In J. Stewart (ed.), *Bridges, not walls* (5th ed.). New York: McGraw-Hill.

Stock, D., and Thelen, H.A. (1958). *Emotional dynamics and group culture*. New York: National Training Laboratories.

Stockton, R., Rhode, R.I., and Haughey, J. (1992). The effects of structured group exercises on cohesion, engagement, avoidance, and conflict. *Small Group Research*, 23, 155–168.

Sue, D.W. (1978). Eliminating cultural oppression in counseling: Toward a general theory. *Journal of Counseling Psychology*, 25, 419–428.

Sue, D.W., and Sue, D. (1990). *Counseling the culturally different: Theory and practice* (2nd ed.). New York: John Wiley and Sons.

Sundel, M., et al., eds. (1985). *Individual change through small groups* (2nd ed.). New York: Free Press.

Tannen, D. (1990). *You just don't understand: Women and men in conversation*. New York: William Morrow.

Ting-Toomey, S. (1988). A face negotiation theory. In Y. Kim and W. Gudykunst (eds.), *Theories in intercultural communication*. Newbury Park, CA: Sage.

Toffler, A. (1970). *Future shock*. New York: Bantam.

Toseland, R.W., and Rivas, R.F. (1995). *An introduction to group work practice* (2nd ed.). Boston: Allyn and Bacon.

———. (1984). *An introduction to group work practice*. New York: Macmillan.

Triandis, H.C. (1988). Collectivism vs. individualism. In G. Verna and C. Bagley (eds.), *Cross-cultural studies of personality, attitudes, and cognition*. London: Macmillan.

Tropp, E. (1979). Whatever happened to group work? *Social Work with Groups*, 1, 85–94.

———. (1977). Social group work: The developmental approach. In *Encyclopedia of social work* (vol. 2). New York: National Association of Social Workers.

———. (1972). *A humanistic foundation for group work practice* (2nd ed.). New York: Selected Academic Readings.

Truax, C.B., and Carkhuff, R.R. (1967). *Toward effective counseling and psychotherapy: Training and practice*. Chicago: Aldine.

Tucker, D.M. (1973). Some relationships between individual and group development. *Human Development*, 16, 249–272.

Tuckman, B.W. (1965). Developmental sequences in small groups. *Psychological Bulletin*, 63, 384–399.

Tuckman, B.W., and Jensen, M.A. (1977). Stages of group development revisited. *Group and Organizational Studies*, 2, 419–427.

Van Dyck, B.J. (1980). An analysis of selection criteria for short-term group counseling clients. *Personnel and Guidance Journal*, 59, 226–230.

Vannicelli, M. (1992). *Removing the roadblocks: Group psychotherapy with substance abusers and family members*. New York: Guilford.

Verdi, A.F., and Wheelan, S.A. (1992). Developmental patterns in same-sex and mixed-sex groups. *Small Group Research*, 23, 356–378.

Vinter, R.D., ed. (1967). *Readings in group work practice*. Ann Arbor, MI: Campus Publishers.

Vorrath, H.H., and Brendtro, L.K. (1985). *Positive peer culture* (2nd ed.). Chicago: Aldine.

Wasserman, H., and Danforth, H.E. (1986). *The human bond: Support groups and mutual aid*. New York: Springer.

Wheelan, S.A., and McKeage, R.L. (1993). Developmental patterns in small and large groups. *Small Group Research*, 24, 60–83.

Whitaker, D.S., and Lieberman, M.A. (1965). *Psychotherapy through group process*. New York: Atherton.

Wickham, E. (1993). *Group treatment in social work: An integration of theory and practice*. Lewiston, NY: Thompson Educational Publishing.

Wile, D.B. (1972). Group leadership questionnaire. In J.W. Pfeiffer and J.E. Jones (eds.), *The 1972 annual handbook for group facilitators*. La Jolla, CA: University Associates.

Williams, R. (1977). *Mutual accommodation: Ethnic conflict and cooperation*. Minneapolis: University of Minnesota Press.

Wilson, G. (1976). From practice to theory: A personalized history. In R.W. Roberts and H. Northen (eds.), *Theories of social work with groups*. New York: Columbia University Press.

Wogan, M., Chionsky, J.M., and Schoeplein, R.N. (1971). Stages of group development in an experimental ghetto program. *American Journal of Orthopsychiatry*, 41, 459–671.

Wogan, M., Getter, H., Amden, J.J., Nichols, M.F., and Okman, G. (1977). Influencing interactions and outcomes in group psychotherapy. *Small Group Behavior*, 8, 25–46.

Woodman, NJ (1995). Lesbians: Direct practice. In R.L. Edwards (ed.), *Encyclopedia of social work* (vol. 19). Washington, DC: National Association of Social Workers.

Woods, M., and Melnick, J. (1979). Review of group therapy selection criteria. *Small Group Behavior*, 10, 155–175.

Yalom, I.D. (1995). *The theory and practice of group psychotherapy* (4th ed.). New York: Basic Books.

———. (1975). *The theory and practice of group psychotherapy*. New York: Basic Books.

Yalom, I.D., and Moos, R. (1967). The use of small interactional groups in the teaching of psychiatry. *Archives of General Psychiatry*, 15, 242–246.

Yalom, V.J., and Yalom, I.D. (1990). Short-term group psychotherapy. *Psychiatric Annals*, 20, 362–367.

Young, R. (1987). Collectivity vs. group: A framework for assessment. *Social Work with Groups*, 9, 33–43.

Zastrow, C. (1985). *Social work with groups*. Chicago: Nelson-Hall.

Zimpfer, D. (1967). Expression of feelings in group counseling. *Personnel and Guidance Journal*, 45, 703–708.

Zinker, J. (1980). Developmental process of a Gestalt therapy group. In B. Feder and R. Ronall (eds.), *Beyond the hot seat: Gestalt approaches to group*. New York: Brunner/Mazel.

———. (1977). *Creative process in Gestalt therapy*. New York: Brunner/Mazel.

Index

About the Author

Joseph Anderson, DSW, ACSW, is Professor of Social Work at the Ethelyn R. Strong School of Social Work at Norfolk State University. He has also been Professor of Social Work at the University of Saint Thomas; the National University of Singapore; and Shippensburg University, where he was chair of the Social Work Department. He received his doctorate from the University of Maryland School of Social Work and Community Planning, where he also has taught. Dr. Anderson currently teaches in the DSW, MSW, and BSW programs at Norfolk State University, chairs the school's Curriculum Committee, and coordinates the group practice content. He has been president of the Central Pennsylvania Chapter of the National Association of Social Workers, chair of the Educational Planning Commission of the Council on Social Work Education (CSWE), and a member of CSWE's Commission on Accreditation. He also is certified as a site visitor for CSWE accreditation. He serves as a member of the Academy of Certified Social Workers, a consulting editor of the *Journal of Social Work Education,* and an editorial board member for the journal *Social Work with Groups.* He is the author of several books, including *Social Work Methods and Processes* and *Counseling through Group Process,* as well as numerous articles on social work with groups and social work practice and education. He resides in Smithfield, Virginia, with his wife, Wanda, his daughters, Bailey and Caitlin, his son, Sean, and two dogs. He enjoys taking long walks, reading, engaging in sports, dancing, and participating in groups of all kinds.